Hippolyte Adolpne Taine

From the etching by Asher B. Durand

THE FIVE-FOOT SHELF OF BOOKS
"THE HARVARD CLASSICS"
EDITED BY CHARLES W ELIOT LL D

PREFACES AND PROLOGUES

TO FAMOUS BOOKS

WITH INTRODUCTIONS AND NOTES

VOLUME 39

P F COLLIER & SON
NEW YORK

Designed, Printed, and Bound at
The Collier Press, New York

CONTENTS

PAGE

Title, Prologue and Epilogues to the Recuyell of the
Histories of Troy...................William Caxton   5
Epilogue to Dictes and Sayings of the Philosophers
William Caxton   10

Prologue to Golden Legend.............William Caxton   14
Prologue to Caton.....................William Caxton   15
Epilogue to Aesop.....................William Caxton   18
Proem to Chaucer's Canterbury Tales..William Caxton   19
Prologue to Malory's King Arthur.....William Caxton   21
Prologue to Virgil's Eneydos...........William Caxton   25

Dedication of the Institutes of the Christian Religion
John Calvin   29
TRANSLATED BY JOHN ALLEN

Dedication of the Revolutions of the Heavenly Bodies
Nicolaus Copernicus   55

Preface to the History of the Reformation in Scotland
John Knox   61

Prefatory Letter to Sir Walter Raleigh on The Faerie
Queene...........................Edmund Spenser   64

Preface to the History of the World
Sir Walter Raleigh   69

Prooemium, Epistle Dedicatory, Preface, and plan of the
Instauratio Magna, Etc..............Francis Bacon 122
TRANSLATION EDITED BY J. SPEDDING

CONTENTS

PAGE

PREFACE TO THE NOVUM ORGANUM..........FRANCIS BACON 150
PREFACE TO THE FIRST FOLIO EDITION OF SHAKESPEARE'S
    PLAYS.........................HEMINGE AND CONDELL 155

PREFACE TO THE PHILOSOPHIAE NATURALIS PRINCIPIA MATHE-
    MATICA........ ... .SIR ISAAC NEWTON 157
        TRANSLATED BY ANDREW MOTTE

PREFACE TO FABLES, ANCIENT AND MODERN....JOHN DRYDEN 160
PREFACE TO JOSEPH ANDREWS..............HENRY FIELDING 184
PREFACE TO THE ENGLISH DICTIONARY.....SAMUEL JOHNSON 191
PREFACE TO SHAKESPEARE................SAMUEL JOHNSON 218
INTRODUCTION TO THE PROPYLÄEN.........J. W. VON GOETHE 264

PREFACES TO VARIOUS VOLUMES OF POEMS
                WILLIAM WORDSWORTH 281
APPENDIX TO LYRICAL BALLADS.....WILLIAM WORDSWORTH 307
ESSAY SUPPLEMENTARY TO PREFACE..WILLIAM WORDSWORTH 327

PREFACE TO CROMWELL.......................VICTOR HUGO 354
PREFACE TO LEAVES OF GRASS.............WALT WHITMAN 409
INTRODUCTION TO THE HISTORY OF ENGLISH LITERATURE
                        H. A. TAINE 433

INTRODUCTORY NOTE

No part of a book is so intimate as the Preface. Here, after the long labor of the work is over, the author descends from his platform, and speaks with his reader as man to man, disclosing his hopes and fears, seeking sympathy for his difficulties, offering defence or defiance, according to his temper, against the criticisms which he anticipates. It thus happens that a personality which has been veiled by a formal method throughout many chapters, is suddenly seen face to face in the Preface; and this alone, if there were no other reason, would justify a volume of Prefaces.

But there are other reasons why a Preface may be presented apart from its parent work, and may, indeed, be expected sometimes to survive it. The Prologues and Epilogues of Caxton were chiefly prefixed to translations which have long been superseded; but the comments of this frank and enthusiastic pioneer of the art of printing in England not only tell us of his personal tastes, but are in a high degree illuminative of the literary habits and standards of western Europe in the fifteenth century. Again, modern research has long ago put Raleigh's "History of the World" out of date; but his eloquent Preface still gives us a rare picture of the attitude of an intelligent Elizabethan, of the generation which colonized America, toward the past, the present, and the future worlds. Bacon's "Great Restoration" is no longer a guide to scientific method; but his prefatory statements as to his objects and hopes still offer a lofty inspiration.

And so with the documents here drawn from the follos of Copernicus and Calvin, with the criticism of Dryden and Wordsworth and Hugo, with Dr. Johnson's Preface to his great Dictionary, with the astounding manifesto of a new poetry from Walt Whitman's "Leaves of Grass"—each of them has a value and significance independent now of the work which it originally introduced, and each of them presents to us a man.

PREFACES AND EPILOGUES

BY WILLIAM CAXTON

THE RECUYELL OF THE HISTORIES OF TROY

TITLE AND PROLOGUE TO BOOK I

HERE beginneth the volume entitled and named the
Recuyell of the Histories of Troy, composed and
drawn out of divers books of Latin into French by
the right venerable person and worshipful man, Raoul le
Feure, priest and chaplain unto the right noble, glorious,
and mighty prince in his time, Philip, Duke of Burgundy,
of Brabant, etc., in the year of the Incarnation of our Lord
God a thousand four hundred sixty and four, and translated
and drawn out of French into English by William Caxton,
mercer, of the city of London, at the commandment of
the right high, mighty, and virtuous Princess, his redoubted
Lady, Margaret, by the grace of God Duchess of Burgundy,
of Lotrylk, of Brabant, etc.; which said translation and
work was begun in Bruges in the County of Flanders, the
first day of March, the year of the Incarnation of our said
Lord God a thousand four hundred sixty and eight, and
ended and finished in the holy city of Cologne the 19th
day of September, the year of our said Lord God a thousand
four hundred sixty and eleven, etc.

William Caxton (1422?—1491), merchant and translator, learned the
art of printing on the Continent, probably at Bruges or Cologne. He
translated "The Recuyell of the Histories of Troy", between 1469 and
1471, and, on account of the great demand for copies, was led to have it
printed—the first English book to be reproduced by this means. The date
was about 1474; the place, probably Bruges. In 1476, Caxton came back
to England, and set up a press of his own at Westminster. In 1477, he
issued the first book known to have been printed in England, "The Dictes
and Sayings of the Philosophers." The following Prefaces and Epilogues
from Caxton's own pen show his attitude towards some of the more important of the works that issued from his press.

And on that other side of this leaf followeth the prologue.
When I remember that every man is bounden by the
commandment and counsel of the wise man to eschew
sloth and idleness, which is mother and nourisher of vices,
and ought to put myself unto virtuous occupation and
business, then I, having no great charge of occupation,
following the said counsel took a French book, and read
therein many strange and marvellous histories, wherein I
had great pleasure and delight, as well for the novelty of
the same as for the fair language of French, which was in
prose so well and compendiously set and written, which
methought I understood the sentence and substance of
every matter. And for so much as this book was new and
late made and drawn into French, and never had seen it
in our English tongue, I thought in myself it should be a
good business to translate it into our English, to the end
that it might be had as well in the royaume of England as
in other lands, and also for to pass therewith the time, and
thus concluded in myself to begin this said work. And
forthwith took pen and ink, and began boldly to run forth
as blind Bayard in this present work, which is named
"The Recuyell of the Trojan Histories." And afterward
when I remembered myself of my simpleness and unper-
fectness that I had in both languages, that is to wit in
French and in English, for in France was I never, and was
born and learned my English in Kent, in the Weald, where
I doubt not is spoken as broad and rude English as in any
place of England; and have continued by the space of 30
years for the most part in the countries of Brabant,
Flanders, Holland, and Zealand. And thus when all these
things came before me, after that I had made and written
five or six quires I fell in despair of this work, and purposed no more to have continued therein, and those
quires laid apart, and in two years after laboured no more
in this work, and was fully in will to have left it, till on
a time it fortuned that the right high, excellent, and right
virtuous princess, my right redoubted Lady, my Lady
Margaret, by the grace of God sister unto the King of
England and of France, my sovereign lord, Duchess of
Burgundy, of Lotryk, of Brabant, of Limburg, and of

Luxembourg, Countess of Flanders, of Artois, and of Burgundy, Palatine of Hainault, of Holland, of Zealand and of Namur, Marquesse of the Holy Empire, Lady of Frisia, of Salins and of Mechlin, sent for me to speak with her good Grace of divers matters, among the which I let her Highness have knowledge of the foresaid beginning of this work, which anon commanded me to show the said five or six quires to her said Grace; and when she had seen them anon she found a default in my English, which she commanded me to amend, and moreover commanded me straitly to continue and make an end of the residue then not translated; whose dreadful commandment I durst in no wise disobey, because I am a servant unto her said Grace and receive of her yearly fee and other many good and great benefits, (and also hope many more to receive of her Highness), but forthwith went and laboured in the said translation after my simple and poor cunning, also nigh as I can following my author, meekly beseeching the bounteous Highness of my said Lady that of her benevolence list to accept and take in gree this simple and rude work here following; and if there be anything written or said to her pleasure, I shall think my labour well employed, and whereas there is default that she arette it to the simpleness of my cunning which is full small in this behalf; and require and pray all them that shall read this said work to correct it, and to hold me excused of the rude and simple translation.

And thus I end my prologue.

EPILOGUE TO BOOK II

Thus endeth the second book of the Recule of the Histories of Troy. Which bookes were late translated into French out of Latin by the labour of the venerable person Raoul le Feure, priest, as afore is said; and by me indigne and unworthy, translated into this rude English by the commandment of my said redoubted Lady, Duchess of Burgundy. And for as much as I suppose the said two books be not had before this time in our English language, therefore I had the better will to accomplish this said

work; which work was begun in Bruges and continued in
Ghent and finished in Cologne, in the time of the troublous
world, and of the great divisions being and reigning, as well
in the royaumes of England and France as in all other
places universally through the world; that is to wit the year
of our Lord a thousand four hundred seventy one. And as
for the third book, which treateth of the general and last
destruction of Troy, it needeth not to translate it into
English, for as much as that worshipful and religious man,
Dan John Lidgate, monk of Bury, did translate it but
late; after whose work I fear to take upon me, that am
not worthy to bear his penner and ink-horn after him, to
meddle me in that work. But yet for as much as I am
bound to contemplate my said Lady's good grace, and also
that his work is in rhyme and as far as I know it is not had
in prose in our tongue, and also, peradventure, he translated after some other author than this is; and yet for as
much as divers men be of divers desires, some to read in
rhyme and metre and some in prose; and also because that
I have now good leisure, being in Cologne, and have none
other thing to do at this time; in eschewing of idleness,
mother of all vices, I have delibered in myself for the
contemplation of my said redoubted lady to take this labour
in hand, by the sufferance and help of Almighty God;
whom I meekly supplye to give me grace to accomplish it
to the pleasure of her that is causer thereof, and that
she receive it in gree of me, her faithful, true, and most
humble servant, etc.

Epilogue to Book III

Thus end I this book, which I have translated after mine
Author as nigh as God hath given me cunning, to whom be
given the laud and praising. And for as much as in the
writing of the same my pen is worn, my hand weary and
not steadfast, mine eyne dimmed with overmuch looking on
the white paper, and my courage not so prone and ready
to labour as it hath been, and that age creepeth on me
daily and feebleth all the body, and also because I have
promised to divers gentlemen and to my friends to address

to them as hastily as I might this said book, therefore I have practised and learned at my great charge and dispense to ordain this said book in print, after the manner and form as ye may here see, and is not written with pen and ink as other books be, to the end that every man may have them at once. For all the books of this story, named "The Recule of the Histories of Troy" thus imprinted as ye here see, were begun in one day and also finished in one day, which book I have presented to my said redoubted Lady, as afore is said. And she hath well accepted it, and largely rewarded me, wherefore I beseech Almighty God to reward her everlasting bliss after this life, praying her said Grace and all them that shall read this book not to disdain the simple and rude work, neither to reply against the saying of the matters touched in this book, though it accord not unto the translation of others which have written it. For divers men have made divers books which in all points accord not, as Dictes, Dares, and Homer. For Dictes and Homer, as Greeks, say and write favorably for the Greeks, and give to them more worship than to the Trojans; and Dares writeth otherwise than they do. And also as for the proper names, it is no wonder that they accord not, for some one name in these days have divers equivocations after the countries that they dwell in; but all accord in conclusion the general destruction of that noble city of Troy, and the death of so many noble princes, as kings, dukes, earls, barons, knights, and common people, and the ruin irreparable of that city that never since was re-edified; which may be example to all men during the world how dreadful and jeopardous it is to begin a war and what harms, losses, and death followeth. Therefore the Apostle saith: "All that is written is written to our doctrine," which doctrine for the common weal I beseech God may be taken in such place and time as shall be most needful in increasing of peace, love, and charity; which grant us He that suffered for the same to be crucified on the rood tree. And say we all Amen for charity!

DICTES AND SAYINGS OF THE PHILOSOPHERS

FIRST EDITION (1477). EPILOGUE

HERE endeth the book named *The Dictes or Sayings of the Philosophers,* imprinted by me, William Caxton, at Westminster, the year of our Lord 1477. Which book is late translated out of French into English by the noble and puissant Lord Lord Antony, Earl of Rivers, Lord of Scales and of the Isle of Wight, defender and director of the siege apostolic for our holy father the Pope in this royaume of England, and governor of my Lord Prince of Wales. And it is so that at such time as he had accomplished this said work, it liked him to send it to me in certain quires to oversee, which forthwith I saw, and found therein many great, notable, and wise sayings of the philosophers, according unto the books made in French which I had often before read; but certainly I had seen none in English until that time. And so afterward I came unto my said Lord, and told him how I had read and seen his book, and that he had done a meritorious deed in the labour of the translation thereof into our English tongue, wherein he had deserved a singular laud and thanks, &c. Then my said Lord desired me to oversee it, and where I should find fault to correct it; whereon I answered unto his Lordship that I could not amend it, but if I should so presume I might apaire it, for it was right well and cunningly made and translated into right good and fair English. Notwithstanding, he willed me to oversee it, and shewed me divers things, which, as seemed to him, might be left out, as divers letters, missives sent from Alexander to Darius and Aristotle, and each to other, which letters were little appertinent unto dictes and sayings aforesaid, forasmuch as they specify of other matters. And also desired me, that done, to put the said book in imprint. And thus obeying his request and commandment, I have put me in devoir to oversee this his said book, and behold as nigh as I could how it accordeth with the original, being in French. And I find nothing discordant therein, save only in the

dictes and sayings of Socrates, wherein I find that my said
Lord hath left out certain and divers conclusions touching
women. Whereof I marvel that my Lord hath not written
them, ne what hath moved him so to do, ne what cause
he had at that time; but I suppose that some fair lady hath
desired him to leave it out of his book; or else he was
amorous on some noble lady, for whose love he would not
set it in his book; or else for the very affection, love, and
good will that he hath unto all ladies and gentlewomen, he
thought that Socrates spared the sooth and wrote of women
more than truth; which I cannot think that so true a man
and so noble a philosopher as Socrates was should write
otherwise than truth. For if he had made fault in writing
of women, he ought not, ne should not, be believed in his
other dictes and sayings. But I perceive that my said
Lord knoweth verily that such defaults be not had ne found
in the women born and dwelling in these parts ne regions
of the world. Socrates was a Greek, born in a far country
from hence, which country is all of other conditions than
this is, and men and women of other nature than they be
here in this country. For I wot well, of whatsoever condition women be in Greece, the women of this country be
right good, wise, pleasant, humble, discreet, sober, chaste,
obedient to their husbands, true, secret, steadfast, ever busy,
and never idle, attemperate in speaking, and virtuous in all
their works—or at least should be so. For which causes
so evident my said Lord, as I suppose, thought it was not
of necessity to set in his book the sayings of his author
Socrates touching women. But forasmuch as I had commandment of my said Lord to correct and amend where
I should find fault, and other find I none save that he hath
left out these dictes and sayings of the women of Greece,
therefore in accomplishing his commandment—forasmuch
as I am not certain whether it was in my Lord's copy or not,
or else, peradventure, that the wind had blown over the leaf
at the time of translation of his book—I purpose to write
those same sayings of that Greek Socrates, which wrote of
the women of Greece and nothing of them of this royaume,
whom, I suppose, he never knew; for if he had, I dare
plainly say that he would have reserved them specially in

his said dictes. Always not presuming to put and set them in my said Lord's book but in the end apart in the rehearsal of the works, humbly requiring all them that shall read this little rehearsal, that if they find any fault to arette it to Socrates, and not to me, which writeth as hereafter followeth.

Socrates said that women be the apparels to catch men, but they take none but them that will be poor or else them that know them not. And he said that there is none so great empechement unto a man as ignorance and women. And he saw a woman that bare fire, of whom he said that the hotter bore the colder. And he saw a woman sick, of whom he said that the evil resteth and dwelleth with the evil. And he saw a woman brought to the justice, and many other women followed her weeping, of whom he said the evil be sorry and angry because the evil shall perish. And he saw a young maid that learned to write, of whom he said that men multiplied evil upon evil. And he said that the ignorance of a man is known in three things, that is to wit, when he hath no thought to use reason; when he cannot refrain his covetise; and when he is governed by the counsel of women, in that he knoweth that they know not. And he said unto his disciples: "Will ye that I enseign and teach you how ye shall now escape from all evil?" And they answered, "Yea." And then he said to them, "For whatsoever thing that it be, keep you and be well ware that ye obey not women." Who answered to him again, "And what sayest thou by our good mothers, and of our sisters?" He said to them, "Suffice you with that I have said to you, for all be semblable in malice." And he said, "Whosoever will acquire and get science, let him never put him in the governance of a woman." And he saw a woman that made her fresh and gay, to whom he said, "Thou resemblest the fire; for the more wood is laid to the fire the more will it burn, and the greater is the heat." And on a time one asked him what him semed of women; he answered that the women resemble a tree called Edelfla, which is the fairest tree to behold and see that may be, but within it is full of venom. And they said to him and demanded wherefore he blamed so women? and that he

himself had not come into this world, ne none other men
also, without them. He answered, " The woman is like
unto a tree named Chassoygnet, on which tree there be
many things sharp and pricking, which hurt and prick them
that approach unto it; and yet, nevertheless, that same
tree bringeth forth good dates and sweet." And they
demanded him why he fled from the women? And he
answered, "Forasmuch as I see them flee and eschew the
good and commonly do evil." And a woman said to him,
" Wilt thou have any other woman than me?" And he
answered to her, "Art not ashamed to offer thyself to
him that demandeth nor desireth thee not?"

So, these be the dictes and sayings of the philosopher
Socrates, which he wrote in his book; and certainly he
wrote no worse than afore is rehearsed. And forasmuch
as it is accordant that his dictes and sayings should be had
as well as others', therefore I have set it in the end of this
book. And also some persons, peradventure, that have read
this book in French would have arette a great default in me
that I had not done my devoir in visiting and overseeing of
my Lord's book according to his desire. And some other
also, haply, might have supposed that Socrates had written
much more ill of women than here afore is specified, wherefore in satisfying of all parties, and also for excuse of the
said Socrates, I have set these said dictes and sayings apart
in the end of this book, to the intent that if my said lord or
any other person, whatsoever he or she be that shall read or
hear it, that if they be not well pleased withal, that they
with a pen race it out, or else rend the leaf out of the book.
Humbly requiring and beseeching my said lord to take no
displeasure on me so presuming, but to pardon whereas he
shall find fault; and that it please him to take the labour of
the imprinting in gree and thanks, which gladly have done
my diligence in the accomplishing of his desire and commandment; in which I am bounden so to do for the good
reward that I have received of his said lordship; whom I
beseech Almighty God to increase and to continue in his
virtuous disposition in this world, and after this life to live
everlastingly in Heaven. Amen.

GOLDEN LEGEND.

First Edition (1483). Prologue

The Holy and blessed doctor Saint Jerome saith this authority, "Do always some good work to the end that the devil find thee not Idle." And the holy doctor Saint Austin saith in the book of the labour of monks, that no man strong or mighty to labour ought to be idle; for which cause when I had performed and accomplished divers works and histories translated out of French into English at the request of certain lords, ladies, and gentlemen, as the Recuyel of the History of Troy, the Book of the Chess, the History of Jason, the history of the Mirror of the World, the 15 books of Metamorphoses in which be contained the fables of Ovid, and the History of Godfrey of Boulogne in the conquest of Jerusalem, with other divers works and books, I ne wist what work to begin and put forth after the said works to-fore made. And forasmuch as idleness is so much blamed, as saith Saint Bernard, the mellifluous doctor, that she is mother of lies and step-dame of virtues, and it is she that overthroweth strong men into sin, quencheth virtue, nourisheth pride, and maketh the way ready to go to hell; and John Cassiodorus saith that the thought of him that is idle thinketh on none other thing but on licorous meats and viands for his belly; and the holy Saint Bernard aforesaid saith in an epistle, when the time shall come that it shall behove us to render and give accounts of our idle time, what reason may we render or what answer shall we give when in idleness is none excuse; and Prosper saith that whosoever liveth in idleness liveth in manner of a dumb beast. And because I have seen the authorities that blame and despise so much idleness, and also know well that it is one of the capital and deadly sins much hateful unto God, therefore I have concluded and firmly purposed in myself no more to be idle, but will apply myself to labour and such occupation as I have been accustomed to do. And forasmuch as Saint Austin aforesaid saith upon a psalm that good work ought not to be done for fear of pain, but for the love of righteousness, and that it be of very and sovereign franchise, and because me-seemeth to be a sovereign weal to incite and exhort men and women to keep them from sloth and idleness, and to let to be understood to such people as be not lettered the nativities, the lives, the passions, the miracles, and the death of the holy saints, and also some other notorious deeds and acts of times past, I have submised myself to translate into English the legend of Saints, which is called *Legenda Aurea* in Latin, that is to say, the *Golden Legend;* for in like wise as gold is most noble above all other metals, in like wise is this legend holden most noble above all other works. Against me here might some persons say that this legend hath been translated before, and truth it is; but forasmuch as I had by me a legend in French, another in Latin, and the third in English, which varied in many and divers places, and also many histories were comprised in the two other books which were not in the English books; and therefore I have written one out of the said three books, which I have ordered otherwise than the said English legend is, which was so to-fore made, beseeching all them that shall see or hear it read to pardon me where I have erred or made fault, which, if any be, is of ignorance and against my will; and submit it wholly of such as can and may, to correct it, humbly beseeching them so to do, and in so doing they shall deserve a singular laud and merit; and I shall pray for them unto Almighty God that He of His benign grace reward them, etc., and that it profit to all them that shall read or hear it read, and may increase in them virtue, and expel vice and sin, that by the example of the holy saints amend their living here in this short life, that by their merits they and I may come to everlasting life and bliss in Heaven. Amen.

CATON (1483)

PROLOGUE

HERE beginneth the prologue of proem of the book called *Caton,* which book hath been translated into English by Master Benet Burgh, late Archdeacon of Colchester, and high canon of St. Stephen's at Westminster, which ful craftily hath made it in ballad royal for the erudition of my lord Bousher, son and heir at that time to my lord the Earl of Essex. And because of late came to my hand a book of the said Cato in French, which rehearseth many a fair learning and notable examples, I have translated it out of French into English, as all along hereafter shall appear, which I present unto the city of London.

Unto the noble, ancient, and renowned city, the city of London, in England, I, William Caxton, citizen and conjury of the same, and of the fraternity and fellowship of the mercery, owe of right my service and good will, and of very duty am bounden naturally to assist, aid, and counsel, as far forth as I can to my power, as to my mother of whom I have received my nurture and living, and shall pray for the good prosperity and policy of the same during my life. For, as me-seemeth, it is of great need, because I have known it in my young age much more wealthy, prosperous, and richer, than it is at this day. And the cause is that there is almost none that intendeth to the common weal, but only every man for his singular profit. Oh! when I remember the noble Romans, that for the common weal of the city of Rome they spent not only their moveable goods but they put their bodies and lives in jeopardy and to the death, as by many a noble example we may see in the acts of Romans, as of the two noble Scipios, African and Asian, Actilius, and many others. And among all others the noble Cato, author and maker of this book, which he hath left for to remain ever to all the people for to learn in it and to know how every man ought to rule and govern him in this life, as well for the life temporal as for the life spiritual. And as in my judgement it is the best book for to be taught to young children in school, and also to people of every age, it is full convenient if it be well understood. And because I see that the children that be born within the said city increase, and profit not like their fathers and elders, but for the most part after that they be come to their perfect years of discretion and ripeness of age, how well that their fathers have left to them great quantity of goods yet scarcely among ten two thrive, [whereas] I have seen and know in other lands in divers cities that of one name and lineage successively have endured prosperously many heirs, yea, a five or six hundred years, and some a thousand; and in this noble city of London it can unneth continue unto the third heir or scarcely to the second,—O blessed Lord, when I remember this I am all abashed; I cannot judge the cause, but fairer ne wiser ne better spoken children in their youth be nowhere than there be in London, but at their full ripening there is no kernel ne good corn found, but chaff for the most part. I wot well there be many noble and wise, and prove well and be better and richer than ever were their fathers. And to the end that many might come to honour and worship, I intend to translate this said book of Cato, in which I doubt not, and if they will read it and understand they shall much the better con rule themselves thereby; for among all other books this is a singular book, and may well be called the regiment or governance of the body and soul.

There was a noble clerk named Pogius of Florence, and was secretary to Pope Eugene and also to Pope Nicholas, which had in the city of Florence a noble and well-stuffed library which all noble strangers coming to Florence desired to see; and therein they found many noble and rare books. And when they had asked of him which was the best book of them all, and that he reputed for best, he said that he held Cato glosed for the best book of his library. Then since that he that was so noble a clerk held this book for the best, doubtless it must follow that this is a noble book and a virtuous, and such one that a man may eschew all vices and ensue virtue. Then to the end that this said book may profit unto the hearers of it, I beseech Almighty God that I may achieve and accomplish it unto his laud and glory, and to the erudition and learning of them that be ignorant, that they may thereby profit and be the better. And I require and beseech all such that find fault or error, that of their charity they correct and amend it, and I shall heartily pray for them to Almighty God, that he reward them.

AESOP. (1483)

Epilogue

Now then I will finish all these fables with this tale that followeth, which a worshipful priest and a parson told me lately. He said that there were dwelling in Oxford two priests, both masters of art, of whom that one was quick and could put himself forth, and that other was a good simple priest. And so it happened that the master that was pert and quick, was anon promoted to a benefice or twain, and after to prebends and for to be a dean of a great prince's chapel, supposing and weening that his fellow the simple priest should never have been promoted, but be alway an Annual, or at the most a parish priest. So after long time that this worshipful man, this dean, came riding into a good parish with a ten or twelve horses, like a prelate, and came into the church of the said parish, and found there this good simple man sometime his fellow, which came and welcomed him lowly; and that other bad him "good morrow, master John," and took him slightly by the hand, and asked him where he dwelt. And the good man said, "In this parish." "How," said he, "are ye here a soul priest or a parish priest?" "Nay, sir," said he, "for lack of a better, though I be not able ne worthy, I am parson and curate of this parish." And then that other availed his bonnet and said, "Master parson, I pray you to be not displeased; I had supposed ye had not been beneficed; but master," said he, "I pray you what is this benefice worth to you a year?" "Forsooth," said the good simple man, "I wot never, for I make never accounts thereof how well I have had it four or five years." "And know ye not," said he, "what it is worth? it should seem a good benefice." "No, forsooth," said he, "but I wot well what it shall be worth to me." "Why," said he, "what shall it be worth?" "Forsooth," said he, "if I do my true diligence in the cure of my parishioners in preaching and teaching, and do my part longing to my cure, I shall have heaven therefore; and if their souls be lost, or any of them by my default, I shall be punished therefore, and hereof am I sure." And with that word the rich dean was abashed, and thought he should do the better and take more heed to his cures and benefices than he had done. This was a good answer of a good priest and an honest. And herewith I finished this book, translated and printed by me, William Caxton, at Westminster in the Abbey, and finished the 26th day of March, the year of our Lord 1484, and the first year of the reign of King Richard the Third.

CHAUCER'S CANTERBURY TALES

Second Edition. (1484)

PROEM

GREAT thanks, laud, and honour ought to be given unto the clerks, poets, and historiographs that have written many noble books of wisedom of the lives, passions, and miracles of holy saints, of histories of noble and famous acts and faites, and of the chronicles since the beginning of the creation of the world unto this present time, by which we be daily informed and have knowledge of many things of whom we should not have known if they had not left to us their monuments written. Among whom and in especial before all others, we ought to give a singular laud unto that noble and great philosopher Geoffrey Chaucer, the which for his ornate writing in our tongue may well have the name of a laureate poet. For to-fore that he by labour embellished, ornated, and made fair our English, in this realm was had rude speech and incongruous, as yet it appeareth by old books, which at this day ought not to have place ne be compared among, ne to, his beauteous volumes and ornate writings, of whom he made many books and treatises of many a noble history, as well in metre as in rhyme and prose; and them so craftily made that he comprehended his matters in short, quick, and high sentences, eschewing prolixity, casting away the chaff of superfluity, and shewing the picked grain of sentence uttered by crafty and sugared eloquence; of whom among all others of his books I purpose to print, by the grace of God, the book of the tales of Canterbury, in which I find many a noble history of every state and degree; first rehearsing the conditions and the array of each of them as properly as possible is to be said. And after their tales which be of nobleness, wisdom, gentleness, mirth and also of very holiness and virtue, wherein he finisheth this said book, which book I have diligently overseen and duly examined, to that end it be made according unto his own making. For I find many of the said books which writers have abridged it, and many things left out; and in some place have set certain verses that he never made ne set in his book; of which books so incorrect was one brought to me, 6 years past, which I supposed had been very true and correct; and according to the same I did so imprint a certain number of them, which anon were sold to many and divers gentlemen, of whom one gentleman came to me and said that this book was not according in many place unto the book that Geoffrey Chaucer had made. To whom I answered that I had made it according to my copy, and by me was nothing added ne minished. Then he said he knew a book which his father had and much loved, that was very true and according unto his own first book by him made; and said more, if I would imprint it again he would get me the same book for a copy, howbeit he wist well that his father would not gladly depart from it. To whom I said, in case that he could get me such a book, true and correct, yet I would once endeavour me to imprint it again for to satisfy the author, whereas before by ignorance I erred in hurting and defaming his book in divers places, in setting in some things that he never said ne made, and leaving out many things that he made which be requisite to be set in it. And thus we fell at accord, and he full gently got of his father the said book and delivered it to me, by which I have corrected my book, as hereafter, all along by the aid of Almighty God, shall follow; whom I humbly beseech to give me grace and aid to achieve and accomplish to his laud, honour, and glory; and that all ye that shall in this book read or hear, will of your charity among your deeds of mercy remember the soul

of the said Geoffrey Chaucer, first author and maker of this
book. And also that all we that shall see and read therein
may so take and understand the good and virtuous tales,
that it may so profit unto the health of our souls that after
this short and transitory life we may come to everlasting
life in Heaven. Amen.

BY WILLIAM CAXTON

MALORY'S KING ARTHUR. (1485)

PROLOGUE

AFTER that I had accomplished and finished divers histories, as well of contemplation as of other historical and
worldly acts of great conquerors and princes, and also
certain books of ensamples and doctrine, many noble and
divers gentlemen of this realm of England came and demanded me many and oft times wherefore that I have
not done made and printed the noble history of the Saint
Graal, and of the most renowned Christian King, first and
chief of the three best Christian and worthy, Arthur, which
ought most to be remembered among us Englishmen before all other Christian Kings. For it is notoyrly known
through the universal world that there be nine worthy
and the best that ever were; that is to wit three Paynims,
three Jews, and three Christian men. As for the Paynims,
they were to-fore the Incarnation of Christ, which were
named—the first, Hector of Troy, of whom the history is
come both in ballad and in prose—the second, Alexander
the Great; and the third, Julius Caesar, Emperor of Rome,
of whom the histories be well known and had. And as
for the three Jews, which also were before the Incarnation
of our Lord of whom the first was Duke Joshua, which
brought the children of Israel into the land of behest;
the second, David, King of Jerusalem; and the third Judas
Maccabæus; of these three the Bible rehearseth all their
noble histories and acts. And since the said Incarnation
have been three noble Christian men, installed and admitted
through the universal world into the number of the nine
best and worthy, of whom was first the noble Arthur, whose

noble acts I purpose to write in this present book here
following. The second was Charlemagne, or Charles the
Great, of whom the history is had in many places both in
French and English; and the third and last was Godfrey
of Boulogne, of whose acts and life I made a book unto the
excellent prince and king of noble memory, King Edward
the Fourth. The said noble gentlemen instantly required
me to print the history of the said noble king and conqueror,
King Arthur, and of his knights, with the history of the
Saint Graal, and of the death and ending of the said Arthur,
affirming that I ought rather to print his acts and noble
feats than of Godfrey of Boulogne or any of the other
eight, considering that he was a man born within this realm,
and king and emperor of the same; and that there be in
French divers and many noble volumes of his acts, and also
of his knights. To whom I answered that divers men hold
opinion that there was no such Arthur, and that all such
books as be made of him be but feigned and fables, because
that some chronicles make of him no mention, ne remember
him nothing ne of his knights; whereto they answered, and
one in special said, that in him that should say or think that
there was never such a king called Arthur, might well be
aretted great folly and blindness; for he said that there were
many evidences of the contrary. First ye may see his sepulchre in the monastery of Glastonbury; and also in 'Poly-
chronicon,' in the fifth book, the sixth chapter, and in the
seventh book, the twenty-third chapter, where his body was
buried, and after found and translated into the said monastery. Ye shall see also in the history of Boccaccio, in
his book 'De casu principum,' part of his noble acts and
also of his fall. Also Galfridus in his British book re-
counteth his life, and in divers places of England many
remembrances be yet of him, and shall remain perpetually,
and also of his knights. First in the Abbey of Westminster at Saint Edward's shrine remaineth the print of
his seal in red wax closed in beryl, in which is written
'Patricius Arthurus, Britanniae Galliae Germaniae Daciae
Imperator.' Item, in the castle of Dover ye may see
Gawain's skull and Caradoc's mantle; at Winchester the
round table; in other places Lancelot's sword, and many

other things. Then all these things considered, there can no man reasonably gainsay but here was a king of this land named Arthur; for in all places, Christian and heathen, he is reputed and taken for one of the nine worthy, and the first of the three Christian men. And also he is more spoken of beyond the sea; more books made of his noble acts than there be in England, as well in Dutch, Italian, Spanish, and Greek as in French; and yet of record remain in witness of him in Wales in the town of Camelot the great stones and marvellous works of iron lying under the ground, and royal vaults, which divers now living hath seen. Wherefore it is a marvel why he is no more renowned in his own country, save only it accordeth to the word of God, which saith that no man is accepted for a prophet in his own country. Then all these things aforesaid alleged, I could not well deny but that there was such a noble king named Arthur, and reputed one of the nine worthy, and first and chief of the Christian men; and many noble volumes be made of him and of his noble knights in French, which I have seen and read beyond the sea, which be not had in our maternal tongue, but in Welsh be many, and also in French, and some in English, but nowhere nigh all. Wherefore such as have lately been drawn out briefly into English, I have, after the simple cunning that God hath sent to me, under the favour and correction of all noble lords and gentlemen, emprised to imprint a book of the noble histories of the said King Arthur and of certain of his knights, after a copy unto me delivered, which copy Sir Thomas Mallory did take out of certain books of French and reduced it into English. And I according to my copy have down set it in print, to the intent that noble men may see and learn the noble acts of chivalry, the gentle and virtuous deeds that some knights used in those days, by which they came to honour, and how they that were vicious were punished and oft put to shame and rebuke; humbly beseeching all noble lords and ladies and all other estates, of what estate or degree they be of, that shall see and read in this said book and work, that they take the good and honest acts in their remembrance and to follow the same, wherein they shall find many joyous and pleasant histories and noble and renowned acts of humanity, gentleness, and chivalry. For herein may be seen noble chivalry, courtesy, humanity, friendliness, hardyhood, love, friendship, cowardice, murder, hate, virtue and sin. Do after the good and leave the evil, and it shall bring you to good' fame and renown. And for to pass the time this book shall be pleasant to read in; but for to give faith and believe that all is true that is contained herein, ye be at your liberty. But all is written for our doctrine, and for to beware that we fall not to vice ne sin, but to exercise and follow virtue, by which we may come and attain to good fame and renown in this life, and after this short and transitory life to come unto everlasting bliss in heaven; the which He grant us that reigneth in Heaven, the Blessed Trinity. Amen.

Then to proceed forth in this said book which I direct unto all noble princes, lords and ladies, gentlemen or gentlewomen, that desire to read or hear read of the noble and joyous history of the great conqueror and excellent king, King Arthur, sometime King of this noble realm then called Britain, I, William Caxton, simple person, present this book following which I have emprised to imprint. And treateth of the noble acts, feats of arms, of chivalry, prowess, hardihood, humanity, love, courtesy, and very gentleness, with many wonderful histories and adventures. And for to understand briefly the contents of this volume, I have divided it into 21 books, and every book chaptered, as hereafter shall by God's grace follow. The first book shall treat how Uther Pendragon begat the noble conqueror, King Arthur, and containeth 28 chapters. The second book treateth of Balyn the noble knight, and containeth 19 chapters. The third book treateth of the marriage of King Arthur to Queen Guinevere, with other matters, and containeth 15 chapters. The fourth book how Merlin was assotted, and of war made to King Arthur, and containeth 29 chapters. The fifth book treateth of the conquest of Lucius the emperor, and containeth 12 chapters. The sixth book treateth of Sir Lancelot and Sir Lionel, and marvellous adventures, and containeth 18 chapters. The seventh book treateth of a noble knight called Sir Gareth, and

named by Sir Kay ' Beaumains,' and containeth 36 chapters.
The eighth book treateth of the birth ot Sir Tristram
the noble knight, and of his acts, and containeth 41 chapters.
The ninth book treateth of a knight named by Sir Kay,
' Le cote mal taillé,' and also of Sir Tristram, and containeth 44 chapters. The tenth book treateth of Sir Tristram, and other marvellous adventures, and containeth 83
chapters. The eleventh book treateth of Sir Lancelot and
Sir Galahad, and containeth 14 chapters. The twelfth
book treateth of Sir Lancelot and his madness, and containeth 14 chapters. The thirteenth book treateth how
Galahad came first to King Arthur's court, and the quest
how the Sangreal was begun, and containeth 20 chapters.
The fourteenth book treateth of the quest of the Sangreal,
and containeth 10 chapters. The fifteenth book treateth
of Sir Lancelot, and containeth 6 chapters. The sixteenth book treateth of Sir Boris and Sir Lionel his brother,
and containeth 17 chapters. The seventeenth book treateth of the Sangreal, and containeth 23 chapters. The
eighteenth book treateth of Sir Lancelot and the Queen,
and containeth 25 chapters. The nineteenth book treateth
of Queen Guinevere, and Lancelot, and containeth 13
chapters. The twentieth book treateth of the piteous death
of Arthur, and containeth 22 chapters. The twenty-first
book treateth of his last departing, and how Sir Lancelot
came to revenge his death, and containeth 13 chapters.
The sum is 21 books, which contain the sum of five hundred and seven chapters, as more plainly shall follow hereafter.

ENEYDOS (1490)

PROLOGUE

AFTER divers work made, translated, and achieved, having
no work in hand, I sitting in my study whereas lay many
divers pamphlets and books, happened that to my hand
came a little book in French, which lately was translated
out of Latin by some noble clerk of France, which book is
named *Aeneidos,* made in Latin by that noble poet and

great clerk, Virgil. Which book I saw over, and read therein how, after the general destruction of the great Troy, Aeneas departed, bearing his old father Anchises upon his shoulders, his little son Iulus on his hand, his wife with much other people following, and how he shipped and departed, with all the history of his adventures that he had ere he came to the achievement of his conquest of Italy, as all along shall be shewed in his present book. In which book I had great pleasure because of the fair and honest terms and words in French; which I never saw before like, ne none so pleasant ne so well ordered; which book as seemed to me should be much requisite to noble men to see, as well for the eloquence as the histories. How well that many hundred years past was the said book of *Aeneidos,* with other works, made and learned daily in schools, especially in Italy and other places; which history the said Virgil made in metre. And when I had advised me in this said book, I delibered and concluded to translate it into English; and forthwith took a pen and ink and wrote a leaf or twain, which I oversaw again to correct it. And when I saw the fair and strange terms therein, I doubted that it should not please some gentlemen which late blamed me, saying that in my translations I had over curious terms, which could not be understood of common people, and desired me to use old and homely terms in my translations. And fain would I satisfy every man, and so to do took an old book and read therein, and certainly the English was so rude and broad that I could not well understood it. And also my Lord Abbot of Westminster did do show to me lately certain evidences written in old English, for to reduce it into our English now used. And certainly it was written in such wise that it was more like to Dutch than English, I could not reduce ne bring it to be understood. And certainly our language now used varieth far from that which was used and spoken when I was born. For we Englishmen be born under the domination of the moon, which is never steadfast but ever wavering, waxing one season and waneth and decreaseth another season. And that common English that is spoken in one shire varieth from another, insomuch that in my days happened that certain merchants were in a ship in Thames for to have sailed over the sea into Zealand, and for lack of wind they tarried at Foreland, and went to land for to refresh them. And one of them named Sheffield, a mercer, came into a house and asked for meat, and especially he asked after eggs; and the good wife answered that she could speak no French, and the merchant was angry, for he also could speak no French, but would have had eggs, and she understood him not. And then at last another said, that he would have " eyren "; then the goodwife said that she understood him well. Lo, what should a man in these days now write, eggs or eyren? Certainly it is hard to please every man because of diversity and change of language. For in these days every man that is in any reputation in his country will utter his communication and matters in such manners and terms that few men shall understand them. And some honest and great clerks have been with me and desired me to write the most curious terms that I could find; and thus between plain, rude and curious I stand abashed. But in my judgment the common terms that be daily used be lighter to be understood than the old and ancient English. And forasmuch as this present book is not for a rude uplandish man to labour therein ne read it, but only for a clerk and a noble gentleman that feeleth and understandeth in feats of arms, in love and in noble chivalry. Therefore in a mean between both I have reduced and translated this said book into our English, not over-rude ne curious; but in such terms as shall be understood, by God's grace, according to my copy. And if any man will intermit in reading of it, and findeth such terms that he cannot understand, let him go read and learn Virgil of the pistles of Ovid, and there he shall see and understand lightly all, if he have a good reader and informer. For this book is not for every rude and uncunning man to see, but to clerks and very gentlemen that understand gentleness and science. Then I pray all them that shall read in this little treatise to hold me for excused for the translating of it, for I acknowledge myself ignorant of cunning to emprise on me so high and noble a work. But I pray Master John Skelton, late **created** poet laureate in the University of Oxenford, to oversee and correct this said book, and to address and expound, wherever shall be found fault, to them that shall require it.

For him I know for sufficient to expound and English every difficulty that is therein; for he hath lately translated the Epistles of Tully, and the book of Diodorus Siculus, and divers other works out of Latin into English, not in rude and old language, but in polished and ornate terms craftily, as he that hath read Virgil, Ovid, Tully, and all the other noble poets and orators to me unknown. And also he hath read the nine Muses, and understands their musical sciences, and to whom of them each science is appropred. I suppose he hath drunken of Helicon's well. Then I pray him and such others to correct, add, or minish whereas he or they shall find fault; for I have but followed my copy in French as nigh as to me is possible. And if any word be said therein well, I am glad; and if otherwise, I submit my said book to their correction. Which book I present unto the high born, my to-coming natural and sovereign lord Arthur, by the grace of God Prince of Wales, Duke of Cornwall and Earl of Chester, first-begotten son and heir unto our most dread natural and sovereign lord and most Christian King, Henry the VII., by the grace of God King of England and of France, and lord of Ireland; beseeching his noble Grace to receive it in thank of me his most humble subject and servant. And I shall pray unto Almighty God for his prosperous increasing in virtue, wisdom, and humanity, that he may be equal with the most renowned of all his noble progenitors; and so to live in this present life that after this transitory life he and we all may come to everlasting life in Heaven. Amen.

DEDICATION
OF THE INSTITUTES OF
THE CHRISTIAN RELIGION
BY JOHN CALVIN (1536)

To His Most Christian Majesty, FRANCIS, King of the French, and his Sovereign, John Calvin wisheth peace and salvation in Christ.

WHEN I began this work, Sire, nothing was further from my thoughts than writing a book which would afterwards be presented to your Majesty. My intention was only to lay down some elementary principles, by which inquirers on the subject of religion might be instructed in the nature of true piety. And this labour I undertook chiefly for my countrymen, the French, of whom I apprehended multitudes to be hungering and thirsting after Christ, but saw very few possessing any real knowledge of him. That this was my design, the book itself proves by its simple method and unadorned composition. But when I perceived that the fury of certain wicked men in your kingdom had grown to such a height, as to leave no room in the land for sound doctrine, I thought I should be usefully employed, if in the same work I delivered my instructions to them, and exhibited my confession to you, that you may know the nature of that doctrine, which is the object of such unbounded rage to those madmen who are now disturbing the country with fire and sword. For I shall not be afraid to acknowledge, that this treatise contains a summary of that very doctrine,

John Calvin was born at Noyon, Picardy, France, in 1509, and died at Geneva in 1564. He joined the Reformation about 1528, and, having been banished from Paris, took refuge in Switzerland. The "Institutes," published at Basle in 1536, contain a comprehensive statement of the beliefs of that school of Protestant theology which bears Calvin's name; and in this "Dedication" we have Calvin's own summing up of the essentials of his creed.

which, according to their clamours, deserves to be punished
with imprisonment, banishment, proscription, and flames,
and to be exterminated from the face of the earth. I well
know with what atrocious insinuations your ears have been
filled by them, in order to render our cause most odious
in your esteem; but your clemency should lead you to
consider that, if accusation be accounted a sufficient evidence of guilt, there will be an end of all innocence in words
and actions. If any one, indeed, with a view to bring
odium upon the doctrine which I am endeavouring to defend, should allege that it has long ago been condemned
by the general consent, and suppressed by many judicial
decisions, this will be only equivalent to saying, that it
has been sometimes violently rejected through the influence
and power of its adversaries, and sometimes insidiously
and fraudulently oppressed by falsehoods, artifices, and
calumnies. Violence is displayed, when sanguinary sentences are passed against it without the cause being heard;
and fraud, when it is unjustly accused of sedition and
mischief. Lest any one should suppose that these our complaints are unfounded, you yourself, Sire, can bear witness
of the false calumnies with which you hear it daily tra-
duced; that its only tendency is to wrest the sceptres of
kings out of their hands, to overturn all the tribunals and
judicial proceedings, to subvert all order and governments,
to disturb the peace and tranquillity of the people, to ab-
rogate all laws, to scatter all properties and possessions,
and, in a word, to involve every thing in total confusion.
And yet you hear the smallest portion of what is alleged
against it; for such horrible things are circulated amongst
the vulgar, that, if they were true, the whole world would
justly pronounce it and its abettors worthy of a thousand
fires and gibbets. Who, then, will wonder at its becoming
the object of public odium, where credit is given to such
most iniquitous accusations? This is the cause of the
general consent and conspiracy to condemn us and our
doctrine. Hurried away with this impulse, those who
sit in judgment pronounce for sentences the prejudices they
brought from home with them; and think their duty fully
discharged if they condemn none to be punished but such

as are convicted by their own confession, or by sufficient proofs. Convicted of what crime? Of this condemned doctrine, they say. But with what justice is it condemned? Now, the ground of defence was not to abjure the doctrine itself, but to maintain its truth. On this subject, however, not a word is allowed to be uttered.

Wherefore I beseech you, Sire,—and surely it is not an unreasonable request,—to take upon yourself the entire cognizance of this cause, which has hitherto been confusedly and carelessly agitated, without any order of law, and with outrageous passion rather than judicial gravity. Think not that I am now meditating my own individual defence, in order to effect a safe return to my native country; for, though I feel the affection which every man ought to feel for it, yet, under the existing circumstances, I regret not my removal from it. But I plead the cause of all the godly, and consequently of Christ himself, which, having been in these times persecuted and trampled on in all ways in your kingdom, now lies in a most deplorable state; and this indeed rather through the tryanny of certain Pharisees, than with your knowledge. How this comes to pass is foreign to my present purpose to say; but it certainly lies in a most afflicted state. For the ungodly have gone to such lengths, that the truth of Christ, if not vanquished, dissipated, and entirely destroyed, is buried, as it were, in ignoble obscurity, while the poor, despised church is either destroyed by cruel massacres, or driven away into banishment, or menaced and terrified into total silence. And still they continue their wonted madness and ferocity, pushing violently against the wall already bent, and finishing the ruin they have begun. In the meantime, no one comes forward to plead the cause against such furies. If there be any persons desirous of appearing most favourable to the truth, they only venture an opinion, that forgiveness should be extended to the error and imprudence of ignorant people. For this is the language of these moderate men, calling that error and imprudence which they know to be the certain truth of God, and those ignorant people, whose understanding they perceive not to have been so despicable to Christ, but that he has favoured them with the mysteries of his heavenly wisdom. Thus all are ashamed of the Gospel. But it shall be yours, Sire, not to turn away your ears or thoughts from so just a defence, especially in a cause of such importance as the maintenance of God's glory unimpaired in the world, the preservation of the honor of divine truth, and the continuance of the kingdom of Christ uninjured among us. This is a cause worthy of your attention, worthy of your cognizance, worthy of your throne. This consideration constitutes true royalty, to acknowledge yourself in the government of your kingdom to be the minister of God. For where the glory of God is not made the end of the government, it is not a legitimate sovereignty, but a usurpation. And he is deceived who expects lasting prosperity in that kingdom which is not ruled by the sceptre of God, that is, his holy word; for that heavenly oracle cannot fail, which declares that " where there is no vision, the people perish."[1] Nor should you be seduced from this pursuit by a contempt of our meanness. We are fully conscious to ourselves how very mean and abject we are, being miserable sinners before God, and accounted most despicable by men; being (if you please) the refuse of the world, deserving of the vilest appellations that can be found; so that nothing remains for us to glory in before God, but his mercy alone, by which, without any merit of ours, we have been admitted to the hope of eternal salvation, and before men nothing but our weakness, the slightest confession of which is esteemed by them as the greatest disgrace. But our doctrine must stand, exalted above all the glory, and invincible by all the power of the world; because it is not ours, but the doctrine of the living God, and of his Christ, whom the Father hath constituted King, that he may have dominion from sea to sea, and from the river even to the ends of the earth, and that he may rule in such a manner, that the whole earth, with its strength of iron and with its splendour of gold and silver, smitten by the rod of his mouth, may be broken to pieces like a potter's vessel;[2] for thus do the prophets foretell the magnificence of his kingdom.

Our adversaries reply, that our pleading the word of God is a false pretence, and that we are nefarious cor-

[1] Prov. xxix. 18.   [2] Daniel ii. 34. Isaiah xi. 4. Psalm ii. 9.

rupters of it. But that this is not only a malicious calumny, but egregious impudence, by reading our confession, you will, in your wisdom, be able to judge. Yet something further is necessary to be said, to excite your attention, or at least to prepare your mind for this perusal. Paul's direction, that every prophecy be framed "according to the analogy of faith,"[3] has fixed an invariable standard by which all interpretation of Scripture ought to be tried. If our principles be examined by this rule of faith, the victory is ours. For what is more consistent with faith than to acknowledge ourselves naked of all virtue, that we may be clothed by God; empty of all good, that we may be filled by him; slaves to sin, that we may be liberated by him; blind, that we may be enlightened by him; lame, that we may be guided; weak, that we may be supported by him; to divest ourselves of all ground of glorying, that he alone may be eminently glorious, and that we may glory in him? When we advance these and similiar sentiments, they interrupt us with complaints that this is the way to overturn, I know not what blind light of nature, pretended preparations, free will, and works meritorious of eternal salvation, together with all their supererogations; because they cannot bear that the praise and glory of all goodness, strength, righteousness, and wisdom, should remain entirely with God. But we read of none being reproved for having drawn too freely from the fountain of living waters; on the contrary, they are severely upbraided who have " hewed them out cisterns, broken cisterns, that can hold no water."[4] Again, what is more consistent with faith, than to assure ourselves of God being a propitious Father, where Christ is acknowledged as a brother and Mediator? than securely to expect all prosperity and happiness from Him, whose unspeakable love towards us went so far, that " he spared not his own Son, but delivered him up for us? "[5] than to rest in the certain expectation of salvation and eternal life, when we reflect upon the Father's gift of Christ, in whom such treasures are hidden? Here they oppose us, and complain that this certainty of confidence is chargeable with arrogance and presumption. But as we ought to presume nothing of

ourselves, so we should presume every thing of God; nor
are we divested of vain glory for any other reason than
that we may learn to glory in the Lord. What shall I say
more? Review, Sire, all the parts of our cause, and consider us worse than the most abandoned of mankind, unless you clearly discover that we thus " both labor and suffer
reproach, because we trust in the living God,"[6] because we
believe that " this is life eternal, to know the only true God,
and Jesus Christ whom he hath sent."[7] For this hope some
of us are bound in chains, others are lashed with scourges,
others are carried about as laughing-stocks, others are out-
lawed, others are cruelly tortured, others escape by flight;
but we are all reduced to extreme perplexities, execrated
with dreadful curses, cruelly slandered and treated with
the greatest indignities. Now, look at our adversaries, (I
speak of the order of priests, at whose will and directions
others carry on these hostilities against us,) and consider a
little with me by what principles they are actuated. The
true religion, which is taught in the Scriptures, and ought
to be universally maintained, they readily permit both themselves and others to be ignorant of, and to treat with
neglect and contempt. They think it unimportant what
any one holds or denies concerning God and Christ, provided he submits his mind with an implicit faith (as they
call it) to the judgment of the Church. Nor are they much
affected, if the glory of God happens to be violated with
open blasphemies, provided no one lift a finger against the
primacy of the Apostolic See, and the authority of their
holy Mother Church. Why, therefore, do they contend with
such extreme bitterness and cruelty for the mass, purgatory,
pilgrimages, and similar trifles, and deny that any piety
can be maintained without a most explicit faith, so to speak,
in these things; whereas they prove none of them from the
word of God? Why, but because their belly is their God,
their kitchen is their religion; deprived of which they consider themselves no longer as Christians, or even as men.
For though some feast themselves in splendour, and others
subsist on slender fare, yet all live on the same pot, which,
without this fuel, would not only cool, but completely freeze.

[6] 1 Tim. iv. 10.   [7] John xvii. 3.

Every one of them, therefore, who is most solicitous for his belly, is found to be a most strenuous champion for their faith. Indeed, they universally exert themselves for the preservation of their kingdom, and the repletion of their bellies; but not one of them discovers the least indication of sincere zeal.

Nor do their attacks on our doctrine cease here; they urge every topic of accusation and abuse to render it an object of hatred or suspicion. They call it novel, and of recent origin,—they cavil at it as doubtful and uncertain,—they inquire by what miracles it is confirmed,—they ask whether it is right for it to be received contrary to the consent of so many holy fathers, and the custom of the highest antiquity,—they urge us to confess that it is schismatical in stirring up opposition against the Church, or that the Church was wholly extinct for many ages, during which no such thing was known.—Lastly, they say all arguments are unnecessary; for that its nature may be determined by its fruits, since it has produced such a multitude of sects, so many factious tumults, and such great licentiousness of vices. It is indeed very easy for them to insult a deserted cause with the credulous and ignorant multitude; but, if we had also the liberty of speaking in our turn, this acrimony, which they now discover in violently foaming against us with equal licentiousness and impunity, would presently cool.

In the first place, their calling it novel is highly injurious to God, whose holy word deserves not to be accused of novelty. I have no doubt of its being new to them, to whom Jesus Christ and the Gospel are equally new. But those who know the antiquity of this preaching of Paul, " that Jesus Christ died for our sins, and rose again for our justification,"[8] will find no novelty among us. That it has long been concealed, buried, and unknown, is the crime of human impiety. Now that the goodness of God has restored it to us, it ought at least to be allowed its just claim of antiquity.

From the same source of ignorance springs the notion of its being doubtful and uncertain. This is the very thing which the Lord complains of by his prophet; that " the ox

8 Rom. iv. 25. 1 Cor. xv. 3, 17.

knoweth his owner, and the ass his master's crib,"[9] but that his people know not him. But however they may laugh at its uncertainty, if they were called to seal their own doctrine with their blood and lives, it would appear how much they value it. Very different is our confidence, which dreads neither the terrors of death, nor even the tribunal of God.

Their requiring miracles of us is altogether unreasonable; for we forge no new Gospel, but retain the very same whose truth was confirmed by all the miracles ever wrought by Christ and the apostles. But they have this peculiar advantage above us, that they can confirm their faith by continual miracles even to this day. But the truth is, they allege miracles which are calculated to unsettle a mind otherwise well established, they are so frivolous and ridiculous, or vain and false. Nor, if they were ever so preternatural, ought they to have any weight in opposition to the truth of God, since the name of God ought to be sanctified in all places and at all times, whether by miraculous events, or by the common order of nature. This fallacy might perhaps be more specious, if the Scripture did not apprize us of the legitimate end and use of miracles. For Mark informs us, that the miracles which followed the preaching of the apostles were wrought in confirmation[10] of it, and Luke tells us, that[11] "the Lord gave testimony to the word of his grace," when "signs and wonders" were "done by the hands" of the apostles. Very similar to which is the assertion of the apostle, that "salvation was confirmed" by the preaching of the Gospel, "God also bearing witness with signs, and wonders, and divers miracles."[12] But those things which we are told were seals of the Gospel, shall we pervert to undermine the faith of the Gospel? Those things which were designed to be testimonials of the truth, shall we accommodate to the confirmation of falsehood? It is right, therefore, that the doctrine, which, according to the evangelist, claims the first attention, be examined and tried in the first place; and if it be approved, then it ought to derive confirmation from miracles. But it is the characteristic of sound doctrine, given by Christ,

[9] Isaiah i. 3.   [10] Mark xvi. 20.   [11] Acts xiv. 3.   [12] Heb. ii. 3-4.

that it tends to promote, not the glory of men, but the glory of God.[13] Christ having laid down this proof of a doctrine, it is wrong to esteem those as miracles which are directed to any other end than the glorification of the name of God alone. And we should remember that Satan has his wonders, which, though they are juggling tricks rather than real miracles, are such as delude the ignorant and inexperienced. Magicians and enchanters have always been famous for miracles; idolatry has been supported by astonishing miracles; and yet we admit them not as proofs of the superstition of magicians or idolaters. With this engine also the simplicity of the vulgar was anciently assailed by the Donatists, who abounded in miracles. We therefore give the same answer now to our adversaries as Augustine[14] gave to the Donatists, that our Lord hath cautioned us against these miracle-mongers by his prediction, that there should arise false prophets, who, by various signs and lying wonders, "should deceive (if possible) the very elect."[15] And Paul has told us, that the kingdom of Antichrist would be "with all power, and signs, and lying wonders."[16] But these miracles (they say) are wrought, not by idols, or sorcerers, or false prophets, but by saints; as if we were ignorant, that it is a stratagem of Satan to "transform" himself "into an angel of light."[17] At the tomb of Jeremiah,[18] who was buried in Egypt, the Egyptians formerly offered sacrifices and other divine honours. Was not this abusing God's holy prophet to the purposes of idolatry? Yet they supposed this veneration of his sepulchre to be rewarded with a cure for the bite of serpents. What shall we say, but that it has been, and ever will be, the most righteous vengeance of God to "send those who receive not the love of the truth strong delusions, that they should believe a lie?"[19] We are by no means without miracles, and such as are certain, and not liable to cavils. But those under which they shelter themselves are mere illusions of Satan, seducing the people from the true worship of God to vanity.

Another calumny is their charging us with opposition to the fathers,—I mean the writers of the earlier and purer

[13] John vii. 18, viii. 50.   [14] In Joan. tract. 13.   [15] Matt. xxiv. 24.
[16] 2 Thess. ii. 9.   [17] 2 Cor. xi. 14.   [18] Hierom. in praef. Jerem.
[19] 2 Thess. ii. 10, 11.

ages,—as if those writers were abettors of their impiety;
whereas, if the contest were to be terminated by this authority, the victory in most parts of the controversy—to speak in
the most modest terms—would be on our side. But though
the writings of those fathers contain many wise and excellent things, yet in some respects they have suffered the common fate of mankind; these very dutiful children reverence
only their errors and mistakes, but their excellences they
either overlook, or conceal, or corrupt; so that it may truly
be said to be their only study to collect dross from the midst
of gold. Then they overwhelm us with senseless clamours,
as despisers and enemies of the fathers. But we do not hold
them in such contempt, but that, if it were consistent with
my present design, I could easily support by their suffrages
most of the sentiments that we now maintain. But while
we make use of their writings, we always remember that
"all things are ours," to serve us, not to have dominion
over us, and that "we are Christ's"[20] alone, and owe him
universal obedience. He who neglects this distinction will
have nothing decided in religion; since those holy men were
ignorant of many things, frequently at variance with each
other, and sometimes even inconsistent with themselves.
There is great reason, they say, for the admonition of
Solomon, "not to transgress or remove the ancient landmarks, which our fathers have set."[21] But the same rule is
not applicable to the bounding of fields, and to the obedience
of faith, which ought to be ready to "forget her own people
and her father's house."[22] But if they are so fond of allego-
rizing, why do they not explain the apostles, rather than any
others, to be those fathers, whose appointed landmarks it is
so unlawful to remove? For this is the interpretation of
Jerome, whose works they have received into their canons.
But if they insist on preserving the landmarks of those
whom they understand to be intended, why do they at
pleasure so freely transgress them themselves? There were
two fathers,[23] of whom one said, that our God neither eats
nor drinks, and therefore needs neither cups nor dishes;
the other, that sacred things require no gold, and that gold

[20] 1 Cor. iii. 21, 23.   [21] Prov. xxii. 28.   [22] Psalm xlv. 10.
[23] Acat. in lib. 11, cap. 16.   Trip. Hist. Amb. lib. 2, de Off. c. 28.

is no recommendation of that which is not purchased with gold. This landmark therefore is transgressed by those who in sacred things are so much delighted with gold, silver, ivory, marble, jewels, and silks, and suppose that God is not rightly worshipped, unless all things abound in exquisite splendour, or rather extravagant profusion. There was a father[24] who said he freely partook of flesh on a day when others abstained from it, because he was a Christian. They transgress the landmarks therefore when they curse the soul that tastes flesh in Lent. There were two fathers,[25] of whom one said, that a monk who labors not with his hands is on a level with a cheat or a robber; and the other, that it is unlawful for monks to live on what is not their own, notwithstanding their assiduity in contemplations, studies, and prayers; and they have transgressed this landmark by placing the idle and distended carcasses of monks in cells and brothels, to be pampered on the substance of others. There was a father[26] who said, that to see a painted image of Christ, or of any other saint, in the temples of Christians, is a dreadful abomination. Nor was this merely the sentence of an individual; it was also decreed by an ecclesiastical council, that the object of worship should not be painted on the walls. They are far from confining themselves within these landmarks, for every corner is filled with images. Another father[27] has advised that, after having discharged the office of humanity towards the dead by the rites of sepulture, we should leave them to their repose. They break through these landmarks by inculcating a constant solicitude for the dead. There was one of the fathers[28] who asserted that the substance of bread and wine in the eucharist ceases not, but remains, just as the substance of the human nature remains in the Lord Christ united with the divine. They transgress this landmark therefore by pretending that, on the words of the Lord being recited, the substance of bread and wine ceases, and is transubstantiated into his body and blood. There were fathers[29] who, while they exhibited to

[24] Spiridion. Trip. Hist. lib. 1, c. 10.
[25] Trip. Hist. lib. 8, c. 1. August. de Opere Mon. c. 17.
[26] Epiph. Epist. ab Hier. vers. Con. Eliber. c. 36.
[27] Amb. de Abra. lib. 1, c. 7.   [28] Gelas. Pap. in Conc. Rom.
[29] Chrys. in 1 Cap. Ephes. Calix. Papa de Cons. dist. 2.

the universal Church only one eucharist, and forbade all
scandalous and immoral persons to approach it, at the same
time severely censured all who, when present, did not par-
take of it. How far have they removed these landmarks,
when they fill not only the churches, but even private houses,
with their masses, admit all who choose to be spectators of
them, and every one the more readily in proportion to the
magnitude of his contribution, however chargeable with
impurity and wickedness! They invite none to faith in
Christ and a faithful participation of the sacraments; but
rather for purposes of gain bring forward their own work
instead of the grace and merit of Christ. There were two
fathers,[30] of whom one contended that the use of Christ's
sacred supper should be wholly forbidden to those who, content with partaking of one kind, abstained from the other;
the other strenuously maintained that Christian people ought
not to be refused the blood of their Lord, for the confession
of whom they are required to shed their own. These landmarks also they have removed, in appointing, by an in-
violable law, that very thing which the former punished with
excommunication, and the latter gave a powerful reason for
disapproving.   There was a father[31] who asserted the
temerity of deciding on either side of an obscure subject,
without clear and evident testimonies of Scripture. This
landmark they forgot when they made so many constitutions,
canons, and judicial determinations, without any authority
from the word of God. There was a father[32] who upbraided
Montanus with having, among other heresies, been the first
imposer of laws for the observance of fasts. They have
gone far beyond this landmark also, in establishing fasts
by the strictest laws. There was a father[33] who denied that
marriage ought to be forbidden to the ministers of the
Church, and pronounced cohabitation with a wife to be real
chastity; and there were fathers who assented to his judgment. They have transgressed these landmarks by enjoining
on their priests the strictest celibacy. There was a father
who thought that attention should be paid to Christ only, of

[30] Gelas. can. Comperimus de Cons. dist. 2. Cypr. Epist. 2, lib. 1, de Laps.
[31] August. lib. 2, de Pec. Mer. cap. ult.
[32] Apollon. de quo Eccl. Hist. lib. 5, cap. 11, 12.
[33] Paphnut. Trip. Hist. lib. 2, c. 14. Cypr. Epist. 2, lib. 2.

whom it is said, " Hear ye him," and that no regard should
be had to what others before us have either said or done,
only to what has been commanded by Christ, who is pre-
eminent over all. This landmark they neither prescribe to
themselves, nor permit to be observed by others, when they
set up over themselves and others any masters rather than
Christ. There was a father[34] who contended that the Church
ought not to take precedence of Christ, because his judgment is always according to truth; but ecclesiastical judges,
like other men, may generally be deceived. Breaking down
this landmark also, they scruple not to assert, that all the
authority of the Scripture depends on the decision of the
Church. All the fathers, with one heart and voice, have
declared it execrable and detestable for the holy word of
God to be contaminated with the subtleties of sophists, and
perplexed by the wrangles of logicians. Do they confine
themselves within these landmarks, when the whole business
of their lives is to involve the simplicity of the Scripture in
endless controversies, and worse than sophistical wrangles?
so that if the fathers were now restored to life, and heard
this art of wrangling, which they call speculative divinity,
they would not suspect the dispute to have the least reference
to God. But if I would enumerate all the instances in which
the authority of the fathers is insolently rejected by those
who would be thought their dutiful children, my address
would exceed all reasonable bounds. Months and years
would be insufficient for me. And yet such is their con-
summate and incorrigible impudence, they dare to censure
us for presuming to transgress the ancient landmarks.

Nor can they gain any advantage against us by their
argument from custom; for, if we were compelled to submit
to custom, we should have to complain of the greatest injustice. Indeed, if the judgments of men were correct,
custom should be sought among the good. But the fact is
often very different. What appears to be practiced by many
soon obtains the force of a custom. And human affairs have
scarcely ever been in so good a state as for the majority to
be pleased with things of real excellence. From the private
vices of multitudes, therefore, has arisen public error, or

[34] Aug. cap. 2, contr. Cresc. Grammatic.

rather a common agreement of vices, which these good men
would now have to be received as law. It is evident to all
who can see, that the world is inundated with more than an
ocean of evils, that it is overrun with numerous destructive
pests, that every thing is fast verging to ruin, so that we
must altogether despair of human affairs, or vigorously and
even violently oppose such immense evils. And the remedy
is rejected for no other reason, but because we have been
accustomed to the evils so long. But let public error be
tolerated in human society; in the kingdom of God nothing
but his eternal truth should be heard and regarded, which
no succession of years, no custom, no confederacy, can circumscribe. Thus Isaiah once taught the chosen people of
God: " Say ye not, A confederacy, to all to whom this people shall say, A confederacy:" that is, that they should not
unite in the wicked consent of the people; " nor fear their
fear, nor be afraid," but rather " sanctify the Lord of hosts,"
that he might " be their fear and their dread."[35]   Now,
therefore, let them, if they please, object against us past
ages and present examples; if we " sanctify the Lord of
hosts," we shall not be much afraid. For, whether many
ages agree in similar impiety, he is mighty to take vengeance on the third and fourth generation; or whether
the whole world combine in the same iniquity, he has given
an example of the fatal end of those who sin with a multitude, by destroying all men with a deluge, and preserving
Noah and his small family, in order that his individual faith
might condemn the whole world. Lastly, a corrupt custom
is nothing but an epidemical pestilence, which is equally
fatal to its objects, though they fall with a multitude. Besides, they ought to consider a remark, somewhere made by
Cyprian,[36] that persons who sin through ignorance, though
they cannot be wholly exculpated, may yet be considered in
some degree excusable; but those who obstinately reject the
truth offered by the Divine goodness, are without any excuse
at all.

Nor are we so embarrassed by their dilemma as to be
obliged to confess, either that the Church was for some

---

[35] Isaiah viii. 12, 13.
[36] Epist. 3, lib. 2, et in Epist. ad. Julian. de Haeret. baptiz.

time extinct, or that we have now a controversy with
the Church. The Church of Christ has lived, and will
continue to live, as long as Christ shall reign at the right
hand of the Father, by whose hand she is sustained, by
whose protection she is defended, by whose power she
is preserved in safety. For he will undoubtedly perform what he once promised, to be with his people " even
to the end of the world."[37] We have no quarrel against
the Church, for with one consent we unite with all
the company of the faithful in worshipping and adoring
the one God and Christ the Lord, as he has been adored
by all the pious in all ages. But our opponents deviate
widely from the truth when they acknowledge no Church
but what is visible to the corporeal eye, and endeavour to
circumscribe it by those limits within which it is far from
being included. Our controversy turns on the two following
points :—first, they contend that the form of the Church is
always apparent and visible; secondly, they place that form
in the see of the Roman Church and her order of prelates.
We assert, on the contrary, first, that the Church may exist
without any visible form; secondly, that its form is not contained in that external splendour which they foolishly
admire, but is distinguished by a very different criterion, viz.
the pure preaching of God's word, and the legitimate administration of the sacraments. They are not satisfied unless the
Church can always be pointed out with the finger. But how
often among the Jewish people was it so disorganized, as to
have no visible form left? What splendid form do we suppose could be seen, when Elias deplored his being left
alone?[38] How long, after the coming of Christ, did it remain
without any external form? How often, since that time,
have wars, seditions, and heresies, oppressed and totally
obscured it? If they had lived at that period, would they
have believed that any Church existed? Yet Elias was informed that there were " left seven thousand" who had " not
bowed the knee to Baal." Nor should we entertain any
doubt of Christ's having always reigned on earth ever since
his ascension to heaven. But if the pious at such periods
had sought for any form evident to their senses, must not

[37] Matt. xxviii. 20.　　[38] I Kings xix. 14, 18.

their hearts have been quite discouraged? Indeed it was
already considered by Hilary in his day as a grievous error,
that people were absorbed in foolish admiration of the
episcopal dignity, and did not perceive the dreadful mischiefs
concealed under that disguise. For this is his language:[39]
" One thing I advise you—beware of Antichrist, for you
have an improper attachment to walls; your veneration for
the Church of God is misplaced on houses and buildings;
you wrongly introduce under them the name of peace. Is
there any doubt that they will be seats of Antichrist? I
think mountains, woods, and lakes, prisons and whirlpools,
less dangerous; for these were the scenes of retirement or
banishment in which the prophets prophesied." But what
excites the veneration of the multitude in the present day
for their horned bishops, but the supposition that those are
the holy prelates of religion whom they see presiding over
great cities? Away, then, with such stupid admiration. Let
us rather leave it to the Lord, since he alone " knoweth them
that are his,"[40] sometimes to remove from human observation
all external knowledge of his Church. I admit this to be a
dreadful judgment of God on the earth; but if it be deserved
by the impiety of men, why do we attempt to resist the
righteous vengeance of God? Thus the Lord punished the
ingratitude of men in former ages; for, in consequence of
their resistance to his truth, and extinction of the light he
had given them, he permitted them to be blinded by sense,
deluded by absurd falsehoods, and immerged in profound
darkness, so that there was no appearance of the true
Church left; yet, at the same time, in the midst of darkness
and errors, he preserved his scattered and concealed people
from total destruction. Nor is this to be wondered at; for
he knew how to save in all the confusion of Babylon, and the
flame of the fiery furnace. But how dangerous it is to
estimate the form of the Church by I know not what vain
pomp, which they contend for; I shall rather briefly suggest
than state at large, lest I should protract this discourse to
an excessive length. The Pope, they say, who holds the
Apostolic see, and the bishops anointed and consecrated by
him, provided they are equipped with mitres and crosiers,

[39] Contr. Auxent.   [40] 2 Tim. ii. 19.

represent the Church, and ought to be considered as the
Church. Therefore they cannot err. How is this?—Because
they are pastors of the Church, and consecrated to the Lord.
And did not the pastoral character belong to Aaron, and
the other rulers of Israel? Yet Aaron and his sons, after
their designation to the priesthood, fell into error when they
made the golden calf.[41] According to this mode of reasoning, why should not the four hundred prophets, who lied to
Ahab, have represented the Church?[42] But the Church remained on the side of Micaiah, solitary and despised as he
was, and out of his mouth proceeded the truth. Did not
those prophets exhibit both the name and appearance of the
Church, who with united violence rose up against Jeremiah,
and threatened and boasted, "the law shall not perish from
the priest, nor counsel from the wise, nor the word from
the prophet?"[43] Jeremiah is sent singly against the whole
multitude of prophets, with a denunciation from the Lord,
that the "law shall perish from the priest, counsel from the
wise, and the word from the prophet."[44] And was there not
the like external respectability in the council convened by the
chief priests, scribes, and Pharisees, to consult about putting
Christ to death?[45] Now, let them go and adhere to the external appearance, and thereby make Christ and all the
prophets schismatics, and, on the other hand, make the
ministers of Satan instruments of the Holy Spirit. But if
they speak their real sentiments, let them answer me sincerely, what nation or place they consider as the seat of the
Church, from the time when, by a decree of the council of
Basil, Eugenius was deposed and degraded from the pontifi-
cate, and Amadeus substituted in his place. They cannot
deny that the council, as far as relates to external forms, was
a lawful one, and summoned not only by one pope, but by
two. There Eugenius was pronounced guilty of schism,
rebellion, and obstinacy, together with all the host of cardinals and bishops who had joined him in attempting a disso-
lution of the council. Yet afterwards, assisted by the favour
of princes, he regained the quiet possession of his former
dignity. That election of Amadeus, though formally made

[41] Exod. xxxii. 4.   [42] 1 Kings xxii. 6, 11-23.   [43] Jer. xviii. 18.
[44] Jer. iv. 9.   [45] Matt. xxvi. 3, 4.

by the authority of a general and holy synod, vanished into smoke; and he was appeased with a cardinal's hat, like a barking dog with a morsel. From the bosom of those heretics and rebels have proceeded all the popes, cardinals, bishops, abbots, and priests ever since. Here they must stop. For to which party will they give the title of the Church? Will they deny that this was a general council, which wanted nothing to complete its external majesty, being solemnly convened by two papal bulls, consecrated by a presiding legate of the Roman see, and well regulated in every point of order, and invariably preserving the same dignity to the last? Will they acknowledge Eugenius to be a schismatic, with all his adherents, by whom they have all been consecrated? Either, therefore, let them give a different definition of the form of the Church, or, whatever be their number, we shall account them all schismatics, as having been knowingly and voluntarily ordained by heretics. But if it had never been ascertained before, that the Church is not confined to external pomps they would themselves afford us abundant proof of it, who have so long superciliously exhibited themselves to the world under the title of the Church, though they were at the same time the deadly plagues of it. I speak not of their morals, and those tragical exploits with which all their lives abound, since they profess themselves to be Pharisees, who are to be heard and not imitated. I refer to the very doctrine itself, on which they found their claim to be considered as the Church. If you devote a portion of your leisure, Sire, to the perusal of our writings, you will clearly discover that doctrine to be a fatal pestilence of souls, the firebrand, ruin, and destruction of the Church.

Finally, they betray great want of candour, by invidiously repeating what great commotions, tumults, and contentions, have attended the preaching of our doctrine, and what effects it produces in many persons. For it is unfair to charge it with those evils which ought to be attributed to the malice of Satan. It is the native property of the Divine word, never to make its appearance without disturbing Satan, and rousing his opposition. This is a most certain and unequivocal criterion by which it is distinguished from false doctrines, which are easily broached when they are heard with general attention, and received with applauses by the world. Thus, in some ages, when all things were immerged in profound darkness, the prince of this world amused and diverted himself with the generality of mankind, and, like another Sardanapalus, gave himself up to his ease and pleasures in perfect peace; for what would he do but amuse and divert himself, in the quiet and undisturbed possession of his kingdom? But when the light shining from above dissipated a portion of his darkness—when that Mighty One alarmed and assaulted his kingdom—then he began to shake off his wonted torpor, and to hurry on his armour. First, indeed, he stirred up the power of men to suppress the truth by violence at its first appearance; and when this proved ineffectual, he had recourse to subtlety. He made the Catabaptists, and other infamous characters, the instruments of exciting dissensions and doctrinal controversies, with a view to obscure and finally to extinguish it. And now he continues to attack it both ways; for he endeavours to root up this genuine seed by means of human force, and at the same time tries every effort to choke it with his tares, that it may not grow and produce fruit. But all his attempts will be vain, if we attend to the admonitions of the Lord, who hath long ago made us acquainted with his devices, that we might not be caught by him unawares, and has armed us with sufficient means of defence against all his assaults. But to charge the word of God with the odium of seditions, excited against it by wicked and rebellious men, or of sects raised by imposters,—is not this extreme malignity? Yet it is not without example in former times. Elias was asked whether it was not he "that troubled Israel."[46] Christ was represented by the Jews as guilty of sedition.[47] The apostles were accused of stirring up popular commotions.[48] Wherein does this differ from the conduct of those who, at the present day, impute to us all the disturbances, tumults, and contentions, that break out against us? But the proper answer to such accusations has been taught us by Elias, that the dissemination of errors and the raising of tumults is not chargeable on us, but on those who are resist-

[46] 1 Kings xviii. 17.   [47] Luke xxiii. 2, 5.   [48] Acts xvii. 6, xxiv. 5.

ing the power of God. But as this one reply is sufficient
to repress their temerity, so, on the other hand, we must
meet the weakness of some persons, who are frequently disturbed with such offences, and become unsettled and wavering in their minds. Now, that they may not stumble and
fall amidst this agitation and perplexity, let them know that
the apostles in their day experienced the same things that
now befall us. There were "unlearned and unstable" men,
Peter says, who "wrested" the inspired writings of Paul
"to their own destruction."[49] There were despisers of God,
who, when they heard that "where sin abounded grace did
much more abound," immediately concluded, Let us "continue in sin, that grace may abound." When they heard that
the faithful were "not under the law," they immediately
croaked, "We will sin, because we are not under the law,
but under grace."[50] There were some who accused him as
an encourager of sin. Many false apostles crept in, to
destroy the churches he had raised. "Some preached" the
gospel "of envy and strife, not in sincerity," maliciously
"supposing to add affliction to his bonds."[51] In some places
the Gospel was attended with little benefit. "All were
seeking their own, not the things of Jesus Christ."[52] Others
returned "like dogs to their vomit, and like swine to their
wallowing in the mire."[53] Many perverted the liberty of the
spirit into the licentiousness of the flesh. Many insinuated
themselves as brethren, who afterwards brought the pious
into dangers. Various contentions were excited among the
brethren themselves. What was to be done by the apostles
in such circumstances? Should they not have dissembled
for a time, or rather have rejected and deserted that Gospel
which appeared to be the nursery of so many disputes, the
cause of so many dangers, the occasion of so many offences?
But in such difficulties as these, their minds were relieved
by this reflection that Christ is the "stone of stumbling and
rock of offence,"[54] "set for the fall and rising again of
many, and for a sign which shall be spoken against;"[55]
and armed with this confidence, they proceeded boldly
through all the dangers of tumults and offences. The same

49 2 Pet. iii. 16.   50 Rom. v. 20, vi. 1, 14, 15.   51 Phil. i. 15, 16.
52 Phil. ii. 21.   53 2 Pet. ii. 22.   54 1 Pet. ii. 8.   55 Luke ii. 34.

consideration should support us, since Paul declares it to
be the perpetual character of the Gospel, that it is a
" savour of death unto death in them that perish," [56] although
it was rather given us to be the " savour of life unto life,"
and " the power of God to " the " salvation " of the faithful;[57] which we also should certainly experience it to be,
if we did not corrupt this eminent gift of God by our ingratitude, and prevert to our destruction what ought to be a
principal instrument of our salvation.

But I return to you, Sire. Let not your Majesty be at
all moved by those groundless accusations with which our
adversaries endeavour to terrify you; as that the sole tendency and design of this new Gospel—for so they call it—
is to furnish a pretext for seditions, and to gain impunity
for all crimes. " For God is not the author of confusion,
but of peace;"[58] nor is " the Son of God," who came to
" destroy the works of the devil, the minister of sin."[59] And
it is unjust to charge us with such motives and designs, of
which we have never given cause for the least suspicion.
Is it probable that we are meditating the subversion of
kingdoms?—we, who were never heard to utter a factious
word, whose lives were ever known to be peaceable and
honest while we lived under your government, and who,
even now in our exile, cease not to pray for all prosperity
to attend yourself and your kingdom ! Is it probable that we
are seeking an unlimited license to commit crimes with
impunity? in whose conduct, though many things may be
blamed, yet there is nothing worthy of such severe reproach ! Nor have we, by Divine Grace, profited so little in
the Gospel, but that our life may be an example to our
detractors of chastity, liberality, mercy, temperance, patience, modesty, and every other virtue. It is an undeniable
fact, that we sincerely fear and worship God, whose name
we desire to be sanctified both by our life and by our death;
and envy itself is constrained to bear testimony to the innocence and civil integrity of some of us, who have suffered
the punishment of death for that very thing which ought to
be accounted their highest praise. But if the Gospel be

[56] 2 Cor. ii. 15, 16.   [57] Rom. i. 16.   [58] 1 Cor. xiv. 33.
          [59] 1 John iii. 8. Gal. ii. 17.

made a pretext for tumults, which has not yet happened in your kingdom; if any persons make the liberty of divine grace an excuse for the licentiousness of their vices, of whom I have known many,—there are laws and legal penalties, by which they may be punished according to their deserts; only let not the Gospel of God be reproached for the crimes of wicked men. You have now, Sire, the virulent iniquity of our calumniators laid before you in a sufficient number of instances, that you may not receive their accusations with too credulous an ear.—I fear I have gone too much into the detail, as this preface already approaches the size of a full apology; whereas I intended it not to contain our defence, but only to prepare your mind to attend to the pleading of our cause; for, though you are now averse and alienated from us, and even inflamed against us, we despair not of regaining your favour, if you will only once read with calmness and composure this our confession, which we intend as our defence before your Majesty. But, on the contrary, if your ears are so preoccupied with the whispers of the malevolent, as to leave no opportunity for the accused to speak for themselves, and if those outrageous furies, with your connivance, continue to persecute with imprisonments, scourges, tortures, confiscations, and flames, we shall indeed, like sheep destined to the slaughter, be reduced to the greatest extremities. Yet shall we in patience possess our souls, and wait for the mighty hand of the Lord, which undoubtedly will in time appear, and show itself armed for the deliverance of the poor from their affliction, and for the punishment of their despisers, who now exult in such perfect security. May the Lord, the King of kings, establish your throne with righteousness, and your kingdom with equity.

Basil, 1st August, 1536.

GENERAL SYLLABUS

THE design of the Author in these Christian Institutes is twofold, relating, First to the knowledge of God, as the way to attain a blessed immortality; and, in connection with and subservience to this, Secondly, to the knowledge of ourselves.

In the prosecution of this design, he strictly follows the method of the Apostles' Creed, as being most familiar to all Christians. For as the Creed consists of four parts, the first relating to God the Father, the second to the Son, the third to the Holy Spirit, the fourth to the Church; so the Author distributes the whole of this work into Four Books, corresponding respectively to the four parts of the Creed; as will clearly appear from the following detail:—

I. The first article of the Creed relates to God the Father, and to the creation, conservation, and government of all things, which are included in his omnipotence.

So the first book is on the knowledge of God, considered as the Creator, Preserver, and Governor of the universe at large, and every thing contained in it. It shows both the nature and tendency of the true knowledge of the Creator—that this is not learned in the schools, but that every man from his birth is self-taught it—Yet that the depravity of men is so great as to corrupt and extinguish this knowledge, partly by ignorance, partly by wickedness; so that it neither leads him to glorify God as he ought, nor conducts him to the attainment of happiness—And though this internal knowledge is assisted by all the creatures around, which serve as a mirror to display the Divine perfections, yet that man does not profit by it—Therefore, that to those, whom it is God's will to bring to an intimate and saving knowledge of himself, he gives his written word; which introduces observations on the sacred Scripture— That he has therein revealed himself; that not the Father only, but the Father, Son, and Holy Spirit, united, is the Creator of heaven and earth; whom neither the knowledge innate by nature, nor the very beautiful mirror displayed to us in the world, can, in consequence of our depravity, teach us to know so as to glorify him. This gives occasion for treating of the revelation of God in the Scripture, of the unity of the Divine Essence, and the trinity of Persons.— To prevent man from attributing to God the blame of his own voluntary blindness, the Author shows the state of man at his creation, and treats of the image of God, free-will, and the primative integrity of nature.—Having finished the subject of creation, he proceeds to the conservation and government of all things, concluding the first book with a full discussion of the doctrine of divine providence.

II. But since man is fallen by sin from the state in which he was created, it is necessary to come to Christ. Therefore it follows in the Creed, "And in Jesus Christ, his only Son our Lord," &c.

So in the second book of the Institutes our Author treats of the knowledge of God as the Redeemer in Christ; and having shown the fall of man, leads him to Christ the Media-tor. Here he states the doctrine of original sin—that man possesses no inherent strength to enable him to deliver himself from sin and the impending curse, but that, on the contrary, nothing can proceed from him, antecedently to reconciliation and renovation, but what is deserving of con-demnation—Therefore, that, man being utterly lost in him-self, and incapable of conceiving even a good thought by which he may restore himself, or perform actions acceptable to God, he must seek redemption out of himself, in Christ—That the Law was given for this purpose, not to confine its observers to itself, but to conduct them to Christ; which gives occasion to introduce an exposition of the Moral Law—That he was known, as the Author of salvation, to the Jews under the Law, but more fully under the Gospel, in which he is manifested to the world.—Hence follows the doctrine of the similiarity and difference of the Old and New Testament, of the Law and Gospel.—It is next stated, that, in order to the complete accomplishment of salva-tion, it was necessary for the eternal Son of God to become man, and that he actually assumed a real human nature:—it is also shown how these two natures constitute one per-son—That the office of Christ, appointed for the acquisition and application of complete salvation by his merit and efficacy, is sacerdotal, regal, and prophetical.—Next follows the manner in which Christ executed his office, or actually performed the part of a Mediator, being an exposition of the Articles respecting his death, resurrection, and ascen-sion to heaven.—Lastly, the Author shows the truth and propriety of affirming that Christ merited the grace of God and salvation for us.

III. As long as Christ is separate from us, he profits us nothing. Hence the necessity of our being ingrafted into him, as branches into a vine. Therefore the doctrine concerning Christ is followed, in the third part of the Creed, by this clause, "I believe in the Holy Spirit," as being the bond of union between us and Christ.

So in the third book our Author treats of the Holy Spirit, who unites us to Christ—and consequently of faith, by which we embrace Christ, with his twofold benefit, free righteousness, which he imputes to us, and regeneration, which he commences within us, by bestowing repentance upon us.—And to show that we have not the least room to glory in such faith as is unconnected with the pursuit of repentance, before proceeding to the full discussion of justification, he treats at large of repentance and the continual exercise of it, which Christ, apprehended by faith, produces in us by his Spirit.—He next fully discusses the first and chief benefit of Christ when united to us by the Holy Spirit that is, justification—and then treats of prayer, which resembles the hand that actually receives those blessings to be enjoyed, which faith knows, from the word of promise, to be laid up with God for our use.—But as all men are not united to Christ, the sole Author of salvation, by the Holy Spirit, who creates and preserves faith in us, he treats of God's eternal election; which is the cause that we, in whom he foresaw no good but what he intended freely to bestow, have been favored with the gift of Christ, and united to God by the effectual call of the Gospel.—Lastly, he treats of complete regeneration, and the fruition of happiness; that is, the final resurrection, towards which our eyes must be directed, since in this world the felicity of the pious, in respect of enjoyment, is only begun.

IV. But as the Holy Spirit does not unite all men to Christ, or make them partakers of faith, and on those to whom he imparts it he does not ordinarily bestow it without means, but employs for this purpose the preaching of the Gospel and the use of the sacraments, with the administration of all discipline, therefore it follows in the Creed,

"I believe in the Holy Catholic Church," whom, although involved in eternal death, yet, in pursuance of the gratuitous election, God has freely reconciled to himself in Christ, and made partakers of the Holy Spirit, that, being ingrafted into Christ, they may have communion with him as their head, whence flows a perpetual remission of sins, and a full restoration to eternal life.

So in the fourth book our Author treats of the Church—then of the means used by the Holy Spirit in effectually calling from spiritual death, and preserving the church—the word and sacraments—baptism and the Lord's supper—which are as it were Christ's regal sceptre, by which he commences his spiritual reign in the Church by the energy of his Spirit, and carries it forwards from day to day during the present life, after the close of which he perfects it without those means.

And as political institutions are the asylums of the Church in this life, though civil government is distinct from the spiritual kingdom of Christ, our Author instructs us respecting it as a signal blessing of God, which the Church ought to acknowledge with gratitude of heart, till we are called out of this transitory state to the heavenly inheritance, where God will be all in all.

This is the plan of the Institutes, which may be comprised in the following brief summary:—

Man, created originally upright, being afterwards ruined, not partially, but totally, finds salvation out of himself, wholly in Christ; to whom being united by the Holy Spirit, freely bestowed, without any regard of future works, he enjoys in him a twofold benefit, the perfect imputation of righteousness, which attends him to the grave, and the commencement of sanctification, which he daily increases, till at length he completes it at the day of regeneration or resurrection of the body, so that in eternal life and the heavenly inheritance his praises are celebrated for such stupendous mercy.

DEDICATION OF THE REVOLUTIONS
OF THE HEAVENLY BODIES
BY NICOLAUS COPERNICUS (1543)

TO POPE PAUL III

I CAN easily conceive, most Holy Father, that as soon as some people learn that in this book which I have written concerning the revolutions of the heavenly bodies, I ascribe certain motions to the Earth, they will cry out at once that I and my theory should be rejected. For I am not so much in love with my conclusions as not to weigh what others will think about them, and although I know that the meditations of a philosopher are far removed from the judgment of the laity, because his endeavor is to seek out the truth in all things, so far as this is permitted by God to the human reason, I still believe that one must avoid theories altogether foreign to orthodoxy. Accordingly, when I considered in my own mind how absurd a performance it must seem to those who know that the judgment of many centuries has approved the view that the Earth remains fixed as center in the midst of the heavens, if I should, on the contrary, assert that the Earth moves; I was for a long time at a loss to know whether I should publish the commentaries which I have written in proof of its motion,

Nicolaus Copernicus was born in 1473 at Thorn in West Prussia, of a Polish father and a German mother. He attended the university of Cracow and Bologna, lectured on astronomy and mathematics at Rome, and later studied medicine at Padua and canon law at Ferrara. He was appointed canon of the cathedral of Frauenburg, and in this town he died in 1543, having devoted the latter part of his life largely to astronomy.

The book which was introduced by this dedication laid the foundations of modern astronomy. At the time when it was written, the earth was believed by all to be the fixed centre of the universe; and although many of the arguments used by Copernicus were invalid and absurd, he was the first modern to put forth the heliocentric theory as " a better explanation." It remained for Kepler, Galileo, and Newton to establish the theory on firm grounds.

or whether it were not better to follow the example of the Pythagoreans and of some others, who were accustomed to transmit the secrets of Philosophy not in writing but orally, and only to their relatives and friends, as the letter from Lysis to Hipparchus bears witness. They did this, it seems to me, not as some think, because of a certain selfish reluctance to give their views to the world, but in order that the noblest truths, worked out by the careful study of great men, should not be despised by those who are vexed at the idea of taking great pains with any forms of literature except such as would be profitable, or by those who, if they are driven to the study of Philosophy for its own sake by the admonitions and the example of others, nevertheless, on account of their stupidity, hold a place among philosophers similar to that of drones among bees. Therefore, when I considered this carefully, the contempt which I had to fear because of the novelty and apparent absurdity of my view, nearly induced me to abandon utterly the work I had begun.

My friends, however, in spite of long delay and even resistance on my part, withheld me from this decision. First among these was Nicolaus Schonberg, Cardinal of Capua, distinguished in all branches of learning. Next to him comes my very dear friend, Tidemann Giese, Bishop of Culm, a most earnest student, as he is, of sacred and, indeed, of all good learning. The latter has often urged me, at times even spurring me on with reproaches, to publish and at last bring to the light the book which had lain in my study not nine years merely, but already going on four times nine. Not a few other very eminent and scholarly men made the same request, urging that I should no longer through fear refuse to give out my work for the common benefit of students of Mathematics. They said I should find that the more absurd most men now thought this theory of mine concerning the motion of the Earth, the more admiration and gratitude it would command after they saw in the publication of my commentaries the mist of absurdity cleared away by most transparent proofs. So, influenced by these advisors and this hope, I have at length allowed my friends to publish the work, as they had long besought me to do.

But perhaps Your Holiness will not so much wonder that I have ventured to publish these studies of mine, after having taken such pains in elaborating them that I have not hesitated to commit to writing my views of the motion of the Earth, as you will be curious to hear how it occurred to me to venture, contrary to the accepted view of mathematicians, and well-nigh contrary to common sense, to form a conception of any terrestrial motion whatsoever. Therefore I would not have it unknown to Your Holiness, that the only thing which induced me to look for another way of reckoning the movements of the heavenly bodies was that I knew that mathematicians by no means agree in their investigations thereof. For, in the first place, they are so much in doubt concerning the motion of the sun and the moon, that they can not even demonstrate and prove by observation the constant length of a complete year; and in the second place, in determining the motions both of these and of the five other planets, they fail to employ consistently one set of first principles and hypotheses, but use methods of proof based only upon the apparent revolutions and motions. For some employ concentric circles only; others, eccentric circles and epicycles; and even by these means they do not completely attain the desired end. For, although those who have depended upon concentric circles have shown that certain diverse motions can be deduced from these, yet they have not succeeded thereby in laying down any sure principle, corresponding indisputably to the phenomena. These, on the other hand, who have devised systems of eccentric circles, although they seem in great part to have solved the apparent movements by calculations which by these eccentrics are made to fit, have nevertheless introduced many things which seem to contradict the first principles of the uniformity of motion. Nor have they been able to discover or calculate from these the main point, which is the shape of the world and the fixed symmetry of its parts; but their procedure has been as if someone were to collect hands, feet, a head, and other members from various places, all very fine in themselves, but not proportionate to one body, and no single one corresponding in its turn to the others, so that a monster rather than a man would be formed from them. Thus in their process of demonstration which they term a "method," they are found to have omitted something essential, or to have included something foreign and not pertaining to the matter in hand. This certainly would never have happened to them if they had followed fixed principles; for if the hypotheses they assumed were not false, all that resulted therefrom would be verified indubitably. Those things which I am saying now may be obscure, yet they will be made clearer in their proper place.

Therefore, having turned over in my mind for a long time this uncertainty of the traditional mathematical methods of calculating the motions of the celestial bodies, I began to grow disgusted that no more consistent scheme of the movements of the mechanism of the universe, set up for our benefit by that best and most law abiding Architect of all things, was agreed upon by philosophers who otherwise investigate so carefully the most minute details of this world. Wherefore I undertook the task of rereading the books of all the philosophers I could get access to, to see whether any one ever was of the opinion that the motions of the celestial bodies were other than those postulated by the men who taught mathematics in the schools. And I found first, indeed, in Cicero, that Niceta perceived that the Earth moved; and afterward in Plutarch I found that some others were of this opinion, whose words I have seen fit to quote here, that they may be accessible to all:—

" Some maintain that the Earth is stationary, but Philolaus the Pythagorean says that it revolves in a circle about the fire of the ecliptic, like the sun and moon. Heraklides of Pontus and Ekphantus the Pythagorean make the Earth move, not changing its position, however, confined in its falling and rising around its own center in the manner of a wheel."

Taking this as a starting point, I began to consider the mobility of the Earth; and although the idea seemed absurd, yet because I knew that the liberty had been granted to others before me to postulate all sorts of little circles for explaining the phenomena of the stars, I thought I also might easily be permitted to try whether by postulating some motion of the Earth, more reliable conclusions could be reached regarding the revolution of the heavenly bodies, than those of my predecessors.

And so, after postulating movements, which, farther on in the book, I ascribe to the Earth, I have found by many and long observations that if the movements of the other planets are assumed for the circular motion of the Earth and are substituted for the revolution of each star, not only do their phenomena follow logically therefrom, but the relative positions and magnitudes both of the stars and all their orbits, and of the heavens themselves, become so closely related that in none of its parts can anything be changed without causing confusion in the other parts and in the whole universe. Therefore, in the course of the work I have followed this plan: I describe in the first book all the .positions of the orbits together with the movements which I ascribe to the Earth, in order that this book might contain, as it were, the general scheme of the universe. Thereafter in the remaining books, I set forth the motions of the other stars and of all their orbits together with the movement of the Earth, in order that one may see from this to what extent the movements and appearances of the other stars and their orbits can be saved, if they are transferred to the movement of the Earth. Nor do I doubt that ingenious and learned mathematicians will sustain me, if they are willing to recognize and weigh, not superficially, but with that thoroughness which Philosophy demands above all things, those matters which have been adduced by me in this work to demonstrate these theories. In order, however, that both the learned and the unlearned equally may see that I do not avoid anyone's judgment, I have preferred to dedicate these lucubrations of mine to Your Holiness rather than to any other, because, even in this remote corner of the world where I live, you are considered to be the most eminent man in dignity of rank and in love of all learning and even of mathematics, so that by your authority and judgment you can easily suppress the bites of slanderers, albeit the proverb hath it that there is no remedy for the bite of a sycophant. If perchance there shall be idle talkers, who, though they are ignorant of all mathematical sciences, nevertheless assume the right to pass judgment on these things, and if they should dare to criticise and attack this theory of mine because of some passage of scripture which they have falsely distorted for their own purpose, I care not at all; I will even despise their judgment as foolish. For it is not unknown that Lactantius, otherwise a famous writer but a poor mathematician, speaks most childishly of the shape of the Earth when he makes fun of those who said that the Earth has the form of a sphere. It should not seem strange then to zealous students, if some such people shall ridicule us also. Mathematics are written for mathematicians, to whom, if my opinion does not deceive me, our labors will seem to contribute something to the ecclesiastical state whose chief office Your Holiness now occupies; for when not so very long ago, under Leo X, in the Lateran Council the question of revising the ecclesiastical calendar was discussed, it then remained unsettled, simply because the length of the years and months, and the motions of the sun and moon were held to have been not yet sufficiently determined. Since that time, I have given my attention to observing these more accurately, urged on by a very distinguished man, Paul, Bishop of Fossombrone, who at that time had charge of the matter. But what I may have accomplished herein I leave to the judgment of Your Holiness in particular, and to that of all other learned mathematicians; and lest I seem to Your Holiness to promise more regarding the usefulness of the work than I can perform, I now pass to the work itself.

PREFACE TO THE HISTORY OF THE REFORMATION IN SCOTLAND

BY JOHN KNOX (C. 1566)

To the gentill readar, grace and peace from God the Father of our Lord Jesus Christ, with the perpetuall encrease of the Holy Spreit.

IT is not unknowen, Christeane Reader, that the same clud of ignorance, that long hath darkened many realmes under this accurssed kingdome of that Romane Antichrist, hath also owercovered this poore Realme; that idolatrie hath bein manteined, the bloode of innocentis hath bene sched, and Christ Jesus his eternall treuth hath bene abhorred, detested, and blasphemed. But that same God that caused light to schyne out of darknes, in the multitud of his mercyes, hath of long tyme opened the eis of some evin within this Realme, to see the vanitie of that which then was universally embrased for trew religioun; and hes gevin unto them strenth to oppone[1] thame selfis unto the same: and now, into these our last and moist[2] corrupt dayis, hath maid his treuth so to triumphe amonges us, that, in despyte of Sathan, hipochrisye is disclosed, and the trew wyrshipping of God is manifested to all the inhabitantis of this realme who eis Sathan blyndis not, eyther by thair fylthy lustes,

John Knox (1505-1572), the leader of the Scottish Reformation and its historian, was educated at Glasgow University; was pastor to English congregations at Frankfort-on-Main and at Geneva, where he met Calvin; returned to Scotland in 1559; and from that time till his death was active in the establishment of the Presbyterian organization, through which his powerful personality has continued to influence the Scottish national character to the present day. His preface, which is printed here in the original Scottish spelling, gives some indication of the sternness, not to say virulence, of his temper towards the Roman Church.

[1] Oppose.   [2] Most.

or ellis by ambitioun, and insatiable covetousness, which mack them repung to[3] the power of God working by his worde.

And becaus we ar not ignorant what diverse bruittis[4] war dispersed of us, the professoures of Jesus Christ within this realme, in the begynnyng of our interprise, ordour was tackin, that all our proceidingis should be committed to register; as that thei war, by such as then paynfullie travailled boith by toung and pen; and so was collected a just volume, (as after will appeir,) conteanyng thingis done frome the fyftie-awght[5] year of God, till the arrivall of the Quenis Majestie[6] furth of France, with the which the Collectour and Writtar for that tyme was content, and never mynded[7] further to have travailled in that kynd of writting. But, after invocatioun of the name of God, and after consultatioun with some faythfull, whai was thought by thame expedient to advance Goddis glorie, and to edifie this present generatioun, and the posteritie to come, it was concluded, that faythfull rehersall should be maid of such personages as God had maid instrumentis of his glorie, by opponyng of thame selfis to manifest abuses, superstitioun, and idolatrie; and albeit thare be no great nomber, yet ar thei mo then the Collectour wold have looked for at the begynnyng, and thairfoir is the volume somewhat enlarged abuif his expectatioun: And yit, in the begynnyng, mon[8] we crave of all the gentill Readaris, not to look[9] of us such ane History as shall expresse all thingis that have occurred within this Realme, during the tyme of this terrible conflict that hes bene betuix the sanctes[10] of God and these bloody wolves who clame to thame selves the titill of clargie, and to have authoritie ower the saules of men; for, with the Pollicey,[11] mynd we to meddill no further then it hath Religioun mixed with it. And thairfoir albeit that many thingis which wer don be omitted, yit, yf we invent no leys,[12] we think our selves blamless in that behalf. Of one other (thing) we mon[8] foirwarne the discreat Readaris, which is, that thei be not offended that the sempill treuth be spokin

[3] Resist. [4] Rumors. [5] I. e., 1558.
[6] Mary, Queen of Scots, arrived in Scotland, Aug. 19, 1561.
[7] Intended. [8] Must. [9] Expect. [10] Saints.
[11] Civil or State politics. [12] Lies.

without partialitie; for seing that of men we neyther hunt
for reward, nor yitt for vane glorie, we litill pass by the ap-
probatioun of such as seldome judge weill of God and of
his workis.   Lett not thairfoar the Readir wonder, albeit
that our style vary and speik diverslie of men, according
as thei have declared thameselves sometymes ennemymes and
sometymes freindis, sometymes fervent, sometymes cold,
sometymes constant, and sometymes changeable in the cause
of God and of his holy religioun: for, in this our simplicitie,
we suppoise that the Godlie shall espy our purpose, which
is, that God may be praised for his mercy schawin,[13] this
present age may be admonished to be thankfull for Goddis
benefittis offerred, and the posteritie to cum may be instructed how wonderouslie hath the light of Christ Jesus
prevailled against darkness in this last and most corrupted
age.

[13] Shown.

PREFATORY LETTER
TO SIR WALTER RALEIGH
ON THE FAERIE QUEENE
BY EDMUND SPENSER (1589)

A LETTER OF THE AUTHORS
EXPOUNDING HIS WHOLE INTENTION IN THE
COURSE OF THIS WORKE: WHICH FOR THAT IT
GIVETH GREAT LIGHT TO THE READER, FOR THE
BETTER UNDERSTANDING IS HEREUNTO ANNEXED

To the Right Noble, and Valorous, Sir Walter Raleigh, Knight, Lord Wardein of the Stanneryes, and Her Majesties Liefetenaunt of the County of Cornewayll

SIR, knowing how doubtfully all allegories may be construed, and this booke of mine, which I have entituled the *Faery Queene,* being a continued allegory, or darke conceit, I have thought good, as well for avoyding of gealous opinions and misconstructions, as also for your better light in reading thereof, (being so by you commanded,) to discover unto you the general intention and meaning, which in the whole course thereof I have fashioned, without expressing of any particular purposes or by accidents therein occasioned. The generall end therefore of all the booke is to fashion a gentleman or noble

Edmund Spenser was born in London about 1552, and died there in 1599. He was the greatest of the non-dramatic poets of the age of Elizabeth; and the "Faerie Queene" is the longest and most famous of his works. The first three books were published in 1590, the second three in 1596; of the remaining six which he had planned some fragments were issued after his death. The poem is a combination of allegory and romance; and in this prefatory letter to Raleigh the poet himself explains the plan of the work and its main allegorical signification.

person in vertuous and gentle discipline: which for that
I conceived shoulde be most plausible and pleasing, being
coloured with an historicall fiction, the which the most
part of men delight to read, rather for variety of matter
then for profite of the ensample, I chose the historye of
King Arthure, as most fitte for the excellency of his person, being made famous by many mens former workes,
and also furthest from the daunger of envy, and suspition
of present time. In which I have followed all the antique
poets historicall: first Homere, who in the persons of
Agamemnon and Ulysses hath ensampled a good governour
and a vertuous man, the one in his Ilias, the other in his
Odysseis; then Virgil, whose like intention was to doe in
the person of Æneas; after him Ariosto comprised them
both in his Orlando; and lately Tasso dissevered them
againe, and formed both parts in two persons, namely that
part which they in philosophy call Ethice, or vertues of a
private man, coloured in his Rinaldo; the other named
Politice in his Godfredo. By ensample of which excellente
poets, I labour to pourtraict in Arthure, before he was king,
the image of a brave knight, perfected in the twelve private
morall vertues, as Aristotle hath devised, the which is the
purpose of these first twelve bookes: which if I finde to
be well accepted, I may be perhaps encoraged to frame the
other part of polliticke vertues in his person, after that hee
came to be king. To some, I know, this methode will
seeme displeasaunt, which had rather have good discipline
delivered plainly in way of precepts, or sermoned at large,
as they use, then thus clowdily enwrapped in allegoricall
devises. But such, me seeme, should be satisfide with the
use of these dayes, seeing all things accounted by their
showes, and nothing esteemed of, that is not delightfull
and pleasing to commune sence. For this cause is Xenophon
preferred before Plato, for that the one, in the exquisite
depth of his judgement, formed a commune welth such as
it should be, but the other in the person of Cyrus and
the Persians fashioned a governement, such as might best
be: so much more profitable and gratious is doctrine by
ensample, then by rule. So have I laboured to doe in the
person of Arthure: whome I conceive, after his long edu-

cation by Timon, to whom he was by Merlin delivered
to be brought up, so soone as he was borne of the Lady
Igrayne, to have seene in a dream or vision the Faery
Queen, with whose excellent beauty ravished, he awaking
resolved to seeke her out, and so being by Merlin armed,
and by Timon throughly instructed, he went to seeke her
forth in Faerye Land. In that Faery Queene I meane
glory in my generall intention, but in my particular I
conceive the most excellent and glorious person of our
soveraine the Queene, and her kingdome in Faery Land.
And yet, in some places els, I doe otherwise shadow her.
For considering she beareth two persons, the one of a
most royall queene or empresse, the other of a most vertuous and beautifull lady, this latter part in some places I
doe expresse in Belphœbe, fashioning her name according
to your owne excellent conceipt of Cynthia, (Phæbe and
Cynthia being both names of Diana.) So in the person
of Prince Arthure I sette forth magnificence in particular,
which vertue, for that (according to Aristotle and the
rest) it is the perfection of all the rest, and conteineth
in it them all, therefore in the whole course I mention the
deedes of Arthure applyable to that vertue which I write
of in that booke. But of the xii. other vertues I make
xii. other knights the patrones, for the more variety of
the history: of which these three bookes contayn three.
The first of the Knight of the Redcrosse, in whome I
expresse holynes: The seconde of Sir Guyon, in whome
I sette forth temperaunce: The third of Britomartis, a
lady knight, in whome I picture chastity. But because
the beginning of the whole worke seemeth abrupte and
as depending upon other antecedents, it needs that ye know
the occasion of these three knights severall adventures.
For the methode of a poet historical is not such as of an
historiographer. For an historiographer discourseth of af-
fayres orderly as they were donne, accounting as well the
times as the actions; but a poet thrusteth into the middest,
even where it most concerneth him, and there recoursing
to the thinges forepaste, and divining of thinges to come,
maketh a pleasing analysis of all.

The beginning therefore of my history, if it were to be

told by an historiographer, should be the twelfth booke, which is the last; where I devise that the Faery Queene kept her annuall feaste xii. dayes, uppon which xii. severall dayes, the occasions of the xii. several adventures hapned, which being undertaken by xii. severall knights, are in these xii. books severally handled and discoursed. The first was this. In the beginning of the feast, there presented him selfe a tall clownish younge man, who, falling before the Queen of Faries, desired a boone (as the manner then was) which during that feast she might not refuse: which was that hee might have the atchievement of any adventure, which during that feaste should happen: that being graunted, he rested him on the floore, unfitte through his rusticity for a better place. Soone after entred a faire ladye in mourning weedes, riding on a white asse, with a dwarfe behind her leading a warlike steed, that bore the armes of a knight, and his speare in the dwarfes hand. Shee, falling before the Queene of Faeries, complayned that her father and mother, an ancient king and queene, had bene by an huge dragon many years shut up in a brasen castle, who thence suffred them not to yssew: and therefore besought the Faery Queene to assygne her some one of her knights to take on him that exployt. Presently that clownish person, upstarting, desired that adventure: whereat the Queene much wondering, and the lady much gaincsaying, yet he earnestly importuned his desire. In the end the lady told him, that unlesse that armour which she brought would serve him (that is, the armour of a Christian man specified by Saint Paul, vi. Ephes.), that he could not succeed in that enterprise: which being forthwith put upon him with dewe furnitures thereunto, he seemed the goodliest man in al that company, and was well liked of the lady. And eftesoones taking on him knighthood, and mounting on that straunge courser, he went forth with her on that adventure: where beginneth the first booke vz.

A gentle knight was pricking on the playne, &c.

The second day ther came in a palmer bearing an infant with bloody hands, whose parents he complained to have bene slayn by an enchaunteresse called Acrasia: and therfore craved of the Faery Queene, to appoint him some knight to performe that adventure; which being assigned to Sir Guyon, he presently went forth with that same palmer: which is the beginning of the second booke and the whole subject thereof. The third day there came in a groome, who complained before the Faery Queene, that a vile enchaunter, called Busirane, had in hand a most faire lady, called Amoretta, whom he kept in most grievous torment, because she would not yield him the pleasure of her body. Whereupon Sir Scudamour, the lover of that lady, presently tooke on him that adventure. But being unable to performe it by reason of the hard enchauntments, after long sorrow, in the end met with Britomartis, who succoured him, and reskewed his love.

But by occasion hereof, many other adventures are intermedled, but rather as accidents then intendments: as the love of Britomart, the overthrow of Marinell, the misery of Florimell, the vertuousnes of Belphœbe, the lasciviousnes of Hellenora, and many the like.

Thus much, Sir, I have briefly overronne, to direct your understanding to the wel-head of the history, that from thence gathering the whole intention of the conceit, ye may, as in a handfull, gripe al the discourse, which otherwise may happily seeme tedious and confused. So humbly craving the continuance of your honourable favour towards me, and th' eternall establishment of your happines, I humbly take leave.

23. January, 1589.
Yours most humbly affectionate,
Ed. Spenser.

PREFACE TO THE
HISTORY OF THE WORLD

BY SIR WALTER RALEIGH (1614)

HOW unfit and how unworthy a choice I have made
of myself, to undertake a work of this mixture,
mine own reason, though exceeding weak, hath
sufficiently resolved me. For had it been begotten then with
my first dawn of day, when the light of common knowledge
began to open itself to my younger years, and before any
wound received either from Fortune or Time, I might yet
well have doubted that the darkness of Age and Death would
have covered over both It and Me, long before the performance. For, beginning with the Creation, I have proceeded
with the History of the World; and lastly purposed (some
few sallies excepted) to confine my discourse with this our
renowned Island of Great Britain. I confess that it had
better sorted with my disability, the better part of whose
times are run out in other travails, to have set together (as
I could) the unjointed and scattered frame of our English
affairs, than of the universal: in whom, had there been no
other defect (who am all defect) than the time of the day,
it were enough; the day of a tempestuous life, drawn on to
the very evening ere I began. But those inmost and soul-
piercing wounds, which are ever aching while uncured; with
the desire to satisfy those few friends, which I have tried by
the fire of adversity, the former enforcing, the latter per-

A sketch of the life of Raleigh will be found prefixed to his "Discovery of Guiana" in the volume of "Voyages and Travels." His "History of the World" was written during his imprisonment in the Tower of
London, which lasted from 1603 to 1616. The Preface is interesting not
only as a fine piece of Elizabethan prose, but as exhibiting the attitude
toward history, and the view of the relation of history to religion and philosophy,
which characterized one who represented with exceptional vigor the typical
Elizabethan man of action and who was also a man of thought and
imagination.

suading; have caused me to make my thoughts legible, and myself the subject of every opinion, wise or weak.

To the world I present them, to which I am nothing indebted: neither have others that were, (Fortune changing) sped much better in any age. For prosperity and adversity have evermore tied and untied vulgar affections. And as we see it in experience, that dogs do always bark at those they know not, and that it is their nature to accompany one another in those clamors: so it is with the inconsiderate multitude; who wanting that virtue which we call honesty in all men, and that especial gift of God which we call charity in Christian men, condemn without hearing, and wound without offence given: led thereunto by uncertain report only; which his Majesty truly acknowledgeth for the author of all lies. "Blame no man," saith Siracides, "before thou have inquired the matter: understand first, and then reform righteously. 'Rumor, res sine teste, sine judice, maligna, fallax'; Rumor is without witness, without judge, malicious and deceivable." This vanity of vulgar opinion it was, that gave St. Augustine argument to affirm, that he feared the praise of good men, and detested that of the evil. And herein no man hath given a better rule, than this of Seneca; "Conscientiæ satisfaciamus: nihil in famam laboremus, sequatur vel mala, dum bene merearis." "Let us satisfy our own consciences, and not trouble ourselves with fame: be it never so ill, it is to be despised so we deserve well."

For myself, if I have in anything served my Country, and prized it before my private, the general acceptation can yield me no other profit at this time, than doth a fair sunshine day to a sea-man after shipwreck; and the contrary no other harm, than an outrageous tempest after the port attained. I know that I lost the love of many, for my fidelity towards Her,[1] whom I must still honor in the dust; though further than the defence of her excellent person, I never persecuted any man. Of those that did it, and by what device they did it, He that is the Supreme Judge of all the world, hath taken the account: so as for this kind of suffering, I must say with Seneca, "Mala opinio, bene parta, delectat."[2]

---

[1] Queen Elizabeth.
[2] "An ill opinion, honorably acquired, is pleasing."

As for other men; if there be any that have made themselves fathers of that fame which hath been begotten for them, I can neither envy at such their purchased glory, nor much lament mine own mishap in that kind; but content myself to say with Virgil, "Sic vos non vobis,"[3] in many particulars. To labor other satisfaction, were an effect of frenzy, not of hope, seeing it is not truth, but opinion, that can travel the world without a passport. For were it otherwise; and were there not as many internal forms of the mind, as there are external figures of men; there were then some possibility to persuade by the mouth of one advocate, even equity alone.

But such is the multiplying and extensive virtue of dead earth, and of that breath-giving life which God hath cast upon time and dust, as that among those that were, of whom we read and hear; and among those that are, whom we see and converse with; everyone hath received a several picture of face, and everyone a diverse picture of mind; everyone a form apart, everyone a fancy and cogitation differing: there being nothing wherein Nature so much triumpheth as in dissimilitude. From whence it cometh that there is found so great diversity of opinions; so strong a contrariety of inclinations; so many natural and unnatural; wise, foolish, manly, and childish affections and passions in mortal men. For it is not the visible fashion and shape of plants, and of reasonable creatures, that makes the difference of working in the one, and of condition in the other; but the form internal.

And though it hath pleased God to reserve the art of reading men's thoughts to himself: yet, as the fruit tells the name of the tree; so do the outward works of men (so far as their cogitations are acted) give us whereof to guess at the rest. Nay, it were not hard to express the one by the other, very near the life, did not craft in many, fear in the most, and the world's love in all, teach every capacity, according to the compass it hath, to qualify and make over their inward deformities for a time. Though it be also true, "Nemo potest diu personam ferre fictam: cito in naturam suam residunt, quibus veritas non subest": "No man can

[3] "So you not to yourselves."

long continue masked in a counterfeit behavior: the things that are forced for pretences having no ground of truth, cannot long dissemble their own natures." Neither can any man (saith Plutarch) so change himself, but that his heart may be sometimes seen at his tongue's end.

In this great discord and dissimilitude of reasonable creatures, if we direct ourselves to the multitude; "omnis honestæ rei malus judex est vulgus": " The common people are evil judges of honest things, and whose wisdom (saith Ecclesiastes) is to be despised": if to the better sort, every understanding hath a peculiar judgment, by which it both censureth other men, and valueth itself. And therefore unto me it will not seem strange, though I find these my worthless papers torn with rats: seeing the slothful censurers of all ages have not spared to tax the Reverend Fathers of the Church, with ambition; the severest men to themselves, with hypocrisy; the greatest lovers of justice, with popularity; and those of the truest valor and fortitude, with vain-glory. But of these natures which lie in wait to find fault, and to turn good into evil, seeing Solomon complained long since: and that the very age of the world renders it every day after other more malicious; I must leave the professors to their easy ways of reprehension, than which there is nothing of more facility.

To me it belongs in the first part of this Preface, following the common and approved custom of those who have left the memories of time past to after ages, to give, as near as I can, the same right to history which they have done. Yet seeing therein I should but borrow other men's words, I will not trouble the Reader with the repetition. True it is that among many other benefits for which it hath been honored, in this one it triumpheth over all human knowledge, that it hath given us life in our understanding, since the world itself had life and beginning, even to this day: yea, it hath triumphed over time, which besides it nothing but eternity hath triumphed over: for it hath carried our knowledge over the vast and devouring space of many thousands of years, and given so fair and piercing eyes to our mind; that we plainly behold living now (as if we had lived then) that great world, " Magni Dei sapiens opus," " The wise work (saith Hermes) of a great God," as it was then, when but new to itself. By it (I say) it is, that we live in the very time when it was created: we behold how it was governed: how it was covered with waters, and again repeopled: how kings and kingdoms have flourished and fallen, and for what virtue and piety God made prosperous; and for what vice and deformity he made wretched, both the one and the other. And it is not the least debt which we owe unto history, that it hath made us acquainted with our dead ancestors; and, out of the depth and darkness of the earth, delivered us their memory and fame. In a word, we may gather out of history a policy no less wise than eternal; by the comparison and application of other men's fore-passed miseries with our own like errors and ill deservings. But it is neither of examples the most lively instruction, nor the words of the wisest men, nor the terror of future torments, that hath yet so wrought in our blind and stupified minds, as to make us remember, that the infinite eye and wisdom of God doth pierce through all our pretences; as to make us remember, that the justice of God doth require none other accuser than our own consciences: which neither the false beauty of our apparent actions, nor all the formality, which (to pacify the opinions of men) we put on, can in any, or the least kind, cover from his knowledge. And so much did that heathen wisdom confess, no way as yet qualified by the knowledge of a true God. If any (saith Euripides) "having in his life committed wickedness, thinks he can hide it from the everlasting gods, he thinks not well."

To repeat God's judgments in particular, upon those of all degrees, which have played with his mercies would require a volume apart: for the sea of examples hath no bottom. The marks, set on private men, are with their bodies cast into the earth; and their fortunes, written only in the memories of those that lived with them: so as they who succeed, and have not seen the fall of others, do not fear their own faults. God's judgments upon the greater and greatest have been left to posterity; first, by those happy hands which the Holy Ghost hath guided; and secondly, by their virtue, who have gathered the acts and ends of men mighty and remarkable in the world. Now to point far off, and to speak of the con-

version of angels into devils; for ambition: or of the greatest and most glorious kings, who have gnawn the grass of
the earth with beasts for pride and ingratitude towards God:
or of that wise working of Pharaoh, when he slew the infants of Israel, ere they had recovered their cradles: or of
the policy of Jezebel, in covering the murder of Naboth by
a trial of the Elders, according to the Law, with many thousands of the like: what were it other, than to make an hopeless proof, that far-off examples would not be left to the
same far-off respects, as heretofore? For who hath not
observed, what labor, practice, peril, bloodshed, and cruelty,
the kings and princes of the world have undergone, exercised, taken on them, and committed; to make themselves
and their issues masters of the world? And yet hath Babylon, Persia, Syria, Macedon, Carthage, Rome, and the rest,
no fruit, no flower, grass, nor leaf, springing upon the face
of the earth, of those seeds: no, their very roots and ruins
do hardly remain. " Omnia quae manu hominum facta sunt,
vel manu hominum evertuntur, vel stando et durando defi-
ciunt ": " All that the hand of man can make, is either overturned by the hand of man, or at length by standing and
continuing consumed." The reasons of whose ruins, are
diversely given by those that ground their opinions on second causes. All kingdoms and states have fallen (say the
politicians) by outward and foreign force, or by inward
negligence and dissension, or by a third cause arising from
both. Others observe, that the greatest have sunk down
under their own weight; of which Livy hath a touch: "eo
crevit, ut magnitudine laboret sua":⁴ Others, That the divine
providence (which Cratippus objected to Pompey) hath set
down the date and period of every estate, before their first
foundation and erection. But hereof I will give myself a
day over to resolve.

For seeing the first books of the following story, have
undertaken the discourse of the first kings and kingdoms:
and that it is impossible for the short life of a Preface, to
travel after, and overtake far-off antiquity, and to judge of
it; I will, for the present, examine what profit hath been
gathered by our own Kings, and their neighbour princes: who

⁴ " He increased, with the result that he is oppressed by his greatness."

having beheld, both in divine and human letters, the success of infidelity, injustice, and cruelty; have (notwithstanding) planted after the same pattern.

True it is, that the judgments of all men are not agreeable; nor (which is more strange) the affection of any one man stirred up alike with examples of like nature: but every one is touched most, with that which most nearly seemeth to touch his own private, or otherwise best suiteth with his apprehension. But the judgments of God are forever unchangeable: neither is He wearied by the long process of time, and won to give His blessing in one age, to that which He hath cursed in another. Wherefor those that are wise, or whose wisdom if it be not great, yet is true and well grounded, will be able to discern the bitter fruits of irreligious policy, as well among those examples that are found in ages removed far from the present, as in those of latter times. And that it may no less appear by evident proof, than by asseveration, that ill doing hath always been attended with ill success; I will here, by way of preface, run over some examples, which the work ensuing hath not reached.

Among our kings of the Norman race, we have no sooner passed over the violence of the Norman Conquest, than we encounter with a singular and most remarkable example of God's justice, upon the children of Henry the First. For that King, when both by force, craft, and cruelty, he had dispossessed, overreached, and lastly made blind and destroyed his elder brother Robert Duke of Normandy, to make his own sons lords of this land: God cast them all, male and female, nephews and nieces (Maud excepted) into the bottom of the sea, with above a hundred and fifty others that attended them; whereof a great many were noble and of the King dearly beloved.

To pass over the rest, till we come to Edward the Second; it is certain, that after the murder of that King, the issue of blood then made, though it had some times of stay and stopping, did again break out, and that so often and in such abundance, as all our princes of the masculine race (very few excepted) died of the same disease. And although the young years of Edward the Third made his

knowledge of that horrible fact no more than suspicious;
yet in that he afterwards caused his own uncle, the Earl of
Kent, to die, for no other offence than the desire of his
brother's redemption, whom the Earl as then supposed to be
living; the King making that to be treated in his uncle,
which was indeed treason in himself, (had his uncle's intelligence been true) this I say made it manifest, that he was
not ignorant of what had past, nor greatly desirous to have
had it otherwise, though he caused Mortimer to die for the
same.

This cruelty the secret and unsearchable judgment of God
revenged on the grandchild of Edward the Third: and so
it fell out, even to the last of that line, that in the second or
third descent they were all buried under the ruins of those
buildings, of which the mortar had been tempered with
innocent blood. For Richard the Second, who saw both
his Treasurers, his Chancellor, and his Steward, with divers
others of his counsellors, some of them slaughtered by the
people, others in his absence executed by his enemies, yet
he always took himself for over-wise to be taught by examples. The Earls of Huntingdon and Kent, Montagu and
Spencer, who thought themselves as great politicians in
those days as others have done in these: hoping to please
the King, and to secure themselves, by the murder of
Gloucester; died soon after, with many other their adherents, by the like violent hands; and far more shamefully
than did that duke. And as for the King himself (who in
regard of many deeds, unworthy of his greatness, cannot be
excused, as the disavowing himself by breach of faith,
charters, pardons, and patents) : he was in the prime of his
youth deposed, and murdered by his cousin-german and
vassal, Henry of Lancaster, afterwards Henry the Fourth.

This King, whose title was weak, and his obtaining the
Crown traitorous; who brake faith with the lords at his
landing, protesting to intend only the recovery of his proper
inheritance, brake faith with Richard himself; and brake
faith with all the kingdom in Parliament, to whom he swore
that the deposed King should live. After that he had enjoyed
this realm some few years, and in that time had been set
upon all sides by his subjects, and never free from con-

spiracies and rebellions: he saw (if souls immortal see and discern anythings after the bodies' death) his grandchild Henry the Sixth, and his son the Prince, suddenly and without mercy, murdered; the possession of the Crown (for which he had caused so much blood to be poured out) transferred from his race, and by the issues of his enemies worn and enjoyed: enemies, whom by his own practice he supposed that he had left no less powerless, than the succession of the Kingdom questionless; by entailing the same upon his own issues by Parliament. And out of doubt, human reason could have judged no otherwise, but that these cautious provisions of the father, seconded by the valor and signal victories of his son Henry the Fifth, had buried the hopes of every competitor, under the despair of all reconquest and recovery. I say, that human reason might so have judged, were not this passage of Casaubon also true; "Dies, hora, momentum, evertendis dominationibus sufficit, quae adamantinis credebantur radicibus esse fundatae:" "A day, an hour, a moment, is enough to overturn the things, that seemed to have been founded and rooted in adamant."

Now for Henry the Sixth, upon whom the great storm of his grandfather's grievous faults fell, as it formerly had done upon Richard the grandchild of Edward: although he was generally esteemed for a gentle and innocent prince, yet as he refused the daughter of Armagnac, of the House of Navarre, the greatest of the Princes of France, to whom he was affianced (by which match he might have defended his inheritance in France) and married the daughter of Anjou, (by which he lost all that he had in France) so in condescending to the unworthy death of his uncle of Gloucester, the main and strong pillar of the House of Lancaster; he drew on himself and this kingdom the greatest joint-loss and dishonor, that ever it sustained since the Norman Conquest. Of whom it may truly be said which a counsellor of his own spake of Henry the Third of France, "Qu'il estait une fort gentile Prince; mais son reigne est advenu en une fort mauvais temps:" "He was a very gentle Prince; but his reign happened in a very unfortunate season."

It is true that Buckingham and Suffolk were the practicers

and contrivers of the Duke's death: Buckingham and Suffolk, because the Duke gave instructions to their authority, which otherwise under the Queen had been absolute; the Queen in respect of her personal wound, " spretaeque injuria formae,"[5] because Gloucester dissuaded her marriage. But the fruit was answerable to the seed; the success to the counsel. For after the cutting down of Gloucester, York grew up so fast, as he dared to dispute his right both by arguments and arms; in which quarrel, Suffolk and Buckingham, with the greatest number of their adherents, were dissolved. And although for his breach of oath by sacrament, it pleased God to strike down York: yet his son the Earl of March, following the plain path which his father had trodden out, despoiled Henry the father, and Edward the son, both of their lives and kingdom. And what was the end now of that politic lady the Queen, other than this, that she lived to behold the wretched ends of all her partakers: that she lived to look on, while her husband the King, and her only son the Prince, were hewn in sunder; while the Crown was set on his head that did it. She lived to see herself despoiled of her estate, and of her moveables: and lastly, her father, by rendering up to the Crown of France the Earldom of Provence and other places, for the payment of fifty thousand crowns for her ransom, to become a stark beggar. And this was the end of that subtility, which Siracides calleth " fine " but " unrighteous: " for other fruit hath it never yielded since the world was.

And now it came to Edward the Fourth's turn (though after many difficulties) to triumph. For all the plants of Lancaster were rooted up, one only Earl of Richmond excepted: whom also he had once bought of the Duke of Brittany, but could not hold him. And yet was not this of Edward such a plantation, as could any way promise itself stability. For this Edward the King (to omit more than many of his other cruelties) beheld and allowed the slaughter which Gloucester, Dorset, Hastings, and others, made of Edward the Prince in his own presence; of which tragical actors, there was not one that escaped the judgment of God in the same kind. And he, which (besides

[5] " The insult done in scorning her beauty."

the execution of his brother Clarence, for none other offence than he himself had formed in his own imagination) instructed Gloucester to kill Henry the Sixth, his predecessor; taught him also by the same art to kill his own sons and successors, Edward and Richard. For those kings which have sold the blood of others at a low rate; have but made the market for their own enemies, to buy of theirs at the same price.

To Edward the Fourth succeeded Richard the Third, the greatest master in mischief of all that fore-went him: who although, for the necessity of his tragedy, he had more parts to play, and more to perform in his own person, than all the rest; yet he so well fitted every affection that played with him, as if each of them had but acted his own interest. For he wrought so cunningly upon the affections of Hastings and Buckingham, enemies to the Queen and to all her kindred, as he easily allured them to condescend, that Rivers and Grey, the King's maternal uncle and half brother, should (for the first) be severed from him: secondly, he wrought their consent to have them imprisoned: and lastly (for the avoiding of future inconvenience) to have their heads severed from their bodies. And having now brought those his chief instruments to exercise that common precept which the Devil hath written on every post, namely, to depress those whom they had grieved, and destroy those whom they had depressed; he urged that argument so far and so forcibly, as nothing but the death of the young King himself, and of his brother, could fashion the conclusion. For he caused it to be hammered into Buckingham's head, that, whensoever the King or his brother should have able years to exercise their power, they would take a most severe revenge of that cureless wrong, offered to their uncle and brother, Rivers and Grey.

But this was not his manner of reasoning with Hastings, whose fidelity to his master's sons was without suspect: and yet the Devil, who never dissuades by impossibility, taught him to try him. And so he did. But when he found by Catesby, who sounded him, that he was not fordable; he first resolved to kill him sitting in council: wherein having failed with his sword, he set the hangman upon him, with a weapon of more weight. And because nothing else could move his appetite, he caused his head to be stricken off, before he ate his dinner. A greater judgment of God than this upon Hastings, I have never observed in any story. For the selfsame day that the Earl Rivers, Grey, and others, were (without trial of law, of offence given) by Hastings' advice executed at Pomfret: I say Hastings himself in the same day, and (as I take it) in the same hour, in the same lawless manner had his head stricken off in the Tower of London. But Buckingham lived a while longer; and with an eloquent oration persuaded the Londoners to elect Richard for their king. And having received the Earldom of Hereford for reward, besides the high hope of marrying his daughter to the King's only son; after many grievous vexations of mind, and unfortunate attempts, being in the end betrayed and delivered up by his trustiest servant; he had his head severed from his body at Salisbury, without the trouble of any of his Peers. And what success had Richard himself after all these mischiefs and murders, policies, and counter-policies to Christian religion: and after such time as with a most merciless hand he had pressed out the breath of his nephews and natural lords; other than the prosperity of so short a life, as it took end, ere himself could well look over and discern it? The great outcry of innocent blood, obtained at God's hands the effusion of his; who became a spectacle of shame and dishonor, both to his friends and enemies.

This cruel King, Henry the Seventh cut off; and was therein (no doubt) the immediate instrument of God's justice. A politic Prince he was if ever there were any, who by the engine of his wisdom, beat down and overturned as many strong oppositions both before and after he wore the Crown, as ever King of England did: I say by his wisdom, because as he ever left the reins of his affections in the hands of his profit, so he always weighed his undertakings by his abilities, leaving nothing more to hazard than so much as cannot be denied it in all human actions. He had well observed the proceedings of Louis the Eleventh, whom he followed in all that was royal or royal-like, but he was far more just, and begun not their processes whom he hated or feared by the execution, as Louis did.

He could never endure any mediation in rewarding his servants, and therein exceeding wise; for whatsoever himself gave, he himself received back the thanks and the love, knowing it well that the affections of men (purchased by nothing so readily as by benefits) were trains that better became great kings, than great subjects. On the contrary, in whatsoever he grieved his subjects, he wisely put it off on those, that he found fit ministers for such actions. Howsoever the taking off of Stanley's head, who set the Crown on his, and the death of the young Earl of Warwick, son to George, Duke of Clarence, shows, as the success also did, that he held somewhat of the errors of his ancestors; for his possession in the first line ended in his grandchildren, as that of Edward the Third and Henry the Fourth had done.

Now for King Henry the Eighth; if all the pictures and patterns of a merciless prince were lost in the world, they might all again be painted to the life, out of the story of this king. For how many servants did he advance in haste (but for what virtue no man could suspect) and with the change of his fancy ruined again; no man knowing for what offence? To how many others of more desert gave he abundant flowers from whence to gather honey, and in the end of harvest burnt them in the hive? How many wives did he cut off, and cast off, as his fancy and affection changed? How many princes of the blood (whereof some of them for age could hardly crawl towards the block) with a world of others of all degrees (of whom our common chronicles have kept the account) did he execute? Yea, in his very death-bed, and when he was at the point to have given his account to God for the abundance of blood already spilt, he imprisoned the Duke of Norfolk the father; and executed the Earl of Surrey the son; the one, whose deservings he knew not how to value, having never omitted anything that concerned his own honor, and the King's service; the other never having committed anything worthy of his least displeasure: the one exceeding valiant and advised; the other no less valiant than learned, and of excellent hope. But besides the sorrows which he heaped upon the fatherless and widows at home: and besides the vain enterprises abroad, wherein it is thought that he consumed more treasure than all our victorious kings did in their several conquests; what causeless and cruel wars did he make upon his own nephew King James the First? What laws and wills did he devise to cut off, and cut down those branches, which sprang from the same root that himself did? And in the end (notwithstanding these his so many irreligious provisions) it pleased God to take away all his own, without increase; though, for themselves in their several kinds, all princes of eminent virtue. For these words of Samuel to Agag King of the Amalekites, have been verified upon many others: "As thy sword hath made other women childless, so shall thy mother be childless among other women." And that blood which the same King Henry affirmed, that the cold air of Scotland had frozen up in the North, God hath diffused by the sunshine of his grace: from whence his Majesty now living, and long to live, is descended. Of whom I may say it truly, "That if all the malice of the world were infused into one eye: yet could it not discern in his life, even to this day, any one of these foul spots, by which the consciences of all the forenamed princes (in effect) have been defiled; nor any drop of that innocent blood on the sword of his justice, with which the most that fore-went him have stained both their hands and fame. And for this Crown of England; it may truly be avowed: that he hath received it even from the hand of God, and hath stayed the time of putting it on, howsoever he were provoked to hasten it: that he never took revenge of any man, that sought to put him beside it: that he refused the assistance of Her enemies, that wore it long, with as great glory as ever princess did: that his Majesty entered not by a breach, nor by blood; but by the ordinary gate, which his own right set open; and into which, by a general love and obedience, he was received. And howsoever his Majesty's preceding title to this Kingdom was preferred by many princes (witness the Treaty at Cambray in the year 1559) yet he never pleased to dispute it, during the life of that renowned lady his predecessor; no, notwithstanding the injury of not being declared heir, in all the time of her long reign.

Neither ought we to forget, or neglect our thankfulness to God for the uniting of the northern parts of Britain to the south, to wit, of Scotland to England, which though they were severed but by small brooks and banks, yet by reason of the long continued war, and the cruelties exercised upon each other, in the affections of the nations, they were infinitely severed. This I say is not the least of God's blessings which his Majesty hath brought with him unto this land: no, put all our petty grievances together, and heap them up to their height, they will appear but as a molehill compared with the mountain of this concord. And if all the historians since then have acknowledged the uniting of the Red Rose, and the White, for the greatest happiness (Christian Religion excepted), that ever this kingdom received from God, certainly the peace between the two lions of gold and gules, and the making them one, doth by many degrees exceed the former; for by it, besides the sparing of our British blood, heretofore and during the difference, so often and abundantly shed, the state of England is more assured, the kingdom more enabled to recover her ancient honor and rights, and by it made more invincible, than by all our former alliances, practises, policies, and conquests. It is true that hereof we do not yet find the effect. But had the Duke of Parma in the year 1588, joined the army which he commanded, with that of Spain, and landed it on the south coast; and had his Majesty at the same time declared himself against us in the North: it is easy to divine what had become of the liberty of England, certainly we would then without murmur have bought this union at far greater price than it hath since cost us. It is true, that there was never any common weal or kingdom in the world, wherein no man had cause to lament. Kings live in the world, and not above it. They are not infinite to examine every man's cause, or to relieve every man's wants. And yet in the latter (though to his own prejudice), his Majesty hath had more comparison of other men's necessities, than of his own coffers. Of whom it may be said, as of Solomon,[6] "Dedit

[6] " God gave to Solomon largeness of heart."—1 Kings iv. 29.

Deus Solomoni latitudinem cordis ": Which if other men
do not understand with Pineda, to be meant by liberality,
but by " latitude of knowledge "; yet may it be better spoken
of His Majesty, than of any king that ever England had;
who as well in divine, as human understanding, hath ex-
ceeded all that fore-went him, by many degrees.

I could say much more of the King's majesty, without
flattery: did I not fear the imputation of presumption, and
withal suspect, that it might befall these papers of mine
(though the loss were little) as it did the pictures of Queen
Elizabeth, made by unskilful and common painters, which
by her own commandment were knocked in pieces and cast
into the fire. For ill artists, in setting out the beauty of the
external; and weak writers, in describing the virtues of the
internal; do often leave to posterity, of well formed faces
a deformed memory; and of the most perfect and princely
minds, a most defective representation. It may suffice, and
there needs no other discourse; if the honest reader but
compare the cruel and turbulent passages of our former
kings, and of other their neighbor-princes (of whom for
that purpose I have inserted this brief discourse) with his
Majesty's temperate, revengeless and liberal disposition: I
say, that if the honest reader weigh them justly, and with
an even hand; and withal but bestow every deformed child
on his true parent; he shall find, that there is no man that
hath so just cause to complain, as the King himself hath.
Now as we have told the success of the trumperies and
cruelties of our own kings, and other great personages: so
we find, that God is everywhere the same God. And as it
pleased him to punish the usurpation, and unnatural cruelty
of Henry the First, and of our third Edward, in their children for many generations: so dealt He with the sons of
Louis Debonnaire, the son of Charles the Great, or Charlemagne. For after such time as Debonnaire of France, had
torn out the eyes of Bernard his nephew, the son of Pepin
the eldest son of Charlemagne, and heir of the Empire, and
then caused him to die in prison, as did our Henry to
Robert his eldest brother: there followed nothing but murders upon murders, poisoning, imprisonments, and civil war;
till the whole race of that famous Emperor was extinguished.

And though Debonnaire, after he had rid himself of his
nephew by a violent death; and of his bastard brothers by
a civil death (having inclosed them with sure guard, all the
days of their lives, within a monastery) held himself secure
from all opposition: yet God raised up against him (which
he suspected not) his own sons, to vex him, to invade him,
to take him prisoner, and to depose him; his own sons, with
whom (to satisfy their ambition) he had shared his estate,
and given them crowns to wear, and kingdoms to govern,
during his own life. Yea his eldest son, Lothair (for he
had four, three by his first wife, and one by his second; to
wit, Lothair, Pepin, Louis, and Charles), made it the cause
of his deposition, that he had used violence towards his
brothers and kinsmen; and that he had suffered his nephew
(whom he might have delivered) to be slain. " Eo quod,"
saith the text,[7] " fratribus, et propinquis violentiam intulerit,
et nepotem suum, quem ipse liberare poterat, interfici per-
miserit ": " Because he used violence to his brothers and
kinsmen, and suffered his nephew to be slain whom he might
have delivered."

Yet did he that which few kings do; namely, repent him
of his cruelty. For, among many other things which he performed in the General Assembly of the States, it follows:
" Post haec autem palam se errasse confessus, et imitatus
Imperatoris Theodosii exemplum, poenitentiam spontaneam
suscepit, tam de his, quam quae in Bernardum proprium
nepotem gesserat ": " After this he did openly confess himself to have erred, and following the example of the Emperor Theodosius, he underwent voluntary penance, as well
for his other offences, as for that which he had done against
Bernard his own nephew."

This he did; and it was praise-worthy. But the blood that
is unjustly spilt, is not again gathered up from the ground
by repentance. These medicines, ministered to the dead,
have but dead rewards.

This king, as I have said, had four sons. To Lothair his
eldest he gave the Kingdom of Italy; as Charlemagne, his
father, had done to Pepin, the father of Bernard, who was
to succeed him in the Empire. To Pepin the second son he

[7] Step. Pasquiere, Recherches, lib. v. cap. i.

gave the Kingdom of Aquitaine: to Louis, the Kingdom of Bavaria: and to Charles, whom he had by a second wife called Judith, the remainder of the Kingdom of France. But this second wife, being a mother-in-law[*] to the rest, persuaded Debonnaire to cast his son Pepin out of Aquitaine, thereby to greaten Charles, which, after the death of his son Pepin, he prosecuted to effect, against his grandchild bearing the same name. In the meanwhile, being invaded by his son Louis of Bavaria, he dies for grief.

Debonnaire dead, Louis of Bavaria, and Charles afterwards called the Bald, and their nephew Pepin, of Aquitaine, join in league against the Emperor Lothair their eldest brother. They fight near to Auxerre the most bloody battle that ever was stroken in France: in which, the marvellous loss of nobility, and men of war, gave courage to the Saracens to invade Italy; to the Huns to fall upon Almaine; and the Danes to enter upon Normandy. Charles the Bald by treason seizeth upon his nephew Pepin, kills him in a cloister: Carloman rebels against his father Charles the Bald, the father burns out the eyes of his son Carloman; Bavaria invades the Emperor Lothair his brother, Lothair quits the Empire, he is assailed and wounded to the heart by his own conscience, for his rebellion against his father, and for his other cruelties, and dies in a monastery. Charles the Bald, the uncle, oppresseth his nephews the sons of Lothair, he usurpeth the Empire to the prejudice of Louis of Bavaria his elder brother; Bavaria's armies and his son Carloman are beaten, he dies of grief, and the usurper Charles is poisoned by Zedechias a Jew, his physician, his son Louis le Bègue dies of the same drink. Bègue had Charles the Simple and two bastards, Louis and Carloman; they rebel against their brother, but the eldest breaks his neck, the younger is slain by a wild boar; the son of Bavaria had the same ill destiny, and brake his neck by a fall out of a window in sporting with his companions. Charles the Gross becomes lord of all that the sons of Debonnaire held in Germany; wherewith not contented, he invades Charles the Simple: but being forsaken of his nobility, of his wife, and of his understanding, he dies a distracted beggar. Charles

[*] Step-mother.

the Simple is held in wardship by Eudes, Mayor of the
Palace, then by Robert the brother of Eudes: and lastly,
being taken by the Earl of Vermandois, he is forced to die
in the prison of Peron. Louis the son of Charles the
Simple breaks his neck in chasing a wolf, and of the two
sons of this Louis, the one dies of poison, the other dies
in the prison of Orleans; after whom Hugh Capet, of another race, and a stranger to the French, makes himself
king.

These miserable ends had the issues of Debonnaire, who
after he had once apparelled injustice with authority, his
sons and successors took up the fashion, and wore that garment so long without other provision, as when the same was
torn from their shoulders, every man despised them as
miserable and naked beggars. The wretched success they
had (saith a learned Frenchman) shows, "que en ceste
mort il y avait plus du fait des hommes que de Dieu, ou de
la justice": "that in the death of that Prince, to wit, of
Bernard the son of Pepin, the true heir of Charlemagne,
men had more meddling than either God or justice had."

But to come nearer home; it is certain that Francis the
First, one of the worthiest kings (except for that fact) that
ever Frenchmen had, did never enjoy himself, after he
had commended the destruction of the Protestants of
Mirandol and Cabrieres, to the Parliament of Provence,
which poor people were thereupon burnt and murdered;
men, women, and children. It is true that the said King
Francis repented himself of the fact, and gave charge to
Henry his son, to do justice upon the murderers, threatening
his son with God's judgments, if he neglected it. But this
unseasonable care of his, God was not pleased to accept for
payment. For after Henry himself was slain in sport by
Montgomery, we all may remember what became of his
four sons, Francis, Charles, Henry, and Hercules. Of
which although three of them became kings, and were married to beautiful and virtuous ladies: yet were they, one
after another, cast out of the world, without stock or seed.
And notwithstanding their subtility, and breach of faith;
with all their massacres upon those of the religion,[*] and

[*] *I. e.,* Protestantism.

great effusion of blood, the crown was set on his head, whom they all labored to dissolve; the Protestants remain more in number than ever they were, and hold to this day more strong cities than ever they had.

Let us now see if God be not the same God in Spain, as in England and France. Towards whom we will look no further back than to Don Pedro of Castile: in respect of which Prince, all the tyrants of Sicil, our Richard the Third, and the great Ivan Vasilowich of Moscow, were but petty ones: this Castilian, of all Christian and heathen kings, having been the most merciless. For, besides those of his own blood and nobility, which he caused to be slain in his own court and chamber, as Sancho Ruis, the great master of Calatrava, Ruis Gonsales, Alphonso Tello, and Don John of Arragon, whom he cut in pieces and cast into the streets, denying him Christian burial: I say, besides these, and the slaughter of Gomes Mauriques, Diego Peres, Alphonso Gomes, and the great commander of Castile; he made away the two infants of Arragon his cousin germans, his brother Don Frederick, Don John de la Cerde, Albuquergues, Nugnes de Guzman, Cornel, Cabrera, Tenorio, Mendes de Toledo, Guttiere his great treasurer and all his kindred; and a world of others. Neither did he spare his two youngest brothers, innocent princes: whom after he had kept in close prison from their cradles, till one of them had lived sixteen years, and the other fourteen, he murdered them there. Nay, he spared not his mother, nor his wife the Lady Blanche of Bourbon. Lastly, as he caused the Archbishop of Toledo, and the Dean to be killed of purpose to enjoy their treasures; so did he put to death Mahomet Aben Alhamar, King of Barbary, with thirty-seven of his nobility, that came unto him for succor, with a great sum of money, to levy (by his favor) some companies of soldiers to return withal. Yea, he would needs assist the hangman with his own hand, in the execution of the old king; in so much as Pope Urban declareth him an enemy both to God and man. But what was his end? Having been formerly beaten out of his kingdom, and re-established by the valor of the English nation, led by the famous Duke of Lancaster: he was stabbed to death by his younger brother the Earl of Astramara, who dispossessed all his children of their inheritance; which, but for the father's injustice and cruelty, had never been in danger of any such thing.

If we can parallel any man with this king, it must be Duke John of Burgogne, who, after his traitorous murder of the Duke of Orleans, caused the Constable of Armagnac, the Chancellor of France, the Bishops of Constance, Bayeux, Eureux, Senlis, Saintes, and other religious and reverend Churchmen, the Earl of Gran Pre, Hector of Chartres, and (in effect) all the officers of justice, of the Chamber of Accounts, Treasury, and Request, (with sixteen hundred others to accompany them) to be suddenly and violently slain. Hereby, while he hoped to govern, and to have mastered France, he was soon after struck with an axe in the face, in the presence of the Dauphin; and, without any leisure to repent his misdeeds, presently[10] slain. *These were the lovers of other men's miseries: and misery found them out.*

Now for the kings of Spain, which lived both with Henry the Seventh, Henry the Eighth, Queen Mary, and Queen Elizabeth; Ferdinand of Arragon was the first: and the first that laid the foundation of the present Austrian greatness. For this King did not content himself to hold Arragon by the usurpation of his ancestor; and to fasten thereunto the Kingdom of Castile and Leon, which Isabel his wife held by strong hand, and his assistance, from her own niece the daughter of the last Henry: but most cruelly and craftily, without all color or pretence of right, he also cast his own niece out of the Kingdom of Navarre, and, contrary to faith, and the promise that he made to restore it, fortified the best places, and so wasted the rest, as there was no means left for any army to invade it. This King, I say, that betrayed also Ferdinand and Frederick, Kings of Naples, princes of his own blood, and by double alliance tied unto him; sold them to the French: and with the same army, sent for their succor under Gonsalvo, cast them out; and shared their kingdom with the French, whom afterwards he most shamefully betrayed.

[10] Instantly.

This wise and politic King, who sold Heaven and his own honor, to make his son, the Prince of Spain, the greatest monarch of the world; saw him die in the flower of his years; and his wife great with child, with her untimely birth, at once and together buried. His eldest daughter married unto Don Alphonso, Prince of Portugal, beheld her first husband break his neck in her presence; and being with child by her second, died with it. A just judgment of God upon the race of John, father to Alphonso, now wholly extinguished; who had not only left many disconsolate mothers in Portugal, by the slaughter of their children; but had formerly slain with his own hand, the son and only comfort of his aunt the Lady Beatrix, Duchess of Viseo.

The second daughter of Ferdinand, married to the Arch-Duke Philip, turned fool, and died mad and deprived.[11] His third daughter, bestowed on King Henry the Eighth, he saw cast off by the King: the mother of many troubles in England; and the mother of a daughter, that in her unhappy zeal shed a world of innocent blood; lost Calais to the French; and died heartbroken without increase. To conclude, all those kingdoms of Ferdinand have masters of a new name; and by a strange family are governed and possessed.

Charles the Fifth, son to the Arch-Duke Philip, in whose vain enterprises upon the French, upon the Almains, and other princes and states, so many multitudes of Christian soldiers, and renowned captains were consumed; who gave the while a most perilous entrance to the Turks, and suffered Rhodes, the Key of Christendom, to be taken; was in conclusion chased out of France, and in a sort out of Germany; and left to the French, Mentz, Toule, and Verdun, places belonging to the Empire, stole away from Inspurg; and scaled the Alps by torchlight, pursued by Duke Maurice; having hoped to swallow up all those dominions wherein he concocted nothing save his own disgraces. And having, after the slaughter of so many millions of men, no one foot of ground in either: he crept into a cloister, and made himself a pensioner of an hundred thousand ducats by the

[11] Dispossessed.

year, to his son Philip, from whom he very slowly received his mean and ordinary maintenance.

His son again King Philip the Second, not satisfied to hold Holland and Zeeland, (wrested by his ancestors from Jacqueline their lawful Princess) and to possess in peace many other provinces of the Netherlands: persuaded by that mischievous Cardinal of Granvile, and other Romish tyrants; not only forgot the most remarkable services done to his father the Emperor by the nobilities of those countries, not only forgot the present made him upon his entry, of forty millions of florins, called the " Novaile aide "; nor only forgot that he had twice most solemnly sworn to the General States, to maintain and preserve their ancient rights, privileges, and customs, which they had enjoyed under their thirty and five earls before him, Conditional Princes of those provinces: but beginning first to constrain them, and en-thrall them by the Spanish Inquisition, and then to im-poverish them by many new devised and intolerable im-positions; he lastly, by strong hand and main force, at-tempted to make himself not only an absolute monarch over them, like unto the kings and sovereigns of England and France; but Turk-like to tread under his feet all their natural and fundamental laws, privileges, and ancient rights. To effect which, after he had easily obtained from the Pope a dispensation of his former oaths (which dispensation was the true cause of the war and bloodshed since then;) and after he had tried what he could perform, by dividing of their own nobility, under the government of his base sister Margaret of Austria, and the Cardinal Granvile; he employed that most merciless Spaniard Don Ferdinand Alvarez of Toledo, Duke of Alva, followed with a powerful army of strange nations: by whom he first slaughtered that renowned captain, the Earl of Egmont, Prince of Gavare: and Philip Montmorency, Earl of Horn: made away Mon-tigue, and the Marquis of Bergues, and cut off in those six years (that Alva governed) of gentlemen and others, eigh-teen thousand and six hundred, by the hands of the hang-man, besides all his other barbarous murders and massacres. By whose ministry when he could not yet bring his affairs to their wished ends, having it in his hope to work that by subtility, which he had failed to perform by force; he sent for governor his bastard brother Don John of Austria, a prince of great hope, and very gracious to those people. But he, using the same papal advantage that his predecessors had done, made no scruple to take oath upon the Holy Evangelists, to observe the treaty made with the General States; and to discharge the Low Countries of all Spaniards, and other strangers therein garrisoned: towards whose pay and passport, the Netherlands strained themselves to make payment of six hundred thousand pounds. Which monies received, he suddenly surprised the citadels of Antwerp and Nemours: not doubting (being unsuspected by the states) to have possessed himself of all the mastering places of those provinces. For whatsoever he overtly pretended, he held in secret a contrary counsel with the Secretary Escovedo, Rhodus, Barlemont, and others, ministers of the Spanish tyranny, formerly practised, and now again intended, But let us now see the effect and end of this perjury and of all other the Duke's cruelties. First, for himself, after he had murdered so many of the nobility; executed (as aforesaid) eighteen thousand and six hundred in six years, and most cruelly slain man, woman, and child, in Mechlin, Zutphen, Naerden, and other places: notwithstanding his Spanish vaunt, that he would suffocate the Hollanders in their own butter-barrels, and milk-tubs; he departed the country no otherwise accompanied, than with the curse and detestation of the whole nation; leaving his master's affairs in a tenfold worse estate, than he found them at his first arrival. For Don John, whose haughty conceit of himself overcame the greatest difficulties; though his judgment were over-weak to manage the least: what wonders did his fearful breach of faith bring forth, other than the King his brother's jealousy and distrust, with the untimely death that seized him, even in the flower of his youth? And for Escovedo his sharp-witted secretary, who in his own imagination had conquered for his master both England and the Netherlands; being sent into Spain upon some new project, he was at the first arrival, and before any access to the King, by certain ruffians appointed by Anthony Peres (though by better warrant than his) rudely murdered in his own lodging. Lastly, if we consider the King of Spain's carriage, his counsel and success in this business, there is nothing left to the memory of man more remarkable. For he hath paid above an hundred millions, and the lives of above four hundred thousand Christians, for the loss of all those countries; which, for beauty, gave place to none; and for revenue, did equal his West Indies: for the loss of a nation which most willingly obeyed him; and who at this day, after forty years war, are in despite of all his forces become a free estate, and far more rich and powerful than they were, when he first began to impoverish and oppress them.

Oh, by what plots, by what forswearings, betrayings, oppressions, imprisonments, tortures, poisonings, and under what reasons of state, and politic subtlety, have these fore-named kings, both strangers, and of our own nation, pulled the vengeance of God upon themselves, upon theirs, and upon their prudent ministers! and in the end have brought those things to pass for their enemies, and seen an effect so directly contrary to all their own counsels and cruelties; as the one could never have hoped for themselves; and the other never have succeeded; if no such opposition had ever been made. God hath said it and performed it ever: "Perdam sapientiam sapientum"; "I will destroy the wisdom of the wise."

But what of all this? and to what end do we lay before the eyes of the living, the fall and fortunes of the dead: seeing the world is the same that it hath been; and the children of the present time, will still obey their parents? It is in the present time that all the wits of the world are exercised. To hold the times we have, we hold all things lawful: and either we hope to hold them forever; or at least we hope that there is nothing after them to be hoped for. For as we are content to forget our own experience, and to counterfeit the ignorance of our own knowledge, in all things that concern ourselves; or persuade ourselves, that God hath given us letters patents to pursue all our irreligious affections, with a "non obstante"[12] so we neither look behind us what hath been, nor before us what shall be. It is true,

[12] "Nothing hindering."

that the quantity which we have, is of the body: we are by it joined to the earth: we are compounded of earth; and we inhabit it. The Heavens are high, far off, and unsearchable: we have sense and feeling of corporal things; and of eternal grace, but by revelation. No marvel then that our thoughts are also earthly: and it is less to be wondered at, that the words of worthless men can not cleanse them: seeing their doctrine and instruction, whose understanding the Holy Ghost vouchsafed to inhabit, have not performed it. For as the Prophet Isaiah cried out long ago, "Lord, who hath believed our reports?" And out of doubt, as Isaiah complained then for himself and others: so are they less believed, every day after other. For although religion, and the truth thereof be in every man's mouth, yea, in the discourse of every woman, who for the greatest number are but idols of vanity: what is it other than an universal dissimulation? We profess that we know God: but by works we deny him. For beatitude doth not consist in the knowledge of divine things, but in a divine life: for the Devils know them better than men. "Beatitudo non est divinorum cognitio, sed vita divina." And certainly there is nothing more to be admired, and more to be lamented, than the private contention, the passionate dispute, the personal hatred, and the perpetual war, massacres, and murders for religion among Christians: the discourse whereof hath so occupied the world, as it hath well near driven the practice thereof out of the world. Who would not soon resolve, that took knowledge but of the religious disputations among men, and not of their lives which dispute, that there were no other thing in their desires, than the purchase of Heaven; and that the world itself were but used as it ought, and as an inn or place, wherein to repose ourselves in passing on towards our celestial habitation? when on the contrary, besides the discourse and outward profession, the soul hath nothing but hypocrisy. We are all (in effect) become comedians in religion: and while we act in gesture and voice, divine virtues, in all the course of our lives we renounce our persons, and the parts we play. For Charity, Justice, and Truth have but their being *in terms,* like the philosopher's *Materia prima.*

Neither is it that wisdom, which Solomon defineth to be the "Schoolmistress of the knowledge of God," that hath valuation in the world: it is enough that we give it our good word: but the same which is altogether exercised in the service of the world as the gathering of riches chiefly, by which we purchase and obtain honor, with the many respects which attend it. These indeed be the marks, which (when we have bent our consciences to the highest) we all shoot at. For the obtaining whereof it is true, that the care is our own; the care our own in this life, the peril our own in the future: and yet when we have gathered the greatest abundance, we ourselves enjoy no more thereof, than so much as belongs to one man. For the rest, he that had the greatest wisdom and the greatest ability that ever man had, hath told us that this is the use: " When goods increase (saith Solomon) they also increase that eat them; and what good cometh to the owners, but the beholding thereof with their eyes? As for those that devour the rest, and follow us in fair weather: they again forsake us in the first tempest of misfortune, and steer away before the sea and wind; leaving us to the malice of our destinies. Of these, among a thousand examples, I will take but one out of Master Danner, and use his own words: " Whilest the Emperor Charles the Fifth, after the resignation of his estates, stayed at Flushing for wind, to carry him his last journey into Spain; he conferred on a time with Seldius, his brother Ferdinand's Ambassador, till the deep of the night. And when Seldius should depart, the Emperor calling for some of his servants, and nobody answering him (for those that attended upon him, were some gone to their lodgings, and all the rest asleep), the Emperor took up the candle himself, and went before Seldius to light him down the stairs; and so did, notwithstanding all the resistance that Seldius could make. And when he was come to the stair's foot, he said thus unto him: " Seldius, remember this of Charles the Emperor, when he shall be dead and gone, that him, whom thou hast known in thy time environed with so many mighty armies and guards of soldiers, thou hast also seen alone, abandoned, and forsaken, yea even of his own domestical servants, &c. I acknowledge this change of Fortune to proceed from the mighty hand of God, which I will by no means go about to withstand."

But you will say, that there are some things else, and of greater regard than the former. The first is the reverend respect that is held of great men, and the honor done unto them by all sorts of people. And it is true indeed: provided, that an inward love for their justice and piety accompany the outward worship given to their places and power; without which what is the applause of the multitude, but as the outcry of an herd of animals, who without the knowledge of any true cause, please themselves with the noise they make? For seeing it is a thing exceeding rare, to distinguish Virtue and Fortune: the most impious (if prosperous) have ever been applauded; the most virtuous (if unprosperous) have ever been despised. For as Fortune's man rides the horse, so Fortune herself rides the man; who when he is descended and on foot, the man taken from his beast, and Fortune from the man, a base groom beats the one, and a bitter contempt spurns at the other, with equal liberty.

The second is the greatening of our posterity, and the contemplation of their glory whom we leave behind us. Certainly, of those which conceive that their souls departed take any comfort therein, it may be truly said of them, which Lactantius spake of certain heathen philosophers, "quod sapientes sunt in re stulta."[13] For when our spirits immortal shall be once separate from our mortal bodies, and disposed by God; there remaineth in them no other joy of their posterity which succeed, than there doth of pride in that stone, which sleepeth in the wall of the king's palace; nor any other sorrow for their poverty, than there doth of shame in that, which beareth up a beggar's cottage. " Nesciunt mortui, etiam sancti, quid agunt vivi, etiam eorum filii, quia animae mortuorum rebus viventium non intersunt ": " The dead, though holy, know nothing of the living, no, not of their own children: for the souls of those departed, are not conversant with their affairs that remain."[14] And if we doubt of St. Augustine, we can not of Job; who tells us, " That we know not if our sons shall be

[13] "That they are wise in a foolish matter."—Lactantius, *De falsa sapientia*, 3, 29.
[14] Augustine, *De cura pro morte*.

honorable: neither shall we understand concerning them, whether they shall be of low degree." Which Ecclesiastes also confirmeth: "Man walketh in a shadow, and disquieteth himself in vain: he heapeth up riches, and can not tell who shall gather them. The living (saith he) know that they shall die, but the dead know nothing at all: for who can show unto man what shall be after him under the sun?" He therefore accounteth it among the rest of worldly vanities, to labor and travail in the world; not knowing after death whether a fool or a wise man should enjoy the fruits thereof: "which made me (saith he) endeavor even to abhor mine own labor." And what can other men hope, whose blessed or sorrowful estates after death God hath reserved? man's knowledge lying but in his hope, seeing the Prophet Isaiah confesseth of the elect, "That Abraham is ignorant of us, and Israel knows us not." But hereof we are assured, that the long and dark night of death (of whose following day we shall never behold the dawn till his return that hath triumphed over it), shall cover us over till the world be no more. After which, and when we shall again receive organs glorified and incorruptible, the seats of angelical affections, in so great admiration shall the souls of the blessed be exercised, as they can not admit the mixture of any second or less joy; nor any return of foregone and mortal affection towards friends, kindred, or children. Of whom whether we shall retain any particular knowledge, or in any sort distinguish them, no man can assure us; and the wisest men doubt. But on the contrary, if a divine life retain any of those faculties which the soul exercised in a mortal body, we shall not at that time so divide the joys of Heaven, as to cast any part thereof on the memory of their felicities which remain in the world. No, be their estates greater than ever the world gave, we shall (by the difference known unto us) even detest their consideration. And whatsoever comfort shall remain of all forepast, the same will consist in the charity which we exercised living; and in that piety, justice, and firm faith, for which it pleased the infinite mercy of God to accept of us, and receive us. Shall we therefore value honor and riches at nothing? and neglect them, as unnecessary and vain? Certainly no. For that infinite

(4) HC XXXIX

wisdom of God, which hath distinguished his angels by
degrees; which hath given greater and less light and beauty
to heavenly bodies; which hath made differences between
beasts and birds; created the eagle and the fly, the cedar and
the shrub; and among stones, given the fairest tincture to
the ruby, and the quickest light to the diamond; hath also
ordained kings, dukes, or leaders of the people, magistrates,
judges, and other degrees among men. And as honor is
left to posterity, for a mark and ensign of the virtue and
understanding of their ancestors: so (seeing Siracides pre-
ferreth death before beggary: and that titles, without pro-
portionable estates, fall under the miserable succor of other
men's pity) I account it foolishness to condemn such a care:
provided, that worldly goods be well gotten, and that we
raise not our own buildings out of other men's ruins. For,
as Plato doth first prefer the perfection of bodily health;
secondly, the form and beauty; and thirdly, "Divitias nulla
fraude quaesitas":²⁸ so Jeremiah cries, "Woe unto them
that erect their houses by unrighteousness, and their chambers without equity": and Isaiah the same, "Woe to those
that spoil and were not spoiled." And it was out of the
true wisdom of Solomon, that he commandeth us, "not to
drink the wine of violence; not to lie in wait for blood, and
not to swallow them up alive, whose riches we covet: for
such are the ways (saith he) of everyone that is greedy
of gain."

And if we could afford ourselves but so much leisure as to
consider, that he which hath most in the world, hath, in
respect of the world, nothing in it: and that he which hath
the longest time lent him to live in it, hath yet no proportion
at all therein, setting it either by that which is past, when
we were not, or by that time which is to come, in which we
shall abide forever: I say, if both, to wit, our proportion
in the world, and our time in the world, differ not much
from that which is nothing; it is not out of any excellency
of understanding, that we so much prize the one, which hath
(in effect) no being: and so much neglect the other, which
hath no ending: coveting those mortal things of the world,
as if our souls were therein immortal; and neglecting those

²⁸ "Wealth acquired without fraud."

things which are immortal, as if ourselves after the world were but mortal.

But let every man value his own wisdom, as he pleaseth. Let the rich man think all fools, that cannot equal his abundance: the revenger esteem all negligent, that have not trodden down their opposites; the politician, all gross that cannot merchandise their faith: yet when we once come in sight of the port of death, to which all winds drive us, and when by letting fall that fatal anchor, which can never be weighed again, the navigation of this life takes end; then it is, I say, that our own cogitations (those sad and severe cogitations, formerly beaten from us by our health and felicity) return again, and pay us to the uttermost for all the pleasing passages of our lives past. It is then that we cry out to God for mercy; then when our selves can no longer exercise cruelty to others; and it is only then, that we are strucken through the soul with this terrible sentence, "That God will not be mocked." For if according to St. Peter, "The righteous scarcely be saved: and that God spared not his angels"; where shall those appear, who, having served their appetites all their lives, presume to think, that the severe commandments of the all-powerful God were given but in sport; and that the short breath, which we draw when death presseth us, if we can but fashion it to the sound of mercy (without any kind of satisfaction or amends) is sufficient? "O quam multi," saith a reverend father, "cum hac spe ad aeternos labores et bella descendunt!"[26] I confess that it is a great comfort to our friends, to have it said, that we ended well; for we all desire (as Balaam did) "to die the death of the righteous." But what shall we call a disesteeming, an opposing, or (indeed) a mocking of God: if those men do not oppose Him, disesteem Him, and mock Him, that think it enough for God, to ask Him forgiveness at leisure, with the remainder and last drawing of a malicious breath? For what do they otherwise, that die this kind of well-dying, but say unto God as followeth? "We beseech Thee, O God, that all the falsehoods, forswearings, and treacheries of our lives past, may be pleasing unto Thee; that Thou wilt for our sakes (that have had no

---

[26] "O how many go down with this hope to endless labors and wars."

leisure to do anything for Thine) change Thy nature (though impossible, and forget to be a just God; that Thou wilt love injuries and oppressions, call ambition wisdom, and charity foolishness. For I shall prejudice my son (which I am resolved not to do) if I make restitution; and confess myself to have been unjust (which I am too proud to do) if I deliver the oppressed." Certainly, these wise worldlings have either found out a new God, or made one: and in all likelihood such a leaden one, as Louis the Eleventh wore in his cap; which when he had caused any that he feared, or hated, to be killed, he would take it from his head and kiss it: beseeching it to pardon him this one evil act more, and it should be the last; which (as at other times) he did, when by the practice of a cardinal and a falsified sacrament, he caused the Earl of Armagnac to be stabbed to death: mockeries indeed fit to be used towards a leaden, but not towards the ever-living God. But of this composition are all devout lovers of the world, that they fear all that is dureless[17] and ridiculous: they fear the plots and practises of their opposites,[18] and their very whisperings: they fear the opinions of men, which beat but upon shadows: they flatter and forsake the prosperous and unprosperous, be they friends or kings: yea they dive under water, like ducks, at every pebblestone, that is but thrown toward them by a powerful hand: and on the contrary, they show an obstinate and giant-like valor, against the terrible judgments of the all-powerful God: yea they show themselves gods against God, and slaves towards men; towards men whose bodies and consciences are alike rotten.

Now for the rest: If we truly examine the difference of both conditions; to wit, of the rich and mighty, whom we call fortunate; and of the poor and oppressed, whom we account wretched: we shall find the happiness of the one, and the miserable estate of the other, so tied by God to the very instant, and both so subject to interchange (witness the sudden downfall of the greatest princes, and the speedy uprising of the meanest persons) as the one hath nothing so certain, whereof to boast; nor the other so uncertain, whereof to bewail itself. For there is no man

<hr />

[17] Transient.   [18] Opponents.

so assured of his honor, of his riches, health, or life; but
that he may be deprived of either, or all, the very next
hour or day to come. "Quid vesper vehat, incertum est,"
"What the evening will bring with it, it is uncertain."
"And yet ye cannot tell (saith St. James) what shall be
tomorrow. Today he is set up, and tomorrow he shall not
be found; for he is turned into dust, and his purpose per-
isheth." And although the air which compasseth adversity
be very obscure; yet therein we better discern God, than
in that shining light which environeth worldly glory; through
which, for the clearness thereof, there is no vanity which
escapeth our sight. And let adversity seem what it will;
to happy men ridiculous, who make themselves merry at
other men's misfortunes; and to those under the cross, grievous: yet this is true, that for all that is past, to the very
instant, the portions remaining are equal to either. For
be it that we have lived many years, "and (according to
Solomon) in them all we have rejoiced;" or be it that we
have measured the same length of days and therein have
evermore sorrowed: yet looking back from our present
being, we find both the one and the other, to wit, the joy
and the woe, sailed out of sight; and death, which doth
pursue us and hold us in chase, from our infancy, hath
gathered it. "Quicquid aetatis retro est, mors tenet:"
"Whatsoever of our age is past, death holds it." So as
whosoever he be, to whom Fortune hath been a servant,
and the Time a friend; let him but take the account of his
memory (for we have no other keeper of our pleasures past),
and truly examine what it hath reserved either beauty and
youth, or foregone delights; what it hath saved, that it might
last, of his dearest affections, or of whatever else the amorous springtime gave his thoughts of contentment, then un-
valuable; and he shall find that all the art which his elder
years have, can draw no other vapor out of these dis-
solutions, than heavy, secret, and sad sighs. He shall find
nothing remaining, but those sorrows, which grow up after
our fast-springing youth; overtake it, when it is at a stand;
and overtopped it utterly, when it begins to wither: in so
much as looking back from the very instant time, and from
our now being, the poor, diseased, and captive creature,

hath as little sense of all his former miseries and pains, as he, that is most blessed in common opinions, hath of his fore-passed pleasure and delights. For whatsoever is cast behind us, is just nothing: and what is to come, deceitful hope hath it: " Omnia quae eventura sunt, in incerto jacent." [19] Only those few black swans, I must except: who having had the grace to value worldly vanities at no more than their own price; do, by retaining the comfortable memory of a well acted life, behold death without dread, and the grave without fear; and embrace both, as necessary guides to endless glory.

For myself, this is my consolation, and all that I can offer to others, that the sorrows of this life are but of two sorts: whereof the one hath respect to God, the other, to the world. In the first we complain to God against ourselves, for our offences against Him; and confess, " Et Tu justus es in omnibus quae venerunt super nos." " And Thou, O Lord, are just in all that hath befallen us." In the second we complain to ourselves against God: as if he had done us wrong, either in not giving us worldly goods and honors, answering our appetites: or for taking them again from us having had them; forgetting that humble and just acknowledgment of Job, " the Lord hath given, and the Lord hath taken." To the first of which St. Paul hath promised blessedness; to the second, death. And out of doubt he is either a fool, or ungrateful to God, or both, that doth not acknowledge, how mean soever his estate be, that the same is yet far greater than that which God oweth him: or doth not acknowledge, how sharp soever his afflictions be, that the same are yet far less, than those which are due unto him. And if an heathen wise man call the adversities of the world but " tributa vivendi," " the tributes of living;" a wise Christian man ought to know them, and bear them, but as the tributes of offending. He ought to bear them manlike, and resolvedly; and not as those whining soldiers do, " qui gementes sequuntur imperatorem." [20]

For seeing God, who is the author of all our tragedies, hath written out for us and appointed us all the parts we

[19] " Everything which is to come lies in uncertainty."
[20] " Who follow their commander with groans."

are to play: and hath not, in their distribution, been partial to the most mighty princes of the world: that gave unto Darius the part of the greatest emperor, and the part of the most miserable beggar, a beggar begging water of an enemy, to quench the great drought of death: that appointed Bajazet to play the Grand Signior of the Turks in the morning, and in the same day the footstool of Tamerlane (both which parts Valerian had also played, being taken by Sapores): that made Belisarius play the most victorious captain, and lastly the part of a blind beggar: of which examples many thousands may be produced: why should other men, who are but as the least worms, complain of wrong? Certainly there is no other account to be made of this ridiculous world, than to resolve, that the change of fortune on the great theatre, is but as the change of garments on the less. For when on the one and the other, every man wears but his own skin, the players are all alike. Now, if any man out of weakness prize the passages of this world otherwise (for saith Petrarch, "Magni ingenii est revocare mentem a sensibus"[21]) it is by reason of that unhappy phantasy of ours, which forgeth in the brains of man all the miseries (the corporal excepted) whereunto he is subject. Therein it is, that misfortunes and adversity work all that they work. For seeing Death, in the end of the play, takes from all whatsoever Fortune or Force takes from any one; it were a foolish madness in the shipwreck of worldly things, where all sinks but the sorrow, to save it. That were, as Seneca saith, "Fortunae succumbere, quod tristius est omni fato:" "To fall under Fortune, of all other the most miserable destiny."

But it is now time to sound a retreat; and to desire to be excused of this long pursuit: and withal, that the good intent, which hath moved me to draw the picture of time past (which we call History) in so large a table, may also be accepted in place of a better reason.

The examples of divine providence, everywhere found (the first divine histories being nothing else but a continuation of such examples) have persuaded me to fetch my beginning from the beginning of all things: to wit, Creation.

[21] "It takes great genius to call back the mind from the senses."

For though these two glorious actions of the Almighty be so near, and (as it were) linked together, that the one necessarily implieth the other: Creation inferring Providence (for what father forsaketh the child that he hath begotten?) and Providence pre-supposing Creation: yet many of those that have seemed to excel in worldly wisdom, have gone about to disjoin this coherence; the epicure denying both Creation and Providence, but granting the world had a beginning; the Aristotelian granting Providence, but denying both the creation and the beginning.

Now although this doctrine of faith, touching the creation in time (for by faith we understand, that the world was made by the word of God), be too weighty a work for Aristotle's rotten ground to bear up, upon which he hath (notwithstanding) founded the defences and fortresses of all his verbal doctrine: yet that the necessity of infinite power, and the world's beginning, and the impossibility of the contrary even in the judgment of natural reason, wherein he believed, had not better informed him; it is greatly to be marvelled at. And it is no less strange, that those men which are desirous of knowledge (seeing Aristotle hath failed in this main point; and taught little other than terms in the rest) have so retrenched their minds from the following and overtaking of truth, and so absolutely subjected themselves to the law of those philosophical principles; as all contrary kind of teaching, in the search of causes, they have condemned either for phantastical, or curious. Both doth it follow, that the positions of heathen philosophers are undoubted grounds and principles indeed, because so called? Or that *ipsi dixerunt,* doth make them to be such? Certainly no. But this is true, that where natural reason hath built anything so strong against itself, as the same reason can hardly assail it, much less batter it down: the same in every question of nature, and infinite power, may be approved for a fundamental law of human knowledge. For saith Charron in his book of wisdom, " Toute proposition humaine a autant d'authorite quel'autre, si la raison n'on fait la difference;" " Every human proposition hath equal authority, if reason make not the difference," the rest being but the fables of principles. But hereof how shall the upright and impartial judgment of man give a sentence, where opposition and examination are not admitted to give in evidence? And to this purpose it was well said of Lactantius, " Sapientiam sibi adimunt, qui sine ullo judicio inventa maiorum probant, et ab aliis pecudum more ducuntur:" " They neglect their own wisdom, who without any judgment approve the invention of those that forewent them; and suffer themselves after the manner of beasts, to be led by them; " by the advantage of which sloth and dullness, ignorance is now become so powerful a tyrant, as it hath set true philosophy, physics, and divinity in a pillory; and written over the first, " Contra negantem principia;"[22] over the second, "Virtus specifica;"[23] over the third, "Ecclesia Romana."[24]

But for myself, I shall never be persuaded, that God hath shut up all light of learning within the lanthorn of Aristotle's brains: or that it was ever said unto him, as unto Esdras, "Accendam in corde tuo Lucernam intellectus":[25] that God hath given invention but to the heathen, and that they only invaded nature, and found the strength and bottom thereof; the same nature having consumed all her store, and left nothing of price to after-ages. That these and these be the causes of these and these effects, time hath taught us; and not reason: and so hath experience without art. The cheese-wife knoweth it as well as the philosopher, that sour rennet doth coagulate her milk into a curd. But if we ask a reason of this cause, why the sourness doth it? whereby it doth it? and the manner how? I think that there is nothing to be found in vulgar philosophy, to satisfy this and many other like vulgar questions. But man to cover his ignorance in the least things, who can not give a true reason for the grass under his feet, why it should be green rather than red, or of any other color; that could never yet discover the way and reason of nature's working, in those which are far less noble creatures than himself; who is far more noble than the heavens themselves: "Man (saith Solomon) that can hardly discern the things that are upon

[22] " Against him who denies the principles."
[23] " Specific virtue, or power."   [24] " The Roman Church."
[25] " I shall light a lamp of understanding in thine heart."—IV. Esdias xiv. 25.

the earth, and with great labor find out the things that are
before us "; that hath so short a time in the world, as he
no sooner begins to learn, than to die; that hath in his
memory but borrowed knowledge; in his understanding,
nothing truly; that is ignorant of the essence of his own
soul, and which the wisest of the naturalists (if Aristotle
be he) could never so much as define, but by the action and
effect, telling us what it works (which all men knew as well
as he) but not what it is, which neither he, nor any else,
doth know, but God that created it; ("For though I were
perfect, yet I know not my soul," saith Job). Man, I say,
that is but an idiot in the next cause of his own life, and
in the cause of all actions of his life, will (notwithstanding)
examine the art of God in creating the world; of God, who
(saith Job) "is so excellent as we know him not"; and examine the beginning of the work, which had end before
mankind had a beginning of being. He will disable God's
power to make a world, without matter to make it of. He
will rather give the motes of the air for a cause; cast the
work on necessity or chance; bestow the honor thereof on nature; make two powers, the one to be the author of the matter,
the other of the form; and lastly, for want of a workman,
have it eternal: which latter opinion Aristotle, to make himself the author of a new doctrine, brought into the world:
and his Sectators[26] have maintained it; "parati ac conjurati,
quos sequuntur, philosophorum animis invictis opiniones
tueri."[27]   For Hermes, who lived at once with, or soon after
Moses, Zoroaster, Musaeus, Orpheus, Linus, Anaximenes,
Anaxagoras, Empedocles, Melissus, Pherecydes, Thales,
Cleanthes, Pythagoras, Plato, and many other (whose opinions are exquisitely gathered by Steuchius Eugubinus) found
in the necessity of invincible reason, "One eternal and infinite Being," to be the parent of the universal. "Horum
omnium sententia quamvis sit incerta, eodem tamen spectat,
ut Providentiam unam esse consentiant: sive enim natura,
sive aether, sive ratio, sive mens, sive fatalis necessitas, sive
divina lex; idem est quod a nobis dicitur Deus": "All these
men's opinions (saith Lactantius) though uncertain, come to

[26] Followers.
[27] "Prepared and sworn to protect with unconquered minds the opinions
of the philosophers whom they follow."

this; That they agree upon one Providence; whether the
same be nature, or light, or reason, or understanding, or
destiny, or divine ordinance, that it is the same which we
call God." Certainly, as all the rivers in the world, though
they have divers risings, and divers runnings; though they
sometimes hide themselves for a while under ground, and
seem to be lost in sea-like lakes; do at last find, and fall
into the great ocean: so after all the searches that human
capacity hath, and after all philosophical contemplation and
curiosity; in the necessity of this infinite power, all the reason of man ends and dissolves itself.

As for the others; the first touching those which conceive
the matter of the world to have been eternal, and that God
did not create the world "Exnihilo,"[28] but " ex materia
praeexistente ":[29] the supposition is so weak, as is hardly
worth the answering. For (saith Eusebius) "Mihi videntur
qui hoc dicunt, fortunam quoque Deo annectere," " They
seem unto me, which affirm this, to give part of the work to
God, and part to Fortune": insomuch as if God had not
found this first matter by chance, He had neither been author nor father, nor creator, nor lord of the universal. For
were the matter or chaos eternal, it then follows, that either
this supposed matter did fit itself to God, or God accommodate Himself to the matter. For the first, it is impossible,
that things without sense could proportion themselves to
the workman's will. For the second: it were horrible to
conceive of God, that as an artificer He applied himself,
according to the proportion of matter which He lighted
upon.

But let it be supposed, that this matter hath been made
by any power, not omnipotent, and infinitely wise; I would
gladly learn how it came to pass, that the same was pro-
portionable to his intention, that was omnipotent and infinitely wise; and no more, nor no less, than served to receive
the form of the universal. For, had it wanted anything of
what was sufficient; then must it be granted, that God created
out of nothing so much new matter, as served to finish the
work of the world: or had there been more of this matter
than sufficed, then God did dissolve and annihilate whatso-

[28] " Out of nothing."   [29] " Out of pre-existing matter."

ever remained and was superfluous. And this must every reasonable soul confess, that it is the same work of God alone, to create anything out of nothing, and by the same art and power, and by none other, can those things, or any part of that eternal matter, be again changed into nothing; by which those things, that once were nothing, obtained a beginning of being.

Again, to say that this matter was the cause of itself; this, of all other, were the greatest idiotism. For, if it were the cause of itself at any time; then there was also a time when itself was not: at which time of not being, it is easy enough to conceive, that it could neither procure itself, nor anything else. For to be, and not to be, at once, is impossible. "Nihil autem seipsum praecedit, neque; seipsum componit corpus": "There is nothing that doth precede itself, neither do bodies compound themselves."

For the rest, those that feign this matter to be eternal, must of necessity confess, that infinite cannot be separate from eternity. And then had infinite matter left no place for infinite form, but that the first matter was finite, the form which it received proves it. For conclusion of this part, whosoever will make choice, rather to believe in eternal deformity, or in eternal dead matter, than in eternal light and eternal life: let eternal death be his reward. For it is a madness of that kind, as wanteth terms to express it. For what reason of man (whom the curse of presumption hath not stupefied) hath doubted, that infinite power (of which we can comprehend but a kind of shadow, "quia comprehensio est intra terminos, qui infinito repugnant"[30]) hath anything wanting in itself, either for matter of form; yea for as many worlds (if such had been God's will) as the sea hath sands? For where the power is without limitation, the work hath no other limitation, than the workman's will. Yea reason itself finds it more easy for infinite power to deliver from itself a finite world, without the help of matter prepared; than for a finite man, a fool and dust, to change the form of matter made to his hands. They are Dionysius his words, "Deus in una existentia omnia prae-

[30] "Because comprehension is between limits, which are opposed to infinity."

habet ":[31] and again, "Esse omnium est ipsa divinitas, omne
quod vides, et quod non vides ":[32] to wit, "causaliter,[33] or in
better terms, "non tanquam forma, sed tanquam causa uni-
versalis."[34] Neither hath the world universal closed up all
of God: "For the most part of his works (saith Siracides)
are hid." Neither can the depth of his wisdom be opened,
by the glorious work of the world: which never brought
to knowledge all it can; for then were his infinite power
bounded and made finite. And hereof it comes; That we
seldom entitle God the all-showing, or the all-willing; but
the Almighty, that is, infinitely able.

But now for those, who from that ground, "that out of
nothing, nothing is made," infer the world's eternity; and yet
not so savage therein, as those are, which give an eternal being to dead matter: it is true if the word (nothing) be taken
in the affirmative; and the making, imposed upon natural
agents and finite power; that out of nothing, nothing is
made. But seeing their great doctor Aristotle himself
confesseth, "quod omnes antiqui decreverunt quasi quodam
rerum principium, ipsumque infinitum:" "That all the ancient decree a kind of beginning, and the same to be infinite";
and a little after, more largely and plainly, "Principium
eius est nullum, sed ipsum omnium cernitur esse principium,
ac omnia complecti ac regere ":[35] it is strange that this
philosopher, with his followers, should rather make choice
out of falsehood, to conclude falsely; than out of truth, to
resolve truly. For if we compare the world universal, and
all the unmeasurable orbs of Heaven, and those marvellous
bodies of the sun, moon, and stars, with "ipsum infinitum":
it may truly be said of them all, which himself affirms of
his imaginary "Materia prima,"[36] that they are neither
"quid, quale," nor "quantum"; and therefore to bring finite
(which hath no proportion with infinite) out of infinite
("qui destruit omnem proportionem"[37]) is no wonder in
God's power. And therefore Anaximander, Melissus, and
Empedocles, call the world universal, but "particulam uni-

[31] "God exhibits all things in one existence."
[32] "The essence of all things, visible and invisible, is divinity itself."
[33] "Causally."   [34] "Not as form, but as universal cause."
[35] "It [*i. e.,* the infinite] has no beginning, but itself is perceived to be
the beginning of all things, and to embrace and govern all things."
[36] "Primal matter."   [37] "Which destroys all proportion."

versitatis" and "infinitatis," a parcel of that which is the universality and the infinity inself; and Plato, but a shadow of God. But the other to prove the world's eternity, urgeth this maxim, "that, a sufficient and effectual cause being granted, an answerable effect thereof is also granted": inferring that God being forever a sufficient and effectual cause of the world, the effect of the cause should also have been forever; to wit, the world universal. But what a strange mockery is this in so great a master, to confess a sufficient and effectual cause of the world, (to wit, an almighty God) in his antecedent; and the same God to be a God restrained in his conclusion; to make God free in power, and bound in will; able to effect, unable to determine; able to make all things, and yet unable to make choice of the time when? For this were impiously to resolve of God, as of natural necessity; which hath neither choice, nor will, nor understanding; which cannot but work matter being present: as fire, to burn things combustible. Again he thus disputeth, that every agent which can work, and doth not work, if it afterward work, it is either thereto moved by itself, or by somewhat else: and so it passeth from power to act. But God (saith he) is immovable, and is neither moved by himself, nor by any other: but being always the same, doth always work. Whence he concludeth, if the world were caused by God, that he was forever the cause thereof: and therefore eternal. The answer to this is very easy, for that God's performing in due time that which he ever determined at length to perform, doth not argue any alteration or change, but rather constancy in him. For the same action of his will, which made the world forever, did also withhold the effect to the time ordained. To this answer, in itself sufficient, others add further, that the pattern or image of the world may be said to be eternal: which the Platonics call "spiritualem mundum";[88] and do in this sort distinguish the idea and creation in time. "Spiritualis ille mundus, mundi huius exemplar, primumque Dei opus, vita aequali est architecto, fuit semper cum illo, eritque semper. Mundus autem corporalis, quod secundum opus est Dei, decedit iam ab opifice

[88] "The spiritual world."

ex parte una, quia non fuit semper: retinet alteram, quia
sit semper futurus ": "That representative, or the inten-
tional world (say they) the sampler of this visible world,
the first work of God, was equally ancient with the architect; for it was forever with him, and ever shall be. This
material world, the second work or creature of God, doth
differ from the worker in this, that it was not from everlasting, and in this it doth agree, that it shall be forever
to come." The first point, that it was not forever, all
Christians confess: the other they understand no otherwise, than that after the consummation of this world, there
shall be a new Heaven and a new earth, without any new
creation of matter. But of these things we need not here
stand to argue: though such opinions be not unworthy the
propounding, in this consideration, of an eternal and unchangeable cause, producing a changeable and temporal
effect. Touching which point Proclus the Platonist disputeth, that the compounded essence of the world (and
because compounded, therefore dissipable) is continued,
and knit to the Divine Being, by an individual and inseparable power, flowing from Divine unity; and that the
world's natural appetite of God showeth, that the same
proceedeth from a good and understanding divine; and
that this virtue, by which the world is continued and knit
together, must be infinite, that it may infinitely and everlastingly continue and preserve the same. Which infinite
virtue, the finite world (saith he) is not capable of, but
receiveth it from the divine infinite, according to the temporal nature it hath, successively every moment by little
and little; even as the whole material world is not altogether: but the abolished parts are departed by small
degrees, and the parts yet to come, do by the same small degrees succeed; as the shadow of a tree in a river seemeth
to have continued the same a long time in the water, but
it is perpetually renewed, in the continual ebbing and flowing thereof.

But to return to them, which denying that ever the
world had any beginning, withal deny that ever it shall have
any end, and to this purpose affirm, that it was never heard,
never read, never seen, no not by any reason perceived,

that the heavens have ever suffered corruption; or that they appear any way the older by continuance; or in any sort otherwise than they were; which had they been subject to final corruption, some change would have been discerned in so long a time. To this it is answered, that the little change as yet perceived, doth rather prove their newness, and that they have not continued so long; than that they will continue forever as they are. And if conjectural arguments may receive answer by conjectures; it then seemeth that some alteration may be found. For either Aristotle, Pliny, Strabo, Beda, Aquinas, and others, were grossly mistaken; or else those parts of the world lying within the burnt zone, were not in elder times habitable, by reason of the sun's heat, neither were the seas, under the equinoctial, navigable. But we know by experience, that those regions, so situate, are filled with people, and exceeding temperate; and the sea, over which we navigate, passable enough. We read also many histories of deluges: and how in the time of Phaeton, divers places in the world were burnt up, by the sun's violent heat.

But in a word, this observation is exceeding feeble. For we know it for certain, that stone walls, of matter mouldering and friable, have stood two, or three thousand years; that many things have been digged up out of the earth, of that depth, as supposed to have been buried by the general flood; without any alteration either of substance or figure: yea it is believed, and it is very probable, that the gold which is daily found in mines, and rocks, under ground, was created together with the earth.

And if bodies elementary, and compounded, the eldest times have not invaded and corrupted: what great alteration should we look for in celestial and quint-essential bodies? And yet we have reason to think, that the sun, by whose help all creatures are generate, doth not in these latter ages assist nature, as heretofore. We have neither giants, such as the eldest world had; nor mighty men, such as the elder world had; but all things in general are reputed of less virtue which from the heavens receive virtue. Whence, if the nature of a preface would permit a larger discourse, we might easily fetch store of proof; as that

this world shall at length have end, as that once it had
beginning.

And I see no good answer that can be made to this objection: if the world were eternal, why not all things in
the world eternal? If there were no first, no cause, no
father, no creator, no incomprehensible wisdom, but that
every nature had been alike eternal; and man more rational
than every other nature: why had not the eternal reason
of man provided for his eternal being in the world? For
if all were equal why not equal conditions to all? Why
should heavenly bodies live forever; and the bodies of men
rot and die?

Again, who was it that appointed the earth to keep
the center, and gave order that it should hang in the air:
that the sun should travel between the tropics, and never
exceed those bounds, nor fail to perform that progress
once in every year: the moon to live by borrowed light:
the fixed stars (according to common opinion) to be fastened
like nails in a cartwheel; and the planets to wander at
their pleasure? Or if none of these had power over
other: was it out of charity and love, that the sun by his
perpetual travel within these two circles, hath visited, given
light unto, and relieved all parts of the earth, and the
creatures therein, by turns and times? Out of doubt, if
the sun have of his own accord kept this course in all
eternity, he may justly be called eternal charity and everlasting love. The same may be said of all the stars; who
being all of them most large and clear fountains of virtue
and operation, may also, be called eternal virtues: the
earth may be called eternal patience; the moon, an eternal
borrower and beggar; and man of all other the most miserable, eternally mortal. And what were this, but to believe again in the old play of the gods? Yea in more gods
by millions, than ever Hesiodus dreamed of. But instead
of this mad folly, we see it well enough with our feeble
and mortal eyes; and the eyes of our reason discern it
better; that the sun, moon, stars, and the earth, are limited
bounded, and constrained: themselves they have not constrained nor could. "Omne determinatum causam habet
aliquam efficientem, quae illud determinaverit:" "Every-

thing bounded hath some efficient cause, by which it is bounded."

Now for Nature; as by the ambiguity of this name, the school of Aristotle hath both commended many errors unto us, and sought also thereby to obscure the glory of the high moderator of all things, shining in the creation, and in the governing of the world: so if the best definition be taken out of the second of Aristotle's "Physics," or "primo de Coelo," or out of the fifth of his "Metaphysics"; I say that the best is but nominal, and serving only to difference the beginning of natural motion from artificial: which yet the Academics open better, when they call it "a seminary strength, infused into matter by the soul of the world": who give the first place to Providence, the second to Fate, and but the third to Nature. "Providentia" (by which they understand God) "dux et caput; Fatum, medium ex providentia prodiens; Natura postremum." [39] But be it what he will, or be it any of these (God excepted) or participating of all: yet that it hath choice or understanding (both which are necessarily in the cause of all things) no man hath avowed. For this is unanswerable of Lactantius, "Is autem facit aliquid, qui aut voluntatem faciendi habet, aut scientiam:" "He only can be said to be the doer of a thing, that hath either will or knowledge in the doing it."

But the will and science of Nature, are in these words truly expressed by Ficinus: "Potest ubique Natura, vel per diversa media, vel ex diversis materiis, diversa facere: sublata vero mediorum materiatumque diversitate, vel unicum, vel similimum operatur, neque potest quando adest materia non operari"; "It is the power of Nature by the diversity of means, or out of diversity of matter, to produce divers things: but taking away the diversity of means, and the diversity of matter, it then works but one or the like work; neither can it but work, matter being present." Now if Nature made choice of diversity of matter, to work all these variable works of heaven and earth, it had then both understanding and will; it had counsel to begin;

---

[39] "Providence, leader and head; Fate, in the middle and proceeding from Providence; Nature, last."

reason to dispose; virtue and knowledge to finish, and power to govern: without which all things had been but one and the same: all of the matter of heaven; or all of the matter of earth. And if we grant Nature this will, and this understanding, this course, reason, and power: "Cur Natura potius quam Deus nominetur?" "Why should we then call such a cause rather Nature, than God?" "God, of whom all men have notion, and give the first and highest place to divine power": "Omnes homines notionem deorum habent, omnesque summum locum divino cuidam numini assignant." And this I say in short; that it is a true effect of true reason in man (were there no authority more binding than reason) to acknowledge and adore the first and most sublime power. "Vera philosophia, est ascensus ab his quae fluunt, et oriuntur, et occidunt, ad ea quae vera sunt, et semper eadem": "True philosophy, is an ascending from the things which flow, and arise, and fall, to the things that are forever the same."

For the rest; I do also account it not the meanest, but an impiety monstrous, to confound God and Nature; be it but in terms. For it is God, that only disposeth of all things according to His own will and maketh of one earth, vessels of honor and dishonor. It is Nature that can dispose of nothing, but according to the will of the matter wherein it worketh. It is God that commandeth all: it is Nature that is obedient to all: it is God that doth good unto all, knowing and loving the good He doth: it is Nature, that secondarily doth also good, but it neither knoweth nor loveth the good it doth. It is God, that hath all things in Himself: Nature, nothing in itself. It is God, which is the Father, and hath begotten all things: it is Nature, which is begotten by all things, in which it liveth and laboreth; for by itself it existeth not. For shall we say, that it is out of affection to the earth, that heavy things fall towards it? Shall we call it reason, which doth conduct every river into the salt sea? Shall we term it knowledge in fire, that makes it to consume combustible matter? If it be affection, reason, and knowledge in these; by the same affection, reason, and knowledge it is, that

Nature worketh. And therefore seeing all things work as they do, (call it by Form, or Nature, or by what you please) yet because they work by an impulsion, which they cannot resist, or by a faculty, infused by the supremest power; we are neither to wonder at, nor to worship, the faculty that worketh, nor the creature wherein it worketh. But herein lies the wonder: and to him is the worship due, who hath created such a nature in things, and such a faculty, as neither knowing itself, the matter wherein it worketh, nor the virtue and power which it hath; do yet work all things to their last and uttermost perfection. And therefore every reasonable man, taking to himself for a ground that which is granted by all antiquity, and by all men truly learned that ever the world had; to wit; that there is a power infinite, and eternal (which also necessity doth prove unto us, without the help of faith, and reason; without the force of authority) all things do as easily follow which have been delivered by divine letters, as the waters of a running river do successfully pursue each other from the first fountains.

This much I say it is, that reason itself hath taught us: and this is the beginning of knowledge. " Sapientia praecedit, Religio sequitur: quia prius est Deum scire, consequens colere "; " Sapience goes before, Religion follows: because it is first to know God, and then to worship Him." This sapience Plato calleth " absoluti boni scientiam," " the science of the absolute good ": and another " scientiam rerum primarum, sempiternarum, perpetuarum."[40] For " faith (saith Isidore) is not extorted by violence; but by reason and examples persuaded ": " fides nequaquam vi extorquetur, sed ratione et exemplis suadetur." I confess it, that to inquire further, as to the essence of God, of His power, of His art, and by what means He created the world: or of His secret judgment, and the causes, is not an effect of reason. " Sed cum ratione insaniunt," but " they grow mad with reason," that inquire after it. For as it is no shame, nor dishonor (saith a French author) " de faire arrest au but qu'on nasceu surpasser," " for a man to rest himself there where he finds it impossible to pass on

---

[40] " The science of things first, eternal, perpetual."

further ": so whatsoever is beyond, and out of the reach of true reason, it acknowledgeth it to be so; as under-standing itself not to be infinite, but according to the name and nature it hath, to be a teacher, that best knows the end of his own art. For seeing both reason and neces-sity teach us (reason, which is "pars divini spiritus in corpus humanum mersi "[41]) that the world was made by a power infinite; and yet how it was made, it cannot teach us: and seeing the same reason and necessity make us know, that the same infinite power is everywhere in the world; and yet how everywhere, it cannot inform us: our belief hereof is not weakened, but greatly strengthened, by our ignorance, because it is the same reason that tells us, that such a nature cannot be said to be God, that can be in all conceived by man.

I have already been over-long, to make any large dis-course either of the parts of the following story, or in mine own excuse: especially in the excuse of this or that passage; seeing the whole is exceeding weak and defec-tive. Among the grossest, the unsuitable division of the books, I could not know how to excuse, had I not been directed to enlarge the building after the foundation was laid, and the first part finished. All men know that there is no great art in the dividing evenly of these things, which are subject to number and measure. For the rest, it suits well enough with a great many books of this age, which speak too much, and yet say little; "Ipsi nobis furto subducimur"; "We are stolen away from ourselves," setting a high price on all that is our own. But hereof, though a late good writer make complaint, yet shall it not lay hold on me, because I believe as he doth; that who so thinks himself the wisest man, is but a poor and mis-erable ignorant. Those that are the best men of war against all the vanities and fooleries of the world, do always keep the strongest guards against themselves, to defend them from themselves; from self-love, self-estimation, and self-opinion.

Generally concerning the order of the work, I have only taken counsel from the argument. For of the Assyrians,

[41] " Part of the divine spirit immersed in the human body."

which after the downfall of Babel take up the first part, and were the first great kings of the world, there came little to the view of posterity: some few enterprises, greater in fame than faith, of Ninus and Semiramis, excepted.

It was the story of the Hebrews, of all before the Olympiads, that overcame the consuming disease of time, and preserved itself, from the very cradle and beginning to this day: and yet not so entire, but that the large discourses thereof (to which in many Scriptures we are referred) are nowhere found. The fragments of other stories, with the actions of those kings and princes which shot up here and there in the same time, I am driven to relate by way of digression: of which we may say with Virgil: "Apparent rari nantes in gurgite vasto"; "They appear here and there floating in the great gulf of time."

To the same first ages do belong the report of many inventions therein found, and from them derived to us; though most of the authors' names have perished in so long a navigation. For those ages had their laws; they had diversity of government; they had kingly rule; nobility; policy in war; navigation, and all, or the most of needful trades. To speak therefore of these (seeing in a general history we should have left a great deal of nakedness, by their omission) it cannot properly be called a digression. True it is, that I have made also many others: which if they shall be laid to my charge, I must cast the fault into the great heap of human error. For seeing we digress in all the ways of our lives: yea, seeing the life of man is nothing else but digression; I may the better be excused, in writing their lives and actions. I am not altogether ignorant in the laws of history and of the kinds.

The same hath been taught by many, but no man better, and with greater brevity, than by that excellent learned gentleman, Sir Francis Bacon. Christian laws are also taught us by the prophets and apostles; and every day preached unto us. But we still make large digressions: yea, the teachers themselves do not (in all) keep the path which they point out to others.

For the rest, after such time as the Persians had wrested the Empire from the Chaldeans, and had raised a great monarchy, producing actions of more importance than were elsewhere to be found; it was agreeable to the order of the story, to attend this Empire; whilst it so flourished, that the affairs of the nations adjoining had reference thereunto. The like observance was to be used towards the fortunes of Greece, when they again began to get ground upon the Persians; as also towards the affairs of Rome, when the Romans grew more mighty than the Greeks.

As for the Medes, the Macedonians, the Sicilians, the Carthaginians, and other nations who resisted the beginnings of the former empires, and afterwards became but parts of their composition and enlargement; it seemed best to remember what was known of them from their several beginnings, in such times and places as they in their flourishing estates opposed those monarchies, which in the end swallowed them up. And herein I have followed the best geographers: who seldom give names to those small brooks, whereof many, joined together, make great rivers: till such times as they become united, and run in main stream to the ocean sea. If the phrase be weak, and the style not everywhere like itself: the first shows their legitimation and true parent; the second will excuse itself upon the variety of matter. For Virgil, who wrote his *Eclogues,* " gracili avena,"[42] used stronger pipes, when he sounded the wars of Aeneas. It may also be laid to my charge, that I use divers Hebrew words in my first book, and elsewhere: in which language others may think and I myself acknowledge it, that I am altogether ignorant: but it is true, that some of them I find in Montanus, others in Latin characters in S. Senensis; and of the rest I have borrowed the interpretation of some of my friends. But say I had been beholding to neither, yet were it not to be wondered at, having had an eleven years' leisure, to attain the knowledge of that, or of any other tongue; howsoever, I know that it will be said by many, that I might have been more pleasing to the reader, if I had written the story of mine own times, having been permitted to draw water as near the well-head as another. To this I answer, that whosoever in writing a modern history, shall follow truth too near the heels, it may haply strike out his

[42] " With delicate pipe."

teeth. There is no mistress or guide, that hath led her
followers and servants into greater miseries. He that goes
after her too far off, loseth her sight, and loseth himself:
and he that walks after her at a middle distance: I know not
whether I should call that kind of course, temper,[43] or baseness. It is true, that I never travelled after men's opinions,
when I might have made the best use of them: and I have
now too few days remaining, to imitate those, that either
out of extreme ambition, or of extreme cowardice, or both,
do yet (when death hath them on his shoulders) flatter the
world, between the bed and the grave. It is enough for
me (being in that state I am) to write of the eldest times:
wherein also why may it not be said, that in speaking of the
past, I point at the present, and tax the vices of those that
are yet living, in their persons that are long since dead; and
have it laid to my charge? But this I cannot help, though
innocent. And certainly, if there be any, that finding themselves spotted like the tigers of old time, shall find fault with
me for painting them over anew, they shall therein accuse
themselves justly, and me falsely.

For I protest before the Majesty of God, that I malice no
man under the sun. Impossible I know it is to please all;
seeing few or none are so pleased with themselves, or so
assured of themselves, by reason of their subjection to their
private passions, but that they seem divers persons in one
and the same day. Seneca hath said it, and so do I: " Unus
mihi pro populo erat ";[44] and to the same effect Epicurus,
"Hoc ego non multis sed tibi ";[45] or (as it hath since lament-
ably fallen out) I may borrow the resolution of an ancient
philosopher, " Satis est unus, satis est nullus."[46] For it was
for the service of that inestimable Prince Henry, the successive hope, and one of the greatest of the Christian world,
that I undertook this work. It pleased him to peruse some
part thereof, and to pardon what was amiss. It is now left
to the world without a master: from which all that is presented, hath received both blows and thanks: " Eadem
probamus, eadem reprehendimus: hic exitus est omnis

---

[43] Moderation.   [44] " To me one man stood for the people."
[45] " I [have done] this not for many, but for thee."
[46] " One is enough, none is enough."

judicii, in quolis secundum plures datur."[47] But these discourses are idle. I know that as the charitable will judge charitably: so against those, " Qui gloriantur in malitia,"[48] my present adversity hath disarmed me. I am on the ground already, and therefore have not far to fall: and for rising again, as in the natural privation there is no recession to habit; so it is seldom seen in the privation politic. I do therefore forbear to style my readers gentle, courteous, and friendly, thereby to beg their good opinions, or to promise a second and third volume (which I also intend) if the first receive grace and good acceptance. For that which is already done, may be thought enough, and too much: and it is certain, let us claw the reader with never so many courteous phrases, yet shall we evermore be thought fools, that write foolishly. For conclusion, all the hope I have lies in this, that I have already found more ungentle and uncourteous readers of my love towards them, and well-deserving of them, than ever I shall do again. For had it been otherwise, I should hardly have had this leisure, to have made myself a fool in print.

[47] " We approve the same things, we blame the same things: this is the result in every case in which the verdict is rendered according to the majority."
[48] " Who glory in malice."

PROŒMIUM, EPISTLE
DEDICATORY, PREFACE,
AND PLAN OF THE INSTAURATIO
MAGNA, ETC.

BY FRANCIS BACON

FRANCIS OF VERULAM REASONED THUS WITH HIMSELF,

And Judged it to be for the Interest of the Present
and Future Generations That They Should be
Made Acquainted with His Thoughts

BEING convinced that the human intellect makes its
own difficulties, not using the true helps which are
at man's disposal soberly and judiciously; whence
follows manifold ignorance of things, and by reason of that
ignorance mischiefs innumerable; he thought all trial should
be made, whether that commerce between the mind of man
and the nature of things, which is more precious than anything on earth, or at least than anything that is of the earth,
might by any means be restored to its perfect and original
condition, or if that may not be, yet reduced to a better condition than that in which it now is. Now that the errors
which have hitherto prevailed, and which will prevail forever, should (if the mind be left to go its own way), either
by the natural force of the understanding or by help of

A sketch of Bacon's life will be found prefixed to his "Essays" in
another volume of the Harvard Classics. His "Instauratio Magna" or
"Great Renewal," the great work by which he hoped to create a scientific
revolution and deliver mankind from Aristotelianism, was left far from
complete; but the nature of his scheme and the scale on which it was
planned are indicated in these Prefaces, which are typical both of the
man and of the age in which he lived.

the aids and instruments of Logic, one by one correct themselves, was a thing not to be hoped for: because the primary
notions of things which the mind readily and passively
imbibes, stores up, and accumulates (and it.is from them that
all the rest flow) are false, confused, and overhastily abstracted from the facts; nor are the secondary and subsequent notions less arbitrary and inconstant; whence it
follows that the entire fabric of human reason which we
employ in the inquisition of nature, is badly put together
and built up, and like some magnificent structure without
any foundation.   For while men are occupied in admiring
and applauding the false powers of the mind, they pass by
and throw away those true powers, which, if it be supplied with the proper aids and can itself be content to wait
upon nature instead of vainly affecting to overrule her,
are within its reach.   There was but one course left, therefore,—to try the whole thing anew upon a better plan, and
to commence a total reconstruction of sciences, arts, and all
human knowledge, raised upon the proper foundations.   And
this, though in the project and undertaking it may seem a
thing infinite and beyond the powers of man, yet when it
comes to be dealt with it will be found sound and sober,
more so than what has been done hitherto.   For of this there
is some issue; whereas in what is now done in the matter of
science there is only a whirling round about, and perpetual
agitation, ending where it began.   And although he was well
aware how solitary an enterprise it is, and how hard a thing
to win faith and credit for, nevertheless he was resolved not
to abandon either it or himself; nor to be deterred from trying and entering upon that one path which is alone open to
the human mind.   For better it is to make a beginning of
that which may lead to something, than to engage in a perpetual struggle and pursuit in courses which have no exit.
And certainly the two ways of contemplation are much like
those two ways of action, so much celebrated, in this—that
the one, arduous and difficult in the beginning, leads out at
last into the open country; while the other, seeming at first
sight easy and free from obstruction, leads to pathless and
precipitous places.

Moreover, because he knew not how long it might be

before these things would occur to any one else, judging especially from this, that he has found no man hitherto who has applied his mind to the like, he resolved to publish at once so much as he has been able to complete. The cause of which haste was not ambition for himself, but solicitude for the work; that in case of his death there might remain some outline and project of that which he had conceived, and some evidence likewise of his honest mind and inclination towards the benefit of the human race. Certain it is that all other ambition whatsoever seemed poor in his eyes compared with the work which he had in hand; seeing that the matter at issue is either nothing, or a thing so great that it may well be content with its own merit, without seeking other recompence.

EPISTLE DEDICATORY

TO THE INSTAURATIO MAGNA

To our Most Gracious and Mighty Prince and Lord

JAMES

BY THE GRACE OF GOD
OF GREAT BRITAIN, FRANCE AND IRELAND
KING, DEFENDER OF THE FAITH, ETC.

Most Gracious and Mighty King,

YOUR Majesty may perhaps accuse me of larceny, having stolen from your affairs so much time as was required for this work. I know not what to say for myself. For of time there can be no restitution, unless it be that what has been abstracted from your business may perhaps go to the memory of your name and the honour of your age; if these things are indeed worth anything. Certainly they are quite new; totally new in their very kind: and yet they are copied from a very ancient model; even the world itself and the nature of things and of the mind. And to say truth, I am wont for my own part to regard this work as a child of time rather than of wit; the only wonder being that the first notion of the thing, and such great suspicions concerning matters long established, should have come into any man's mind. All the rest follows readily enough. And no doubt there is something of accident (as we call it) and luck as well in what men think as in what they do or say. But for this accident which I speak of, I wish that if there be any good in what I have to offer, it may be ascribed to the infinite mercy and goodness of God, and to the felicity of your Majesty's times; to which as I have been an honest and affectionate servant in my life, so after my death I may yet perhaps, through the kindling of this new light in the darkness of philosophy, be the means of making this age famous to posterity; and surely to the times of the wisest and most learned of kings belongs of right the regeneration and restoration of the sciences. Lastly, I have a request to make—a request no way unworthy of your Majesty, and which especially concerns the work in hand; namely, that you who resemble Solomon in so many things—in the gravity of your judgments, in the peacefulness of your reign, in the largeness of your heart, in the noble variety of the books which you have composed—would further follow his example in taking order for the collecting and perfecting of a Natural and Experimental History, true and severe (unincumbered with literature and book-learning), such as philosophy may be built upon,—such, in fact, as I shall in its proper place describe: that so at length, after the lapse of so many ages, philosophy and the sciences may no longer float in air, but rest on the solid foundation of experience of every kind, and the same well examined and weighed. I have provided the machine, but the stuff must be gathered from the facts of nature. May God Almighty long preserve your Majesty!

Your Majesty's

Most bounden and devoted Servant,

FRANCIS VERULAM,

Chancellor.

PREFACE

TO THE INSTAURATIO MAGNA

That the state of knowledge is not prosperous nor greatly advancing; and that a way must be opened for the human understanding entirely different from any hitherto known, and other helps provided, in order that the mind may exercise over the nature of things the authority which properly belongs to it.

IT SEEMS to me that men do not rightly understand either their store or their strength, but overrate the one and underrate the other. Hence it follows, that either from an extravagant estimate of the value of the arts which they possess, they seek no further; or else from too mean an estimate of their own powers, they spend their strength in small matters and never put it fairly to the trial in those which go to the main. These are as the pillars of fate set in the path of knowledge; for men have neither desire nor hope to encourage them to penetrate further. And since opinion of store is one of the chief causes of want, and satisfaction with the present induces neglect of provision for the future, it becomes a thing not only useful, but absolutely necessary, that the excess of honour and admiration with which our existing stock of inventions is regarded be in the very entrance and threshold of the work, and that frankly and without circumlocution, stripped off, and men be duly warned not to exaggerate or make too much of them. For let a man look carefully into all that variety of books with which the arts and sciences abound, he will find everywhere endless repetitions of the same thing, varying in the method of treatment, but not new in substance, insomuch that the whole stock, numerous as it appears at first view, proves on examination to be but scanty. And for its value and utility it must be plainly avowed that that wisdom which we have

derived principally from the Greeks is but like the boyhood
of knowledge, and has the characteristic property of boys:
it can talk, but it cannot generate; for it is fruitful of controversies but barren of works. So that the state of learning
as it now is appears to be represented to the life in the old
fable of Scylla, who had the head and face of a virgin, but
her womb was hung round with barking monsters, from
which she could not be delivered. For in like manner the
sciences to which we are accustomed have certain general
positions which are specious and flattering; but as soon as
they come to particulars, which are as the parts of generation, when they should produce fruit and works, then arise
contentions and barking disputations, which are the end of
the matter and all the issue they can yield. Observe also, that
if sciences of this kind had any life in them, that could
never have come to pass which has been the case now for
many ages—that they stand almost at a stay, without receiving any augmentations worthy of the human race; insomuch
that many times not only what was asserted once is asserted
still, but what was a question once is a question still, and
instead of being resolved by discussion is only fixed and
fed; and all the tradition and succession of schools is still
a succession of masters and scholars, not of inventors and
those who bring to further perfection the things invented.
In the mechanical arts we do not find it so; they, on the
contrary, as having in them some breath of life, are continually growing and becoming more perfect. As originally
invented they are commonly rude, clumsy, and shapeless;
afterwards they acquire new powers and more commodious
arrangements and constructions; in so far that men shall
sooner leave the study and pursuit of them and turn to
something else, than they arrive at the ultimate perfection
of which they are capable. Philosophy and the intellectual
sciences, on the contrary, stand like statues, worshiped and
celebrated, but not moved or advanced. Nay, they sometimes flourish most in the hands of the first author, and
afterwards degenerate. For when men have once made over
their judgments to others' keeping, and (like those senators
whom they called *Pedarii*) have agreed to support some one
person's opinion, from that time they make no enlargement

of the sciences themselves, but fall to the servile office of embellishing certain individual authors and increasing their retinue. And let it not be said that the sciences have been growing gradually till they have at last reached their full stature, and so (their course being completed) have settled in the works of a few writers; and that there being now no room for the invention of better, all that remains is to embellish and cultivate those things which have been invented already. Would it were so! But the truth is that this appropriating of the sciences has its origin in nothing better than the confidence of a few persons and the sloth and indolence of the rest. For after the sciences had been in several parts perhaps cultivated and handled diligently, there has risen up some man of bold disposition, and famous for methods and short ways which people like, who has in appearance reduced them to an art, while he has in fact only spoiled all that the others had done. And yet this is what posterity like, because it makes the work short and easy, and saves further inquiry, of which they are weary and impatient. And if any one take this general acquiescence and consent for an argument of weight, as being the judgment of Time, let me tell him that the reasoning on which he relies is most fallacious and weak. For, first, we are far from knowing all that in the matter of sciences and arts has in various ages and places been brought to light and published; much less, all that has been by private persons secretly attempted and stirred; so neither the births nor the miscarriages of Time are entered in our records. Nor, secondly, is the consent itself and the time it has continued a consideration of much worth. For however various are the forms of civil politics, there is but one form of polity in the sciences; and that always has been and always will be popular. Now the doctrines which find most favour with the populace are those which are either contentious and pugnacious, or specious and empty; such, I say, as either entangle assent or tickle it. And therefore no doubt the greatest wits in each successive age have been forced out of their own course; men of capacity and intellect above the vulgar having been fain, for reputation's sake, to bow to the judgment of the time and the multitude; and thus if any contemplations of a higher order took light anywhere, they were presently blown out by the winds of vulgar opinions. So that Time is like a river, which has brought down to us things light and puffed up, while those which are weighty and solid have sunk. Nay, those very authors who have usurped a kind of dictatorship in the sciences and taken upon them to lay down the law with such confidence, yet when from time to time they come to themselves again, they fall to complaints of the subtlety of nature, the hiding-places of truth, the obscurity of things, the entanglement of causes, the weakness of the human mind; wherein nevertheless they show themselves never the more modest, seeing that they will rather lay the blame upon the common condition of man and nature than upon themselves. And then whatever any art fails to attain, they ever set it down upon the authority of that art itself as impossible of attainment; and how can art be found guilty when it is judge in its own cause? So it is but a device for exempting ignorance from ignominy. Now for those things which are delivered and received, this is their condition: barren of works, full of questions; in point of enlargement slow and languid; carrying a show of perfection in the whole, but in the parts ill filled up; in selection popular, and unsatisfactory even to those who propound them; and therefore fenced round and set forth with sundry artifices. And if there be any who have determined to make trial for themselves, and put their own strength to the work of advancing the boundaries of the sciences, yet have they not ventured to cast themselves completely loose from received opinions or to seek their knowledge at the fountain; but they think they have done some great thing if they do but add and introduce into the existing sum of science something of their own; prudently considering with themselves that by making the addition they can assert their liberty, while they retain the credit of modesty by assenting to the rest. But these mediocrities and middle ways so much praised, in deferring to opinions and customs, turn to the great detriment of the sciences. For it is hardly possible at once to admire an author and to go beyond him; knowledge being as water, which will not rise above the level from which it fell. Men of this kind, therefore, amend some things, but advance little; and improve the condition of knowledge, but do not extend its range. Some, indeed, there have been who have gone more boldly to work, and taking it all for an open matter and giving their genius full play, have made a passage for themselves and their own opinions by pulling down and demolishing former ones; and yet all their stir has but little advanced the matter; since their aim has been not to extend philosophy and the arts in substance and value, but only to change doctrines and transfer the kingdom of opinions to themselves; whereby little has indeed been gained, for though the error be the opposite of the other, the causes of erring are the same in both. And if there have been any who, not binding themselves either to other men's opinions or to their own, but loving liberty, have desired to engage others along with themselves in search, these, though honest in intention, have been weak in endeavour. For they have been content to follow probable reasons, and are carried round in a whirl of arguments, and in the promiscuous liberty of search have relaxed the severity of inquiry. There is none who has dwelt upon experience and the facts of nature as long as is necessary. Some there are indeed who have committed themselves to the waves of experience, and almost turned mechanics; yet these again have in their very experiments pursued a kind of wandering inquiry, without any regular system of operations. And besides they have mostly proposed to themselves certain petty tasks, taking it for a great matter to work out some single discovery;—a course of proceeding at once poor in aim and unskilful in design. For no man can rightly and successfully investigate the nature of anything in the thing itself; let him vary his experiments as laboriously as he will, he never comes to a resting-place, but still finds something to seek beyond. And there is another thing to be remembered; namely, that all industry in experimenting has begun with proposing to itself certain definite works to be accomplished, and has pursued them with premature and unseasonable eagerness; it has sought, I say, experiments of Fruit, not experiments of Light; not imitating the divine procedure, which in its first day's work created light only

and assigned to it one entire day; on which day it produced
no material work, but proceeded to that on the days following. As for those who have given the first place to Logic,
supposing that the surest helps to the sciences were to be
found in that, they have indeed most truly and excellently
perceived that the human intellect left to its own course
is not to be trusted; but then the remedy is altogether too
weak for the disease; nor is it without evil in itself. For
the Logic which is received, though it be very properly applied to civil business and to those arts which rest in discourse and opinion, is not nearly subtle enough to deal with
nature; and in offering at what it cannot master, has done
more to establish and perpetuate error than to open the
way to truth.

Upon the whole therefore, it seems that men have not
been happy hitherto either in the trust which they have
placed in others or in their own industry with regard to
the sciences; especially as neither the demonstrations nor
the experiments as yet known are much to be relied upon.
But the universe to the eye of the human understanding is
framed like a labyrinth; presenting as it does on every side
so many ambiguities of way, such deceitful resemblances
of objects and signs, natures so irregular in their lines, and
so knotted and entangled. And then the way is still to be
made by the uncertain light of the sense, sometimes shining
out, sometimes clouded over, through the woods of experience and particulars; while those who offer themselves for
guides are (as was said) themselves also puzzled, and increase the number of errors and wanderers. In circumstances so difficult neither the natural force of man's judgment nor even any accidental felicity offers any chance of
success. No excellence of wit, no repetition of chance experiments, can overcome such difficulties as these. Our
steps must be guided by a clue, and the whole way from
the very first perception of the senses must be laid out upon
a sure plan. Not that I would be understood to mean that
nothing whatever has been done in so many ages by so
great labours. We have no reason to be ashamed of the
discoveries which have been made, and no doubt the ancients
proved themselves in everything that turns on wit and

abstract meditation, wonderful men. But as in former ages when men sailed only by observation of the stars, they could indeed coast along the shores of the old continent or cross a few small and mediterranean seas; but before the ocean could be traversed and the new world discovered, the use of the mariner's needle, as a more faithful and certain guide, had to be found out; in like manner the discoveries which have been hitherto made in the arts and sciences are such as might be made by practice, meditation, observation, argumentation,—for they lay near to the senses, and immediately beneath common notions; but before we can reach the remoter and more hidden parts of nature, it is necessary that a more perfect use and application of the human mind and intellect be introduced.

For my own part at least, in obedience to the everlasting love of truth, I have committed myself to the uncertainties and difficulties and solitudes of the ways, and relying on the divine assistance have upheld my mind both against the shocks and embattled ranks of opinion, and against my own private and inward hesitations and scruples, and against the fogs and clouds of nature, and the phantoms flitting about on every side; in the hope of providing at last for the present and future generations guidance more faithful and secure. Wherein if I have made any progress, the way has been opened to me by no other means than the true and legitimate humiliation of the human spirit. For all those who before me have applied themselves to the invention of arts have but cast a glance or two upon facts and examples and experience, and straightway proceeded, as if invention were nothing more than an exercise of thought, to invoke their own spirits to give them oracles. I, on the contrary, dwelling purely and constantly among the facts of nature, withdraw my intellect from them no further than may suffice to let the images and rays of natural objects meet in a point, as they do in the sense of vision; whence it follows that the strength and excellency of the wit has but little to do in the matter. And the same humility which I use in inventing I employ likewise in teaching. For I do not endeavour either by triumphs of confutation, or pleadings of antiquity, or assumption of authority, or even by the veil of obscurity, to invest these inventions of mine with any majesty; which might easily be done by one who sought to give lustre to his own name rather than light to other men's minds. I have not sought (I say) nor do I seek either to force or ensnare men's judgments, but I lead them to things themselves and the concordances of things, that they may see for themselves what they have, what they can dispute, what they can add and contribute to the common stock. And for myself, if in anything I have been either too credulous or too little awake and attentive, or if I have fallen off by the way and left the inquiry incomplete, nevertheless I so present these things naked and open, that my errors can be marked and set aside before the mass of knowledge be further infected by them; and it will be easy also for others to continue and carry on my labours. And by these means I suppose that I have established for ever a true and lawful marriage between the empirical and the rational faculty, the unkind and ill-starred divorce and separation of which has thrown into confusion all the affairs of the human family.

Wherefore, seeing that these things do not depend upon myself, at the outset of the work I most humbly and fervently pray to God the Father, God the Son, and God the Holy Ghost, that remembering the sorrows of mankind and the pilgrimage of this our life wherein we wear out days few and evil, they will vouchsafe through my hands to endow the human family with new mercies. This likewise I humbly pray, that things human may not interfere with things divine, and that from the opening of the ways of sense and the increase of natural light there may arise in our minds no incredulity or darkness with regard to the divine mysteries; but rather that the understanding being thereby purified and purged of fancies and vanity, and yet not the less subject and entirely submissive to the divine oracles, may give to faith that which is faith's. Lastly, that knowledge being now discharged of that venom which the serpent infused into it, and which makes the mind of man to swell, we may not be wise above measure and sobriety, but cultivate truth in charity.

And now having said my prayers I turn to men; to whom I have certain salutary admonitions to offer and certain fair requests to make. My first admonition (which was also my prayer) is that men confine the sense within the limits of duty in respect to things divine: for the sense is like the sun, which reveals the face of earth, but seals and shuts up the face of heaven. My next, that in flying from this evil they fall not into the opposite error, which they will surely do if they think that the inquisition of nature is in any part interdicted or forbidden. For it was not that pure and uncorrupted natural knowledge whereby Adam gave names to the creatures according to their propriety, which gave occasion to the fall. It was the ambitious and proud desire of moral knowledge to judge of good and evil, to the end that man may revolt from God and give laws to himself, which was the form and manner of the temptation. Whereas of the sciences which regard nature, the divine philosopher declares that " it is the glory of God to conceal a thing, but it is the glory of the King to find a thing out." Even as though the divine nature took pleasure in the innocent and kindly sport of children playing at hide and seek, and vouchsafed of his kindness and goodness to admit the human spirit for his playfellow at that game. Lastly, I would address one general admonition to all; that they consider what are the true ends of knowledge, and that they seek it not either for pleasure of the mind, or for contention, or for superiority to others, or for profit, or fame, or power, or any of these inferior things; but for the benefit and use of life; and that they perfect and govern it in charity. For it was from lust of power that the angels fell, from lust of knowledge that man fell; but of charity there can be no excess, neither did angel or man ever come in danger by it.

The requests I have to make are these. Of myself I say nothing; but in behalf of the business which is in hand I entreat men to believe that it is not an opinion to be held, but a work to be done; and to be well assured that I am ' labouring to lay the foundation, not of any sect or doctrine, but of human utility and power. Next, I ask them to deal fairly by their own interests, and laying aside all emulations and prejudices in favour of this or that opinion, to join in consultation for the common good; and being now freed and guarded by the securities and helps which I offer from the errors and impediments of the way, to come forward themselves and take part in that which remains to be done. Moreover, to be of good hope, nor to imagine that this Instauration of mine is a thing infinite and beyond the power of man, when it is in fact the true end and termination of infinite error, and seeing also that it is by no means forgetful of the conditions of mortality and humanity, (for it does not suppose that the work can be altogether completed within one generation, but provides for its being taken up by another); and finally that it seeks for the sciences not arrogantly in the little cells of human wit, but with reverence in the greater world. But it is the empty things that are vast: things solid are most contracted and lie in little room. And now I have only one favour more to ask (else injustice to me may perhaps imperil the business itself)—that men will consider well how far, upon that which I must needs assert (if I am to be consistent with myself), they are entitled to judge and decide upon these doctrines of mine; inasmuch as all that premature human reasoning which anticipates inquiry, and is abstracted from the facts rashly and sooner than is fit, is by me rejected (so far as the inquisition of nature is concerned), as a thing uncertain, confused, and ill built up; and I cannot be fairly asked to abide by the decision of a tribunal which is itself on its trial.

THE PLAN OF THE INSTAURATIO MAGNA

The work is in six Parts:—

1. *The Divisions of the Sciences.*
2. *The New Organon; or Directions concerning the Interpretation of Nature.*
3. *The Phenomena of the Universe; or a Natural and Experimental History for the foundation of Philosophy.*
4. *The Ladder of the Intellect.*
5. *The Forerunners; or Anticipations of the New Philosophy.*
6. *The New Philosophy; or Active Science.*

The Arguments of the several Parts.

It being part of my design to set everything forth, as far as may be, plainly and perspicuously (for nakedness of the mind is still, as nakedness of the body once was, the companion of innocence and simplicity), let me first explain the order and plan of the work. I distribute it into six parts.

The first part exhibits a summary or general description of the knowledge which the human race at present possesses. For I thought it good to make some pause upon that which is received; that thereby the old may be more easily made perfect and the new more easily approached. And I hold the improvement of that which we have to be as much an object as the acquisition of more. Besides which it will make me the better listened to; for "He that is ignorant (says the proverb) receives not the words of knowledge, unless thou first tell him that which is in his own heart." We will therefore make a coasting voyage along the shores of the arts and sciences received; not without importing into them some useful things by the way.

In laying out the divisions of the sciences however, I take into account not only things already invented and known, but likewise things omitted which ought to be there. For there are found in the intellectual as in the terrestial globe waste regions as well as cultivated ones. It is no wonder therefore if I am sometimes obliged to depart from the ordinary divisions. For in adding to the total you necessarily alter the parts and sections; and the received divisions of the sciences are fitted only to the received sum of them as it stands now.

With regard to those things which I shall mark down as omitted, I intend not merely to set down a simple title or a concise argument of that which is wanted. For as often as I have occasion to report anything as deficient, the nature of which is at all obscure, so that men may not perhaps easily understand what I mean or what the work is which I have in my head, I shall always (provided it be a matter of any worth) take care to subjoin either directions for the execution of such work, or else a portion of the work itself executed by myself as a sample of the whole: thus giving assistance in every case either by work or by counsel. For if it were for the sake of my reputation only and other men's interests were not concerned in it, I would not have any man think that in such cases merely some light and vague notion has crossed my mind, and that the things which I desire and offer at are no better than wishes; when they are in fact things which men may certainly command if they will, and of which I have formed in my own mind a clear and detailed conception. For I do not propose merely to survey these regions in my mind, like an augur taking auspices, but to enter them like a general who means to take possession.—So much for the first part of the work.

Having thus coasted past the ancient arts, the next point is to equip the intellect for passing beyond. To the second part therefore belongs the doctrine concerning the better and more perfect use of human reason in the inquisition of things, and the true helps of the understanding: that thereby (as far as the condition of mortality and humanity allows) the intellect may be raised and exalted, and made capable

of overcoming the difficulties and obscurities of nature.
The art which I introduce with this view (which I call
Interpretation of Nature) is a kind of logic; though the
difference between it and the ordinary logic is great; indeed immense. For the ordinary logic professes to contrive
and prepare helps and guards for the understanding, as
mine does; and in this one point they agree. But mine differs
from it in three points especially; viz. in the end aimed at;
in the order of demonstration; and in the starting point
of the inquiry.

For the end which this science of mine proposes is the invention not of arguments but of arts; not of things in accordance with principles, but of principles themselves; not
of probable reasons, but of designations and directions for
works. And as the intention is different, so accordingly is
the effect; the effect of the one being to overcome an oppo-
nent in argument, of the other to command nature in action.

In accordance with this end is also the nature and order
of the demonstrations. For in the ordinary logic almost all
the work is spent about the syllogism. Of induction the
logicians seem hardly to have taken any serious thought, but
they pass it by with a slight notice, and hasten on to the
formulæ of disputation. I on the contrary reject demonstration by syllogism, as acting too confusedly, and letting nature
slip out of its hands. For although no one can doubt that
things which agree in a middle term agree with one another
(which is a proposition of mathematical certainty), yet it
leaves an opening for deception; which is this. The syllogism
consists of propositions; propositions of words; and words
are the tokens and signs of notions. Now if the very notions
of the mind (which are as the soul of words and the basis
of the whole structure) be improperly and over-hastily abstracted from facts, vague, not sufficiently definite, faulty
in short in many ways, the whole edifice tumbles. I therefore reject the syllogism; and that not only as regards
principles (for to principles the logicians themselves do not
apply it) but also as regards middle propositions; which,
though obtainable no doubt by the syllogism, are, when so
obtained, barren of works, remote from practice, and altogether unavailable for the active department of the sciences

Although therefore I leave to the syllogism and these famous and boasted modes of demonstration their jurisdiction
over popular arts and such as are matter of opinion (in
which department I leave all as it is), yet in dealing with
the nature of things I use induction throughout, and that
in the minor propositions as well as the major. For I
consider induction to be that form of demonstration which
upholds the sense, and closes with nature, and comes to the
very brink of operation, if it does not actually deal with it.

Hence it follows that the order of demonstration is likewise inverted. For hitherto the proceeding has been to fly
at once from the sense and particulars up to the most general propositions, as certain fixed poles for the argument to
turn upon, and from these to derive the rest by middle terms:
a short way, no doubt, but precipitate; and one which will
never lead to nature, though it offers an easy and ready
way to disputation. Now my plan is to proceed regularly
and gradually from one axiom to another, so that the most
general are not reached till the last: but then when you
do come to them you find them to be not empty notions,
but well defined, and such as nature would really recognise
as her first principles, and such as lie at the heart and mar-
row of things.

But the greatest change I introduce is in the form itself
of induction and the judgment made thereby. For the induction of which the logicians speak, which proceeds by
simple enumeration, is a puerile thing; concludes at hazard;
is always liable to be upset by a contradictory instance;
takes into account only what is known and ordinary; and
leads to no result.

Now what the sciences stand in need of is a form of induction which shall analyse experience and take it to pieces,
and by a due process of exclusion and rejection lead to an inevitable conclusion. And if that ordinary mode of judgment practised by the logicians was so laborious, and found
exercise for such great wits, how much more labour must we
be prepared to bestow upon this other, which is extracted not
merely out of the depths of the mind, but out of the very
bowels of nature.

Nor is this all. For I also sink the foundations of the

sciences deeper and firmer; and I begin the inquiry nearer the source than men have done heretofore; submitting to examination those things which the common logic takes on trust. For first, the logicians borrow the principles of each science from the science itself; secondly, they hold in reverence the first notions of the mind; and lastly, they receive as conclusive the immediate informations of the sense, when well disposed. Now upon the first point, I hold that true logic ought to enter the several provinces of science armed with a higher authority than belongs to the principles of those sciences themselves, and ought to call those putative principles to account until they are fully established. Then with regard to the first notions of the intellect; there is not one of the impressions taken by the intellect when left to go its own way, but I hold it for suspected, and no way established, until it has submitted to a new trial and a fresh judgment has been thereupon pronounced. And lastly, the information of the sense itself I sift and examine in many ways. For certain it is that the senses deceive; but then at the same time they supply the means of discovering their own errors; only the errors are here, the means of discovery are to seek.

The sense fails in two ways. Sometimes it gives no information, sometimes it gives false information. For first, there are very many things which escape the sense, even when best disposed and no way obstructed; by reason either of the subtlety of the whole body, or the minuteness of the parts, or distance of place, or slowness or else swiftness of motion, or familiarity of the object, or other causes. And again when the sense does apprehend a thing its apprehension is not much to be relied upon. For the testimony and information of the sense has reference always to man, not to the universe; and it is a great error to assert that the sense is the measure of things.

To meet these difficulties, I have sought on all sides diligently and faithfully to provide helps for the sense—substitutes to supply its failures, rectifications to correct its errors; and this I endeavour to accomplish not so much by instruments as by experiments. For the subtlety of experiments is far greater than that of the sense itself, even when assisted by exquisite instruments; such experiments, I mean, as are skilfully and artificially devised for the express purpose of determining the point in question. To the immediate and proper perception of the sense therefore I do not give much weight; but I contrive that the office of the sense shall be only to judge of the experiment, and that the experiment itself shall judge of the thing. And thus I conceive that I perform the office of a true priest of the sense (from which all knowledge in nature must be sought, unless men mean to go mad) and a not unskilful interpreter of its oracles; and that while others only profess to uphold and cultivate the sense, I do so in fact. Such then are the provisions I make for finding the genuine light of nature and kindling and bringing it to bear. And they would be sufficient of themselves, if the human intellect were even, and like a fair sheet of paper with no writing on it. But since the minds of men are strangely possessed and beset, so that there is no true and even surface left to reflect the genuine rays of things, it is necessary to seek a remedy for this also.

Now the idols, or phantoms, by which the mind is occupied are either adventitious or innate. The adventitious come into the mind from without; namely, either from the doctrines and sects of philosophers, or from perverse rules of demonstration. But the innate are inherent in the very nature of the intellect, which is far more prone to error than the sense is. For let men please themselves as they will in admiring and almost adoring the human mind, this is certain: that as an uneven mirror distorts the rays of objects according to its own figure and section, so the mind, when it receives impressions of objects through the sense, cannot be trusted to report them truly, but in forming its notions mixes up its own nature with the nature of things.

And as the first two kinds of idols are hard to eradicate, so idols of this last kind cannot be eradicated at all. All that can be done is to point them out, so that this insidious action of the mind may be marked and reproved (else as fast as old errors are destroyed new ones will spring up out of the ill complexion of the mind itself, and so we shall have but a change or errors, and not a clearance); and to lay it down once for all as a fixed and established maxim, that the intellect is not qualified to judge except by means of induction, and induction in its legitimate form. This doctrine then of the expurgation of the intellect to qualify it for dealing with truth, is comprised in three refutations: the refutation of the Philosophies; the refutation of the Demonstrations; and the refutation of the Natural Human Reason. The explanation of which things, and of the true relation between the nature of things and the nature of the mind, is as the strewing and decoration of the bridal chamber of the Mind and the Universe, the Divine Goodness assisting; out of which marriage let us hope (and be this the prayer of the bridal song) there may spring helps to man, and a line and race of inventions that may in some degree subdue and overcome the necessities and miseries of humanity. This is the second part of the work.

But I design not only to indicate and mark out the ways, but also to enter them. And therefore the third part of the work embraces the Phenomena of the Universe; that is to say, experience of every kind, and such a natural history as may serve for a foundation to build philosophy upon. For a good method of demonstration or form of interpreting nature may keep the mind from going astray or stumbling, but it is not any excellence of method that can supply it with the material of knowledge. Those however who aspire not to guess and divine, but to discover and know; who propose not to devise mimic and fabulous worlds of their own, but to examine and dissect the nature of this very world itself; must go to facts themselves for everything. Nor can the place of this labour and search and worldwide perambulation be supplied by any genius or meditation or argumentation; no, not if all men's wits could meet in one. This therefore we must have, or the business must be for ever abandoned. But up to this day such has been the condition of men in this matter, that it is no wonder if nature will not give herself into their hands.

For first, the information of the sense itself, sometimes failing, sometimes false; observation, careless, irregular, and led by chance; tradition, vain and fed on rumour; practice, slavishly bent upon its work; experiment, blind, stupid, vague, and prematurely broken off; lastly, natural history, trivial and poor;—all these have contributed to supply the understanding with very bad materials for philosophy and the sciences.

Then an attempt is made to mend the matter by a preposterous subtlety and winnowing of argument. But this comes too late, the case being already past remedy; and is far from setting the business right or sifting away the errors. The only hope therefore of any greater increase or progress lies in a reconstruction of the sciences.

Of this reconstruction the foundation must be laid in natural history, and that of a new kind and gathered on a new principle. For it is in vain that you polish the mirror if there are no images to be reflected; and it is as necessary that the intellect should be supplied with fit matter to work upon, as with safeguards to guide its working. But my history differs from that in use (as my logic does) in many things,— in end and office, in mass and composition, in subtlety, in selection also and setting forth, with a view to the operations which are to follow.

For first, the object of a natural history which I propose is not so much to delight with variety of matter or to help with present use of experiments, as to give light to the discovery of causes and supply a suckling philosophy with its first food. For though it be true that I am principally in pursuit of works and the active department of the sciences, yet I wait for harvest-time, and do not attempt to mow the moss or to reap the green corn. For I well know that axioms once rightly discovered will carry whole troops of works along with them, and produce them, not here and there one, but in clusters. And that unseasonable and puerile hurry to snatch by way of earnest at the first works which come within reach, I utterly condemn and reject, as an Atalanta's apple that hinders the race. Such then is the office of this natural history of mine.

Next, with regard to the mass and composition of it: I mean it to be a history not only of nature free and at large (when she is left to her own course and does her work her own way)—such as that of the heavenly bodies, meteors, earth and sea, minerals, plants, animals,—but much more of nature under constraint and vexed; that is to say, when by art and the hand of man she is forced out of her natural state, and squeezed and moulded. Therefore I set down at length all experiments of the mechanical arts, of the operative part of the liberal arts, of the many crafts which have not yet grown into arts properly so called, so far as I have been able to examine them and as they conduce to the end in view. Nay (to say the plain truth) I do in fact (low and vulgar as men may think it) count more upon this part both for helps and safeguards than upon the other; seeing that the nature of things betrays itself more readily under the vexations of art than in its natural freedom.

Nor do I confine the history to Bodies; but I have thought it my duty besides to make a separate history of such Virtues as may be considered cardinal in nature. I mean those original passions or desires of matter which constitute the primary elements of nature; such as Dense and Rare, Hot and Cold, Solid and Fluid, Heavy and Light, and several others.

Then again, to speak of subtlety: I seek out and get together a kind of experiments much subtler and simpler than those which occur accidentally. For I drag into light many things which no one who was not proceeding by a regular and certain way to the discovery of causes would have thought of inquiring after; being indeed in themselves of no great use; which shows that they were not sought for on their own account; but having just the same relation to things and works which the letters of the alphabet have to speech and words—which, though in themselves useless, are the elements of which all discourse is made up.

Further, in the selection of the relation and experiments I conceive I have been a more cautious purveyor than those who have hitherto dealt with natural history. For I admit nothing but on the faith of eyes, or at least of careful and severe examination; so that nothing is exaggerated for wonder's sake, but what I state is sound and without mixture of fables or vanity. All received or current falsehoods also (which by strange negligence have been allowed for many ages to prevail and become established) I proscribe and brand by name; that the sciences may be no more troubled with them. For it has been well observed that the fables and superstitions and follies which nurses instil into children do serious injury to their minds; and the same consideration makes me anxious, having the management of the childhood as it were of philosophy in its course of natural history, not to let it accustom itself in the beginning to any vanity. Moreover, whenever I come to a new experiment of any subtlety (though it be in my own opinion certain and approved), I nevertheless subjoin a clear account of the manner in which I made it; that men knowing exactly how each point was made out, may see whether there be any error connected with it, and may arouse themselves to devise proofs more trustworthy and exquisite, if such can be found; and finally, I interpose everywhere admonitions and scruples and cautions, with a religious care to eject, repress, and as it were exorcise every kind of phantasm.

Lastly, knowing how much the sight of man's mind is distracted by experience and history, and how hard it is at the first (especially for minds either tender or preoccupied) to become familiar with nature, I not unfrequently subjoin observations of my own, being as the first offers, inclinations, and as it were glances of history towards philosophy; both by way of an assurance to men that they will be kept for ever tossing on the waves of experience, and also that when the time comes for the intellect to begin its work, it may find everything the more ready. By such a natural history then as I have described, I conceive that a safe and convenient approach may be made to nature, and matter supplied of good quality and well prepared for the understanding to work upon.

And now that we have surrounded the intellect with faithful helps and guards, and got together with most careful selection a regular army of divine works, it may seem that we have no more to do but to proceed to philosophy itself. And yet in a matter so difficult and doubtful there are still some things which it seems necessary to premise, partly for convenience of explanation, partly for present use.

Of these the first is to set forth examples of inquiry and invention according to my method, exhibited by anticipation in some particular subjects; choosing such subjects as are at once the most noble in themselves among those under inquiry, and most different one from another; that there may be an example in every kind. I do not speak of those examples which are joined to the several precepts and rules by way of illustration (for of these I have given plenty in the second part of the work); but I mean actual types and models, by which the entire process of the mind and the whole fabric and order of invention from the beginning to the end, in certain subjects, and those various and remarkable, should be set as it were before the eyes. For I remember that in the mathematics it is easy to follow the demonstration when you have a machine beside you; whereas without that help all appears involved and more subtle than it really is. To examples of this kind,—being in fact nothing more than an application of the second part in detail and at large,—the fourth part of the work is devoted.

The fifth part is for temporary use only, pending the completion of the rest; like interest payable from time to time until the principal be forthcoming. For I do not make so blindly for the end of my journey, as to neglect anything useful that may turn up by the way. And therefore I include in this fifth part such things as I have myself discovered, proved, or added,—not however according to the true rules and methods of interpretation, but by the ordinary use of the understanding in inquiring and discovering. For besides that I hope my speculations may in virtue of my continual conversancy with nature have a value beyond the pretensions of my wit, they will serve in the meantime for wayside inns, in which the mind may rest and refresh itself on its journey to more certain conclusions. Nevertheless I wish it to be understood in the meantime that they are conclusions by which (as not being discovered and proved by the true form of interpretation) I do not at all mean to bind myself. Nor need any one be alarmed at such suspension of judgment, in one who maintains not simply that nothing can be known, but only that nothing can be known except in a certain course and way; and yet establishes provisionally certain degrees of assurance, for use and relief until the mind shall arrive at a knowledge of causes in which it can rest. For even those schools of philosophy which held the absolute impossibility of knowing anything were not inferior to those which took upon them to pronounce. But then they did not provide helps for the sense and understanding, as I have done, but simply took away all their authority: which is quite a different thing—almost the reverse.

The sixth part of my work (to which the rest is subservient and ministrant) discloses and sets forth that philosophy which by the legitimate, chaste, and severe course of inquiry which I have explained and provided is at length developed and established. The completion however of this last part is a thing both above my strength and beyond my hopes. I have made a beginning of the work—a beginning, as I hope, not unimportant:—the fortune of the human race will give the issue;—such an issue, it may be, as in the present condition of things and men's minds cannot easily be conceived or imagined. For the matter in hand is no mere felicity of speculation, but the real business and fortunes of the human race, and all power of operation. For man is but the servant and interpreter of nature: what he does and what he knows is only what he has observed of nature's order in fact or in thought; beyond this he knows nothing and can do nothing. For the chain of causes cannot by any force be loosed or broken, nor can nature be commanded except by being obeyed. And so those twin objects, human Knowledge and human Power, do really meet in one; and it is from ignorance of causes that operation fails.

And all depends on keeping the eye steadily fixed upon the facts of nature and so receiving their images simply as they are. For God forbid that we should give out a dream of our own imagination for a pattern of the world; rather may he graciously grant to us to write an apocalypse or true vision of the footsteps of the Creator imprinted on his creatures.

Therefore do thou, O Father, who gavest the visible light

as the first fruits of creation, and didst breathe into the face of man the intellectual light as the crown and consummation thereof, guard and protect this work, which coming from thy goodness returneth to thy glory. Thou when thou turnedst to look upon the works which thy hands had made, sawest that all was very good, and didst rest from thy labours. But man, when he turned to look upon the work which his hands had made, saw that all was vanity and vexation of spirit, and could find no rest therein. Wherefore if we labour in thy works with the sweat of our brows thou wilt make us partakers of thy vision and thy sabbath. Humbly we pray that this mind may be steadfast in us, and that through these our hands, and the hands of others to whom thou shalt give the same spirit, thou wilt vouchsafe to endow the human family with new mercies.

PREFACE

TO THE NOVUM ORGANUM

THOSE who have taken upon them to lay down the law of nature as a thing already searched out and understood, whether they have spoken in simple assurance or professional affectation, have therein done philosophy and the sciences great injury. For as they have been successful in inducing belief, so they have been effective in quenching and stopping inquiry; and have done more harm by spoiling and putting an end to other men's efforts than good by their own. Those on the other hand who have taken a contrary course, and asserted that absolutely nothing can be known,—whether it were from hatred of the ancient sophists, or from uncertainty and fluctuation of mind, or even from a kind of fulness of learning, that they fell upon this opinion,—have certainly advanced reasons for it that are not to be despised; but yet they have neither started from true principles nor rested in the just conclusion, zeal and affectation having carried them much too far. The more ancient of the Greeks (whose writings are lost) took up with better judgment a position between these two extremes,—between the presumption of pronouncing on everything, and the despair of comprehending anything; and though frequently and bitterly complaining of the difficulty of inquiry and the obscurity of things, and like impatient horses champing the bit, they did not the less follow up their object and engage with Nature; thinking (it seems) that this very question,— viz. whether or no anything can be known,—was to be settled not by arguing, but by trying. And yet they too, trusting entirely to the force of their understanding, applied no rule, but made everything turn upon hard thinking and perpetual working and exercise of the mind.

Now my method, though hard to practise, is easy to explain; and it is this. I propose to establish progressive stages of certainty. The evidence of the sense, helped and guarded by a certain process of correction, I retain. But the mental operation which follows the act of sense I for the most part reject; and instead of it I open and lay out a new and certain path for the mind to proceed in, starting directly from the simple sensuous perception. The necessity of this was felt no doubt by those who attributed so much importance to Logic; showing thereby that they were in search of helps for the understanding, and had no confidence in the native and spontaneous process of the mind. But ' this remedy comes too late to do any good, when the mind is already, through the daily intercourse and conversation of life, occupied with unsound doctrines and beset on all sides by vain imaginations. And therefore that art of Logic, coming (as I said) too late to the rescue, and no way able to set matters right again, has had the effect of fixing errors rather than disclosing truth. There remains but one course for the recovery of a sound and healthy condition,— namely, that the entire work of the understanding be commenced afresh, and the mind itself be from the very outset not left to take its own course, but guided at every step; and the business be done as if by machinery. Certainly if in things mechanical men had set to work with their naked hands, without help or force of instruments, just as in things intellectual they have set to work with little else than the naked forces of the understanding, very small would the matters have been which, even with their best efforts applied in conjunction, they could have attempted or accomplished. Now (to pause while upon this example and look in it as in a glass) let us suppose that some vast obelisk were (for the decoration of a triumph or some such magnificence) to be removed from its place, and that men should set to work upon it with their naked hands; would not any sober spectator think them mad? And if they should then send for more people, thinking that in that way they might manage it, would he not think them all the madder? And if they then proceeded to make a selection, putting away the weaker hands, and using only the strong and vigorous, would he not think them madder than ever? And if lastly, not content with this, they resolved to call in aid the art of athletics, and required all their men to come with hands, arms, and sinews well anointed and medicated according to the rules of art, would he not cry out that they were only taking pains to show a kind of method and discretion in their madness? Yet just so it is that men proceed in matters intellectual,—with just the same kind of mad effort and useless combination of forces,—when they hope great things either from the number and cooperation or from the excellency and acuteness of individual wits; yea, and when they endeavour by Logic (which may be considered as a kind of athletic art) to strengthen the sinews of the understanding; and yet with all this study and endeavour it is apparent to any true judgment that they are but applying the naked intellect all the time; whereas in every great work to be done by the hand of man it is manifestly impossible, without instruments or machinery, either for the strength of each to be exerted or the strength of all to be united.

Upon these premises two things occur to me of which, that they may not be overlooked, I would have men reminded. First it falls out fortunately as I think for the allaying of contradictions and heart-burnings, that the honour and reverence due to the ancients remains untouched and undiminished; while I may carry out my designs and at the same time reap the fruit of my modesty. For if I should profess that I, going the same road as the ancients, have something better to produce, there must needs have been some comparison or rivalry between us (not to be avoided by any art of words) in respect of excellency or ability of wit; and though in this there would be nothing unlawful or new (for if there be anything misapprehended by them, or falsely laid down, why may not I, using a liberty common to all, take exception to it?) yet the contest, however just and allowable, would have been an unequal one perhaps, in respect of the measure of my own powers. As it is however,—my object being to open a new way for the understanding, a way by them untried and unknown,—the case is altered; party zeal and emulation are at an end; and I appear merely as a guide to point out the road; an office of small authority, and depending more upon a kind of luck than upon any ability or excellency. And thus much relates to the persons only. The other point of which I would have men reminded relates to the matter itself.

Be it remembered then that I am far from wishing to interfere with the philosophy which now flourishes, or with any other philosophy more correct and complete than this which has been or may hereafter be propounded. For I do not object to the use of this received philosophy, or others like it, for supplying matter for disputations or ornaments for discourse,—for the professor's lecture and for the business of life. Nay more, I declare openly that for these uses the philosophy which I bring forward will not be much available. It does not lie in the way. It cannot be caught up in passage. It does not flatter the understanding by conformity with preconceived notions. Nor will it come down to the apprehension of the vulgar except by its utility and effects.

Let there be therefore (and may it be for the benefit of both) two streams and two dispensations of knowledge; and in like manner two tribes or kindreds of students in philosophy—tribes not hostile or alien to each other, but bound together by mutual services;—let there in short be one method for the cultivation, another for the invention, of knowledge.

And for those who prefer the former, either from hurry or from considerations of business or for want of mental power to take in and embrace the other (which must needs be most men's case), I wish that they may succeed to their desire in what they are about, and obtain what they are pursuing. But if any man there be who, not content to rest in and use the knowledge which has already been discovered, aspires to penetrate further; to overcome, not an adversary in argument, but nature in action; to seek, not pretty and probable conjectures, but certain and demonstrable knowledge;—I invite all such to join themselves, as true sons of knowledge, with me, that passing by the outer courts of nature, which numbers have trodden, we may find a way at length into her inner chambers. And to make my meaning clearer and to familiarise the thing by giving it a name, I have chosen to call one of these methods or ways *Anticipation of the Mind,* the other *Interpretation of Nature.*

Moreover I have one request to make. I have on my own part made it my care and study that the things which I shall propound should not only be true, but should also be presented to men's minds, how strangely soever preoccupied and obstructed, in a manner not harsh or unpleasant. It is but reasonable however (especially in so great a restoration of learning and knowledge) that I should claim of men one favour in return; which is this; If any one would form an opinion or judgment either out of his own observation, or out of the crowd of authorities, or out of the forms of demonstration (which have now acquired a sanction like that of judicial laws), concerning these speculations of mine, let him not hope that he can do it in passage or by the by; but let him examine the thing thoroughly; let him make some little trial for himself of the way which I describe and lay out; let him familiarise his thoughts with that subtlety of nature to which experience bears witness; let him correct by seasonable patience and due delay the depraved and deep-rooted habits of his mind; and when all this is done and he has begun to be his own master, let him (if he will) use his own judgment.

PREFACE TO THE
FIRST FOLIO EDITION
OF SHAKESPEARE'S PLAYS
(1623)

To the Great Variety of Readers

FROM the most able, to him that can but spell: There you are number'd. We had rather you were weighd. Especially, when the fate of all Bookes depends vpon your capacities: and not of your heads alone, but of your purses. Well! it is now publique, & you wil stand for your priuiledges wee know: to read, and censure. Do so, but buy it first. That doth best commend a Booke, the Stationer saies. Then, how odde soeuer your braines be, or your wise-domes, make your licence the same, and spare not. Iudge your sixe-pen'orth, your shillings worth, your fiue shillings worth at a time, or higher, so you rise to the iust rates, and welcome. But, what euer you do, Buy. Censure will not driue a Trade, or make the Iacke go. And though you be a Magistrate of wit, and sit on the Stage at *Black-Friers,* or the *Cock-pit,* to arraigne Playes dailie, know, these Playes haue had their triall alreadie, and stood out all Appeals; and do now come forth quitted rather by a Decree of Court, then any purchas'd Letters of commendation.

It had bene a thing, we confesse, worthie to haue bene

Little more than half of Shakespeare's plays were published during his lifetime; and in the publication of these there is no evidence that the author had any hand. Seven years after his death, John Heminge and Henry Condell, two of his fellow-actors, collected the unpublished plays, and in 1623, issued them along with the others in a single volume, usually known as the First Folio. When one considers what would have been lost had it not been for the enterprise of these men, it seems safe to say that the volume they introduced by this quaint and not too accurate preface, is the most important single book in the imaginative literature of the world.

wished, that the Author himselfe had liu'd to haue set forth, and ouerseen his owne writings; But since it hath bin ordain'd otherwise, and he by death departed from that right, we pray you do not envie his Friends, the office of their care, and paine, to haue collected & publish'd them; and so to haue publish'd them, as where (before) you were abus'd with diuerse stolne, and surreptitious copies, maimed, and deformed by the frauds and stealthes of iniurious imposters, that expos'd them: euen those, are now offer'd to your view cur'd, and perfect of their limbes; and all the rest, absolute in their numbers, as he conceiued them. Who, as he was a happie imitator of Nature, was a most gentle expresser of it. His mind and hand went together: And what he thought, he vttered with that easinesse, that wee haue scarse receiued from him a blot in his papers. But it is not our prouince, who onely gather his works, and giue them you, to praise him. It is yours that reade him. And there we hope, to your diuers capacities, you will finde enough, both to draw, and hold you: for his wit can no more lie hid, then it could be lost. Reade him, therefore; and againe, and againe: And if then you doe not like him, surely you are in some manifest danger, not to vnderstand him. And so we leaue you to other of his Friends, whom if you need, can bee your guides: if you neede them not, you can leade your selues, and others. And such Readers we wish him.

IOHN HEMINGE.
HENRIE CONDELL.

PREFACE TO THE PHILOSOPHIAE NATURALIS PRINCIPIA MATHEMATICA

BY SIR ISAAC NEWTON. (1686)

SINCE the ancients (as we are told by Pappus) made great account of the science of mechanics in the investigation of natural things; and the moderns, laying aside substantial forms and occult qualities, have endeavored to subject the phenomena of nature to the laws of mathematics, I have in this treatise cultivated mathematics so far as it regards philosophy. The ancients considered mechanics in a twofold respect; as rational, which proceeds accurately by demonstration, and practical. To practical mechanics all the manual arts belong, from which mechanics took its name. But as artificers do not work with perfect accuracy, it comes to pass that mechanics is so distinguished from geometry, that what is perfectly accurate is called geometrical; what is less so is called mechanical. But the errors are not in the art, but in the artificers. He that works with less accuracy is an imperfect mechanic; and if any could work with perfect accuracy, he would be the most perfect mechanic of all; for the description of right lines and circles, upon which geometry is founded, belongs to mechanics. Geometry does not teach us to draw these lines, but requires them to be drawn; for it requires that the learner should first be taught to describe these accurately, before he

Sir Isaac Newton, the great English mathematician and physicist, was born at Woolsthorpe in 1642, and died at Kensington in 1727. He held a professorship at Cambridge, represented the University in Parliament, as master of the mint reformed the English coinage, and for twenty-five years was president of the Royal Society. His theory of the law of universal gravitation, the most important of his many discoveries, is expounded in his " Philosophiae Naturalis Principia Mathematica," usually known merely as the " Principia," from which this Preface is translated.

enters upon geometry; then it shows how by these operations problems may be solved. To describe right lines and circles are problems, but not geometrical problems. The solution of these problems is required from mechanics; and by geometry the use of them, when so solved, is shown; and it is the glory of geometry that from those few principles, fetched from without, it is able to produce so many things. Therefore geometry is founded in mechanical practice, and is nothing but that part of universal mechanics which accurately proposes and demonstrates the art of measuring. But since the manual arts are chiefly conversant in the moving of bodies, it comes to pass that geometry is commonly referred to their magnitudes, and mechanics to their motion. In this sense rational mechanics will be the science of motions resulting from any forces whatsoever, and of the forces required to produce any motions, accurately proposed and demonstrated. This part of mechanics was cultivated by the ancients in the five powers which relate to manual arts, who considered gravity (it not being a manual power) no otherwise than as it moved weights by those powers. Our design, not respecting arts, but philosophy, and our subject, not manual, but natural powers, we consider chiefly those things which relate to gravity, levity, elastic force, the resistance of fluids, and the like forces, whether attractive or impulsive; and therefore we offer this work as mathematical principles of philosophy; for all the difficulty of philosophy seems to consist in this—from the phenomena of motions to investigate the forces of nature, and then from these forces to demonstrate the other phenomena; and to this end the general propositions in the first and second book are directed. In the third book we give an example of this in the explication of the system of the World; for by the propositions mathematically demonstrated in the first book, we there derive from the celestial phenomena the forces of gravity with which bodies tend to the sun and the several planets. Then, from these forces, by other propositions which are also mathematical, we deduce the motions of the planets, the comets, the moon, and the sea. I wish we could derive the rest of the phenomena of nature by the same kind of reasoning from mechanical principles; for I am induced by many reasons to suspect that they may all depend upon certain forces by which the particles of bodies, by some causes hitherto unknown, are either mutually impelled towards each other, and cohere in regular figures, or are repelled and recede from each other; which forces being unknown, philosophers have hitherto attempted the search of nature in vain; but I hope the principles here laid down will afford some light either to that or some truer method of philosophy.

In the publication of this work, the most acute and universally learned Mr. Edmund Halley not only assisted me with his pains in correcting the press and taking care of the schemes, but it was to his solicitations that its becoming public is owing; for when he had obtained of me my demonstrations of the figure of the celestial orbits, he continually pressed me to communciate the same to the Royal Society, who afterwards, by their kind encouragement and entreaties, engaged me to think of publishing them. But after I had begun to consider the inequalities of the lunar motions, and had entered upon some other things relating to the laws and measures of gravity, and other forces; and the figures that would be described by bodies attracted according to given laws; and the motion of several bodies moving among themselves; the motion of bodies in resisting mediums; the forces, densities, and motions of mediums; the orbits of the comets, and such like; I put off that publication till I had made a search into those matters, and could put out the whole together. What relates to the lunar motions (being imperfect) I have put all together in the corollaries of proposition 66, to avoid being obliged to propose and distinctly demonstrate the several things there contained in a method more prolix than the subject deserved, and interrupt the series of the several propositions. Some things, found out after the rest, I chose to insert in places less suitable, rather than change the number of the propositions and the citations. I heartily beg that what I have here done may be read with candor; and that the defects I have been guilty of upon this difficult subject may be not so much reprehended as kindly supplied, and investigated by new endeavors of my readers.

Cambridge, Trinity College,   ISAAC NEWTON.
  May 8, 1686.

PREFACE TO FABLES,
ANCIENT AND MODERN
BY JOHN DRYDEN. (1700)

'TIS with a poet, as with a man who designs to build, and is very exact, as he supposes, in casting up the cost beforehand; but, generally speaking, he is mistaken in his account, and reckons short of the expense he first intended. He alters his mind as the work proceeds, and will have this or that convenience more, of which he had not thought when he began. So has it happen'd to me; I have built a house, where I intended but a lodge; yet with better success than a certain nobleman,[1] who, beginning with a dog kennel, never liv'd to finish the palace he had contriv'd.

From translating the first of Homer's *Iliads* (which I intended as an essay to the whole work) I proceeded to the translation of the twelfth book of Ovid's *Metamorphoses,* because it contains, among other things, the causes, the beginning, and ending, of the Trojan war. Here I ought in reason to have stopp'd; but the speeches of Ajax and Ulysses lying next in my way, I could not balk 'em. When I had compass'd them, I was so taken with the former part of the fifteenth book, (which is the masterpiece of the whole *Metamorphoses,*) that I enjoin'd myself the pleasing task of rend'ring it into English. And now I found, by the number of my verses, that they began to swell into a little volume; which gave me an occasion of looking backward on some beauties of my author, in his former books. There

John Dryden (1631-1700), the great dramatic and satirical poet of the later seventeenth century, whose translation of Virgil's " Æneid " appears in another volume of the Harvard Classics, deserves hardly less distinction as a prose writer than as a poet. The present essay, prefixed to a volume of narrative poems, is largely concerned with Chaucer; and in its genial and penetrating criticism, expressed with characteristic clearness and vigor, can be seen the ground for naming Dryden the first of English literary critics, and the founder of modern prose style.

[1] Scott suggests that the allusion is to the Duke of Buckingham, who was often satirized for the slow progress of his great mansion at Cliefden.

occurr'd to me the *Hunting of the Boar, Cinyras and Myr-rha,* the good-natur'd story of *Baucis and Philemon,* with the rest, which I hope I have translated closely enough, and given them the same turn of verse which they had in the original; and this, I may say without vanity, is not the talent of every poet. He who has arriv'd the nearest to it, is the ingenious and learned Sandys, the best versifier of the former age; if I may properly call it by that name, which was the former part of this concluding century. For Spenser and Fairfax both flourish'd in the reign of Queen Elizabeth; great masters in our language, and who saw much farther into the beauties of our numbers than those who immediately follow'd them. Milton was the poetical son of Spenser, and Mr. Waller of Fairfax, for we have our lineal descents and clans as well as other families. Spenser more than once insinuates that the soul of Chaucer was transfus'd into his body, and that he was begotten by him two hundred years after his decease. Milton has acknowledg'd to me that Spenser was his original, and many besides myself have heard our famous Waller own that he deriv'd the harmony of his numbers from the *Godfrey of Bulloign,* which was turn'd into English by Mr. Fairfax. But to return. Having done with Ovid for this time, it came into my mind that our old English poet, Chaucer, in many things resembled him, and that with no disadvantage on the side of the modern author, as I shall endeavor to prove when I compare them; and as I am, and always have been, studious to promote the honor of my native country, so I soon resolv'd to put their merits to the trial, by turning some of the *Canterbury Tales* into our language, as it is now refin'd; for by this means, both the poets being set in the same light, and dress'd in the same English habit, story to be compar'd with story, a certain judgment may be made betwixt them by the reader, without obtruding my opinion on him. Or, if I seem partial to my countryman and predecessor in the laurel, the friends of antiquity are not few; and besides many of the learn'd, Ovid has almost all the beaux, and the whole fair sex, his declar'd patrons. Perhaps I have assum'd somewhat more to myself than they allow me, because I have adventur'd to sum up the evidence; but the readers are the jury, and their privilege remains entire, to decide, according to the merits of the cause, or if they please, to bring it to another hearing before some other court. In the mean time, to follow the thrid of my discourse, (as thoughts, according to Mr. Hobbes, have always some connection,) so from Chaucer I was led to think on Boccace, who was not only his contemporary, but also pursued the same studies; wrote novels in prose, and many works in verse; particularly is said to have invented the octave rhyme,[2] or stanza of eight lines, which ever since has been maintain'd by the practice of all Italian writers, who are, or at least assume the title of, heroic poets. He and Chaucer, among other things, had this in common, that they refin'd their mother tongues; but with this difference, that Dante had begun to file their language, at least in verse, before the time of Boccace, who likewise receiv'd no little help from his master Petrarch. But the reformation of their prose was wholly owing to Boccace himself, who is yet the standard of purity in the Italian tongue; tho' many of his phrases are become obsolete, as in process of time it must needs happen. Chaucer (as you have formerly been told by our learn'd Mr. Rymer) first adorn'd and amplified our barren tongue from the Provençal,[3] which was then the most polish'd of all the modern languages; but this subject has been copiously treated by that great critic, who deserves no little commendation from us his countrymen. For these reasons of time, and resemblance of genius in Chaucer and Boccace, I resolv'd to join them in my present work; to which I have added some original papers of my own; which, whether they are equal or inferior to my other poems, an author is the most improper judge, and therefore I leave them wholly to the mercy of the reader. I will hope the best, that they will not be condemn'd; but if they should, I have the excuse of an old gentleman, who mounting on horseback before some ladies, when I was present, got up somewhat heavily, but desir'd of the fair spectators that

---

[2] Boccaccio did not invent this stanza, which had been used in both French and Italian before his day, but he did constitute it the Italian form for heroic verse.

[3] Rymer misled Dryden. There is no trace of Provençal influence on Chaucer.

they would count fourscore and eight before they judg'd
him. By the mercy of God, I am already come within
twenty years of his number, a cripple in my limbs; but what
decays are in my mind, the reader must determine. I think
myself as vigorous as ever in the faculties of my soul, excepting only my memory, which is not impair'd to any great
degree; and if I lose not more of it, I have no great reason
to complain. What judgment I had, increases rather than
diminishes; and thoughts, such as they are, come crowding in so fast upon me, that my only difficulty is to choose
or to reject; to run them into verse, or to give them the
other harmony of prose. I have so long studied and practic'd
both, that they are grown into a habit, and become familiar to me. In short, tho' I may lawfully plead some part
of the old gentleman's excuse, yet I will reserve it till I
think I have greater need, and ask no grains of allowance
for the faults of this my present work, but those which are
given of course to human frailty. I will not trouble my
reader with the shortness of time in which I writ it, or the
several intervals of sickness. They who think too well of
their own performances are apt to boast in their prefaces
how little time their works have cost them, and what other
business of more importance interfer'd; but the reader will
be as apt to ask the question, why they allow'd not a longer
time to make their works more perfect, and why they had
so despicable an opinion of their judges as to thrust their
indigested stuff upon them, as if they deserv'd no better.

With this account of my present undertaking, I conclude
the first part of this discourse; in the second part, as at a
second sitting, tho' I alter not the draught, I must touch
the same features over again, and change the dead coloring* of the whole. In general, I will only say that I have
written nothing which savors of immorality or profaneness;
at least, I am not conscious to myself of any such intention. If there happen to be found an irreverent expression,
or a thought too wanton, they are crept into my verses thro'
my inadvertency; if the searchers find any in the cargo, let
them be stav'd or forfeited, like counterbanded goods; at
least, let their authors be answerable for them, as being

* The foundation layer of color in a painting.

but imported merchandise, and not of my own manufacture. On the other side, I have endeavor'd to choose such fables, both ancient and modern, as contain in each of them some instructive moral; which I could prove by induction, but the way is tedious, and they leap foremost into sight, without the reader's trouble of looking after them. I wish I could affirm, with a safe conscience, that I had taken the same care in all my former writings; for it must be own'd, that supposing verses are never so beautiful or pleasing, yet if they contain anything which shocks religion, or good manners, they are at best what Horace says of good numbers without good sense, *Versus inopes rerum, nugæque canoræ.*[5] Thus far, I hope, I am right in court, without renouncing to my other right of self-defense, where I have been wrongfully accus'd, and my sense wiredrawn into blasphemy or bawdry, as it has often been by a religious lawyer,[6] in a late pleading against the stage; in which he mixes truth with falsehood, and has not forgotten the old rule of calumniating strongly, that something may remain.

I resume the thrid of my discourse with the first of my translations, which was the *First Iliad* of Homer. If it shall please God to give me longer life, and moderate health, my intentions are to translate the whole *Ilias;* provided still that I meet with those encouragements from the public which may enable me to proceed in my undertaking with some cheerfulness. And this I dare assure the world beforehand, that I have found by trial Homer a more pleasing task than Virgil, (tho' I say not the translation will be less laborious). For the Grecian is more according to my genius than the Latin poet. In the works of the two authors we may read their manners and natural inclinations, which are wholly different. Virgil was of a quiet, sedate temper; Homer was violent, impetuous, and full of fire. The chief talent of Virgil was propriety of thoughts, and ornament of words; Homer was rapid in his thoughts, and took all the liberties, both of numbers and of expressions, which his language, and the age in which he liv'd,

---

[5] "Verses without content, melodious trifles."—*Ars Poet.* 322.
[6] Jeremy Collier, in his *Short View of the Immortality and Profaneness of the Stage,* 1698.

allow'd him. Homer's invention was more copious, Virgil's more confin'd; so that if Homer had not led the way, it was not in Virgil to have begun heroic poetry; for nothing can be more evident than that the Roman poem is but the second part of the *Ilias;* a continuation of the same story, and the persons already form'd; the manners of Æneas are those of Hector superadded to those which Homer gave him. The adventures of Ulysses in the *Odysseis* are imitated in the first six books of Virgil's *Æneis;* and tho' the accidents are not the same, (which would have argued him of a servile, copying, and total barrenness of invention,) yet the seas were the same, in which both the heroes wander'd; and Dido cannot be denied to be the poetical daughter of Calypso. The six latter books of Virgil's poem are the four and twenty *Iliads* contracted: a quarrel occasion'd by a lady, a single combat, battles fought, and a town besieg'd. I say not this in derogation to Virgil, neither do I contradict anything which I have formerly said in his just praise: for his episodes are almost wholly of his own invention; and the form which he has given to the telling makes the tale his own, even tho' the original story had been the same. But this proves, however, that Homer taught Virgil to design; and if invention be the first virtue of an epic poet, then the Latin poem can only be allow'd the second place. Mr. Hobbes, in the preface to his own bald translation of the *Ilias* (studying poetry as he did mathematics, when it was too late)—Mr. Hobbes, I say, begins the praise of Homer where he should have ended it. He tells us that the first beauty of an epic poem consists in diction, that is, in the choice of words, and harmony of numbers; now the words are the coloring of the work, which in the order of nature is last to be consider'd. The design, the disposition, the manners, and the thoughts, are all before it: where any of those are wanting or imperfect, so much wants or is imperfect in the imitation of human life; which is in the very definition of a poem. Words, indeed, like glaring colors, are the first beauties that arise and strike the sight: but if the draught be false or lame, the figures ill dispos'd, the manners obscure or inconsistent, or the thoughts unnatural, then the finest colors are but daubing, and the piece is a beautiful monster at the best. Neither Virgil nor Homer were deficient in any of the former beauties; but in this last, which is expression, the Roman poet is at least equal to the Grecian, as I have said elsewhere; supplying the poverty of his language by his musical ear, and by his diligence. But to return: our two great poets, being so different in their tempers, one choleric and sanguine, the other phlegmatic and melancholic; that which makes them them excel in their several ways is that each of them has follow'd his own natural inclination, as well in forming the design as in the execution of it. The very heroes shew their authors: Achilles is hot, impatient, revengeful, *Impiger, iracundus, inexorabilis, acer,*[7] &c.; Æneas patient, considerate, careful of his people, and merciful to his enemies; ever submissive to the will of Heaven —*Quo fata trahunt retrahuntque sequamur.*[8] I could please myself with enlarging on this subject, but am forc'd to defer it to a fitter time. From all I have said I will only draw this inference, that the action of Homer being more full of vigor than that of Virgil, according to the temper of the writer, is of consequence more pleasing to the reader. One warms you by degrees: the other sets you on fire all at once, and never intermits his heat. 'Tis the same difference which Longinus makes betwixt the effects of eloquence in Demosthenes and Tully. One persuades; the other commands. You never cool while you read Homer, even not in the second book (a graceful flattery to his countrymen); but he hastens from the ships, and concludes not that book till he has made you an amends by the violent playing of a new machine. From thence he hurries on his action with variety of events, and ends it in less compass than two months. This vehemence of his, I confess, is more suitable to my temper; and therefore I have translated his first book with greater pleasure than any part of Virgil; but it was not a pleasure without pains. The continual agitations of the spirits must needs be a weak'ning of any constitution, especially in age; and many pauses are requir'd for refreshment

---

[7] " Energetic, irascible, unyielding, vehement."—Horace, *Ars Poet.* 121.
[8] " Whithersoever the fates drag us to and fro, let us follow."—Virgil, *Æneid,* v. 709.

betwixt the heats; the *Iliad* of itself being a third part longer than all Virgil's works together.

This is what I thought needful in this place to say of Homer. I proceed to Ovid and Chaucer, considering the former only in relation to the latter. With Ovid ended the golden age of the Roman tongue; from Chaucer the purity of the English tongue began. The manners of the poets were not unlike: both of them were well bred, well natur'd, amorous, and libertine, at least in their writings, it may be also in their lives. Their studies were the same, philosophy and philology. Both of them were knowing in astronomy, of which Ovid's books of the Roman feasts, and Chaucer's treatise of the Astrolabe, are sufficient witnesses. But Chaucer was likewise an astrologer, as were Virgil, Horace, Persius, and Manilius. Both writ with wonderful facility and clearness: neither were great inventors; for Ovid only copied the Grecian fables; and most of Chaucer's stories were taken from his Italian contemporaries, or their predecessors.* Boccace his *Decameron* was first publish'd; and from thence our Englishman has borrow'd many of his *Canterbury Tales;* yet that of *Palamon and Arcite* was written in all probability by some Italian wit in a former age, as I shall prove hereafter. The tale of Grizild was the invention of Petrarch; by him sent to Boccace; from whom it came to Chaucer. *Troilus and Cressida* was also written by a Lombard author; but much amplified by our English translator, as well as beautified; the genius of our countrymen, in general, being rather to improve an invention, than to invent themselves; as is evident not only in our poetry, but in many of our manufactures. I find I have anticipated already, and taken up from Boccace before I come to him; but there is so much less behind; and I am of the temper of most kings, *who love to be in debt,* are all for present money, no matter how they pay it afterwards: besides, the nature of a preface is rambling; never wholly out of the way, nor in it. This I have learn'd from the practice of honest Montaigne, and return at my pleasure to Ovid and Chaucer, of whom I have little more to say.

* The statements that follow as to Chaucer's sources are mostly not in accord with the results of modern scholarship.

Both of them built on the inventions of other men; yet
since Chaucer had something of his own, as *The Wife of
Bath's Tale, The Cock and the Fox,*[10] which I have translated, and some others, I may justly give our countryman
the precedence in that part; since I can remember nothing
of Ovid which was wholly his. Both of them understood
the manners, under which name I comprehend the passions,
and, in a larger sense, the descriptions of persons, and their
very habits; for an example, I see Baucis and Philemon as
perfectly before me, as if some ancient painter had drawn
them; and all the pilgrims in the *Canterbury Tales,* their
humors, their features, and the very dress, as distinctly as if
I had supp'd with them at the Tabard in Southwark; yet
even there too the figures of Chaucer are much more lively,
and set in a better light: which tho' I have not time to prove,
yet I appeal to the reader, and am sure he will clear me
from partiality. The thoughts and words remain to be
consider'd in the comparison of the two poets; and I have
sav'd myself one half of that labor, by owning that Ovid
liv'd when the Roman tongue was in its meridian, Chaucer
in the dawning of our language; therefore that part of the
comparison stands not on an equal foot, any more than the
diction of Ennius and Ovid, or of Chaucer and our present
English. The words are given up as a post not to be defended in our poet, because he wanted the modern art of
fortifying. The thoughts remain to be consider'd, and they
are to be measur'd only by their propriety; that is, as they
flow more or less naturally from the persons describ'd, on
such and such occasions. The vulgar judges, which are
nine parts in ten of all nations, who call conceits and jingles
wit, who see Ovid full of them, and Chaucer altogether without them, will think me little less than mad, for preferring
the Englishman to the Roman: yet, with their leave, I must
presume to say that the things they admire are only glitter-
ing trifles, and so far from being witty, that in a serious
poem they are nauseous, because they are unnatural. Would
any man who is ready to die for love describe his passion
like Narcissus? Would he think of *inopem me copia
fecit,*[11] and a dozen more of such expressions, pour'd on

---

[10] The plot of neither of these poems was original with Chaucer.

the neck of one another, and signifying all the same thing?
If this were wit, was this a time to be witty, when the poor
wretch was in the agony of death? This is just John Little-
wit in *Bartholomew Fair*,[12] who had a conceit (as he tells
you) left him in his misery; a miserable conceit. On these
occasions the poet should endeavor to raise pity; but instead
of this, Ovid is tickling you to laugh. Virgil never made use
of such machines, when he was moving you to commiser-
ate the death of Dido: he would not destroy what he was
building. Chaucer makes Arcite violent in his love, and unjust in the pursuit of it; yet when he came to die, he made
him think more reasonably: he repents not of his love, for
that had alter'd his character; but acknowledges the injustice of his proceedings, and resigns Emilia to Palamon.
What would Ovid have done on this occasion? He would
certainly have made Arcite witty on his deathbed. He had
complain'd he was farther off from possession by being so
near, and a thousand such boyisms, which Chaucer rejected
as below the dignity of the subject. They who think otherwise would by the same reason prefer Lucan and Ovid to
Homer and Virgil, and Martial to all four of them. As for
the turn of words, in which Ovid particularly excels all
poets, they are sometimes a fault, and sometimes a beauty,
as they are us'd properly or improperly; but in strong passions always to be shunn'd, because passions are serious, and
will admit no playing. The French have a high value for
them; and I confess, they are often what they call delicate,
when they are introduc'd with judgment; but Chaucer writ
with more simplicity, and follow'd nature more closely, than
to use them. I have thus far, to the best of my knowledge,
been an upright judge betwixt the parties in competition,
not meddling with the design nor the disposition of it;
because the design was not their own, and in the disposing
of it they were equal. It remains that I say somewhat of
Chaucer in particular.

In the first place, as he is the father of English poetry, so
I hold him in the same degree of veneration as the Grecians
held Homer or the Romans Virgil. He is a perpetual fountain of good sense, learn'd in all sciences, and therefore

[11] "Plenty has made me poor."—*Meta.* iii. 466.   [12] By Ben Jonson.

speaks properly on all subjects: as he knew what to say, so he knows also when to leave off, a continence which is practic'd by few writers, and scarcely by any of the ancients, excepting Virgil and Horace. One of our late great poets[13] is sunk in his reputation, because he could never forgive any conceit which came in his way, but swept like a drag-net, great and small. There was plenty enough, but the dishes were ill sorted; whole pyramids of sweetmeats for boys and women, but little of solid meat for men. All this proceeded not from any want of knowledge, but of judgment; neither did he want that in discerning the beauties and faults of other poets; but only indulg'd himself in the luxury of writing; and perhaps knew it was a fault, but hop'd the reader would not find it. For this reason, tho' he must always be thought a great poet, he is no longer esteem'd a good writer; and for ten impressions, which his works have had in so many successive years, yet at present a hundred books are scarcely purchas'd once a twelvemonth: for, as my last Lord Rochester said, tho' somewhat profanely, "Not being of God, he could not stand."

Chaucer follow'd Nature everywhere, but was never so bold to go beyond her; and there is a great difference of being *poeta* and *nimis poeta*,[14] if we may believe Catullus, as much as betwixt a modest behavior and affectation. The verse of Chaucer, I confess, is not harmonious to us; but 't is like the eloquence of one whom Tacitus commends, it was *auribus istius temporis accommodata*:[15] they who liv'd with him, and some time after him, thought it musical; and it continued so even in our judgment, if compar'd with the numbers of Lydgate and Gower, his contemporaries: there is the rude sweetness of a Scotch tune in it, which is natural and pleasing, tho' not perfect. 'T is true, I cannot go so far as he who publish'd the last edition of him;[16] for he would make us believe the fault is in our ears, and that there were really ten syllables in a verse where we find but nine: but this opinion is not worth confuting; 't is so gross and obvious an error, that common sense (which is a rule in

[13] Cowley.   [14] " Too much a poet."—Martial iii. 44 (not Catullus).
[15] " Suited to the ears of that time."
[16] Speght, whom modern scholarship has shown to be right in this matter.

everything but matters of faith and revelation) must convince the reader that equality of numbers in every verse which we call heroic was either not known, or not always practic'd, in Chaucer's age. It were an easy matter to produce some thousands of his verses, which are lame for want of half a foot, and sometimes a whole one, and which no pronunciation can make otherwise. We can only say, that he liv'd in the infancy of our poetry, and that nothing is brought to perfection at the first. We must be children before we grow men. There was an Ennius, and in process of time a Lucilius and a Lucretius, before Virgil and Horace; even after Chaucer there was a Spenser, a Harrington, a Fairfax, before Waller and Denham were in being: and our numbers were in their nonage till these last appear'd. I need say little of his parentage, life, and fortunes;[17] they are to be found at large in all the editions of his works. He was employ'd abroad and favor'd by Edward the Third, Richard the Second, and Henry the Fourth, and was poet, as I suppose, to all three of them. In Richard's time, I doubt, he was a little dipp'd in the rebellion of the commons, and being brother-in-law to John of Ghant, it was no wonder if he follow'd the fortunes of that family, and was well with Henry the Fourth when he had depos'd his predecessor. Neither is it to be admir'd,[18] that Henry, who was a wise as well as a valiant prince, who claim'd by succession, and was sensible that his title was not sound, but was rightfully in Mortimer, who had married the heir of York; it was not to be admir'd, I say, if that great politician should be pleas'd to have the greatest wit of those times in his interests, and to be the trumpet of his praises. Augustus had given him the example, by the advice of Mæcenas, who recommended Virgil and Horace to him; whose praises help'd to make him popular while he was alive, and after his death have made him precious to posterity. As for the religion of our poet, he seems to have some little bias towards the opinions of Wycliffe, after John of Ghant his patron; somewhat of which appears in the tale of Piers Plowman.[19] Yet I cannot blame him for inveighing so sharply against the

---

[17] What follows on Chaucer's life is full of errors.   [18] Wondered at.
[19] A spurious " Plowman's Tale " was included in the older editions of Chaucer.

vices of the clergy in his age; their pride, their ambition,
their pomp, their avarice, their worldly interest, deserv'd
the lashes which he gave them, both in that and in most of
his *Canterbury Tales:* neither has his contemporary Boccace
spar'd them. Yet both those poets liv'd in much esteem with
good and holy men in orders; for the scandal which is given
by particular priests reflects not on the sacred function.
Chaucer's Monk, his Canon, and his Friar, took not from
the character of his Good Parson. A satirical poet is the
check of the laymen on bad priests. We are only to take
care that we involve not the innocent with the guilty in the
same condemnation. The good cannot be too much honor'd,
nor the bad too coarsely us'd: for the corruption of the best
becomes the worst. When a clergyman is whipp'd, his gown
is first taken off, by which the dignity of his order is se-
cur'd: if he be wrongfully accus'd, he has his action of slander; and 't is at the poet's peril if he transgress the law.
But they will tell us that all kind of satire, tho' never so
well deserv'd by particular priests, yet brings the whole order into contempt. Is then the peerage of England anything
dishonor'd, when a peer suffers for his treason? If he be
libel'd or any way defam'd, he has his *scandalum magna-
tum*[20] to punish the offender. They who use this kind of
argument seem to be conscious to themselves of somewhat
which has deserv'd the poet's lash, and are less concern'd for
their public capacity than for their private; at least there is
pride at the bottom of their reasoning. If the faults of men
in orders are only to be judg'd among themselves, they are
all in some sort parties: for, since they say the honor of
their order is concern'd in every member of it, how can we
be sure that they will be impartial judges? How far I may
be allow'd to speak my opinion in this case, I know not;
but I am sure a dispute of this nature caus'd mischief in
abundance betwixt a king of England and an archbishop of
Canterbury;[21] one standing up for the laws of his land, and
the other for the honor (as he call'd it) of God's Church;
which ended in the murther of the prelate, and in the
whipping of his Majesty from post to pillar for his penance.

[20] A law term for slander of a man of high rank, involving more severe
punishment than ordinary slander.   [21] Henry II. and Thomas à Becket.

The learn'd and ingenious Dr. Drake [22] has sav'd me the labour of inquiring into the esteem and reverence which the priests have had of old, and I would rather extend than diminish any part of it: yet I must needs say, that when a priest provokes me without any occasion given him, I have no reason, unless it be the charity of a Christian, to forgive him: *prior læsit* [23] is justification sufficient in the civil law. If I answer him in his own language, self-defense, I am sure, must be allow'd me; and if I carry it farther, even to a sharp recrimination, somewhat may be indulg'd to human frailty. Yet my resentment has not wrought so far, but that I have follow'd Chaucer in his character of a holy man, and have enlarg'd on that subject with some pleasure, reserving to myself the right, if I shall think fit hereafter, to describe another sort of priests, such as are more easily to be found than the Good Parson; such as have given the last blow to Christianity in this age, by a practice so contrary to their doctrine. But this will keep cold till another time. In the mean while I take up Chaucer where I left him. He must have been a man of a most wonderful comprehensive nature, because, as it has been truly observ'd of him, he has taken into the compass of his *Canterbury Tales* the various manners and humors (as we now call them) of the whole English nation, in his age. Not a single character has escap'd him. All his pilgrims are severally distinguish'd from each other; and not only in their inclinations, but in their very physiognomies and persons. Bapista Porta [24] could not have describ'd their natures better, than by the marks which the poet gives them. The matter and manner of their tales, and of their telling, are so suited to their different educations, humors, and callings, that each of them would be improper in any other mouth. Even the grave and serious characters are distinguish'd by their several sorts of gravity: their discourses are such as belong to their age, their calling, and their breeding; such as are becoming of them, and of them only. Some of his persons are vicious, and some virtuous; some are unlearn'd, or (as Chaucer calls them) lewd, and some are learn'd. Even the

[22] Dr. James Drake wrote a reply to Jeremy Collier's *Short View.*
[23] " He did the first injury."
[24] A Neapolitan physician who wrote on physiognomy.

ribaldry of the low characters is different: the Reeve, the
Miller, and the Cook are several men, and distinguish'd
from each other, as much as the mincing Lady Prioress
and the broad-speaking gap-tooth'd Wife of Bath. But
enough of this: there is such a variety of game springing
up before me, that I am distracted in my choice, and know
not which to follow. 'Tis sufficient to say, according to
the proverb, that here is God's plenty. We have our fore-
fathers and great-grandames all before us, as they were in
Chaucer's days; their general characters are still remaining
in mankind, and even in England, tho' they are call'd by
other names than those of Monks and Friars, and Canons,
and Lady Abbesses, and Nuns: for mankind is ever the
same, and nothing lost out of nature, tho' everything is
alter'd. May I have leave to do myself the justice—since
my enemies will do me none, and are so far from granting
me to be a good poet, that they will not allow me so
much as to be a Christian, or a moral man—may I have
leave, I say, to inform my reader that I have confin'd my
choice to such tales of Chaucer as savor nothing of im-
modesty. If I had desir'd more to please than to instruct,
the Reeve, the Miller, the Shipman, the Merchant, the
Sumner, and, above all, the Wife of Bath, in the prologue
to her tale, would have procur'd me as many friends and
readers, as there are beaux and ladies of pleasure in the
town. But I will no more offend against good manners:
I am sensible, as I ought to be, of the scandal I have given
by my loose writings; and make what reparation I am able,
by this public acknowledgment. If anything of this nature,
or of profaneness, be crept into these poems, I am so far
from defending it, that I disown it. *Totum hoc indictum
volo.*[25] Chaucer makes another manner of apology for his
broad speaking, and Boccace makes the like; but I will follow neither of them. Our countryman, in the end of his
characters, before the *Canterbury Tales,* thus excuses the
ribaldry, which is very gross in many of his novels:

> But first, I pray you of your courtesy,
> That ye ne arrete[26] it nought my villany,
> Though that I plainly speak in this mattere

[25] "I wish all this unsaid."   [26] Reckon.

To tellen you her[27] words, and eke her chere:
Ne though I speak her words properly,
For this ye knowen as well as I,
Who shall tellen a tale after a man,
He mote rehearse as nye as ever he can:
Everich word of it been in his charge,
All speke he never so rudely ne large.
Or else he mote tellen his tale untrue,
Or feine things, or find words new:
He may not spare, altho he were his brother,
He mote as well say o word as another.
Christ spake himself full broad in holy writ,
And well I wote no villany is it.
Eke Plato saith, who so can him rede,
The words mote[28] been cousin to the dede.[29]

Yet if a man should have enquir'd of Boccace or of
Chaucer, what need they had of introducing such characters, where obscene words were proper in their mouths,
but very undecent to be heard; I know not what answer
they could have made: for that reason such tales shall be
left untold by me. You have here a specimen of Chaucer's
language, which is so obsolete that his sense is scarce to
be understood; and you have likewise more than one example of his unequal numbers, which were mention'd before. Yet many of his verses consist of ten syllables, and
the words not much behind our present English: as for
example, these two lines, in the description of the carpenter's young wife:

Wincing she was, as is a jolly colt,
Long as a mast, and upright as a bolt.

I have almost done with Chaucer, when I have answer'd
some objections relating to my present work. I find some
people are offended that I have turn'd these tales into
modern English; because they think them unworthy of
my pains, and look on Chaucer as a dry, old-fashion'd wit,
not worth reviving. I have often heard the late Earl of
Leicester say that Mr. Cowley himself was of that opinion;
who having read him over at my lord's request, declar'd
he had no taste of him. I dare not advance my opinion

[27] Their.   [28] Must.
[29] The corrupt state of the text of this passage is enough to explain
why Dryden found Chaucer rough.

against the judgment of so great an author; but I think it fair, however, to leave the decision to the public: Mr. Cowley was too modest to set up for a dictator; and being shock'd perhaps with his old style, never examin'd into the depth of his good sense. Chaucer, I confess, is a rough diamond, and must first be polish'd, ere he shines. I deny not, likewise, that, living in our early days of poetry, he writes not always of a piece, but sometimes mingles trivial things with those of greater moment. Sometimes also, tho' not often, he runs riot, like Ovid, and knows not when he has said enough. But there are more great wits, beside Chaucer, whose fault is their excess of conceits, and those ill sorted. An author is not to write all he can, but only all he ought. Having observ'd this redundancy in Chaucer, (as it is an easy matter for a man of ordinary parts to find a fault in one of greater,) I have not tied myself to a literal translation; but have often omitted what I judg'd unnecessary, or not of dignity enough to appear in the company of better thoughts. I have presum'd farther, in some places, and added somewhat of my own where I thought my author was deficient, and had not given his thoughts their true luster, for want of words in the beginning of our language. And to this I was the more embolden'd, because (if I may be permitted to say it of myself) I found I had a soul congenial to his, and that I had been conversant in the same studies. Another poet, in another age, may take the same liberty with my writings; if at least they live long enough to deserve correction. It was also necessary sometimes to restore the sense of Chaucer, which was lost or mangled in the errors of the press. Let this example suffice at present; in the story of *Palamon and Arcite,* where the temple of Diana is describ'd, you find these verses, in all the editions of our author:

> There saw I Danè turned unto a tree,
> I mean not the goddess Diane,
> But Venus daughter, which that hight Danè;

which after a little consideration I knew was to be reform'd into this sense, that Daphne, the daughter of Peneus, was turn'd into a tree. I durst not make thus bold with Ovid, lest some future Milbourne should arise, and say I varied from my author, because I understood him not.

But there are other judges, who think I ought not to have translated Chaucer into English, out of a quite contrary notion: they suppose there is a certain veneration due to his old language; and that it is little less than profanation and sacrilege to alter it. They are farther of opinion that somewhat of his good sense will suffer in this transfusion, and much of the beauty of his thoughts will infallibly be lost, which appear with more grace in their old habit. Of this opinion was that excellent person whom I mention'd, the late Earl of Leicester, who valued Chaucer as much as Mr. Cowley despis'd him. My lord dissuaded me from this attempt, (for I was thinking of it some years before his death,) and his authority prevail'd so far with me as to defer my undertaking while he liv'd, in deference to him: yet my reason was not convinc'd with what he urg'd against it. If the first end of a writer be to be understood, then as his language grows obsolete, his thoughts must grow obscure:

> Multa renascentur quæ nunc cecidere; cadentque,
> Quæ nunc sunt in honore vocabula, si volet usus,
> Quem penes arbitrium est et jus et norma loquendi.[30]

When an ancient word for its sound and significancy deserves to be reviv'd, I have that reasonable veneration for antiquity, to restore it. All beyond this is superstition. Words are not like landmarks, so sacred as never to be remov'd; customs are chang'd, and even statutes are silently repeal'd, when the reason ceases for which they were enacted. As for the other part of the argument, that his thoughts will lose of their original beauty, by the innovation of words; in the first place, not only their beauty, but their being is lost, where they are no longer understood, which is the present case. I grant that something must be lost in all transfusion, that is, in all translations; but the sense will remain, which would otherwise be lost, or at

---

[30] " Many words which have now fallen out of use shall be born again; and others which are now in honor shall fall, if custom wills it, in the force of which lie the judgement and law and rules of speech."—Horace *Ars Poet.* 70-72.

least be maim'd, when it is scarce intelligible; and that but to a few. How few are there who can read Chaucer so as to understand him perfectly! And if imperfectly, then with less profit and no pleasure. 'Tis not for the use of some old Saxon friends that I have taken these pains with him: let them neglect my version, because they have no need of it. I made it for their sakes who understand sense and poetry as well as they, when that poetry and sense is put into words which they understand. I will go farther, and dare to add, that what beauties I lose in some places, I give to others which had them not originally; but in this I may be partial to myself; let the reader judge, and I submit to his decision. Yet I think I have just occasion to complain of them, who, because they understand Chaucer, would deprive the greater part of their countrymen of the same advantage, and hoard him up, as misers do their grandam gold, only to look on it themselves and hinder others from making use of it. In sum, I seriously protest that no man ever had, or can have, a greater veneration for Chaucer, than myself. I have translated some part of his works, only that I might perpetuate his memory, or at least refresh it, amongst my countrymen. If I have alter'd him anywhere for the better, I must at the same time acknowledge that I could have done nothing without him: *facile est inventis addere*,[81] is no great commendation; and I am not so vain to think I have deserv'd a greater. I will conclude what I have to say of him singly, with this one remark: a lady of my acquaintance, who keeps a kind of correspondence with some authors of the fair sex in France, has been inform'd by them, that Mademoiselle de Scudéry, who is as old as Sibyl, and inspir'd like her by the same God of Poetry, is at this time translating Chaucer into modern French. From which I gather that he has been formerly translated into the old Provençal (for how she should come to understand old English I know not). But the matter of fact being true, it makes me think that there is something in it like fatality; that, after certain periods of time, the fame and memory of great wits should be renew'd, as Chaucer is both in France and

[81] " It is easy to add to what is already invented."

England. If this be wholly chance, 't is extraordinary, and I dare not call it more, for fear of being tax'd with superstition.

Boccace comes last to be consider'd, who living in the same age with Chaucer, had the same genius, and follow'd the same studies: both writ novels, and each of them cultivated his mother tongue. But the greatest resemblance of our two modern authors being in their familiar style, and pleasing way of relating comical adventures, I may pass it over, because I have translated nothing from Boccace of that nature. In the serious part of poetry, the advantage is wholly on Chaucer's side; for tho' the Englishman has borrow'd many tales from the Italian, yet it appears that those of Boccace were not generally of his own making, but taken from authors of former ages, and by him only model'd; so that what there was of invention in either of them may be judg'd equal. But Chaucer has refin'd on Boccace, and has mended the stories which he has borrow'd, in his way of telling; tho' prose allows more liberty of thought, and the expression is more easy when unconfin'd by numbers. Our countryman carries weight, and yet wins the race at disadvantage. I desire not the reader should take my word, and therefore I will set two of their discourses on the same subject, in the same light, for every man to judge betwixt them. I translated Chaucer first, and, amongst the rest, pitch'd on *The Wife of Bath's Tale;* not daring, as I have said, to adventure on her prologue, because 't is too licentious: there Chaucer introduces an old woman of mean parentage, whom a youthful knight of noble blood was forc'd to marry, and consequently loath'd her; the crone being in bed with him on the wedding night, and finding his aversion, endeavors to win his affection by reason, and speaks a good word for herself (as who could blame her?) in hope to mollify the sullen bridegroom. She takes her topics from the benefits of poverty, the advantages of old age and ugliness, the vanity of youth, and the silly pride of ancestry and titles without inherent virtue, which is the true nobility. When I had clos'd Chaucer, I return'd to Ovid, and translated some more of his fables; and by this time had so far forgotten *The Wife of Bath's Tale,* that, when I took up Boccace,

unawares I fell on the same argument of preferring virtue
to nobility of blood, and titles, in the story of Sigismonda;
which I had certainly avoided for the resemblance of the
two discourses, if my memory had not fail'd me. Let the
reader weigh them both; and if he thinks me partial to
Chaucer, 't is in him to right Boccace.

I prefer in our countryman, far above all his other stories,
the noble poem of *Palamon and Arcite,* which is of the epic
kind, and perhaps not much inferior to the *Ilias* or the
Æneis: the story is more pleasing than either of them, the
manners as perfect, the diction as poetical, the learning as
deep and various, and the disposition full as artful; only it
includes a greater length of time, as taking up seven years
at least; but Aristotle has left undecided the duration of the
action; which yet is easily reduc'd into the compass of a
year, by a narration of what preceded the return of Palamon to Athens. I had thought for the honor of our nation,
and more particularly for his, whose laurel, tho' unworthy,
I have worn after him, that this story was of English
growth, and Chaucer's own; but I was undeceiv'd by Boccace; for, casually looking on the end of his seventh
Giornata, I found Dioneo (under which name he shadows
himself) and Fiametta (who represents his mistress, the
natural daughter of Robert, King of Naples), of whom these
words are spoken: *Dioneo e Fiametta gran pezza cantarono
insieme d' Arcita, e di Palamone:*[32] by which it appears that
this story was written before the time of Boccace; but, the
name of its author being wholly lost, Chaucer is now become
an original; and I question not but the poem has receiv'd
many beauties by passing thro' his noble hands. Besides
this tale, there is another of his own invention, after the
manner of the Provençals, call'd *The Flower and the Leaf,*[33]
with which I was so particularly pleas'd, both for the invention and the moral, that I cannot hinder myself from recommending it to the reader.

As a corollary to this preface, in which I have done justice
to others, I owe somewhat to myself: not that I think it
worth my time to enter the lists with one M——,[34] or one

[32] Dioneo and Fiametta sang together a long time of Arcite and Palamon.
[33] Not by Chaucer.
[34] Rev. Luke Milbourne, who had attacked Dryden's Virgil.

B——,[35] but barely to take notice, that such men there are
who have written scurrilously against me, without any
provocation. M——, who is in orders, pretends amongst the
rest this quarrel to me, that I have fallen foul on priesthood:
if I have, I am only to ask pardon of good priests, and am
afraid his part of the reparation will come to little. Let
him to satisfied that he shall not be able to force himself
upon me for an adversary. I contemn him too much to enter
into competition with him. His own translations of Virgil
have answer'd his criticisms on mine. If (as they say he
has declar'd in print) he prefers the version of Ogleby to
mine, the world has made him the same compliment: for
't is agreed on all hands, that he writes even below Ogleby:
that, you will say, is not easily to be done; but what cannot
M—— bring about? I am satisfied, however, that while he
and I live together, I shall not be thought the worst poet of
the age. It looks as if I had desir'd him underhand to write
so ill against me; but upon my honest word I have not
brib'd him to do me this service, and am wholly guiltless of
his pamphlet. 'T is true, I should be glad if I could persuade
him to continue his good offices, and write such another
critique on anything of mine: for I find by experience he
has a great stroke with the reader, when he condemns any
of my poems, to make the world have a better opinion of
them. He has taken some pains with my poetry, but nobody
will be persuaded to take the same with his. If I had taken
to the Church, (as he affirms, but which was never in my
thoughts,) I should have had more sense, if not more grace,
than to have turn'd myself out of my benefice by writing libels
on my parishioners. But his account of my manners and my
principles are of a piece with his cavils and his poetry; and
so I have done with him for ever.

As for the City Bard, or Knight Physician, I hear his
quarrel to me is that I was the author of *Absalom and
Achitophel,* which, he thinks, is a little hard on his fanatic
patrons in London.

But I will deal the more civilly with his two poems, because nothing ill is to be spoken of the dead; and therefore

[35] Sir Richard Blackmore, who had censured Dryden for the indecency
of his writings.

peace be to the *manes* of his *Arthurs*. I will only say that it was not for this noble knight that I drew the plan of an epic poem on King Arthur, in my preface to the translation of Juvenal. The guardian angels of kingdoms were machines too ponderous for him to manage; and therefore he rejected them, as Dares did the whirlbats of Eryx, when they were thrown before him by Entellus. Yet from that preface he plainly took his hint: for he began immediately upon the story, tho' he had the baseness not to acknowledge his benefactor but, instead of it, to traduce me in a libel.

I shall say the less of Mr. Collier, because in many things he has tax'd me justly; and I have pleaded guilty to all thoughts and expressions of mine which can be truly argued of obscenity, profaneness, of immorality; and retract them. If he be my enemy, let him triumph; if he be my friend, as I have given him no personal occasion to be otherwise, he will be glad of my repentance. It becomes me not to draw my pen in the defense of a bad cause, when I have so often drawn it for a good one. Yet it were not difficult to prove that in many places he has perverted my meaning by his glosses, and interpreted my words into blasphemy and bawdry, of which they were not guilty. Besides that, he is too much given to horseplay in his raillery, and comes to battle like a dictator from the plow. I will not say: "The zeal of God's house has eaten him up;" but I am sure it has devour'd some part of his good manners and civility. It might also be doubted whether it were altogether zeal which prompted him to this rough manner of proceeding: perhaps it became not one of his function to rake into the rubbish of ancient and modern plays; a divine might have employ'd his pains to better purpose than in the nastiness of Plautus and Aristophanes; whose examples, as they excuse not me, so it might be possibly suppos'd that he read them not without some pleasure. They who have written commentaries on those poets, or on Horace, Juvenal, and Martial, have explain'd some vices which, without their interpretation, had been unknown to modern times. Neither has he judg'd impartially betwixt the former age and us.

There is more bawdry in one play of Fletcher's, call'd *The Custom of the Country,* than in all ours together. Yet this has been often acted on the stage in my remembrance. Are the times so much more reform'd now than they were five and twenty years ago? If they are, I congratulate the amendment of our morals. But I am not to prejudice the cause of my fellow poets, tho' I abandon my own defense: they have some of them answer'd for themselves, and neither they nor I can think Mr. Collier so formidable an enemy that we should shun him. He has lost ground at the latter end of the day, by pursuing his point too far, like the Prince of Condé at the battle of Seneffe: from immoral plays to no plays, *ab abusu ad usum, non valet consequentia.*[36] But being a party, I am not to erect myself into a judge. As for the rest of those who have written against me, they are such scoundrels that they deserve not the least notice to be taken of them. B—— and M—— are only distinguish'd from the crowd by being remember'd to their infamy:

—— Demetri, teque Tigelli[37]
Discipulorum inter jubeo plorare cathedras.

[36] " The argument from abuse to use is not valid."
[37] " You, Demetrius and Tigellius, I bid lament among the chairs of your scholars." Blackmore had once been a schoolmaster.—Noyes.

PREFACE TO
JOSEPH ANDREWS

BY HENRY FIELDING (1742)

THE COMIC EPIC IN PROSE

AS IT is possible the mere English reader may have a different idea of romance with the author of these little volumes; and may consequently expect a kind of entertainment, not to be found, nor which was even intended, in the following pages; it may not be improper to premise a few words concerning this kind of writing, which I do not remember to have seen hitherto attempted in our language.

The EPIC, as well as the DRAMA, is divided into tragedy and comedy. HOMER, who was the father of this species of poetry, gave us the pattern of both these, tho' that of the latter kind is entirely lost; which Aristotle tells us, bore the same relation to comedy which his Iliad bears to tragedy. And perhaps, that we have no more instances of it among the writers of antiquity, is owing to the loss of this great pattern, which, had it survived, would have found its imitators equally with the other poems of this great original.

And farther, as this poetry may be tragic or comic, I will not scruple to say it may be likewise either in verse or prose: for tho' it wants one particular, which the critic enumerates in the constituent parts of an epic poem, namely, metre; yet, when any kind of writing contains all its other parts, such

Henry Fielding, dramatist, novelist, and judge, was born near Glastonbury, Somersetshire, April 22, 1707, and died at Lisbon, October 8, 1754. Though seldom spoken of as an essayist, Fielding scattered through his novels a large number of detached or detachable discussions which are essentially essays, of which the preface to "Joseph Andrews," on the "Comic Epic in Prose," is a favorable specimen. The novel which it introduces was begun as a parody on Richardson's "Pamela," and the preface gives Fielding's conception of this form of fiction.

as fable, action, characters, sentiments, and diction, and is
deficient in metre only, it seems, I think, reasonable to refer
it to the epic; at least, as no critic hath thought proper to
range it under any other head, nor to assign it a particular
name to itself.

Thus the Telemachus of the archbishop of Cambray appears to me of the epic kind, as well as the Odyssey of
Homer; indeed, it is much fairer and more reasonable to give
it a name common with that species from which it differs
only in a single instance, than to confound it with those
which it resembles in no other.   Such are those voluminous
works, commonly called Romances, namely Clelia, Cleopatra,
Astræa, Cassandra, the Grand Cyrus, and innumerable others
which contain, as I apprehend, very little instruction or entertainment.

Now, a comic romance is a comic epic-poem in prose;
differing from comedy, as the serious epic from tragedy: its
action being more extended and comprehensive; containing
a much larger circle of incidents, and introducing a greater
variety of characters.   It differs from the serious romance in
its fable and action, in this: that as in the one these are
grave and solemn, so in the other they are light and ridiculous; it differs in its characters, by introducing persons of inferiour rank, and consequently of inferiour manners, whereas
the grave romance sets the highest before us; lastly in its sentiments and diction; by preserving the ludicrous instead of
the sublime.   In the diction I think, burlesque itself may be
sometimes admitted; of which many instances will occur in
this work, as in the description of the battles, and some other
places not necessary to be pointed out to the classical reader;
for whose entertainment those parodies or burlesque imitations are chiefly calculated.

But tho' we have sometimes admitted this in our diction,
we have carefully excluded it from our sentiments and characters; for there it is never properly introduced, unless in
writings of the burlesque kind, which this is not intended to
be.   Indeed, no two species of writing can differ more widely
than the comic and the burlesque: for as the latter is ever the
exhibition of what is monstrous and unnatural, and where
our delight, if we examine it, arises from the surprising ab-

surdity, as in appropriating the manners of the highest to the lowest, or *è converso;* so in the former, we should ever confine ourselves strictly to nature, from the just imitation of which, will flow all the pleasure we can this way convey to a sensible reader. And perhaps, there is one reason, why a comic writer should of all others be the least excused for deviating from nature, since it may not be always so easy for a serious poet to meet with the great and the admirable; but life everywhere furnishes an accurate observer with the ridiculous.

I have hinted this little, concerning burlesque; because I have often heard that name given to performances, which have been truly of the comic kind, from the author's having sometimes admitted it in his diction only; which as it is the dress of poetry, doth like the dress of men establish characters, (the one of the whole poem, and the other of the whole man), in vulgar opinion, beyond any of their greater excellences: but surely, a certain drollery in style, where characters and sentiments are perfectly natural, no more constitutes the burlesque, than an empty pomp and dignity of words, where everything else is mean and low, can entitle any performance to the appellation of the true sublime.

And I apprehend, my Lord Shaftesbury's opinion of mere burlesque agrees with mine, when he asserts, " There is no such thing to be found in the writings of the antients." But perhaps I have less abhorrence than he professes for it: and that not because I have had some little success on the stage this way; but rather as it contributes more to exquisite mirth and laughter than any other; and these are probably more wholesome physic for the mind, and conduce better to purge away spleen, melancholy, and ill affections, than is generally imagined. Nay, I will appeal to common observation, whether the same companies are not found more full of good-humour and benevolence, after they have been sweetened for two or three hours with entertainments of this kind, than soured by a tragedy or a grave lecture.

But to illustrate all this by another science, in which, perhaps, we shall see the distinction more clearly and plainly: let us examine the works of a comic history-painter, with those performances which the Italians call *Caricatura,* where we shall find the greatest excellence of the former to consist in the exactest copy of nature; insomuch, that a judicious eye instantly rejects anything *outré;* any liberty which the painter hath taken with the features of that *alma mater.* Whereas in the *Caricatura* we allow all licence. Its aim is to exhibit monsters, not men; and all distortions and exaggerations whatever are within its proper province.

Now what Caricatura is in painting, Burlesque is in writing; and in the same manner the comic writer and painter correlate to each other. And here I shall observe, that as in the former, the painter seems to have the advantage; so it is in the latter infinitely on the side of the writer: for the Monstrous is much easier to paint than describe, and the Ridiculous to describe than paint.

And tho' perhaps this latter species doth not in either science so strongly affect and agitate the muscles as the other; yet it will be owned, I believe, that a more rational and useful pleasure arises to us from it. He who should call the ingenious Hogarth a burlesque painter, would, in my opinion, do him very little honour: for sure it is much easier, much less the subject of admiration, to paint a man with a nose, or any other feature of a preposterous size, or to expose him in some absurd or monstrous attitude, than to express the affections of men on canvas. It hath been thought a vast commendation of a painter to say his figures *seem to breathe;* but surely it is a much greater and nobler applause, *that they appear to think.*

But to return. The Ridiculous only, as I have before said, falls within my province in the present work. Nor will some explanation of this word be thought impertinent by the reader, if he considers how wonderfully it hath been mistaken, even by writers who have profess'd it: for to what but such a mistake, can we attribute the many attempts to ridicule the blackest villainies; and what is yet worse, the most dreadful calamities? What could exceed the absurdity of an author, who should write the comedy of Nero, with the merry incident of ripping up his mother's belly; or what would give a greater shock to humanity than an attempt to expose the miseries of poverty and distress to ridicule? And yet, the reader will not want much learning to suggest such instances to himself.

Besides, it may seem remarkable, that Aristotle, who is so fond and free of definitions, hath not thought proper to define the Ridiculous. Indeed, where he tells us it is proper to comedy, he hath remarked that villainy is not its object: but that he hath not, as I remember, positively asserted what is. Nor doth the Abbé Bellegarde, who hath written a treatise on this subject, tho' he shows us many species of it, once trace it to its fountain.

The only source of the true Ridiculous (as it appears to me) is affectation. But tho' it arises from one spring only, when we consider the infinite streams into which this one branches, we shall presently cease to admire at the copious field it affords to an observer. Now affectation proceeds from one of these two causes; vanity, or hypocrisy: for as vanity puts us on affecting false characters, in order to purchase applause; so hypocrisy sets us on an endeavour to avoid censure by concealing our vices under an appearance of their opposite virtues. And tho' these two causes are often confounded, (for they require some distinguishing;) yet, as they proceed from very different motives, so they are as clearly distinct in their operations: for indeed, the affectation which arises from vanity is nearer to truth than the other; as it hath not that violent repugnancy of nature to struggle with, which that of the hypocrite hath. It may be likewise noted, that affectation doth not imply an absolute negation of those qualities which are affected: and therefore, tho', when it proceeds from hypocrisy, it be nearly allied to deceit; yet when it comes from vanity only, it partakes of the nature of ostentation: for instance, the affectation of liberality in a vain man, differs visibly from the same affectation in the avaricious; for tho' the vain man is not what he would appear, or hath not the virtue he affects, to the degree he would be thought to have it; yet it sits less awkwardly on him than on the avaricious man, who is the very reverse of what he would seem to be.

From the discovery of this affectation arises the Ridiculous—which always strikes the reader with surprize and pleasure; and that in a higher and stronger degree when the affectation arises from hypocrisy, than when from vanity: for to discover any one to be the exact reverse of what he affects, is more surprizing, and consequently more ridiculous, than to find him a little deficient in the quality he desires the reputation of. I might observe that our Ben Jonson, who of all men understood the Ridiculous the best, hath chiefly used the hypocritical affectation.

Now from affectation only, the misfortunes and calamities of life, or the imperfections of nature, may become the objects of ridicule. Surely he hath a very ill-framed mind, who can look on ugliness, infirmity, or poverty, as ridiculous in themselves: nor do I believe any man living who meets a dirty fellow riding through the streets in a cart, is struck with an idea of the Ridiculous from it; but if he should see the same figure descend from his coach and six, or bolt from his chair with his hat under his arm, he would then begin to laugh, and with justice. In the same manner, were we to enter a poor house and behold a wretched family shivering with cold and languishing with hunger, it would not incline us to laughter, (at least we must have very diabolical natures, if it would): but should we discover there a grate, instead of coals, adorned with flowers, empty plate or china dishes on the side-board, or any other affectation of riches and finery either on their persons or in their furniture; we might then indeed be excused, for ridiculing so fantastical an appearance. Much less are natural imperfections the object of derision: but when ugliness aims at the applause of beauty, or lameness endeavours to display agility; it is then that these unfortunate circumstances, which at first moved our compassion, tend only to raise our mirth.

The poet carries this very far;

> None are for being what they are in fault,
> But for not being what they would be thought.

Where if the metre would suffer the word Ridiculous to close the first line, the thought would be rather more proper. Great vices are the proper objects of our detestation, smaller faults of our pity: but affectation appears to me the only true source of the Ridiculous

But perhaps it may be objected to me, that I have against

my own rules introduced vices, and of a very black kind into this work. To this I shall answer: First, that it is very difficult to pursue a series of human actions and keep clear from them. Secondly, that the vices to be found here, are rather the accidental consequences of some human frailty, or foible, than causes habitually existing in the mind. Thirdly, that they are never set forth as the objects of ridicule, but detestation. Fourthly, that they are never the principal figure at that time on the scene; lastly, they never produce the intended evil.

PREFACE TO THE
ENGLISH DICTIONARY

BY SAMUEL JOHNSON (1755)

IT IS the fate of those who toil at the lower employments of life, to be rather driven by the fear of evil, than attracted by the prospect of good; to be exposed to censure, without hope of praise; to be disgraced by miscarriage, or punished for neglect, where success would have been without applause, and diligence without reward.

Among these unhappy mortals is the writer of dictionaries; whom mankind have considered, not as the pupil, but the slave of science, the pioneer of literature, doomed only to remove rubbish and clear obstructions from the paths through which Learning and Genius press forward to conquest and glory, without bestowing a smile on the humble drudge that facilitates their progress. Every other author may aspire to praise; the lexicographer can only hope to escape reproach, and even this negative recompense has been yet granted to very few.

I have, notwithstanding this discouragement, attempted a Dictionary of the English Language, which, while it was employed in the cultivation of every species of literature, has itself been hitherto neglected; suffered to spread, under the direction of chance, into wild exuberance; resigned to the tyranny of time and fashion; and exposed to the corruptions of ignorance, and caprices of innovation.

For a sketch of Johnson's life, see the introduction to "Life of Addison" in the volume of English Essays. The interest of his preface to the great Dictionary need hardly be pointed out, since the work itself is a landmark in the history of our language. The letter to Chesterfield, short though it is, is a document of great importance in the freeing of literature from patronage, and is in itself a notable piece of literature. The preface to Johnson's edition of Shakespeare's plays not only explains the editor's conception of his task, but contains what is perhaps the best appreciation of the dramatist written in the eighteenth century.

When I took the first survey of my undertaking, I found our speech copious without order, and energetic without rule: wherever I turned my view, there was perplexity to be disentangled and confusion to be regulated; choice was to be made out of boundless variety, without any established principle of selection; adulterations were to be detected, without a settled test of purity; and modes of expression to be rejected or received, without the suffrages of any writers of classical reputation or acknowledged authority.

Having therefore no assistance but from general grammar, I applied myself to the perusal of our writers; and noting whatever might be of use to ascertain or illustrate any word or phrase, accumulated in time the materials of a dictionary, which, by degrees, I reduced to method, establishing to myself, in the progress of the work, such as experience and analogy suggested to me; experience, which practice and observation were continually increasing; and analogy, which, though in some words obscure, was evident in others.

In adjusting the ORTHOGRAPHY, which has been to this time unsettled and fortuitous, I found it necessary to distinguish those irregularities that are inherent in our tongue, and perhaps coeval with it, from others which the ignorance or negligence of later writers has produced. Every language has its anomalies, which though inconvenient, and in themselves once unnecessary, must be tolerated among the imperfections of human things, and which require only to be registered, that they may not be increased; and ascertained, that they may not be confounded: but every language has likewise its improprieties and absurdities, which it is the duty of the lexicographer to correct or proscribe.

As language was at its beginning merely oral, all words of necessary or common use were spoken before they were written; and while they were unfixed by any visible signs, must have been spoken with great diversity, as we now observe those who cannot read to catch sounds imperfectly, and utter them negligently. When this wild and barbarous jargon was first reduced to an alphabet, every penman endeavored to express, as he could, the sounds which he was accustomed to pronounce or to receive, and vitiated in writing such words as were already vitiated in speech. The powers of the letters, when they were applied to a new language, must have been vague and unsettled, and therefore different hands would exhibit the same sound by different combinations.

From this uncertain pronunciation arise in a great part the various dialects of the same country, which will always be observed to grow fewer, and less different, as books are multiplied; and from this arbitrary representation of sounds by letters proceeds that diversity of spelling observable in the Saxon remains, and I suppose in the first books of every nation, which perplexes or destroys analogy, and produces anomalous formations, which, being once incorporated can never be afterward dismissed or reformed.

Of this kind are the derivatives *length* from *long, strength* from *strong, darling* from *dear, breadth* from *broad,* from *dry, drought,* and from *high, height,* which Milton, in zeal for analogy, writes highth. ' Quid te exempta juvat spinis de pluribus una?' To change all would be too much, and to change one is nothing.

This uncertainty is most frequent in the vowels, which are so capriciously pronounced, and so differently modified, by accident or affectation, not only in every province, but in every mouth, that to them, as is well known to etymologists, little regard is to be shown in the deduction of one language from another.

Such defects are not errors in orthography, but spots of barbarity impressed so deep in the English language, that criticism can never wash them away: these, therefore, must be permitted to remain untouched; but many words have likewise been altered by accident, or depraved by ignorance, as the pronunciation of the vulgar has been weakly followed; and some still continue to be variously written, as authors differ in their care or skill: of these it was proper to inquire the true orthography, which I have always considered as depending on their derivation, and have therefore referred them to their original languages; thus I write *enchant, enchantment, enchanter,* after the French, and *incantation* after the Latin; thus *entire* is chosen rather than *intire,* because it passed to us not from the Latin *integer,* but from the French *entier.*

Of many words it is difficult to say whether they were immediately received from the Latin or the French, since at the time when we had dominions in France, we had Latin service in our churches. It is, however, my opinion that the French generally supplied us; for we have few Latin words, among the terms of domestic use, which are not French; but many French, which are very remote from Latin.

Even in words of which the derivation is apparent, I have been often obliged to sacrifice uniformity to custom; thus I write, in compliance with a numberless majority, *convey* and *inveigh, deceit* and *receipt, fancy* and *phantom;* sometimes the derivative varies from the primitive, as *explain* and *explanation, repeat* and *repetition.*

Some combinations of letters having the same power, are used indifferently without any discoverable reason of choice, as in *choak, choke; soap, sope; fewel, fuel,* and many others; which I have sometimes inserted twice, that those who search for them under either form, may not search in vain.

In examining the orthography of any doubtful word, the mode of spelling by which it is inserted in the series of the dictionary, is to be considered as that to which I give, perhaps not often rashly, the preference. I have left, in the examples, to every author his own practice unmolested, that the reader may balance suffrages, and judge between us: but this question is not always to be determined by reputed or by real learning; some men, intent upon greater things, have thought little on sounds and derivations; some, knowing in the ancient tongues, have neglected those in which our words are commonly to be sought. Thus Hammond writes *fecibleness* for *feasibleness,* because I suppose he imagined it derived immediately from the Latin; and some words, such as *dependant, dependent; dependance, dependence,* vary their final syllable, as one or other language is present to the writer.

In this part of the work, where caprice has long wantoned without control, and vanity sought praise by petty reformation, I have endeavored to proceed with a scholar's reverence for antiquity, and a grammarian's regard to the genius of our tongue. I have attempted few alterations, and among those few, perhaps the greater part is from the modern to the ancient practice; and I hope I may be allowed to recommend to those, whose thoughts have been perhaps employed too anxiously on verbal singularities, not to disturb, upon narrow views, or for minute propriety, the orthography of their fathers. It has been asserted, that for the law to be *known,* is of more importance than to be *right.* 'Change,' says Hooker, 'is not made without inconvenience, even from worse to better.' There is in constancy and stability a general and lasting advantage, which will always overbalance the slow improvements of gradual correction. Much less ought our written language to comply with the corruptions of oral utterance, or copy that which every variation of time or place makes different from itself, and imitate those changes, which will again be changed, while imitation is employed in observing them.

This recommendation of steadiness and uniformity does not proceed from an opinion that particular combinations of letters have much influence on human happiness; or that truth may not be successfully taught by modes of spelling fanciful and erroneous; I am not yet so lost in lexicography as to forget that 'words are the daughters of earth, and that things are the sons of heaven.' Language is only the instrument of science, and words are but the signs of ideas: I wish, however, that the instrument might be less apt to decay, and that signs might be permanent, like the things which they denote.

In settling the orthography, I have not wholly neglected the pronunciation, which I have directed, by printing an accent upon the acute or elevated syllable. It will sometimes be found that the accent is placed by the author quoted, on a different syllable from that marked in the alphabetical series; it is then to be understood, that custom has varied, or that the author has, in my opinion, pronounced wrong. Short directions are sometimes given where the sound of letters is irregular; and if they are sometimes omitted, defect in such minute observations will be more easily excused, than superfluity.

In the investigation, both of the orthography and signification of words, their ETYMOLOGY was necessarily to be considered, and they were therefore to be divided into primitives and derivatives. A primitive word is that which can be traced no further to any English root; thus *circumspect, circumvent, circumstance, delude, concave,* and *complicate,* though compounds in the Latin, are to us primitives. Derivatives, are all those that can be referred to any word in English of greater simplicity.

The derivatives I have referred to their primitives, with an accuracy sometimes needless; for who does not see that *remoteness* comes from *remote, lovely* from *love, concavity* from *concave,* and *demonstrative* from *demonstrate?* But this grammatical exuberance the scheme of my work did not allow me to repress. It is of great importance, in examining the general fabric of a language, to trace one word from another, by noting the usual modes of derivation and inflection; and uniformity must be preserved in systematical works; though sometimes at the expense of particular propriety.

Among other derivatives I have been careful to insert and elucidate the anomalous plurals of nouns and preterites of verbs, which in the Teutonic dialects are very frequent, and, though familiar to those who have always used them, interrupt and embarrass the learners of our language.

The two languages from which our primitives have been derived, are the Roman and Teutonic: under the Roman, I comprehend the French and provincial tongues; and under the Teutonic, range the Saxon, German, and all their kindred dialects. Most of our polysyllables are Roman, and our words of one syllable are very often Teutonic.

In assigning the Roman original, it has perhaps sometimes happened that I have mentioned only the Latin, when the word was borrowed from the French; and considering myself as employed only in the illustration of my own language, I have not been very careful to observe whether the Latin would be pure or barbarous, or the French elegant or obsolete.

For the Teutonic etymologies, I am commonly indebted to Junius and Skinner, the only names which I have forborne to quote when I copied their books; not that I might appropriate their labors or usurp their honors, but that I might spare perpetual repetition by one general acknowledgment. Of these, whom I ought not to mention but with the reverence due to instructors and benefactors, Junius appears to have excelled in extent of learning, and Skinner in rectitude of understanding. Junius was accurately skilled in all the northern languages, Skinner probably examined the ancient and remoter dialects only by occasional inspection into dictionaries; but the learning of Junius is often of no other use than to show him a track by which he may deviate from his purpose, to which Skinner always presses forward by the shortest way. Skinner is often ignorant, but never ridiculous: Junius is always full of knowledge; but his variety distracts his judgment, and his learning is very frequently disgraced by his absurdities.

The votaries of the northern muses will not perhaps easily restrain their indignation, when they find the name of Junius thus degraded by a disadvantageous comparison; but whatever reverence is due to his diligence, or his attainments, it can be no criminal degree of censoriousness to charge that etymologist with want of judgment, who can seriously derive *dream* from *drama,* because ' life is a drama and a drama is a dream '; and who declares with a tone of defiance, that no man can fail to derive *moan* from *µóvos, monos, single* or *solitary,* who considers that grief naturally loves to be alone.

Our knowledge of the northern literature is so scanty, that of words undoubtedly Teutonic, the original is not always to be found in an ancient language; and I have therefore inserted Dutch or German substitutes, which I consider not as radical, but parallel, not as the parents, but sisters of the English.

The words which are represented as thus related by descent or cognation, do not always agree in sense; for it is incident to words, as to their authors, to degenerate from their ancestors, and to change their manners when they change their country. It is sufficient, in etymological inquiries, if the senses of kindred words be found such as may easily pass into each other, or such as may both be referred to one general idea.

The etymology, so far as it is yet known, was easily found

in the volumes, where it is particularly and professedly delivered; and, by proper attention to the rules of derivation, the orthography was soon adjusted. But to COLLECT THE WORDS of our language was a task of greater difficulty: the deficiency of dictionaries was immediately apparent; and when they were exhausted, what was yet wanting must be sought by fortuitous and unguided excursions into books and gleaned as industry should find, or chance should offer it, in the boundless chaos of a living speech. My search, however, has been either skilful or lucky; for I have much augmented the vocabulary.

As my design was a dictionary, common or appellative, I have omitted all words which have relation to proper names; such as *Arian, Socinian, Calvinist, Benedictine, Mahometan;* but have retained those of a more general nature, as *Heathen, Pagan.*

Of the terms of art I have received such as could be found either in books of science or technical dictionaries; and have often inserted, from philosophical writers, words which are supported perhaps only by a single authority, and which, being not admitted into general use, stand yet as candidates or probationers, and must depend for their adoption on the suffrage of futurity. The words which our authors have introduced by their knowledge of foreign languages, or ignorance of their own, by vanity or wantonness, by compliance with fashion or lust of innovation, I have registered as they occurred, though commonly only to censure them, and warn others against the folly of naturalizing useless foreigners to the injury of the natives.

I have not rejected any by design, merely because they were unnecessary or exuberant; but have received those which by different writers have been differently formed, as *viscid,* and *viscidity, viscous,* and *viscosity.*

Compounded or double words I have seldom noted, except when they obtain a signification different from that which the components have in their simple state.

Thus *highwayman, woodman,* and *horsecourser,* require an explanation; but of *thieflike;* or *coachdriver,* no notice was needed, because the primitives contain the meaning of the compounds.

Words arbitrarily formed by a constant and settled analogy, like diminutive adjectives in *ish, as greenish, bluish;* adverbs in *ly,* as *dully, openly;* substantives in *ness,* as *vileness, faultiness;* were less diligently sought, and many sometimes have been omitted, when I had no authority that invited me to insert them; not that they are not genuine, and regular offsprings of English roots, but because their relation to the primitive being always the same, their signification cannot be mistaken.

The verbal nouns in *ing,* such as the *keeping* of the *castle,* the *leading* of the *army,* are always neglected, or placed only to illustrate the sense of the verb, except when they signify things as well as actions, and have therefore a plural number, as *dwelling, living;* or have an absolute and abstract signification, as *coloring, painting, learning.*

The participles are likewise omitted, unless, by signifying rather habit or quality than action, they take the nature of adjectives; as a *thinking* man, a man of prudence; a *pacing* horse, a horse that can pace: these I have ventured to call *participial adjectives.* But neither are these always inserted, because they are commonly to be understood without any danger of mistake, by consulting the verb.

Obsolete words are admitted when they are found in authors not obsolete, or when they have any force or beauty that may deserve revival.

As composition is one of the chief characteristics of a language, I have endeavored to make some reparation for the universal negligence of my predecessors, by inserting great numbers of compounded words, as may be found under *after, fore, new, night, fair,* and many more. These, numerous as they are, might be multiplied, but that use and curiosity are here satisfied, and the frame of our language and modes of our combination amply discovered.

Of some forms of composition, such as that by which *re* is prefixed to note *repetition,* and *un* to signify *contrariety* or *privation,* all the examples cannot be accumulated, because the use of these particles, if not wholly arbitrary, is so little limited, that they are hourly affixed to new words as occasion requires, or is imagined to require them.

There is another kind of composition more frequent in

our language than perhaps in any other, from which arises
to foreigners the greatest difficulty. We modify the signification of many verbs by a particle subjoined; as to *come
off,* to escape by a fetch; to *fall on,* to attack; *fall off,* to
apostatize; to *break off,* to stop abruptly; to *bear out,* to
justify; *to fall in,* to comply; to *give over,* to cease; to *set
off,* to embellish; to *set in,* to begin a continual tenor; to *set
out,* to begin a course or journey; to *take off,* to copy; with
innumerable expressions of the same kind, of which some
appear wildly irregular, being so far distant from the sense
of the simple words, that no sagacity will be able to trace
the steps by which they arrived at the present use. These I
have noted with great care; and though I cannot flatter myself that the collection is complete, I believe I have so far
assisted the students of our language that this kind of phraseology will be no longer insuperable; and the combinations
of verbs and particles, by chance omitted, will be easily explained by comparison with those that may be found.

Many words yet stand supported only by the name of
Bailey, Ainsworth, Philips, or the contracted *Dict.* for Dictionaries, subjoined; of these I am not always certain that
they are read in any book but the works of lexicographers.
Of such I have omitted many, because I had never read
them; and many I have inserted, because they may perhaps
exist, though they have escaped my notice: they are, however, to be yet considered as resting only upon the credit of
former dictionaries. Others, which I considered as useful, or
know to be proper, though I could not at present support
them by authorities, I have suffered to stand upon my own
attestation, claiming the same privilege with my predecessors, of being sometimes credited without proof.

The words, thus selected and disposed, are grammatically
considered; they are referred to the different parts of speech;
traced when they are irregularly inflected, through their
various terminations; and illustrated by observations, not
indeed of great or striking importance, separately considered,
but necessary to the elucidation of our language, and hitherto
neglected or forgotten by English grammarians.

That part of my work on which I expect malignity most
frequently to fasten, is the EXPLANATION; in which I cannot

hope to satisfy those, who are perhaps not inclined to be pleased, since I have not always been able to satisfy myself. To interpret a language by itself is very difficult; many words cannot be explained by synonimes, because the idea signified by them has not more than one appellation; nor by paraphrase, because simple ideas cannot be described. When the nature of things is unknown, or the notion unsettled and indefinite, and various in various minds, the words by which such notions are conveyed, or such things denoted, will be ambiguous and perplexed. And such is the fate of hapless lexicography, that not only darkness, but light impedes and distresses it; things may be not only too little, but too much known, to be happily illustrated. To explain, requires the use of terms less abstruse than that which is to be explained, and such terms cannot always be found; for as nothing can be proved but by supposing something intuitively known, and evident without proof, so nothing can be defined but by the use of words too plain to admit a definition.

Other words there are, of which the sense is too subtle and evanescent to be fixed in a paraphrase; such are all those which are by the grammarians termed expletives, and, in dead languages, are suffered to pass for empty sounds, of no other use than to fill a verse, or to modulate a period, but which are easily perceived in living tongues to have power and emphasis, though it be sometimes such as no other form of expression can convey.

My labor has likewise been much increased by a class of verbs too frequent in the English language, of which the signification is so loose and general, the use so vague and indeterminate, and the senses detorted so widely from the first idea, that it is hard to trace them through the maze of variation, to catch them on the brink of utter inanity, to circumscribe them by any limitations, or interpret them by any words of distinct and settled meaning; such are *bear, break, come, cast, full, get, give, do, put, set, go, run, make, take, turn, throw.* If of these the whole power is not accurately delivered, it must be remembered, that while our language is yet living, and variable by the caprice of every one that speaks it, these words are hourly shifting their relations, and can no more be ascertained in a dictionary, than a grove, in the agitation of a storm, can be accurately delineated from its picture in the water.

The particles are among all nations applied with so great latitude, that they are not easily reducible under any regular scheme of explication: this difficulty is not less, nor perhaps greater, in English, than in other languages. I have labored them with diligence, I hope with success; such at least as can be expected in a task, which no man, however learned or sagacious, has yet been able to perform.

Some words there are which I cannot explain, because I do not understand them; these might have been omitted very often with little inconvenience, but I would not so far indulge my vanity as to decline this confession: for when Tully owns himself ignorant whether *lessus,* in the twelve tables, means a *funeral song,* or *mourning garment;* and Aristotle doubts whether οὐρεύς in the *Iliad* signifies a *mule, or muleteer,* I may surely without shame, leave some obscurities to happier industry, or future information.

The rigor of interpretative lexicography requires that *the explanation,* and *the word explained should be always reciprocal;* this I have always endeavoured, but could not always attain. Words are seldom exactly synonymous; a new term was not introduced, but because the former was thought inadequate: names, therefore, have often many ideas, but few ideas have many names. It was then necessary to use the proximate word, for the deficiency of single terms can very seldom be supplied by circumlocution; nor is the inconvenience great of such mutilated interpretations, because the sense may easily be collected entire from the examples.

In every word of extensive use, it was requisite to mark the progress of its meaning, and show by what gradations of intermediate sense it has passed from its primitive to its remote and accidental signification; so that every foregoing explanation should tend to that which follows, and the series be regularly concatenated from the first notion to the last.

This is specious, but not always practicable; kindred senses may be so interwoven, that the perplexity cannot be disentangled, nor any reason be assigned why one should be ranged before the other. When the radical idea branches out into parallel ramifications, how can a consecutive series be formed of senses in their nature collateral? The shades of meaning sometimes pass imperceptibly into each other, so that though on one side they apparently differ, yet it is impossible to mark the point of contact. Ideas of the same race, though not exactly alike, are sometimes so little different, that no words can express the dissimilitude, though the mind easily perceives it when they are exhibited together; and sometimes there is such a confusion of acceptations, that discernment is wearied and distinction puzzled, and perseverance herself hurries to an end, by crowding together what she cannot separate.

These complaints of difficulty will, by those that have never considered words beyond their popular use, be thought only the jargon of a man willing to magnify his labors, and procure veneration to his studies by involution and obscurity. But every art is obscure to those that have not learned it; this uncertainty of terms, and commixture of ideas, is well known to those who have joined philosophy with grammar; and if I have not expressed them very clearly, it must be remembered that I am speaking of that which words are insufficient to explain.

The original sense of words is often driven out of use by their metaphorical acceptations, yet must be inserted for the sake of a regular origination. Thus I know not whether *ardor* is used for *material heat,* or whether *flagrant,* in English, ever signifies the same with *burning;* yet such are the primitive ideas of these words, which are therefore set first, though without examples, that the figurative senses may be commodiously deduced.

Such is the exuberance of signification which many words have obtained, that it was scarcely possible to collect all their senses; sometimes the meaning of derivatives must be sought in the mother term, and sometimes deficient explanations of the primitive may be supplied in the train of derivation. In any case of doubt or difficulty, it will be always proper to examine all the words of the same race; for some words are slightly passed over to avoid repetition, some admitted easier and clearer explanation than others, and all will be better understood, as they are considered in greater variety of structures and relations.

All the interpretations of words are not written with the same skill, or the same happiness: things equally easy in themselves, are not all equally easy to any single mind. Every writer of a long word commits errors, where there appears neither ambiguity to mislead, nor obscurity to confound him; and in a search like this, many felicities of expression will be casually overlooked, many convenient parallels will be forgotten, and many particulars will admit improvement from a mind utterly unequal to the whole performance.

But many seeming faults are to be imputed rather to the nature of the undertaking, than the negligence of the performer. Thus some explanations are unavoidably reciprocal or circular, as *hind, the female of the stag; stag, the male of the hind:* sometimes easier words are changed into harder, as *burial* into *sepulture, or interment, drier* into *desiccative, dryness* into *siccity* or *aridity, fit* into *paroxysm;* for the easiest word, whatever it be, can never be translated into one more easy. But easiness and difficulty are merely relative; and if the present prevalence of our language should invite foreigners to this Dictionary, many will be assisted by those words which now seem only to increase or produce obscurity. For this reason I have endeavoured frequently to join a Teutonic and Roman interpretation, as to *cheer,* to *gladden* or *exhilarate,* that every learner of English may be assisted by his own tongue.

The solution of all difficulties, and the supply of all defects must be sought in the examples, subjoined to the various senses of each word, and ranged according to the time of their authors.

When I first collected these authorities, I was desirous that every quotation should be useful to some other end than the illustration of a word; I therefore extracted from philosophers principles of science; from historians remarkable facts; from chymists complete processes; from divines striking exhortations; and from poets beautiful descriptions. Such is design, while it is yet at a distance from execution.

When the time called upon me to range this accumulation of elegance and wisdom into an alphabetical series, I soon discovered that the bulk of my volumes would fright away the student, and was forced to depart from my scheme of including all that was pleasing or useful in English literature, and reduce my transcripts very often to clusters of words, in which scarcely any meaning is retained; thus to the weariness of copying, I was condemned to add the vexation of expunging. Some passages I have yet spared, which may relieve the labor of verbal searches, and intersperse with verdure and flowers the dusty desarts of barren philology.

The examples, thus mutilated, are no longer to be considered as conveying the sentiments or doctrine of their authors; the word for the sake of which they are inserted, with all its appendant clauses, has been carefully preserved; but it may sometimes happen, by hasty detruncation, that the general tendency of the sentence may be changed: the divine may desert his tenets, or the philosopher his system.

Some of the examples have been taken from writers who were never mentioned as masters of elegance, or models of style; but words must be sought where they are used; and in what pages, eminent for purity, can terms of manufacture or agriculture be found? Many quotations serve no other purpose than that of proving the bare existence of words, and are therefore selected with less scrupulousness than those which are to teach their structures and relations.

My purpose was to admit no testimony of living authors, that I might not be misled by partiality, and that none of my contemporaries might have reason to complain; nor have I departed from this resolution, but when some performance of uncommon excellence excited my veneration, when my memory supplied me, from late books, with an example that was wanting, or when my heart, in the tenderness of friendship, solicited admission for a favorite name.

So far have I been from any care to grace my pages with modern decorations, that I have studiously endeavored to collect examples and authorities from the writers before the Restoration, whose works I regard as the ' wells of English undefiled,' as the pure sources of genuine diction. Our language, for almost a century, has, by the concurrence of many causes, been gradually departing from its original Teutonic character and deviating towards a Gallic structure and phraseology, from which it ought to be our endeavor to recall it, by making our ancient volumes the ground-work of style, admitting among the additions of later times, only such as may supply real deficiencies, such as are readily adopted by the genius of our tongue, and incorporate easily with our native idioms.

But as every language has a time of rudeness antecedent to perfection, as well as of false refinement and declension, I have been cautious lest my zeal for antiquity might drive me into times too remote, and crowd my book with words now no longer understood. I have fixed Sidney's work for the boundary, beyond which I make few excursions. From the authors which rose in the time of Elizabeth, a speech might be formed adequate to all the purposes of use and elegance. If the language of theology were extracted from Hooker and the translation of the Bible; the terms of natural knowledge from Bacon; the phrases of policy, war, and navigation from Raleigh; the dialect of poetry and fiction from Spenser and Sidney; and the diction of common life from Shakespeare, few ideas would be lost to mankind, for want of English words in which they might be expressed.

It is not sufficient that a word is found, unless it be so combined as that its meaning is apparently determined by the tract and tenor of the sentence; such passages I have therefore chosen, and when it happened that any author gave a definition of a term, or such an explanation as is equivalent to a definition, I have placed his authority as a supplement to my own, without regard to the chronological order that is otherwise observed.

Some words, indeed, stand unsupported by any authority, but they are commonly derivative nouns or adverbs, formed from their primitives by regular and constant analogy, or names of things seldom occurring in books, or words of which I have reason to doubt the existence.

There is more danger of censure from the multiplicity than paucity of examples; authorities will sometimes seem to have been accumulated without necessity or use, and perhaps some will be found, which might, without loss, have been omitted. But a work of this kind is not hastily to be charged with superfluities; those quotations, which to careless or unskillful perusers appear only to repeat the same sense, will often exhibit, to a more accurate examiner, diversities of signification, or, at least, afford different shades of the same meaning: one will show the word applied to persons, another to things; one will express an ill, another a good, and a third a neutral sense; one will prove the expression genuine from an ancient author; another will show it elegant from a modern: a doubtful authority is corroborated by another of more credit; an ambiguous sentence is ascertained by a passage clear and determinate: the word, how often soever repeated, appears with new associates and in different combinations, and every quotation contributes something to the stability or enlargement of the language.

When words are used equivocally, I receive them in either sense; when they are metaphorical, I adopt them in their primitive acceptation.

I have sometimes, though rarely, yielded to the temptation of exhibiting a genealogy of sentiments, by showing how one author copied the thoughts and diction of another: such quotations are indeed little more than repetitions, which might justly be censured, did they not gratify the mind, by affording a kind of intellectual history.

The various syntactical structures occurring in the examples have been carefully noted; the license or negligence with which many words have been hitherto used, has made our style capricious and indeterminate; when the different combinations of the same word are exhibited together, the preference is readily given to propriety, and I have often endeavored to direct the choice.

Thus have I labored by settling the orthography, displaying the analogy, regulating the structures, and ascertaining the signification of English words, to perform all the parts of a faithful lexicographer: but I have not always executed my own scheme, or satisfied my own expectations. The work, whatever proofs of diligence and attention it may exhibit, is yet capable of many improvements: the orthography which I recommend is still controvertible; the etymology which I adopt is uncertain, and perhaps frequently erroneous; the explanations are sometimes too much contracted, and sometimes too much diffused, the significations are distinguished rather with subtlety than skill, and the attention is harassed with unnecessary minuteness.

The examples are too often injudiciously truncated, and perhaps sometimes—I hope very rarely—alleged in a mistaken sense; for in making this collection I trusted more to memory, than, in a state of disquiet and embarrassment, memory can contain, and purposed to supply at the review what was left incomplete in the first transcription.

Many terms appropriated to particular occupations, though necessary and significant, are undoubtedly omitted; and of the words most studiously considered and exemplified, many senses have escaped observation.

Yet these failures, however frequent, may admit extenuation and apology. To have attempted much is always laudable, even when the enterprise is above the strength that undertakes it: to rest below his own aim is incident to every one whose fancy is active, and whose views are comprehensive; nor is any man satisfied with himself because he has done much, but because he can conceive little. When first I engaged in this work, I resolved to leave neither words nor things unexamined, and pleased myself with a prospect of the hours which I should revel away in feasts of literature, the obscure recesses of northern learning which I should enter and ransack, the treasures with which I expected every search into those neglected mines to reward my labor, and the triumph with which I should display my acquisitions to mankind. When I had thus inquired into the original of words, I resolved to show likewise my attention to things; to pierce deep into every science, to inquire the nature of every substance of which I inserted the name, to limit every idea by a definition strictly logical, and exhibit every production of art or nature in an accurate description, that my book might be in place of all other dictionaries whether appellative or technical. But these were the dreams of a poet doomed at last to wake a lexicographer. I soon found that it is too late to look for instruments, when the work calls for execution, and that whatever abilities I had brought to my task, with those I must finally perform it. To deliberate whenever I doubted, to inquire whenever I was ignorant, would have protracted the undertaking without end, and, perhaps, without much improvement; for I did not find by my first experiments, that what I had not of my own was easily to be obtained: I saw that one inquiry only gave occasion to another, that book referred to book, that to search was not always to find, and to find was not always to be informed; and that thus to pursue perfection, was, like the first inhabitants of Arcadia, to chase the sun, which, when they had reached the hill where he seemed to rest, was still beheld at the same distance from them.

I then contracted my design, determining to confide in myself, and no longer to solicit auxiliaries which produced more incumbrance than assistance; by this I obtained at least one advantage, that I set limits to my work, which would in time be ended, though not completed.

Despondency has never so far prevailed as to depress me to negligence; some faults will at last appear to be the effects of anxious diligence and persevering activity. The nice and subtle ramifications of meaning were not easily avoided by a mind intent upon accuracy, and convinced of the necessity of disentangling combinations, and separating similitudes. Many of the distinctions which to common readers appear useless and idle, will be found real and important by men versed in the school philosophy, without which no dictionary can ever be accurately compiled, or skillfully examined.

Some senses, however, there are, which, though not the same, are yet so nearly allied, that they are often confounded. Most men think indistinctly, and therefore cannot speak with exactness; and consequently some examples might be indifferently put to either signification: this uncertainty is not to be imputed to me, who do not form, but register the language; who do not teach men how they should think, but relate how they have hitherto expressed their thoughts.

The imperfect sense of some examples I lamented, but could not remedy, and hope they will be compensated by innumerable passages selected with propriety, and preserved with exactness; some shining with sparks of imagination, and some replete with treasures of wisdom.

The orthography and etymology, though imperfect, are not imperfect for want of care, but because care will not always be successful, and recollection or information come too late for use.

That many terms of art and manufacture are omitted, must be frankly acknowledged; but for this defect I may boldly allege that it is unavoidable; I could not visit caverns to learn the miner's language, nor take a voyage to perfect my skill in the dialect of navigation, nor visit the warehouses of merchants, and shops of artificers, to gain the names of wares, tools, and operations, of which no mention is found in books; what favorable accident or easy inquiry brought within my reach, has not been neglected; but it had been a hopeless labor to glean up words, by courting living information, and contesting with the sullenness of one, and the roughness of another.

To furnish the Academicians *della Crusca* with words of this kind, a series of comedies called *La Fiera,* or *The Fair,* was professedly written by Buonaroti; but I had no such assistant, and therefore was content to want what they must have wanted likewise, had they not luckily been so supplied.

Nor are all words which are not found in the vocabulary, to be lamented as omissions. Of the laborious and mercantile part of the people, the diction is in a great measure casual and mutable; many of their terms are formed for some temporay or local convenience, and though current at certain times and places, are in others utterly unknown. This fugitive cant, which is always in a state of increase or decay, cannot be regarded as any part of the durable materials of a language, and therefore must be suffered to perish with other things unworthy of preservation.

Care will sometimes betray to the appearance of negligence. He that is catching opportunities which seldom occur, will suffer those to pass by unregarded, which he expects hourly to return; he that is searching for rare and remote things, will neglect those that are obvious and familiar: thus many of the most common and cursory words have been inserted with little illustration, because in gathering the authorities, I forebore to copy those which I thought likely to occur whenever they were wanted. It is remarkable that, in reviewing my collection, I found the word *sea* unexemplified.

Thus it happens, that in things difficult there is danger from ignorance, and in things easy, from confidence; the mind, afraid of greatness, and disdainful of littleness, hastily withdraws herself from painful searches, and passes with scornful rapidity over tasks not adequate to her powers; sometimes too secure for caution, and again too anxious for vigorous effort; sometimes idle in a plain path, and sometimes distracted in labyrinths, and dissipated by different intentions.

A large work is difficult because it is large, even though all its parts might singly be performed with facility; where there are many things to be done, each must be allowed its share of time and labor, in the proportion only which it bears to the whole; nor can it be expected, that the stones which form the dome of a temple, should be squared and polished like the diamond of a ring.

Of the event of this work, for which, having labored it with so much application, I cannot but have some degree of parental fondness, it is natural to form conjectures. Those who have been persuaded to think well of my design, will require that it should fix our language, and put a stop to those alterations which time and chance have hitherto been suffered to make in it without opposition. With this consequence I will confess that I flattered myself for a while; but now begin to fear that I have indulged expectation which neither reason nor experience can justify. When we see men grow old and die at a certain time one after another, from century to century, we laugh at the elixir that promises to prolong life to a thousand years; and with equal justice may the lexicographer be derided, who being able to produce no example of a nation that has preserved their words and phrases from mutability, shall imagine that his dictionary can embalm his language, and secure it from corruption and decay, that it is in his power to change sublunary nature, and clear the world at once from folly, vanity, and affectation.

With this hope, however, academies have been instituted, to guard the avenues of their languages, to retain fugitives, and repulse intruders; but their vigilance and activity have hitherto been vain; sounds are too volatile and subtile for legal restraints; to enchain syllables, and to lash the wind, are equally the undertakings of pride, unwilling to measure its desires by its strength. The French language has visibly changed under the inspection of the Academy; the style of Amelot's translation of Father Paul is observed by Le Courayer to be *un peu passé;* and no Italian will maintain that the diction of any modern writer is not perceptibly different from that of Boccace, Machiavel, or Caro.

Total and sudden transformations of a language seldom happen; conquests and migrations are now very rare: but there are other causes of change, which, though slow in their operation, and invisible in their progress, are perhaps as much superior to human resistance, as the revolutions of the sky, or intumescence of the tide. Commerce, however necessary, however lucrative, as it depraves the manners, corrupts the language; they that have frequent intercourse with strangers, to whom they endeavor to accommodate themselves, must in time learn a mingled dialect, like the jargon which serves the traffickers on the Mediterranean and Indian coasts. This will not always be confined to the exchange, the warehouse, or the port, but will be communicated by degrees to other ranks of the people, and be at last incorporated with the current speech.

There are likewise internal causes equally forcible. The language most likely to continue long without alterations, would be that of a nation raised a little, and but a little, above barbarity, secluded from strangers, and totally employed in procuring the conveniences of life; either without books, or, like some of the Mahometan countries, with every few: men thus busied and unlearned, having only such words as common use requires, would perhaps long continue to express the same notions by the same signs. But no such constancy can be expected in a people polished by arts, and classed by subordination, where one part of the community is sustained and accommodated by the labor of the other. Those who have much leisure to think, will always be enlarging the stock of ideas; and every increase of knowledge, whether real or fancied, will produce new words, or combination of words. When the mind is unchained from necessity, it will range after convenience; when it is left at large in the fields of speculation, it will shift opinions; as any custom is disused, the words that expressed it must perish with it; as any opinion grows popular, it will innovate speech in the same proportion as it alters practice.

As by the cultivation of various sciences a language is amplified, it will be more furnished with words deflected from their original sense; the geometrician will talk of a courtier's zenith or the eccentric virtue of a wild hero, and the physician, of sanguine expectations and phlegmatic delays. Copiousness of speech will give opportunities to capricious choice, by which some words will be preferred, and others degraded; vicissitudes of fashion will enforce the use of new, or extend the signification of known terms. The tropes of poetry will make hourly encroachments, and the metaphorical will become the current sense: pronunciation will be varied by levity or ignorance, and the pen must at length comply with the tongue; illiterate writers will, at one time or other, by public infatuation, rise into renown, who, not knowing the original import of words, will use them with colloquial licentiousness, confound distinction, and forget propriety. As politeness increases, some expressions will be considered as too gross and vulgar for the delicate, others as too formal and ceremonious for the gay and airy; new phrases are therefore adopted, which must for the same reasons be in time dismissed. Swift, in his petty treatise on the English language, allows that new words must sometimes be introduced, but proposes that none should be suffered to become obsolete. But what makes a word obsolete, more than general agreement to forbear it? and how shall it be continued, when it conveys an offensive idea, or recalled again into the mouths of mankind, when it has once become unfamiliar by disuse, and unpleasing by unfamiliarity?

There is another cause of alteration more prevalent than any other, which yet in the present state of the world cannot be obviated. A mixture of two languages will produce a third distinct from both, and they will always be mixed, where the chief parts of education, and the most conspicuous accomplishment, is skill in ancient or in foreign tongues. He that has long cultivated another language, will find its words and combinations crowd upon his memory; and haste and negligence, refinement and affectation, will obtrude borrowed terms and exotic expressions.

The great pest of speech is frequency of translation. No book was ever turned from one language into another, without imparting something of its native idiom; this is the most mischievous and comprehensive innovation; single words may enter by thousands, and the fabric of the tongue continue the same; but new phraseology changes much at once; it alters not the single stones of the building, but the order of the columns. If an academy should be established for the cultivation of our style—which I, who can never wish to see dependence multiplied, hope the spirit of English liberty will hinder or destroy—let them, instead of compiling grammars and dictionaries, endeavor, with all their influence, to stop the license of translators, whose idleness and ignorance, if it be suffered to proceed, will reduce us to babble a dialect of France.

If the changes that we fear be thus irresistible, what remains but to acquiesce with silence, as in the other insurmountable distresses of humanity? It remains that we retard what we cannot repel, that we palliate what we cannot cure. Life may be lengthened by care, though death cannot be ultimately defeated: tongues, like governments, have a natural tendency to degeneration; we have long preserved our constitution, let us make some struggles for our language.

In hope of giving longevity to that which its own nature forbids to be immortal, I have devoted this book, the labor of years, to the honor of my country, that we may no longer yield the palm of philology, without a contest, to the nations

of the continent. The chief glory of every people arises
from its authors: whether I shall add any thing by my own
writings to the reputation of English literature, must be left
to time: much of my life has been lost under the pressures
of disease; much has been trifled away; and much has always been spent in provision for the day that was passing
over me; but I shall not think my employment useless or
ignoble, if by my assistance foreign nations, and distant ages,
gain access to the propagators of knowledge, and understand
the teachers of truth; if my labors afford light to the re-
positories of science, and add celebrity to Bacon, to Hooker,
to Milton, and to Boyle.

When I am animated by this wish, I look with pleasure on
my book, however defective, and deliver it to the world with
the spirit of a man that has endeavored well. That it will
immediately become popular I have not promised to myself:
a few wild blunders, and risible absurdities, from which no
work of such multiplicity was ever free, may for a time
furnish folly with laughter, and harden ignorance into contempt; but useful diligence will at last prevail, and there
never can be wanting some who distinguish desert; who will
consider that no dictionary of a living tongue ever can be
perfect, since, while it is hastening to publication, some
words are budding, and some falling away; that a whole life
cannot be spent upon syntax and etymology, and that even a
whole life would not be sufficient; that he, whose design
includes whatever language can express, must often speak
of what he does not understand; that a writer will sometimes be hurried by eagerness to the end, and sometimes
faint with weariness under a task which Scaliger compares
to the labors of the anvil and the mine; that what is obvious
is not always known, and what is known is not always
present; that sudden fits of inadvertency will surprise
vigilance, slight avocations will seduce attention, and casual
eclipses of the mind will darken learning; and that the
writer shall often in vain trace his memory at the moment
of need, for that which yesterday he knew with intuitive
readiness, and which will come uncalled into his thoughts
to-morrow.

In this work, when it shall be found that much is omitted,

let it not be forgotten that much likewise is performed; and though no book was ever spared out of tenderness to the author, and the world is little solicitous to know whence proceed the faults of that which it condemns; yet it may gratify curiosity to inform it, that the English Dictionary was written with little assistance of the learned, and without any patronage of the great; not in the soft obscurities of retirement, or under the shelter of academic bowers, but amidst inconvenience and distraction, in sickness and in sorrow. It may repress the triumph of malignant criticism to observe, that if our language is not here fully displayed, I have only failed in an attempt which no human powers have hitherto completed. If the lexicons of ancient tongues, now immutably fixed, and comprised in a few volumes, be yet, after the toil of successive ages, inadequate and delusive; if the aggregated knowledge, and co-operating diligence of the Italian academicians, did not secure them from the censure of Beni; if the embodied critics of France, when fifty years had been spent upon their work, were obliged to change its economy, and give their second edition another form, I may surely be contented without the praise of perfection, which, if I could obtain, in this gloom of solitude, what would it avail me? I have protracted my work till most of those whom I wished to please have sunk into the grave, and success and miscarriage are empty sounds: I therefore dismiss it with frigid tranquillity, having little to fear or hope from censure or from praise.

TO THE RIGHT HONORABLE THE EARL OF CHESTERFIELD

February 7, 1755.

My Lord:

I have lately been informed by the proprietor of *The World*, that two papers, in which my *Dictionary* is recommended to the public, were written by your Lordship. To be so distinguished is an honor which, being very little accustomed to favours from the great, I know not well how to receive, or in what terms to acknowledge.

When, upon some slight encouragement, I first visited your Lordship, I was overpowered, like the rest of mankind, by the enchantment of your address; and I could not forbear to wish that I might boast myself 'Le vainqueur du vainqueur de la terre'; that I might obtain that regard for which I saw the world contending; but I found my attendance so little encouraged, that neither pride nor modesty would suffer me to continue it. When I had once addressed your Lordship in public, I had exhausted all the art of pleasing which a retired and uncourtly scholar can possess. I had done all that I could; and no man is well pleased to have his all neglected, be it ever so little.

Seven years, my Lord, have now passed, since I waited in your outward rooms, or was repulsed from your door; during which time I have been pushing on my work through difficulties, of which it is useless to complain, and have brought it at last to the verge of publication, without one act of assistance, one word of encouragement, or one smile of favor. Such treatment I did not expect, for I never had a Patron before.

The shepherd in Virgil grew at last acquainted with Love, and found him a native of the rocks.

Is not a Patron, my Lord, one who looks with unconcern on a man struggling for life in the water, and, when he has reached ground, encumbers him with help? The notice which you have been pleased to take of my labors, had it been early, had been kind; but it has been delayed till I am indifferent, and cannot enjoy it; till I am solitary, and cannot impart it; till I am known, and do not want it. I hope it is no very cynical asperity not to confess obligations where no benefit has been received, or to be unwilling that the Public should consider me as owing that to a Patron, which Providence has enabled me to do for myself.

Having carried on my work thus far with so little obligation to any favorer of learning, I shall not be disappointed though I should conclude it, if less be possible, with less; for I have been long wakened from that dream of hope, in which I once boasted myself with so much exultation,

My Lord, Your Lordship's most humble,

Most obedient servant, SAM. JOHNSON.

PREFACE TO SHAKESPEARE

BY SAMUEL JOHNSON. (1765)

THAT praises are without reason lavished on the dead, and that the honours due only to excellence are paid to antiquity, is a complaint likely to be always continued by those, who, being able to add nothing to truth, hope for eminence from the heresies of paradox; or those, who, being forced by disappointment upon consolatory expedients, are willing to hope from posterity what the present age refuses, and flatter themselves that the regard which is yet denied by envy, will be at last bestowed by time.

Antiquity, like every other quality that attracts the notice of mankind, has undoubtedly votaries that reverence it, not from reason, but from prejudice. Some seem to admire indiscriminately whatever has been long preserved, without considering that time has sometimes co-operated with chance; all perhaps are more willing to honour past than present excellence; and the mind contemplates genius through the shades of age, as the eye surveys the sun through artificial opacity. The great contention of criticism is to find the faults of the moderns, and the beauties of the ancients. While an author is yet living we estimate his powers by his worst performance, and when he is dead, we rate them by his best.

To works, however, of which the excellence is not absolute and definite, but gradual and comparative; to works not raised upon principles demonstrative and scientifick, but appealing wholly to observation and experience, no other test can be applied than length of duration and continuance of esteem. What mankind have long possessed they have often examined and compared; and if they persist to value the possession, it is because frequent comparisons have confirmed opinion in its favour. As among the works of nature no man can properly call a river deep, or a mountain high, without the knowledge of many mountains, and many rivers; so in the productions of genius, nothing can be stiled excellent till it has been compared with other works of the same kind. Demonstration immediately displays its power, and has nothing to hope or fear from the flux of years; but works tentative and experimental must be estimated by their proportion to the general and collective ability of man, as it is discovered in a long succession of endeavours. Of the first building that was raised, it might be with certainty determined that it was round or square; but whether it was spacious or lofty must have been referred to time. The Pythagorean scale of numbers was at once discovered to be perfect; but the poems of *Homer* we yet know not to transcend the common limits of human intelligence, but by remarking, that nation after nation, and century after century, has been able to do little more than transpose his incidents, new-name his characters, and paraphrase his sentiments.

The reverence due to writings that have long subsisted arises therefore not from any credulous confidence in the superior wisdom of past ages, or gloomy persuasion of the degeneracy of mankind, but is the consequence of acknowledged and indubitable positions, that what has been longest known has been most considered, and what is most considered is best understood.

The Poet, of whose works I have undertaken the revision, may now begin to assume the dignity of an ancient, and claim the privilege of established fame and prescriptive veneration. He has long outlived his century, the term commonly fixed as the test of literary merit. Whatever advantages he might once derive from personal allusions, local customs, or temporary opinions, have for many years been lost; and every topick of merriment, or motive of sorrow, which the modes of artificial life afforded him, now only obscure the scenes which they once illuminated. The effects of favour and competition are at an end; the tradition of his friendships and his enemies has perished; his works support no opinion with arguments, nor supply any faction with invectives; they can neither indulge vanity nor gratify malignity; but are read without any other reason than the desire of pleasure, and are therefore praised only as pleasure is obtained; yet, thus unassisted by interest or passion, they have past through variations of taste and changes of manners, and, as they devolved from one generation to another, have received new honours at every transmission.

But because human judgment, though it be gradually gaining upon certainty, never becomes infallible; and approbation, though long continued, may yet be only the approbation of prejudice or fashion; it is proper to inquire, by what peculiarities of excellence *Shakespeare* has gained and kept the favour of his countrymen.

Nothing can please many, and please long, but just representations of general nature. Particular manner, can be known to few, and therefore few only can judge how nearly they are copied. The irregular combinations of fanciful invention may delight a-while, by that novelty of which the common satiety of life sends us all in quest; but the pleasures of sudden wonder are soon exhausted, and the mind can only repose on the stability of truth.

Shakespeare is above all writers, at least above all modern writers, the poet of nature; the poet that holds up to his readers a faithful mirrour of manners and of life. His characters are not modified by the customs of particular places, unpractised by the rest of the world; by the peculiarities of studies or professions, which can operate but upon small numbers; or by the accidents of transient fashions or temporary opinions: they are the genuine progeny of common humanity, such as the world will always supply, and observation will always find. His persons act and speak by the influence of those general passions and principles by which all minds are agitated, and the whole system of life is continued in motion. In the writings of other poets a character is too often an individual; in those of *Shakespeare* it is commonly a species.

It is from this wide extension of design that so much instruction is derived. It is this which fills the plays of *Shakespeare* with practical axioms and domestic wisdom. It was said of *Euripides,* that every verse was a precept; and it may be said of *Shakespeare,* that from his works may be collected a system of civil and oeconomical prudence.

Yet his real power is not shewn in the splendour of particular passages, but by the progress of his fable, and the tenour of his dialogue; and he that tries to recommend him by select quotations, will succeed like the pedant in *Hierocles,* who, when he offered his house to sale, carried a brick in his pocket as a specimen.

It will not easily be imagined how much *Shakespeare* excells in accommodating his sentiments to real life, but by comparing him with other authors. It was observed of the ancient schools of declamation, that the more diligently they were frequented, the more was the student disqualified for the world, because he found nothing there which he should ever meet in any other place. The same remark may be applied to every stage but that of *Shakespeare.* The theatre, when it is under any other direction, is peopled by such characters as were never seen, conversing in a language which was never heard, upon topicks which will never rise in the commerce of mankind. But the dialogue of this author is often so evidently determined by the incident which produces it, and is pursued with so much ease and simplicity, that it seems scarcely to claim the merit of fiction, but to have been gleaned by diligent selection out of common conversation, and common occurrences.

Upon every other stage the universal agent is love, by whose power all 'good and evil is distributed, and every action quickened or retarded. To bring a lover, a lady and a rival into the fable; to entangle them in contradictory obligations, perplex them with oppositions of interest, and harrass them with violence of desires inconsistent with each other; to make them meet in rapture and part in agony; to fill their mouths with hyperbolical joy and outrageous sorrow; to distress them as nothing human ever was distressed; to deliver them as nothing human ever was delivered; is the business of a modern dramatist. For this probability is violated, life is misrepresented, and language is depraved. But love is only one of many passions; and as it has no great influence upon the sum of life, it has little operation in the dramas of a poet, who caught his ideas from the living world, and exhibited only what he saw before him.

He knew, that any other passion, as it was regular or exorbitant, was a cause of happiness or calamity.

Characters thus ample and general were not easily discriminated and preserved, yet perhaps no poet ever kept his personages more distinct from each other. I will not say with *Pope,* that every speech may be assigned to the proper speaker, because many speeches there are which have nothing characteristical; but perhaps, though some may be equally adapted to every person, it will be difficult to find any that can be properly transferred from the present possessor to another claimant. The choice is right, when there is reason for choice.

Other dramatists can only gain attention by hyperbolical or aggravated characters, by fabulous and unexampled excellence or depravity, as the writers of barbarous romances invigorated the reader by a giant and a dwarf; and he that should form his expectations of human affairs from the play, or from the tale, would be equally deceived. *Shakespeare* has no heroes; his scenes are occupied only by men, who act and speak as the reader thinks that he should himself have spoken or acted on the same occasion: Even where the agency is supernatural the dialogue is level with life. Other writers disguise the most natural passions and most frequent incidents; so that he who contemplates them in the book will not know them in the world: *Shakespeare* approximates the remote, and familiarizes the wonderful; the event which he represents will not happen, but if it were possible, its effects would probably be such as he has assigned; and it may be said, that he has not only shewn human nature as it acts in real exigencies, but as it would be found in trials, to which it cannot be exposed.

This therefore is the praise of *Shakespeare,* that his drama is the mirrour of life; that he who has mazed his imagination, in following the phantoms which other writers raise up before him, may here be cured of his delirious extasies, by reading human sentiments in human language, by scenes from which a hermit may estimate the transactions of the world, and a confessor predict the progress of the passions.

His adherence to general nature has exposed him to the censure of criticks, who form their judgments upon narrow principles. *Dennis* and *Rhymer* think his *Romans* not sufficiently *Roman;* and *Voltaire* censures his kings as not completely royal. *Dennis* is offended, that *Menenius,* a senator of *Rome,* should play the buffoon; and *Voltaire* perhaps thinks decency violated when the *Danish* Usurper is represented as a drunkard. But *Shakespeare* always makes nature predominate over accident; and if he preserves the essential character, is not very careful of distinctions superinduced and adventitious. His story requires Romans or kings, but he thinks only on men. He knew that *Rome,* like every other city, had men of all dispositions; and wanting a buffoon, he went into the senate-house for that which the senate-house would certainly have afforded him. He was inclined to shew an usurper and a murderer not only odious but despicable, he therefore added drunkenness to his other qualities, knowing that kings love wine like other men, and that wine exerts its natural power upon kings. These are the petty cavils of petty minds; a poet overlooks the casual distinction of country and condition, as a painter, satisfied with the figure, neglects the drapery.

The censure which he has incurred by mixing comick and tragick scenes, as it extends to all his works, deserves more consideration. Let the fact be first stated, and then examined.

Shakespeare's plays are not in the rigorous and critical sense either tragedies or comedies, but compositions of a distinct kind; exhibiting the real state of sublunary nature, which partakes of good and evil, joy and sorrow, mingled with endless variety of proportion and innumerable modes of combination; and expressing the course of the world, in which the loss of one is the gain of another; in which, at the same time, the reveller is hasting to his wine, and the mourner burying his friend; in which the malignity of one is sometimes defeated by the frolick of another; and many mischiefs and many benefits are done and hindered without design.

Out of this chaos of mingled purposes and casualties the ancient poets, according to the laws which custom had prescribed, selected some the crimes of men, and some their absurdities; some the momentous vicissitudes of life, and some the lighter occurrences; some the terrours of distress, and some the gayeties of prosperity. Thus rose the two modes of imitation, known by the names of *tragedy* and *comedy*, compositions intended to promote different ends by contrary means, and considered as so little allied, that I do not recollect among the *Greeks* or *Romans* a single writer who attempted both.

Shakespeare has united the powers of exciting laughter and sorrow not only in one mind, but in one composition. Almost all his plays are divided between serious and ludicrous characters, and, in the successive evolutions of the design, sometimes produce seriousness and sorrow, and sometimes levity and laughter.

That this is a practice contrary to the rules of criticism will be readily allowed; but there is always an appeal open from criticism to nature. The end of writing is to instruct; the end of poetry is to instruct by pleasing. That the mingled drama may convey all the instruction of tragedy or comedy cannot be denied, because it includes both in its alterations of exhibition and approaches nearer than either to the appearance of life, by shewing how great machinations and slender designs may promote or obviate one another, and the high and the low co-operate in the general system by unavoidable concatenation.

It is objected, that by this change of scenes the passions are interrupted in their progression, and that the principal event, being not advanced by a due gradation of preparatory incidents, wants at last the power to move, which constitutes the perfection of dramatick poetry. This reasoning is so specious, that it is received as true even by those who in daily experience feel it to be false. The interchanges of mingled scenes seldom fail to produce the intended vicissitudes of passion. Fiction cannot move so much, but that the attention may be easily transferred; and though it must be allowed that pleasing melancholy be sometimes interrupted by unwelcome levity, yet let it be considered likewise, that melancholy is often not pleasing, and that the disturbance of one man may be the relief of another; that different auditors have different habitudes; and that, upon the whole, all pleasure consists in variety.

The players, who in their edition divided our authour's works into comedies, histories, and tragedies, seem not to have distinguished the three kinds by any very exact or definite ideas.

And action which ended happily to the principal persons, however serious or distressful through its intermediate incidents, in their opinion, constituted a comedy. This idea of a comedy continued long amongst us; and plays were written, which, by changing the catastrophe, were tragedies to-day, and comedies to-morrow.

Tragedy was not in those times a poem of more general dignity or elevation than comedy; it required only a calamitous conclusion, with which the common criticism of that age was satisfied, whatever lighter pleasure it afforded in its progress.

History was a series of actions, with no other than chronological succession, independent on each other, and without any tendency to introduce or regulate the conclusion. It is not always very nicely distinguished from tragedy. There is not much nearer approach to unity of action in the tragedy of *Antony and Cleopatra,* than in the history of *Richard the Second.* But a history might be continued through many plays; as it had no plan, it had no limits.

Through all these denominations of the drama, *Shakespeare's* mode of composition is the same; an interchange of seriousness and merriment, by which the mind is softened at one time, and exhilarated at another. But whatever be his purpose, whether to gladden or depress, or to conduct the story, without vehemence or emotion, through tracts of easy and familiar dialogue, he never fails to attain his purpose; as he commands us, we laugh or mourn, or sit silent with quiet expectation, in tranquillity without indifference.

When *Shakespeare's* plan is understood, most of the criticisms of *Rhymer* and *Voltaire* vanish away. The play of *Hamlet* is opened, without impropriety, by two sentinels; *Iago* bellows at *Brabantio's* window, without injury to the scheme of the play, though in terms which a modern audience would not easily endure; the character of *Polonius* is seasonable and useful; and the Grave-diggers themselves may be heard with applause.

Shakespeare engaged in dramatick poetry with the world open before him; the rules of the ancients were yet known to few; but publick judgment was unformed; he had no example of such fame as might force him upon imitation, nor criticks of such authority as might restrain his extravagance: He therefore indulged his natural disposition, and his disposition, as *Rhymer* has remarked, led him to comedy. In tragedy he often writes, with great appearance of toil and study, what is written at last with little felicity; but in his comick scenes, he seems to produce without labour what no labour can improve. In tragedy he is always struggling after some occasion to be comick; but in comedy he seems to repose, or to luxuriate, as in a mode of thinking congenial to his nature. In his tragick scenes there is always something wanting, but his comedy often surpasses expectation or desire. His comedy pleases by the thoughts and the language, and his tragedy for the greater part by incident and action. His tragedy seems to be skill, his comedy to be instinct.

The force of his comick scenes has suffered little diminution from the changes made by a century and a half, in manners or in words. As his personages act upon principles arising from genuine passion, very little modified by particular forms, their pleasures and vexations are communicable to all times and to all places; they are natural, and therefore durable; the adventitious peculiarities of personal habits, are only superficial dies, bright and pleasing for a little while, yet soon fading to a dim tinct, without any remains of former lustre; but the discriminations of true passion are the colours of nature; they pervade the whole mass, and can only perish with the body that exhibits them. The accidental compositions of heterogeneous modes are dissolved by the chance which combined them; but the uniform simplicity of primitive qualities neither admits increase, nor suffers decay. The sand heap by one flood is scattered by another, but the rock always continues in its place. The stream of time, which is continually washing the dissoluble fabricks of other poets, passes without injury by the adamant of *Shakespeare*.

If there be, what I believe there is, in every nation, a

stile which never becomes obsolete, a certain mode of phraseology so consonant and congenial to the analogy and principles of its respective language as to remain settled and unaltered; this style is probably to be sought in the common intercourse of life, among those who speak only to be understood, without ambition of elegance. The polite are always catching modish innovations, and the learned depart from established forms of speech, in hope of finding or making better; those who wish for distinction forsake the vulgar, when the vulgar is right; but there is ' a conversation above grossness and below refinement, where propriety resides, and where this poet seems to have gathered his comick dialogue. He is therefore more agreeable to the ears of the present age than any other authour equally remote, and among his other excellencies deserves to be studied as one of the original masters of our language.

These observations are to be considered not as unexceptionally constant, but as containing general and predominant truth. *Shakespeare's* familiar dialogue is affirmed to be smooth and clear, yet not wholly without ruggedness or difficulty; as a country may be eminently fruitful, though it has spots unfit for cultivation: His characters are praised as natural, though their sentiments are sometimes forced, and their actions improbable; as the earth upon the whole is spherical, though its surface is varied with protuberances and cavities.

Shakespeare with his excellencies has likewise faults, and faults sufficient to obscure and overwhelm any other merit. I shall shew them in the proportion in which they appear to me, without envious malignity or superstitious veneration. No question can be more innocently discussed than a dead poet's pretensions to renown; and little regard is due to that bigotry which sets candour higher than truth.

His first defect is that to which may be imputed most of the evil in books or in men. He sacrifices virtue to convenience, and is so much more careful to please than to instruct, that he seems to write without any moral purpose. From his writings indeed a system of social duty may be selected, for he that thinks reasonably must think morally; but his precepts and axioms drop casually from him; he makes no just distribution of good or evil, nor is always careful to shew in the virtuous a disapprobation of the wicked; he carries his persons indifferently through right and wrong, and at the close dismisses them without further care, and leaves their examples to operate by chance. This fault the barbarity of his age cannot extenuate; for it is always a writer's duty to make the world better, and justice is a virtue independent on time or place.

The plots are often so loosely formed, that a very slight consideration may improve them, and so carelessly pursued, that he seems not always fully to comprehend his own design. He omits opportunities of instructing or delighting which the train of his story seems to force upon him, and apparently rejects those exhibitions which would be more affecting, for the sake of those which are more easy.

It may be observed, that in many of his plays the latter part is evidently neglected. When he found himself near the end of his work, and, in view of his reward, he shortened the labour to snatch the profit. He therefore remits his efforts where he should most vigorously exert them, and his catastrophe is improbably produced or imperfectly represented.

He had no regard to distinction of time or place, but gives to one age or nation, without scruple, the customs, institutions, and opinions of another, at the expence not only of likelihood, but of possibility. These faults *Pope* has endeavoured, with more zeal than judgment, to transfer to his imagined interpolators. We need not wonder to find *Hector* quoting *Aristotle,* when we see the loves of *Theseus* and *Hippolyta* combined with the *Gothick* mythology of fairies. *Shakespeare,* indeed, was not the only violator of chronology, for in the same age *Sidney,* who wanted not the advantages of learning, has, in his *Arcadia,* confounded the pastoral with the feudal times, the days of innocence, quiet and security, with those of turbulence, violence, and adventure.

In his comick scenes he is seldom very successful, when he engages his characters in reciprocations of smartness and contests of sarcasm; their jests are commonly gross, and their pleasantry licentious; neither his gentlemen nor his ladies have much delicacy, nor are sufficiently distinguished from his clowns by any appearance of refined manners. Whether he represented the real conversation of his time is not easy to determine; the reign of *Elizabeth* is commonly supposed to have been a time of stateliness, formality and reserve; yet perhaps the relaxations of that severity were not very elegant. There must, however, have been always some modes of gayety preferable to others, and a writer ought to chuse the best.

In tragedy his performance seems constantly to be worse, as his labour is more. The effusions of passion which exigence forces out are for the most part striking and energetick; but whenever he solicits his invention, or strains his faculties, the offspring of his throes is tumour, meanness, tediousness, and obscurity.

In narration he affects a disproportionate pomp of diction, and a wearisome train of circumlocution, and tells the incident imperfectly in many words, which might have been more plainly delivered in few. Narration in dramatick poetry is naturally tedious, as it is unanimated and inactive, and obstructs the progress of the action; it should therefore always be rapid, and enlivened by frequent interruption. *Shakespeare* found it an encumberance, and instead of lightening it by brevity, endeavoured to recommend it by dignity and splendour.

His declamations or set speeches are commonly cold and weak, for his power was the power of nature; when he endeavoured, like other tragick writers, to catch opportunities of amplification, and instead of inquiring what the occasion demanded, to show how much his stores of knowledge could supply, he seldom escapes without the pity or resentment of his reader.

It is incident to him to be now and then entangled with an unwieldy sentiment, which he cannot well express, and will not reject; he struggles with it a while, and if it continues stubborn, comprises it in words such as occur, and leaves it to be disentangled and evolved by those who have more leisure to bestow upon it.

Not that always where the language is intricate the thought is subtle, or the image always great where the line is bulky; the equality of words to things is very often neglected, and trivial sentiments and vulgar ideas disappoint the attention, to which they are recommended by sonorous epithets and swelling figures.

But the admirers of this great poet have never less reason to indulge their hopes of supreme excellence, than when he seems fully resolved to sink them in dejection, and mollify them with tender emotions by the fall of greatness, the danger of innocence, or the crosses of love. He is not long soft and pathetick without some idle conceit, or contemptible equivocation. He no sooner begins to move, than he counteracts himself; and terrour and pity, as they are rising in the mind, are checked and blasted by sudden frigidity.

A quibble is to *Shakespeare,* what luminous vapours are to the traveller; he follows it at all adventures; it is sure to lead him out of his way, and sure to engulf him in the mire. It has some malignant power over his mind, and its fascinations are irresistible. Whatever be the dignity or profundity of his disquisition, whether he be enlarging knowledge or exalting affection, whether he be amusing attention with incidents, or enchaining it in suspense, let but a quibble spring up before him, and he leaves his work unfinished. A quibble is the golden apple for which he will always turn aside from his career, or stoop from his elevation. A quibble, poor and barren as it is, gave him such delight, that he was content to purchase it, by the sacrifice of reason, propriety and truth. A quibble was to him the fatal *Cleopatra* for which he lost the world, and was content to lose it.

It will be thought strange, that, in enumerating the defects of this writer, I have not yet mentioned his neglect of the unities; his violation of those laws which have been instituted and established by the joint authority of poets and criticks.

For his other deviations from the art of writing I resign him to critical justice, without making any other demand in his favour, than that which must be indulged to all human excellence: that his virtues be rated with his failings: But, from the censure which this irregularity may bring upon him, I shall, with due reverence to that learning which I must oppose, adventure to try how I can defend him.

His histories, being neither tragedies nor comedies are not subject to any of their laws; nothing more is necessary to all the praise which they expect, than that the changes of action be so prepared as to be understood, that the incidents be various and affecting, and the characters consistent, natural, and distinct. No other unity is intended, and therefore none is to be sought.

In his other works he has well enough preserved the unity of action. He has not, indeed, an intrigue regularly perplexed and regularly unravelled: he does not endeavour to hide his design only to discover it, for this is seldom the order of real events, and *Shakespeare* is the poet of nature: But his plan has commonly what *Aristotle* requires, a beginning, a middle, and an end; one event is concatenated with another, and the conclusion follows by easy consequence. There are perhaps some incidents that might be spared, as in other poets there is much talk that only fills up time upon the stage; but the general system makes gradual advances, and the end of the play is the end of expectation.

To the unities of time and place he has shewn no regard; and perhaps a nearer view of the principles on which they stand will diminish their value, and withdraw from them the veneration which, from the time of *Corneille,* they have very generally received, by discovering that they have given more trouble to the poet, than pleasure to the auditor.

The necessity of observing the unities of time and place arises from the supposed necessity of making the drama credible. The criticks hold it impossible, that an action of months or years can be possibly believed to pass in three hours; or that the spectator can suppose himself to sit in the theatre, while ambassadors go and return between distant kings while armies are levied and towns besieged, while an exile wanders and returns, or till he whom they saw courting his mistress, shall lament the untimely fall of his son. The mind revolts from evident falsehood, and fiction loses its force when it departs from the resemblance of reality

From the narrow limitation of time necessarily arises the

contraction of place. The spectator, who knows that he saw the first act at *Alexandria,* cannot suppose that he sees the next at *Rome,* at a distance to which not the dragons of *Medea* could, in so short a time, have transported him; he knows with certainty that he has not changed his place, and he knows that place cannot change itself; that what was a house cannot become a plain; that what was *Thebes* can never be *Persepolis.*

Such is the triumphant language with which a critick exults over the misery of an irregular poet, and exults commonly without resistance or reply. It is time therefore to tell him by the authority of *Shakespeare,* that he assumes, as an unquestionable principle, a position, which, while his breath is forming it into words, his understanding pronounces to be false. It is false, that any representation is mistake for reality; that any dramatick fable in its materiality was ever credible, or, for a single moment, was ever credited.

The objection arising from the impossibility of passing the first hour at *Alexandria,* and the next at *Rome,* supposes, that when the play opens, the spectator really imagines himself at *Alexandria,* and believes that his walk to the theatre has been a voyage to *Egypt,* and that he lives in the days of *Antony* and *Cleopatra.* Surely he that imagines this may imagine more. He that can take the stage at one time for the palace of the *Ptolemies,* may take it in half an hour for the promontory of *Actium.* Delusion, if delusion be admitted, has no certain limitation; if the spectator can be once persuaded, that his old acquaintance are *Alexander* and *Cæsar,* that a room illuminated with candles is the plain of *Pharsalia,* or the bank of *Granicus,* he is in a state of elevation above the reach of reason, or of truth, and from the heights of empyrean poetry, may despise the circumscriptions of terrestrial nature. There is no reason why a mind thus wandering in extacy should count the clock, or why an hour should not be a century in that calenture of the brains that can make the stage a field.

The truth is, that the spectators are always in their senses, and know, from the first act to the last, that the stage is only a stage, and that the players are only players. They came to hear a certain number of lines recited with just gesture and elegant modulation. The lines relate to some action, and an action must be in some place; but the different actions that complete a story may be in places very remote from each other; and where is the absurdity of allowing that space to represent first *Athens,* and then *Sicily,* which was always known to be neither *Sicily* nor *Athens,* but a modern theatre?

By supposition, as place is introduced, times may be extended; the time required by the fable elapses for the most part between the acts; for, of so much of the action as is represented, the real and poetical duration is the same. If, in the first act, preparations for war against *Mithridates* are represented to be made in *Rome,* the event of the war may, without absurdity, be represented, in the catastrophe, as happening in *Pontus;* we know that there is neither war, nor preparation for war; we know that we are neither in *Rome* nor *Pontus;* that neither *Mithridates* nor *Lucullus* are before us. The drama exhibits successive imitations of successive actions; and why may not the second imitation represent an action that happened years after the first, if it be so connected with it, that nothing but time can be supposed to intervene? Time is, of all modes of existence, most obsequious to the imagination; a lapse of years is as easily conceived as a passage of hours. In contemplation we easily contract the time of real actions, and therefore willingly permit it to be contracted when we only see their imitation.

It will be asked, how the drama moves, if it is not credited. It is credited with all the credit due to a drama. It is credited, whenever it moves, as a just picture of a real original; as representing to the auditor what he would himself feel, if he were to do or suffer what is there feigned to be suffered or to be done. The reflection that strikes the heart is not, that the evils before us are real evils, but that they are evils to which we ourselves may be exposed. If there be any fallacy, it is not that we fancy the players, but that we fancy ourselves unhappy for a moment; but we rather lament the possibility than suppose the presence of misery, as a mother weeps over her babe, when she remembers that death may take it from her. The delight of tragedy proceeds from our consciousness of fiction; if we thought murders and treasons real, they would please no more.

Imitations produce pain or pleasure, not because they are mistaken for realities, but because they bring realities to mind. When the imagination is recreated by a painted landscape, the trees are not supposed capable to give us shade, or the fountains coolness; but we consider, how we should be pleased with such fountains playing beside us, and such woods waving over us. We are agitated in reading the history of *Henry* the Fifth, yet no man takes his book for the field of *Agencourt*. A dramatick exhibition is a book recited with concomitants that encrease or diminish its effect. Familiar comedy is often more powerful in the theatre, than on the page; imperial tragedy is always less. The humour of *Petruchio* may be heightened by grimace; but what voice or what gesture can hope to add dignity or force to the soliloquy of *Cato*.

A play read, affects the mind like a play acted. It is therefore evident, that the action is not supposed to be real; and it follows, that between the acts a longer or shorter time may be allowed to pass, and that no more account of space or duration is to be taken by the auditor of a drama, than by the reader of a narrative, before whom may pass in an hour the life of a hero, or the revolutions of an empire.

Whether *Shakespeare* knew the unities, and rejected them by design, or deviated from them by happy ignorance, it is, I think, impossible to decide, and useless to enquire. We may reasonably suppose, that, when he rose to notice, he did not want the counsels and admonitions of scholars and criticks, and that he at last deliberately persisted in a practice, which he might have begun by chance. As nothing is essential to the fable, but unity of action, and as the unities of time and place arise evidently from false assumptions, and, by circumscribing the extent of the drama, lessen its variety, I cannot think it much to be lamented, that they were not known by him, or not observed: Nor, if such another poet could arise, should I very vehemently reproach him, that his first act passed at *Venice,* and his next in *Cyprus.* Such violations of rules merely positive, become the comprehensive genius of *Shakespeare,* and such censures are suitable to the minute and slender criticism of *Voltaire:*

> Non usque adeo permiscuit imis
> Longus summa dies, ut non, si voce Metelli
> Serventur leges, malint a Cæsare tolli.

Yet when I speak thus slightly of dramatick rules, I cannot but recollect how much wit and learning may be produced against me; before such authorities I am afraid to stand, not that I think the present question one of those that are to be decided by mere authority, but because it is to be suspected, that these precepts have not been so easily received but for better reasons than I have yet been able to find. The result of my enquiries, in which it would be ludicrous to boast of impartiality, is, that the unities of time and place are not essential to a just drama, that though they may sometimes conduce to pleasure, they are always to be sacrificed to the nobler beauties of variety and instruction; and that a play, written with nice observation of critical rules, is to be contemplated as an elaborate curiosity, as the product of superfluous and ostentatious art, by which is shewn, rather what is possible, than what is necessary.

He that, without diminution of any other excellence, shall preserve all the unities unbroken, deserves the like applause with the architect, who shall display all the orders of architecture in a citadel, without any deduction from its strength; but the principal beauty of a citadel is to exclude the enemy; and the greatest graces of a play, are to copy nature and instruct life.

Perhaps what I have here not dogmatically but deliberatively written, may recal the principles of the drama to a new examination. I am almost frighted at my own temerity; and when I estimate the fame and the strength of those that maintain the contrary opinion, am ready to sink down in reverential silence; as *Æneas* withdrew from the defence of *Troy,* when he saw *Neptune* shaking the wall, and *Juno* heading the besiegers.

Those whom my arguments cannot persuade to give their

appr obation to the judgment of *Shakespeare*, will easily, if they consider the condition of his life, make some allowance for his ignorance.

Every man's performances, to be rightly estimated, must be compared with the state of the age in which he lived, and with his own particular opportunities; and though to the reader a book be not worse or better for the circumstances of the authour, yet as there is always a silent reference of human works to human abilities, and as the enquiry, how far man may extend his designs, or how high he may rate his native force, is of far greater dignity than in what rank we shall place any particular performance, curiosity is always busy to discover the instruments, as well as to survey the workmanship, to know how much is to be ascribed to original powers, and how much to casual and adventitious help. The palaces of *Peru* or *Mexico* were certainly mean and incommodious habitations, if compared to the houses of *European* monarchs; yet who could forbear to view them with astonishment, who remembered that they were built without the use of iron?

The *English* nation, in the time of *Shakespeare*, was yet struggling to emerge from barbarity. The philology of *Italy* had been transplanted hither in the reign of *Henry* the Eighth; and the learned languages had been successfully cultivated by *Lilly, Linacer,* and *More;* by *Pole, Cheke,* and *Gardiner;* and afterwards by *Smith, Clerk, Haddon,* and *Ascham.* Greek was now taught to boys in the principal schools; and those who united elegance with learning, read, with great diligence, the *Italian* and *Spanish* poets. But literature was yet confined to professed scholars, or to men and women of high rank. The publick was gross and dark; and to be able to read and write, was an accomplishment still valued for its rarity.

Nations, like individuals, have their infancy. A people newly awakened to literary curiosity, being yet unacquainted with the true state of things, knows not how to judge of that which is proposed as its resemblance. Whatever is remote from common appearances is always welcome to vulgar, as to childish credulity; and of a country unenlightened by learning, the whole people is the vulgar.

The study of those who then aspired to plebeian learning was laid out upon adventures, giants, dragons, and enchantments. *The Death of Arthur* was the favourite volume.

The mind, which has feasted on the luxurious wonders of fiction, has no taste of the insipidity of truth. A play which imitated only the common occurrences of the world, would, upon the admirers of *Palmerin* and *Guy* of *Warwick,* have made little impression; he that wrote for such an audience was under the necessity of looking round for strange events and fabulous transactions, and that incredibility, by which maturer knowledge is offended, was the chief recommendation of writings, to unskilful curiosity.

Our authour's plots are generally borrowed from novels, and it is reasonable to suppose, that he chose the most popular, such as were read by many, and related by more; for his audience could not have followed him through the intricacies of the drama, had they not held the thread of the story in their hands.

The stories, which we now find only in remoter authours, were in his time accessible and familiar. The fable of *As you like it,* which is supposed to be copied from *Chaucer's* Gamelyn, was a little pamphlet of those times; and old Mr. *Cibber* remembered the tale of *Hamlet* in plain *English* prose, which the criticks have now to seek in *Saxo Grammaticus.*

His *English* histories he took from *English* chronicles and *English* ballads; and as the ancient writers were made known to his countrymen by versions, they supplied him with new subjects; he dilated some of *Plutarch's* lives into plays, when they had been translated by *North.*

His plots, whether historical or fabulous, are always crouded with incidents, by which the attention of a rude people was more easily caught than by sentiment or argumentation; and such is the power of the marvellous even over those who despise it, that every man finds his mind more strongly seized by the tragedies of *Shakespeare* than of any other writer; others please us by particular speeches, but he always makes us anxious for the event, and has perhaps excelled all but *Homer* in securing the first purpose of a writer, by exciting restless and unquenchable curiosity

and compelling him that reads his work to read it through.
The shows and bustle with which his plays abound have
the same original. As knowledge advances, pleasure passes
from the eye to the ear, but returns, as it declines, from
the ear to the eye. Those to whom our authour's labours
were exhibited had more skill in pomps or processions than
in poetical language, and perhaps wanted some visible and
discriminated events, as comments on the dialogue. He
knew how he should most please; and whether his practice
is more agreeable to nature, or whether his example has
prejudiced the nation, we still find that on our stage something must be done as well as said, and inactive declamation is very coldly heard, however musical or elegant, passionate or sublime.

Voltaire expresses his wonder, that our authour's extravagances are endured by a nation, which has seen the tragedy
of *Cato*. Let him be answered, that *Addison* speaks the language of poets, and *Shakespeare,* of men. We find in *Cato*
innumerable beauties which enamour us of its authour, but
we see nothing that acquaints us with human sentiments or
human actions; we place it with the fairest and the noblest
progeny which judgment propagates by conjunction with
learning, but *Othello* is the vigorous and vivacious offspring
of observation impregnated by genius. *Cato* affords a splendid exhibition of artificial and fictitious manners, and de-
livers just and noble sentiments, in diction easy, elevated
and harmonious, but its hopes and fears communicate no
vibration to the heart; the composition refers us only to
the writer; we pronounce the name of *Cato,* but we think
on *Addison.*

The work of a correct and regular writer is a garden
accurately formed and diligently planted, varied with shades,
and scented with flowers; the composition of *Shakespeare*
is a forest, in which oaks extend their branches, and pines
tower in the air, interspersed sometimes with weeds and
brambles, and sometimes giving shelter to myrtles and to
roses; filling the eye with awful pomp, and gratifying the
mind with endless diversity. Other poets display cabinets
of precious rarities, minutely finished, wrought into shape,
and polished into brightness. *Shakespeare* opens a mine

which contains gold and diamonds in unexhaustible plenty, though clouded by incrustations, debased by impurities, and mingled with a mass of meaner minerals.

It has been much disputed, whether *Shakespeare* owed his excellence to his own native force, or whether he had the common helps of scholastick education, the precepts of critical science, and the examples of ancient authours.

There has always prevailed a tradition, that *Shakespeare* wanted learning, that he had no regular education, nor much skill in the dead languages. *Johnson,* his friend, affirms, that *he had small Latin, and no Greek;* who, besides that he had no imaginable temptation to falsehood, wrote at a time when the character and acquisitions of *Shakespeare* were known to multitudes. His evidence ought therefore to decide the controversy, unless some testimony of equal force could be opposed.

Some have imagined, that they have discovered deep learning in many imitations of old writers; but the examples which I have known urged, were drawn from books translated in his time; or were such easy coincidences of thought, as will happen to all who consider the same subjects; or such remarks on life or axioms of morality as float in conversation, and are transmitted through the world in proverbial sentences.

I have found it remarked, that, in this important sentence, *Go before, I'll follow,* we read a translation of, *I prae, sequar.* I have been told, that when *Caliban,* after a pleasing dream, says, *I cry'd to sleep again,* the authour imitates *Anacreon,* who had, like every other man, the same wish on the same occasion.

There are a few passages which may pass for imitations, but so few, that the exception only confirms the rule; he obtained them from accidental quotations, or by oral communication, and as he used what he had, would have used more if he had obtained it.

The *Comedy of Errors* is confessedly taken from the *Menæchmi* of *Plautus;* from the only play of *Plautus* which was then in *English.* What can be more probable, than that he who copied that, would have copied more; but that those which were not translated were inaccessible?

Whether he knew the modern languages is uncertain. That his plays have some *French* scenes proves but little; he might easily procure them to be written, and probably, even though he had known the language in the common degree, he could not have written it without assistance. In the story of *Romeo* and *Juliet* he is observed to have followed the *English* translation, where it deviates from the *Italian;* but this on the other part proves nothing against his knowledge of the original. He was to copy, not what he knew himself, but what was known to his audience.

It is most likely that he had learned *Latin* sufficiently to make him acquainted with construction, but that he never advanced to an easy perusal of the *Roman* authours. Concerning his skill in modern languages, I can find no sufficient ground of determination; but as no imitations of *French* or *Italian* authours have been discovered, though the *Italian* poetry was then high in esteem, I am inclined to believe, that he read little more than *English,* and chose for his fables only such tales as he found translated.

That much knowledge is scattered over his works is very justly observed by *Pope,* but it is often such knowledge as books did not supply. He that will understand *Shakespeare,* must not be content to study him in the closet, he must look for his meaning sometimes among the sports of the field, and sometimes among the manufactures of the shop.

There is however proof enough that he was a very diligent reader, nor was our language then so indigent of books, but that he might very liberally indulge his curiosity without excursion into foreign literature. Many of the *Roman* authours were translated, and some of the *Greek;* the reformation had filled the kingdom with theological learning; most of the topicks of human disquisition had found *English* writers; and poetry had been cultivated, not only with diligence, but success. This was a stock of knowledge sufficient for a mind so capable of appropriating and improving it.

But the greater part of his excellence was the product of his own genius. He found the *English* stage in a state of the utmost rudeness; no essays either in tragedy or comedy had appeared, from which it could be discovered to what degree of delight either one or other might be carried. Neither character nor dialogue were yet understood. *Shakespeare* may be truly said to have introduced them both amongst us, and in some of his happier scenes to have carried them both to the utmost height.

By what gradations of improvement he proceeded, is not easily known; for the chronology of his works is yet unsettled. *Rowe* is of opinion, that *perhaps we are not to look for his beginning, like those of other writers, in his least perfect works; art had so little, and nature so large a share in what he did, that for ought I know,* says he, *the performances of his youth, as they were the most vigorous, were the best.* But the power of nature is only the power of using to any certain purpose the materials which diligence procures, or opportunity supplies. Nature gives no man knowledge, and when images are collected by study and experience, can only assist in combining or applying them. *Shakespeare,* however favoured by nature, could impart only what he had learned; and as he must increase his ideals, like other mortals, by gradual acquisition, he, like them, grew wiser as he grew older, could display life better, as he knew it more, and instruct with more efficacy, as he was himself more amply instructed.

There is a vigilance of observation and accuracy of distinction which books and precepts cannot confer; from this almost all original and native excellence proceeds. *Shakespeare* must have looked upon mankind with perspicacity, in the highest degree curious and attentive. Other writers borrow their characters from preceding writers, and diversify them only by the accidental appendages of present manners; the dress is a little varied, but the body is the same. Our authour had both matter and form to provide; for except the characters of *Chaucer,* to whom I think he is not much indebted, there were no writers in *English,* and perhaps not many in other modern languages, which shewed life in its native colours.

The contest about the original benevolence or malignity of man had not yet commenced. Speculation had not yet attempted to analyse the mind, to trace the passions to their sources, to unfold the seminal principles of vice and virtue,

or sound the depths of the heart for the motives of action.
All those enquiries, which from that time that human
nature became the fashionable study, have been made
sometimes with nice discernment, but often with idle subtilty, were yet unattempted. The tales, with which the
infancy of learning was satisfied, exhibited only the superficial appearances of action, related the events but omitted
the causes, and were formed for such as delighted in wonders
rather than in truth. Mankind was not then to be studied
in the closet; he that would know the world, was under the
necessity of gleaning his own remarks, by mingling as he
could in its business and amusements.

Boyle congratulated himself upon his high birth, because
it favoured his curiosity, by facilitating his access. *Shakespeare* had no such advantage; he came to *London* a needy
adventurer, and lived for a time by very mean employments.
Many works of genius and learning have been performed in
states of life, that appear very little favourable to thought
or to enquiry; so many, that he who considers them is inclined to think that he sees enterprise and perseverance pre-
dominating over all external agency, and bidding help and
hindrance vanish before them. The genius of *Shakespeare*
was not to be depressed by the weight of poverty, nor limited
by the narrow conversation to which men in want are inevitably condemned; the incumbrances of his fortune were
shaken from his mind, *as dewdrops from a lion's mane.*

Though he had so many difficulties to encounter, and so
little assistance to surmount them, he has been able to
obtain an exact knowledge of many modes of life, and many
casts of native dispositions; to vary them with great multiplicity; to mark them by nice distinctions; and to shew
them in full view by proper combinations. In this part of
his performances he had none to imitate, but has himself
been imitated by all succeeding writers; and it may be
doubted, whether from all his successors more maxims of
theoretical knowledge, or more rules of practical prudence,
can be collected, than he alone has given to his country.

Nor was his attention confined to the actions of men;
he was an exact surveyor of the inanimate world; his
descriptions have always some peculiarities, gathered by

contemplating things as they really exist. It may be observed, that the oldest poets of many nations preserve their reputation, and that the following generations of wit, after a short celebrity, sink into oblivion. The first, whoever they be, must take their sentiments and descriptions immediately from knowledge; the resemblance is therefore just, their descriptions are verified by every eye, and their sentiments acknowledged by every breast. Those whom their fame invites to the same studies, copy partly them, and partly nature, till the books of one age gain such authority, as to stand in the place of nature to another, and imitation, always deviating a little, becomes at last capricious and casual. *Shakespeare,* whether life or nature be his subject, shews plainly, that he has seen with his own eyes; he gives the image which he receives, not weakened or distorted by the intervention of any other mind; the ignorant feel his representations to be just, and the learned see that they are compleat.

Perhaps it would not be easy to find any authour, except *Homer,* who invented so much as *Shakespeare,* who so much advanced the studies which he cultivated, or effused so much novelty upon his age or country. The form, the characters, the language, and the shows of the *English* drama are his. *He seems,* says *Dennis, to have been the very original of our* English *tragical harmony, that is, the harmony of blank verse, diversified often by dissyllable and trissyllable terminations. For the diversity distinguishes it from heroick harmony, and by bringing it nearer to common use makes it more proper to gain attention, and more fit for action and dialogue. Such verse we make when we are writing prose; we make such verse in common conversation.*

I know not whether this praise is rigorously just. The dissyllable termination, which the critic rightly appropriates to the drama, is to be found, though, I think, not in *Gorboduc* which is confessedly before our author; yet in *Hieronnymo,* of which the date is not certain, but which there is reason to believe at least as old as his earliest plays. This however is certain, that he is the first who taught either tragedy or comedy to please, there being no theatrical piece of any older writer, of which the name is known, except to antiquaries and collectors of books, which are sought because they are scarce, and would not have been scarce, had they been much esteemed.

To him we must ascribe the praise, unless *Spenser* may divide it with him, of having first discovered to how much smoothness and harmony the *English* language could be softened. He has speeches, perhaps sometimes scenes, which have all the delicacy of *Rowe*, without his effeminacy. He endeavours indeed commonly to strike by the force and vigour of his dialogue, but he never executes his purpose better, than when he tries to sooth by softness.

Yet it must be at last confessed, that as we owe every thing to him, he owes something to us; that, if much of his praise is paid by perception and judgement, much is likewise given by custom and veneration. We fix our eyes upon his graces, and turn them from his deformities, and endure in him what we should in another loath or despise. If we endured without praising, respect for the father of our drama might excuse us; but I have seen, in the book of some modern critick, a collection of anomalies, which shew that he has corrupted language by every mode of depravation, but which his admirer has accumulated as a monument of honour.

He has scenes of undoubted and perpetual excellence, but perhaps not one play, which, if it were now exhibited as the work of a contemporary writer, would be heard to the conclusion. I am indeed far from thinking, that his works were wrought to his own ideas of perfection; when they were such as would satisfy the audience, they satisfied the writer. It is seldom that authours, though more studious of fame than *Shakespeare,* rise much above the standard of their own age; to add a little of what is best will always be sufficient for present praise, and those who find themselves exalted into fame, are willing to credit their encomiasts, and to spare the labour of contending with themselves.

It does not appear, that *Shakespeare* thought his works worthy of posterity, that he levied any ideal tribute upon future times, or had any further prospect, than of present popularity and present profit. When his plays had been acted, his hope was at an end; he solicited no addition of honour from the reader. He therefore made no scruple to repeat the same jests in many dialogues, or to entangle different plots by the same knot of perplexity, which may be at least forgiven him, by those who recollect, that of *Congreve's* four comedies, two are concluded by a marriage in a mask, by a deception, which perhaps never happened, and which, whether likely or not, he did not invent.

So careless was this great poet of future fame, that, though he retired to ease and plenty, while he was yet little *declined into the vale of years,* before he could be disgusted with fatigue, or disabled by infirmity, he made no collection of his works, nor desired to rescue those that had been already published from the depravations that obscured them, or secure to the rest a better destiny, by giving them to the world in their genuine state.

Of the plays which bear the name of *Shakespeare* in the late editions, the greater part were not published till about seven years after his death, and the few which appeared in his life are apparently thrust into the world without the care of the authour, and therefore probably without his knowledge.

Of all the publishers, clandestine or professed, their negligence and unskilfulness has by the late revisers been sufficiently shown. The faults of all are indeed numerous and gross, and have not only corrupted many passages perhaps beyond recovery, but have brought others into suspicion, which are only obscured by obsolete phraseology, or by the writer's unskilfulness and affectation. To alter is more easy than to explain, and temerity is a more common quality than diligence. Those who saw that they must employ conjecture to a certain degree, were willing to indulge it a little further. Had the author published his own works, we should have sat quietly down to disentangle his intricacies, and clear his obscurities; but now we tear what we cannot loose, and eject what we happen not to understand.

The faults are more than could have happened without the concurrence of many causes. The stile of *Shakespeare* was in itself ungrammatical, perplexed and obscure; his works were transcribed for the players by those who may be supposed to have seldom understood them; they were transmitted by copiers equally unskilful, who still multiplied errours; they were perhaps sometimes mutilated by the actors, for the sake of shortening the speeches; and were at last printed without correction of the press.

In this state they remained, not as Dr. *Warburton* supposes, because they were unregarded, but because the editor's art was not yet applied to modern languages, and our ancestors were accustomed to so much negligence of *English* printers, that they could very patiently endure it. At last an edition was undertaken by *Rowe;* not because a poet was to be published by a poet, for *Rowe* seems to have thought very little on correction or explanation, but that our authour's works might appear like those of his fraternity, with the appendages of a life and recommendatory preface. *Rowe* has been clamorously blamed for not performing what he did not undertake, and it is time that justice be done him, by confessing, that though he seems to have had no thought of corruption beyond the printer's errours, yet he has made many emendations, if they were not made before, which his successors have received without acknowledgement, and which, if they had produced them, would have filled pages and pages with censures of the stupidity by which the faults were committed, with displays of the absurdities which they involved, with ostentatious expositions of the new reading, and self congratulations on the happiness of discovering it.

Of *Rowe,* as of all the editors, I have preserved the preface, and have likewise retained the authour's life, though not written with much elegance or spirit; it relates however what is now to be known, and therefore deserves to pass through all succeeding publications.

The nation had been for many years content enough with Mr. *Rowe's* performance, when Mr. *Pope* made them acquainted with the true state of *Shakespeare's* text, shewed that it was extremely corrupt, and gave reason to hope that there were means of reforming it. He collated the old copies, which none had thought to examine before, and restored many lines to their integrity; but, by a very com-

pendious criticism, he rejected whatever he disliked, and
thought more of amputation than of cure.

I know not why he is commended by Dr. *Warburton* for
distinguishing the genuine from the spurious plays. In
this choice he exerted no judgement of his own; the plays
which he received, were given by *Hemings* and *Condel,*
the first editors; and those which he rejected, though, according to the licentiousness of the press in those times,
they were printed during *Shakespeare's* life, with his
name, had been omitted by his friends, and were never added
to his works before the edition of 1664, from which they were
copied by the later printers.

This was a work which *Pope* seems to have thought unworthy of his abilities, being not able to suppress his contempt of *the dull duty of an editor.* He understood but
half his undertaking. The duty of a collator is indeed dull,
yet, like other tedious tasks, is very necessary; but an
emendatory critick would ill discharge his duty, without
qualities very different from dullness. In perusing a corrupted piece, he must have before him all possibilities of
meaning, with all possibilities of expression. Such must be
his comprehension of thought, and such his copiousness of
language. Out of many readings possible, he must be able
to select that which best suits with the state, opinions, and
modes of language prevailing in every age, and with his
authour's particular cast of thought, and turn of expression.
Such must be his knowledge, and such his taste. Conjectural criticism demands more than humanity possesses,
and he that exercises it with most praise has very frequent
need of indulgence. Let us now be told no more of the dull
duty of an editor.

Confidence is the common consequence of success. They
whose excellence of any kind has been loudly celebrated, are
ready to conclude, that their powers are universal. *Pope's*
edition fell below his own expectations, and he was so much
offended, when he was found to have left any thing for others
to do, that he past the latter part of his life in a state of
hostility with verbal criticism.

I have retained all his notes, that no fragment of so great
a writer may be lost; his preface, valuable alike for elegance

of composition and justness of remark, and containing a general criticism on his authour, so extensive, that little can be added, and so exact, that little can be disputed, every editor has an interest to suppress, but that every reader would demand its insertion.

Pope was succeeded by *Theobald,* a man of narrow comprehension and small acquisitions, with no native and intrinsick splendour of genius, with little of the artificial light of learning, but zealous for minute accuracy, and not negligent in pursuing it. He collated the ancient copies, and rectified many errours. A man so anxiously scrupulous might have been expected to do more, but what little he did was commonly right.

In his report of copies and editions he is not to be trusted, without examination. He speaks sometimes indefinitely of copies, when he has only one. In his enumeration of editions, he mentions the two first folios as of high, and the third folio as of middle authority; but the truth is, that the first is equivalent to all others, and that the rest only deviate from it by the printer's negligence. Whoever has any of the folios has all, excepting those diversities which mere reiteration of editions will produce. I collated them all at the beginning, but afterwards used only the first.

Of his notes I have generally retained those which he retained himself in his second edition, except when they were confuted by subsequent annotators, or were too minute to merit preservation. I have sometimes adopted his restoration of a comma, without inserting the panegyrick in which he celebrated himself for his atchievement. The exuberant excrescence of his diction I have often lopped, his triumphant exultations over *Pope* and *Rowe* I have sometimes suppressed, and his contemptible ostentation I have frequently concealed; but I have in some places shewn him, as he would have shewn himself, for the reader's diversion, that the inflated emptiness of some notes may justify or excuse the contraction of the rest.

Theobald, thus weak and ignorant, thus mean and faithless, thus petulant and ostentatious, by the good luck of having *Pope* for his enemy, has escaped, and escaped alone, with reputation, from this undertaking. So willingly does the world support those who solicite favour, against those who command reverence; and so easily is he praised, whom no man can envy.

Our authour fell then into the hands of Sir *Thomas Hanmer,* the *Oxford* editor, a man, in my opinion, eminently qualified by nature for such studies. He had, what is the first requisite to emendatory criticism, that intuition by which the poet's intention is immediately discovered, and that dexterity of intellect which despatches its work by the easiest means. He had undoubtedly read much; his acquaintance with customs, opinions, and traditions, seems to have been large; and he is often learned without shew. He seldom passes what he does not understand, without an attempt to find or to make a meaning, and sometimes hastily makes what a little more attention would have found. He is solicitous to reduce to grammar, what he could not be sure that his authour intended to be grammatical. *Shakespeare* regarded more the series of ideas, than of words; and his language, not being designed for the reader's desk, was all that he desired it to be, if it conveyed his meaning to the audience.

Hanmer's care of the metre has been too violently censured. He found the measures reformed in so many passages, by the silent labours of some editors, with the silent acquiescence of the rest, that he thought himself allowed to extend a little further the license, which had already been carried so far without reprehension; and of his corrections in general, it must be confessed, that they are often just, and made commonly with the least possible violation of the text.

But, by inserting his emendations, whether invented or borrowed, into the page, without any notice of varying copies, he has appropriated the labour of his predecessors, and made his own edition of little authority. His confidence indeed, both in himself and others, was too great; he supposes all to be right that was done by *Pope* and *Theobald;* he seems not to suspect a crick of fallibility, and it was but reasonable that he should claim what he so liberally granted.

As he never writes without careful enquiry and diligent consideration, I have received all his notes, and believe that every reader will wish for more.

Of the last editor it is more difficult to speak. Respect is due to high place, tenderness to living reputation, and veneration to genius and learning; but he cannot be justly offended at that liberty of which he has himself so frequently given an example, nor very solicitous what is thought of notes, which he ought never to have considered as part of his serious employments, and which, I suppose, since the ardour of composition is remitted, he no longer numbers among his happy effusions.

The original and predominant errour of his commentary, is acquiescence in his first thoughts; that precipitation which is produced by consciousness of quick discernment; and that confidence which presumes to do, by surveying the surface, what labour only can perform, by penetrating the bottom. His notes exhibit sometimes perverse interpretations, and sometimes improbable conjectures; he at one time gives the authour more profundity of meaning, than the sentence admits, and at another discovers absurdities, where the sense is plain to every other reader. But his emendations are likewise often happy and just; and his interpretation of obscure passages learned and sagacious.

Of his notes, I have commonly rejected those, against which the general voice of the publick has exclaimed, or which their own incongruity immediately condemns, and which, I suppose, the authour himself would desire to be forgotten. Of the rest, to part I have given the highest approbation, by inserting the offered reading in the text; part I have left to the judgment of the reader, as doubtful, though specious; and part I have censured without reserve, but I am sure without bitterness of malice, and, I hope, without wantonness of insult.

It is no pleasure to me, in revising my volumes, to observe how much paper is wasted in confutation. Whoever considers the revolutions of learning, and the various questions of greater or less importance, upon which wit and reason have exercised their powers, must lament the unsuccessfulness of enquiry, and the slow advances of truth, when he reflects, that great part of the labour of every writer is only the destruction of those that went before him. The first care of the builder of a new system, is to demolish the fabricks which are standing. The chief desire of him that comments an authour, is to shew how much other commentators have corrupted and obscured him. The opinions prevalent in one age, as truths above the reach of controversy, are confuted and rejected in another, and rise again to reception in remoter times. Thus the human mind is kept in motion without progress. Thus sometimes truth and errour, and sometimes contrarieties of errour, take each other's place by reciprocal invasion. The tide of seeming knowledge which is poured over one generation, retires and leaves another naked and barren; the sudden meteors of intelligence which for a while appear to shoot their beams into the regions of obscurity, on a sudden withdraw their lustre, and leave mortals again to grope their way.

These elevations and depressions of renown, and the contradictions to which all improvers of knowledge must for ever be exposed, since they are not escaped by the highest and brightest of mankind, may surely be endured with patience by criticks and annotators, who can rank themselves but as the satellites of their authours. How canst thou beg for life, says *Achilles* to his captive, when thou knowest that thou art now to suffer only what must another day be suffered by *Achilles?*

Dr. *Warburton* had a name sufficient to confer celebrity on those who could exalt themselves into antagonists, and his notes have raised a clamour too loud to be distinct. His chief assailants are the authours of *the Canons of criticism* and of the *Review of* Shakespeare's *text;* of whom one ridicules his errours with airy petulance, suitable enough to the levity of the controversy; the other attacks them with gloomy malignity, as if he were dragging to justice an assassin or incendiary. The one stings like a fly, sucks a little blood, takes a gay flutter, and returns for more; the other bites like a viper, and would be glad to leave inflammations and gangrene behind him. When I think on one, with his confederates, I remember the danger of *Coriolanus,* who was afraid that *girls with spits, and boys with stones, should slay him in puny battle;* when the other crosses my imagination, I remember the prodigy in *Macbeth,*

An eagle tow'ring in his pride of place,
Was by a mousing owl hawk'd at and kill'd.

Let me however do them justice. One is a wit, and one a scholar. They have both shown acuteness sufficient in the discovery of faults, and have both advanced some probable interpretations of obscure passages; but when they aspire to conjecture and emendation, it appears how falsely we all estimate our own abilities, and the little which they have been able to perform might have taught them more candour to the endeavours of others.

Before Dr. *Warburton's* edition, *Critical observations on* Shakespeare had been published by Mr. *Upton,* a man skilled in languages, and acquainted with books, but who seems to have had no great vigour of genius or nicety of taste. Many of his explanations are curious and useful, but he likewise, though he professed to oppose the licentious confidence of editors, and adhere to the old copies, is unable to restrain the rage of emendation, though his ardour is ill seconded by his skill. Every cold empirick, when his heart is expanded by a successful experiment, swells into a theorist, and the laborious collator at some unlucky moment frolicks in conjecture.

Critical, historical and explanatory notes have been likewise published upon *Shakespeare* by Dr. *Grey,* whose diligent perusal of the old *English* writers has enabled him to make some useful observations. What he undertook he has well enough performed, but as he neither attempts judicial nor emendatory criticism, he employs rather his memory than his sagacity. It were to be wished that all would endeavour to imitate his modesty who have not been able to surpass his knowledge.

I can say with great sincerity of all my predecessors, what I hope will hereafter be said of me, that not one has left *Shakespeare* without improvement, nor is there one to whom I have not been indebted for assistance and information. Whatever I have taken from them it was my intention to refer to its original authour, and it is certain, that what I have not given to another, I believed when I wrote it to be my own. In some perhaps I have been anticipated; but if I am ever found to encroach upon the remarks of any other commentator, I am willing that the honour, be it more or less, should be transferred to the first claimant, for his right, and his alone, stands above dispute; the second can prove his pretensions only to himself, nor can himself always distinguish invention, with sufficient certainty, from recollection.

They have all been treated by me with candour, which they have not been careful of observing to one another. It is not easy to discover from what cause the acrimony of a scholiast can naturally proceed. The subjects to be discussed by him are of very small importance; they involve neither property nor liberty; nor favour the interest of sect or party. The various readings of copies, and different interpretations of a passage, seem to be questions that might exercise the wit, without engaging the passions. But, whether it be, that *small things make mean men proud,* and vanity catches small occasions; or that all contrariety of opinion, even in those that can defend it no longer, makes proud men angry; there is often found in commentaries a spontaneous strain of invective and contempt, more eager and venomous than is vented by the most furious controvertist in politicks against those whom he is hired to defame.

Perhaps the lightness of the matter may conduce to the vehemence of the agency; when the truth to be investigated is so near to inexistence, as to escape attention, its bulk is to be enlarged by rage and exclamation: That to which all would be indifferent in its original state, may attract notice when the fate of a name is appended to it. A commentator has indeed great temptations to supply by turbulence what he wants of dignity, to beat his little gold to a spacious surface, to work that to foam which no art or diligence can exalt to spirit.

The notes which I have borrowed or written are either illustrative, by which difficulties are explained; or judicial by which faults and beauties are remarked; or emendatory, by which depravations are corrected.

The explanations transcribed from others, if I do not subjoin any other interpretation, I suppose commonly to be right, at least I intend by acquiescence to confess, that I have nothing better to propose.

After the labours of all the editors, I found many passages which appeared to me likely to obstruct the greater number of readers, and thought it my duty to facilitate their passage. It is impossible for an expositor not to write too little for some, and too much for others. He can only judge what is necessary by his own experience; and how long soever he may deliberate, will at last explain many lines which the learned will think impossible to be mistaken, and omit many for which the ignorant will want his help. These are censures merely relative, and must be quietly endured. I have endeavoured to be neither superfluously copious, nor scrupulously reserved, and hope that I have made my authour's meaning accessible to many who before were frighted from perusing him, and contributed something to the publick, by diffusing innocent and rational pleasure.

The compleat explanation of an authour not systematick and consequential, but desultory and vagrant, abounding in casual allusions and light hints, is not to be expected from any single scholiast. All personal reflections, when names are suppressed, must be in a few years irrecoverably obliterated; and customs, too minute to attract the notice of law, such as modes of dress, formalities of conversation, rules of visits, disposition of furniture, and practices of ceremony, which naturally find places in familiar dialogue, are so fugitive and unsubstantial, that they are not easily retained or recovered. What can be known, will be collected by chance, from the recesses of obscure and obsolete papers, perused commonly with some other view. Of this knowledge every man has some, and none has much; but when an authour has engaged the publick attention, those who can add any thing to his illustration, communicate their discoveries, and time produces what had eluded diligence.

To time I have been obliged to resign many passages, which, though I did not understand them, will perhaps hereafter be explained, having, I hope, illustrated some, which others have neglected or mistaken, sometimes by short remarks, or marginal directions, such as every editor has added at his will, and often by comments more laborious than the matter will seem to deserve; but that which is most difficult is not always most important, and to an editor nothing is a trifle by which his authour is obscured.

The poetical beauties or defects I have not been very diligent to observe. Some plays have more, and some fewer judicial observations, not in proportion to their difference of merit, but because I gave this part of my design to chance and to caprice. The reader, I believe, is seldom pleased to find his opinion anticipated; it is natural to delight more in what we find or make, than in what we receive. Judgement, like other faculties, is improved by practice, and its advancement is hindered by submission to dictatorial decisions, as the memory grows torpid by the use of a table book. Some initiation is however necessary; of all skill, part is infused by precept, and part is obtained by habit; I have therefore shewn so much as may enable the candidate of criticism to discover the rest.

To the end of most plays, I have added short strictures, containing a general censure of faults, or praise of excellence; in which I know not how much I have concurred with the current opinion; but I have not, by any affectation of singularity, deviated from it. Nothing is minutely and particularly examined, and therefore it is to be supposed, that in the plays which are condemned there is much to be praised, and in these which are praised much to be condemned.

The part of criticism in which the whole succession of editors has laboured with the greatest diligence, which has occasioned the most arrogant ostentation, and excited the keenest acrimony, is the emendation of corrupted passages, to which the publick attention having been first drawn by the violence of contention between *Pope* and *Theobald,* has been continued by the persecution, which, with a kind of conspiracy, has been since raised against all the publishers of *Shakespeare.*

That many passages have passed in a state of depravation through all the editions is indubitably certain; of these the restoration is only to be attempted by collation of copies or sagacity of conjecture. The collator's province is safe and easy, the conjecturer's perilous and difficult. Yet as the greater part of the plays are extant only in one copy, the peril must not be avoided, nor the difficulty refused.

Of the readings which this emulation of amendment has hitherto produced, some from the labours of every publisher I have advanced into the text; those are to be considered as in my opinion sufficiently supported; some I have rejected without mention, as evidently erroneous; some I have left in the notes without censure or approbation, as resting in equipoise between objection and defence; and some, which seemed specious but not right, I have inserted with a subsequent animadversion.

Having classed the observations of others, I was at last to try what I could substitute for their mistakes, and how I could supply their omissions. I collated such copies as I could procure, and wished for more, but have not found the collectors of these rarities very communicative. Of the editions which chance or kindness put into my hands I have given an enumeration, that I may not be blamed for neglecting what I had not the power to do.

By examining the old copies, I soon found that the later publishers, with all their boasts of diligence, suffered many passages to stand unauthorised, and contented themselves with *Rowe's* regulation of the text, even where they knew it to be arbitrary, and with a little consideration might have found it to be wrong. Some of these alterations are only the ejection of a word for one that appeared to him more elegant or more intelligible. These corruptions I have often silently rectified; for the history of our language, and the true force of our words, can only be preserved, by keeping the text of authours free from adulteration. Others, and those very frequent, smoothed the cadence, or regulated the measure; on these I have not exercised the same rigour; if only a word was transposed, or a particle inserted or omitted, I have sometimes suffered the line to stand; for the inconstancy of the copies is such, as that some liberties may be easily permitted. But this practice I have not suffered to proceed far, having restored the primitive diction wherever it could for any reason be preferred.

The emendations, which comparison of copies supplied, I have inserted in the text; sometimes where the improvement was slight, without notice, and sometimes with an account of the reasons of the change.

Conjecture, though it be sometimes unavoidable, I have not wantonly nor licentiously indulged. It has been my settled principle, that the reading of the ancient books is probably true, and therefore is not to be disturbed for the sake of elegance, perspicuity, or mere improvement of the sense. For though much credit is not due to the fidelity, nor any to the judgement of the first publishers, yet they who had the copy before their eyes were more likely to read it right, than we who read it only by imagination. But it is evident that they have often made strange mistakes by ignorance or negligence, and that therefore something may be properly attempted by criticism, keeping the middle way between presumption and timidity.

Such criticism I have attempted to practice, and where any passage appeared inextricably perplexed, have endeavoured to discover how it may be recalled to sense, with least violence. But my first labour is, always to turn the old text on every side, and try if there be any interstice, through which light can find its way; nor would *Huetius* himself condemn me, as refusing the trouble of research, for the ambition of alteration. In this modest industry I have not been unsuccessful. I have rescued many lines from the violations of temerity, and secured many scenes from the inroads of correction. I have adopted the *Roman* sentiment, that it is more honourable to save a citizen, than to kill an enemy, and have been more careful to protect than to attack.

I have preserved the common distribution of the plays into acts, though I believe it to be in almost all the plays void of authority. Some of those which are divided in the later editions have no division in the first folio, and some that are divided in the folio have no division in the preceding copies. The settled mode of the theatre requires four intervals in the play, but few, if any, of our authour's compositions can be properly distributed in that manner. An act is so much of the drama as passes without intervention of time or change of place. A pause makes a new act. In every real, and therefore in every imitative action, the intervals may be more or fewer, the restriction of five acts being accidental and arbitrary. This *Shakespeare* knew, and this he practised; his plays were written, and at first printed in one unbroken continuity, and ought now to be exhibited with short pauses, interposed as often as the scene is changed, or any considerable time is required to pass. This method would at once quell a thousand absurdities.

In restoring the author's works to their integrity, I have considered the punctuation as wholly in my power; for what could be their care of colons and commas, who corrupted words and sentences. Whatever could be done by adjusting points is therefore silently performed, in some plays with much diligence, in others with less; it is hard to keep a busy eye steadily fixed upon evanescent atoms, or a discursive mind upon evanescent truth.

The same liberty has been taken with a few particles, or other words of slight effect. I have sometimes inserted or omitted them without notice. I have done that sometimes, which the other editors have done always, and which indeed the state of the text may sufficiently justify.

The greater part of readers, instead of blaming us for passing trifles, will wonder that on mere trifles so much labour is expended, with such importance of debate, and such solemnity of diction. To these I answer with confidence, that they are judging of an art which they do not understand; yet cannot much reproach them with their ignorance, nor promise that they would become in general, by learning criticism, more useful, happier or wiser.

As I practised conjecture more, I learned to trust it less; and after I had printed a few plays, resolved to insert none of my own readings in the text. Upon this caution I now congratulate myself, for every day encreases my doubt of my emendations.

Since I have confined my imagination to the margin, it must not be considered as very reprehensible, if I have suffered it to play some freaks in its own dominion. There is no danger in conjecture, if it be proposed as conjecture; and while the text remains uninjured, those changes may be safely offered, which are not considered even by him that offers them as necessary or safe.

If my readings are of little value, they have not been ostentatiously displayed or importunately obtruded. I could have written longer notes, for the art of writing notes is not of difficult attainment. The work is performed, first by railing at the stupidity, negligence, ignorance, and asinine tasteless-ness of the former editors, and shewing, from all that goes before and all that follows, the inelegance and absurdity of the old reading; then by proposing something which to superficial readers would seem specious, but which the editor rejects with indignation; then by producing the true reading, with a long paraphrase, and concluding with loud acclama-tions on the discovery, and a sober wish for the advance-ment and prosperity of genuine criticism.

All this may be done, and perhaps done sometimes with-out impropriety. But I have always suspected that the read-ing is right, which requires many words to prove it wrong; and the emendation wrong, that cannot without so much labour appear to be right. The justness of a happy restora-tion strikes at once, and the moral precept may be well ap-plied to criticism, *quod dubitas ne feceris.*

To dread the shore which he sees spread with wrecks, is natural to the sailor. I had before my eye, so many critical adventures ended in miscarriage, that caution was forced upon me. I encountered in every page Wit struggling with its own sophistry, and Learning confused by the multi-plicity of its views. I was forced to censure those whom I admired, and could not but reflect, while I was dispossessing their emendations, how soon the same fate might happen to my own, and how many of the readings which I have cor-rected may be by some other editor defended and established.

> Criticks, I saw, that other's names efface,
> And fix their own, with labour, in the place;
> Their own, like others, soon their place resign'd,
> Or disappear'd, and left the first behind.
> POPE.

That a conjectural critick should often be mistaken, cannot be wonderful, either to others or himself, if it be considered, that in his art there is no system, no principal and axiomat-ical truth that regulates subordinate positions. His chance of errour is renewed at every attempt; an oblique view of the passage, a slight misapprehension of a phrase, a casual inattention to the parts connected, is sufficient to make him not only fails, but fail ridiculously; and when he succeeds best, he produces perhaps but one reading of many probable, and he that suggests another will always be able to dispute his claims.

It is an unhappy state, in which danger is hid under pleasure. The allurements of emendation are scarcely resistible. Conjecture has all the joy and all the pride of invention, and he that has once started a happy change, is too much delighted to consider what objections may rise against it.

Yet conjectural criticism has been of great use in the learned world; nor is it my intention to depreciate a study, that has exercised so many mighty minds, from the revival of learning to our own age, from the Bishop of *Aleria* to English *Bentley*. The criticks on ancient authours have, in the exercise of their sagacity, many assistances, which the editor of *Shakespeare* is condemned to want. They are employed upon grammatical and settled languages, whose construction contributes so much to perspicuity, that *Homer* has fewer passages unintelligible than *Chaucer*. The words have not only a known regimen, but invariable quantities, which direct and confine the choice. There are commonly more manuscripts than one; and they do not often conspire in the same mistakes. Yet *Scaliger* could confess to *Salmasius* how little satisfaction his emendations gave him. *Illudunt nobis conjecturæ nostræ, quarum nos pudet, posteaquam in meliores codices incidimus.* And *Lipsius* could complain, that criticks were making faults, by trying to remove them, *Ut olim vitiis, ita nunc remediis laboratur.* And indeed, where mere conjecture is to be used, the emendations of *Scaliger* and *Lipsius,* notwithstanding their wonderful sagacity and erudition, are often vague and disputable, like mine or *Theobald*'s.

Perhaps I may not be more censured for doing wrong, than for doing little; for raising in the publick expectations, which at last I have not answered. The expectation of ignorance is indefinite, and that of knowledge is often tyrannical. It is hard to satisfy those who know not what to demand, or those who demand by design what they think impossible to be done. I have indeed disappointed no opinion more than my own; yet I have endeavoured to perform my task with no slight solicitude. Not a single passage in the whole work has appeared to me corrupt, which I have not attempted to restore; or obscure, which I have not endeavoured to illustrate. In many I have failed like others; and from many, after all my efforts, I have retreated, and confessed the repulse. I have not passed over, with affected superiority, what is equally difficult to the reader and to myself, but where I could not instruct him, have owned my ignorance. I might easily have accumulated a mass of seeming learning upon easy scenes; but it ought not to be imputed to negligence, that, where nothing was necessary, nothing has been done, or that, where others have said enough, I have said no more.

Notes are often necessary, but they are necessary evils. Let him, that is yet unacquainted with the powers of *Shakespeare,* and who desires to feel the highest pleasure that the drama can give, read every play from the first scene to the last, with utter negligence of all his commentators. When his fancy is once on the wing, let it not stoop at correction or explanation. When his attention is strongly engaged, let it disdain alike to turn aside to the name of *Theobald* and of *Pope.* Let him read on through brightness and obscurity, through integrity and corruption; let him preserve his comprehension of the dialogue and his interest in the fable. And when the pleasures of novelty have ceased, let him attempt exactness, and read the commentators.

Particular passages are cleared by notes, but the general effect of the work is weakened. The mind is refrigerated by interruption; the thoughts are diverted from the principal subject; the reader is weary, he suspects not why; and at last throws away the book, which he has too diligently studied.

Parts are not to be examined till the whole has been surveyed; there is a kind of intellectual remoteness necessary for the comprehension of any great work in its full design and its true proportions; a close approach shews the smaller niceties, but the beauty of the whole is discerned no longer

It is not very grateful to consider how little the succession
of editors has added to this authour's power of pleasing.
He was read, admired, studied, and imitated, while he was
yet deformed with all the improprieties which ignorance and
neglect could accumulate upon him; while the reading was
yet not rectified, nor his allusions understood; yet then did
Dryden pronounce " that *Shakespeare* was the man, who,
of all modern and perhaps ancient poets, had the largest and
most comprehensive soul." All the images of nature were
still present to him, and he drew them not laboriously, but
luckily: when he describes any thing, you more than see
it, you feel it too. Those who accuse him to have wanted
learning, give him the greater commendation: he was
naturally learned: he needed not the spectacles of books to
read nature; he looked inwards, and found her there. I
cannot say he is every where alike; were he so, I should do
him injury to compare him with the greatest of mankind.
He is many times flat and insipid; his comick wit degenerat-
ing into clenches, his serious swelling into bombast. But
he is always great, when some great occasion is presented to
him: No man can say, he ever had a fit subject for his
wit, and did not then raise himself as high above the rest
of poets,

" Quantum lenta solent inter viburna cupressi."

It is to be lamented, that such a writer should want a
commentary; that his language should become obsolete, or
his sentiments obscure. But it is vain to carry wishes beyond the condition of human things; that which must happen to all, has happened to · *Shakespeare,* by accident and
time; and more than has been suffered by any other writer
since the use of types, has been suffered by him through
his own negligence of fame, or perhaps by that superiority
of mind, which despised its own performances, when it
compared them with its powers, and judged those works
unworthy to be preserved, which the criticks of following ages were to contend for the fame of restoring and
explaining.

Among these candidates of inferiour fame, I am now to

stand the judgment of the publick; and wish that I could confidently produce my commentary as equal to the encouragement which I have had the honour of receiving. Every work of this kind is by its nature deficient, and I should feel little solicitude about the sentence, were it to be pronounced only by the skilful and the learned.

INTRODUCTION
TO THE PROPYLÄEN

BY J. W. VON GOETHE. (1798)

THE youth, when Nature and Art attract him, thinks that with a vigorous effort he can soon penetrate into the innermost sanctuary; the man, after long wanderings, finds himself still in the outer court.

Such an observation has suggested our title. It is only on the step, in the gateway, the entrance, the vestibule, the space between the outside and the inner chamber, between the sacred and the common, that we may ordinarily tarry with our friends.

If the word *Propylaea* recalls particularly the structure through which was reached the citadel of Athens and the temple of Minerva, this is not inconsistent with our purpose; but the presumption of intending to produce here a similar work of art and splendor should not be laid to our charge. The name of the place may be understood as symbolizing what might have happened there; one may expect conversations and discussions such as would perhaps not be unworthy of that place.

Are not thinkers, scholars, artists, in their best hours allured to those regions, to dwell (at least in imagination) among a people to whom a perfection which we desire but never attain was natural, among whom in the course of time and life, a culture developed in a beautiful continuity, which to us appears only in passing fragments? What modern nation

---

The Propyläen was a periodical founded in July, 1798, by Goethe and his friend Heinrich Meyer. During its short existence of three years, there were published in it, besides the writings of the editors, short contributions by Schiller and Humboldt. Its purpose was to spread sound ideas about the aims and methods of art; and in this notable introduction Goethe set forth with clearness and profundity his fundamental ideas on these subjects. The present translation has been made expressly for the Harvard Classics.

does not owe its artistic culture to the Greeks, and, in certain branches, what nation more than the German?

So much by way of excuse for the symbolic title, if indeed an excuse be necessary. May the title be a reminder that we are to depart as little as possible from classic ground; may it, through its brevity and signification, modify the demands of the friends of art whom we hope to interest through the present work, which is to contain observations and reflections concerning Nature and Art by a harmonious circle of friends.

He who is called to be an artist will give careful heed to everything around him; objects and their parts will attract his attention, and by making practical use of such experience he will gradually train himself to observe more sharply. He will, in his early career, apply everything, so far as possible, to his own advantage; later he will gladly make himself serviceable to others. Thus we also hope to present and relate to our readers many things which we regard as useful and agreeable, things which, under various circumstances, have been noted by us during a number of years.

But who will not willingly agree that pure observation is more rare than is believed? We are apt to confuse our sensations, our opinion, our judgment, with what we experience, so that we do not remain long in the passive attitude of the observer, but soon go on to make reflections; and upon these no greater weight can be placed than may be more or less justified by the nature and quality of our individual intellects.

In this matter we are able to gain stronger confidence from our harmony with others, and from the knowledge that we do not think and work alone, but in common. The perplexing doubt whether our method of thought belongs only to us—a doubt which often comes over us when others express the direct opposite of our convictions—is softened, even dispelled, when we find ourselves in agreement with others; only then do we go on rejoicing with assurance in the possession of those principles which a long experience, on our own part and on the part of others, has gradually confirmed.

When several persons thus live united, so that they may

call one another friends, because they have a common interest
in bringing about their progressive cultivation and in advancing towards closely related aims, then they may be certain
that they will meet again in the most varied ways, and that
even the courses which seemed to separate them from one another will nevertheless soon bring them happily together again.

Who has not experienced what advantages are afforded
in such cases by conversation? But conversation is ephemeral; and while the results of a mutual development are imper-
ishable, the memory of the means by which it was reached
disappears. Letters preserve better the stages of a progress
which friends achieve together; every moment of growth is
fixed, and if the result attained affords us agreeable satisfaction, a look backward at the process of development is
instructive since it permits us to hope for an unflagging advance in the future.

Short papers, in which are set down from time to time one's
thoughts, convictions, and wishes, in order to find entertainment in one's past self after a lapse of time, are excellent
auxiliary means for the development of oneself and of
others, none of which should be neglected when one considers the brief period allotted to life and the many obstacles
that stand in the way of every advance.

It is self evident that we are talking here particularly of
an exchange of ideas between such friends as are striving for
cultivation in the sphere of science and art; although life
in the world of affairs and industry should not lack similar
advantages.

In the arts and sciences, however, in addition to this close
association among their votaries, a relation to the public is
as favorable as it is necessary. Whatever of universal interest one thinks or accomplishes belongs to the world, and the
world brings to maturity whatever it can utilize of the efforts
of the individual. The desire for approval which the author
feels is an impulse implanted by Nature to draw him toward
something higher; he thinks he has attained the laurel wreath,
but soon becomes aware that a more laborious training of
every native talent is necessary in order to retain the public
favor; though it may be attained for a short moment through
fortune or accident also.

The relation of the author to his public is important in his early period; even in later days he cannot dispense with it. However little he may be fitted to teach others, he wishes to share his thoughts with those whom he feels congenial, but who are scattered far and wide in the world. By this means he wishes to re-establish his relation with his old friends, to continue it with new ones, and to gain in the younger generation still others for the remainder of his life. He wishes to spare youth the circuitous paths upon which he himself went astray, and while observing and utilizing the advantages of the present, to maintain the memory of his praiseworthy earlier efforts.

With this serious view, a small society has been brought together; may cheerfulness attend our undertakings, and time may show whither we are bound.

The papers which we intend to present, though they are composed by several authors, will, it is hoped, never be contradictory in the main points, even though the methods of thought may not be the same in all. No two persons regard the world in exactly the same way, and different characters will often apply in different ways a principle which they all acknowledge. Indeed, a person is not always consistent with himself in his views and judgments: early convictions must give way to later ones. The individual opinions that a man holds and expresses may stand all tests or not; the main thing is that he continue on his way, true to himself and to others!

Much as the authors wish and hope to be in harmony with one another and with a large part of the public, they must not shut their eyes to the fact that from various quarters many a discord will ring out. They must expect this all the more since they differ from prevailing opinions in more than one point. Though far from wishing to dominate or change the way of thinking of a third person, still they will firmly express their own opinion, and, as circumstances dictate, will avoid or take up a quarrel. On the whole, however, they will adhere to one creed, and especially will they repeat again and again those conditions which seem to them indispensable in the training of an artist. Whoever takes an interest in this matter, must be ready to take sides; otherwise he does not deserve to be effective anywhere.

If, therefore, we promise to present reflections and observations concerning Nature, we must at the same time indicate that these remarks will chiefly have reference, first, to plastic art; then, to art in general; finally, to the general training of the artist.

The highest demand that is made on an artist is this: that he be true to Nature, study her, imitate her, and produce something that resembles her phenomena. How great, how enormous, this demand is, is not always kept in mind; and the true artist himself learns it by experience only, in the course of his progressive development. Nature is separated from Art by an enormous chasm, which genius itself is unable to bridge without external assistance.

All that we perceive around us is merely raw material; if it happens rarely enough that an artist, through instinct and taste, through practice and experiment, reaches the point of attaining the beautiful exterior of things, of selecting the best from the good before him, and of producing at least an agreeable appearance, it is still more rare, particularly in modern times, for an artist to penetrate into the depths of things as well as into the depths of his own soul, in order to produce in his works not only something light and superficially effective, but, as a rival of Nature, to produce something spiritually organic, and to give his work of art a content and a form through which it appears both natural and beyond Nature.

Man is the highest, the characteristic subject of plastic art; to understand him, to extricate oneself from the labyrinth of his anatomy, a general knowledge of organic nature is imperative. The artist should also acquaint himself theoretically with inorganic bodies and with the general operations of Nature, particularly if, as in the case of sound and color, they are adaptable to the purposes of art; but what a circuitous path he would be obliged to take if he wanted to seek laboriously in the schools of the anatomist, the naturalist, and the physicist, for that which serves his purposes! It is, indeed, a question whether he would find there what must be most important for him. Those men have the entirely different needs of their own pupils to satisfy, so that they cannot be expected to think of the limited and special needs of the artist. For that reason it is our intention to take a hand, and, even though we cannot see prospects of completing the necessary work ourselves, both to give a view of the whole and to begin the elaboration of details.

The human figure cannot be understood merely through observation of its surface; the interior must be laid bare, its parts must be separated, the connections perceived, the differences noted, action and reaction observed, the concealed, constant, and fundamental elements of the phenomena impressed on the mind, if one really wishes to contemplate and imitate what moves before our eyes in living waves as a beautiful, undivided whole. A glance at the surface of a living being confuses the observer; we may cite here, as in other cases, the true proverb, " One sees only what one knows." For just as a short-sighted man sees more clearly an object from which he draws back than one to which he draws near, because his intellectual vision comes to his aid, so the perfection of observation really depends on knowledge. How well an expert naturalist, who can also draw, imitates objects by recognizing and emphasizing the important and significant parts from which is derived the character of the whole!

Just as the artist is greatly helped by an exact knowledge of the separate parts of the human figure, which he must in the end regard again as a whole, so a general view, a side glance at related objects, is highly advantageous, provided the artist is capable of rising to ideas and of grasping the close relationship of things apparently remote. Comparative anatomy has prepared a general conception of organic creatures; it leads us from form to form, and by observing organisms closely or distantly related, we rise above them all to see their characteristics in an ideal picture. If we keep this picture in mind, we find that in observing objects our attention takes a definite direction, that scattered facts can be learned and retained more easily by comparison, that in the practice of art we can finally vie with Nature only when we have learned from her, at least to some extent, her method of procedure in the creation of her works.

Furthermore, we would encourage the artist to gain

knowledge also of the inorganic world; this can be done all
the more easily since now we can conveniently and quickly
acquire knowledge of the mineral kingdom. The painter
needs some knowledge of stones in order to imitate their
characteristics; the sculptor and architect, in order to utilize
them; the cutter of precious stones cannot be without a
knowledge of their nature; the connoisseur and amateur,
too, will strive for such information.

Now that we have advised the artist to gain a conception
of the general operations of Nature, in order to become
acquainted with those which particularly interest him, partly
to develop himself in more directions, partly to understand
better that which concerns him; we shall add a few further
remarks on this significant point.

Up to the present the painter has been able merely to
wonder at the physicist's theory of colors, without gaining
any advantage from it. The natural feeling of the artist,
however, constant training, and a practical necessity led
him into a way of his own. He felt the vivid contrasts out
of the union of which harmony of color arises, he designated
certain characteristics through approximate sensations, he
had warm and cold colors, colors which express proximity,
others which express distance, and what not; and thus in his
own way he brought these phenomena closer to the most general laws of Nature. Perhaps the supposition is confirmed
that the operations of Nature in colors, as well as mag-
netic, electric, and other operations, depend upon a mutual
relation, a polarity, or whatever else we might call the twofold or manifold aspects of a distinct unity.

We shall make it our duty to present this matter in detail
and in a form comprehensible to the artist; and we can be
the more hopeful of doing something welcome to him, since
we shall be concerned only with explaining and tracing to
fundamental principles things which he has hitherto done
by instinct.

So much for what we hope to impart in regard to Nature;
now for what is most necessary in regard to Art.

Since the arrangement of this work proposes the presentation of single treatises, some of these only in part, and
since it is not our desire to dissect a whole, but rather to

build up a whole from many parts, it will be necessary to present, as soon as possible and in a general summary, those things which the reader will gradually find unfolded in our detailed elaborations. We shall, therefore, be occupied first with an essay on plastic art, in which the familiar rubrics will be presented according to our interpretation and method. Here it will be our main concern to emphasize the importance of every branch of Art, and to show that the artist must not neglect a single one, as has unfortunately often happened, and still happens.

Hitherto we have regarded Nature as the treasure chamber of material in general; now, however, we reach the important point where it is shown how Art prepares its materials for itself.

When the artist takes any object of Nature, the object no longer belongs to Nature; indeed, we can say that the artist creates the object in that moment, by extracting from it all that is significant, characteristic, interesting, or rather by putting into it a higher value. In this way finer proportions, nobler forms, higher characteristics are, as it were, forced upon the human figure; the circle of regularity, perfection, signification, and completeness is drawn, in which Nature gladly places her best possessions even though elsewhere in her vast extent she easily degenerates into ugliness and loses herself in indifference.

The same is true of composite works of art, of their subject and content, whether the theme be fable or history. Happy the artist who makes no mistake in undertaking the work, who knows how to choose, or rather to determine what is suitable for art! He who wanders uneasily among scattered myths and far-stretching history in search of a theme, he who wishes to be significantly scholarly or allegorically interesting, will often be checked in the midst of his work by unexpected obstacles, or will miss his finest aim after the completion of the work. He who does not speak clearly to the senses, will not address himself clearly to the mind; and we regard this point as so important, that we insert at the very outset a more extended discussion of it.

A theme having been happily found or invented, it is subjected to treatment which we would divide into the spiritual, the sensuous, and the mechanical. The spiritual develops the subject according to its inner relations, it discovers subordinate motives; and, if we can at all judge the depth of an artistic genius by the choice of subject, we can recognize in his selection of themes his breadth, wealth, fullness, and power of attraction. The sensuous treatment we should define as that through which the work becomes thoroughly comprehensible to the senses, agreeable, delightful, and irresistible through its gentle charm. The mechanical treatment, finally, is that which works upon given material through any bodily organ, and thus brings the work into existence and gives it reality.

While we hope to be useful to the artist in this way, and earnestly wish that he may avail himself of advice and of suggestions in his work, the disquieting observation is forced upon us that every undertaking, like every man, is likely to suffer just as much from its period as it is to derive occasional advantage from it, and in our own case we cannot altogether put aside the question concerning the reception we are likely to meet with.

Everything is subject to constant change, and since certain things cannot exist side by side, they displace one another. This is true of kinds of knowledge, of certain methods of instruction, of methods of representation, and of maxims. The aims of men remain nearly always the same: they still desire to become good artists or poets as they did centuries ago; but the means through which the goal is reached are not clear to everybody, and why should it be denied that nothing would be more agreeable than to be able to carry out joyfully a great design?

Naturally the public has a great influence upon Art, since in return for its approval and its money it demands work that may give satisfaction and immediate enjoyment; and the artist will for the most part be glad to adapt himself to it, for he also is a part of the public, he has received his training during the same years, he feels the same needs, strives in the same direction, and thus moves along happily with the multitude which supports him and which is invigorated by him. In this matter we see whole nations and epochs delighted by their artists, just as the artist sees himself reflected in his nation and his epoch, without either having even the slightest suspicion that their path might not be right, that their taste might be at least one-sided, their art on the decline, and their progress in the wrong direction.

Instead of proceeding to further generalities on this point, we shall make a remark which refers particularly to plastic art.

For the German artist, in fact for modern and northern artists in general, it is difficult—indeed almost impossible—to make the transition from formless matter to form, and to maintain himself at that point, even should he succeed in reaching it. Let every artist who has lived for a time in Italy ask himself whether the presence of the best works of ancient and modern art have not aroused in him the incessant endeavour to study and imitate the human figure in its proportions, forms, and characteristics, to apply all diligence and care in the execution in order to approach those artistic works, so entirely complete in themselves, in order to produce a work which, in gratifying the sense, exalts the spirit to the greatest heights. Let him also admit, however, that after his return he must gradually relax his efforts, because he finds few persons who will really see, enjoy, and comprehend what is depicted; but, for the most part, finds only those who look at a work superficially, receive from it mere random impressions, and in some way of their own try to get out of it any kind of sensation and pleasure.

The worst picture can appeal to our senses and imagination by arousing their activity, setting them free, and leaving them to themselves; the best work of art also appeals to our senses, but in a higher language which, of course, we must understand; it enchains the feelings and imagination; it deprives us of caprice, we cannot deal with a perfect work at our will; we are forced to give ourselves up to it, in order to receive ourselves from it again, exalted and refined.

That these are no dreams we shall try to show gradually, in detail, and as clearly as possible; we shall call attention particularly to a contradiction in which the moderns are often involved. They call the ancients their teachers, they acknowledge in their works an unattainable excellence, yet they depart both in theory and practice far from the maxims which the ancients continually observed. In starting from this important point and in returning to it often, we shall find others about which something falls to be said.

One of the principal signs of the decay of art is the mixture of its various kinds. The arts themselves, as well as their branches, are related to one another, and have a certain tendency to unite, even to lose themselves in one another; but it is in this that the duty, the merit, the dignity of the real artist consists, namely, in being able to separate the field of art in which he works from others, in placing every art and every branch of art on its own footing, and in isolating it as far as possible.

It has been noticed that all plastic art strives toward painting, all literary art toward the drama, and this observation may in the future give us occasion for important reflections.

The genuine law-giving artist strives for the truth of art, the lawless artist who follows a blind impulse strives for the reality of Nature; through the former, art reaches its highest summit, through the latter its lowest stage.

What holds good of art in general holds good also of the kinds of art. The sculptor must think and feel differently from the painter, indeed he must proceed when he wishes to produce a work in relief, in a different fashion from that which he will employ for a work in the round. By the raising of low reliefs higher and higher, by the making of various parts and figures stand out completely, and finally by the adding of buildings and landscapes, so that work was produced which was half painting and half puppet-show, true art steadily declined. Excellent artists of modern times have unfortunately pursued this course.

When in the future we express such maxims as we think sound, we should like, since they are deduced from works of art, to have them put to the test of practice by the artist. How rarely one can come to a theoretical agreement with anyone else on a fundamental principle. That which is applicable and useful, on the other hand, is decided upon much more quickly. How often we see artists in embarrassment over the choice of subjects, over the general type of composition adapted to their art, and the detailed arrangement; how often the painter over the choice of colors! Then is the time to test a principle, then will it be easier to decide whether it is bringing us closer to the great models and to everything that we value and love in them, or whether it leaves us entangled in the empirical confusion of an experience that has not been sufficiently thought out.

If such maxims hold good in training the artist, in guiding him in many an embarrassment, they will serve also in the development, valuation, and judgment of old and new works of art, and will in turn arise from an observation of these works. Indeed, it is all the more necessary to adhere to this, because, notwithstanding the universally praised excellences of antiquity, individuals and whole nations among the moderns often fail to recognize wherein lies the highest excellence of those works.

An exact test will protect us best from this evil. For that reason let us cite only one example to show what usually happens to the amateur in plastic art, so that we may make clear how necessary it is that criticism of ancient as well as modern works should be exact if it is to be of any use.

Upon him who has an eye for beauty, though untrained, even a blurred, imperfect plaster cast of an excellent antique will always have a great effect; for in such a reproduction there always remain the idea, the simplicity and greatness of form, in short, the general outlines; as much, at all events, as one could perceive with poor eyes at a distance.

It may be noticed that a strong inclination toward art is often enkindled by such quite imperfect reproductions. But the effect is like the object; it is rather that an obscure indefinite feeling is aroused, than that the object in all its worth and dignity really appears to such beginners in art. These are they who usually express the theory that too minute a critical investigation destroys the enjoyment, who are accustomed to oppose and resist regard for details.

If gradually, however, after further experience and training, they are confronted with a sharp cast instead of a blurred one, an original instead of a cast, their pleasure grows with their insight, and increases when the originals themselves, the perfect originals, finally become known to them.

The labyrinth of exact observations is willingly entered when the details as well as the whole are perfect; indeed one learns to realize that the excellences can be appreciated only in proportion as the defects are perceived. To discriminate the restoration from the genuine parts, and the copy from the original, to see in the smallest fragments the ruined glory of the whole—this is the joy of the finished expert; and there is a great difference between observing and comprehending an imperfect whole with obscured vision, and a perfect whole with clear vision.

He who concerns himself with any branch of knowledge, should strive for the highest! Insight is different from practice, for in practical work everyone must soon resign himself to the fact that only a certain measure of strength is alloted to him; far more people, however, are capable of knowledge and insight. Indeed, one may well say that everyone is thus capable who can deny himself and subordinate himself to external objects, everyone who does not strive with rigid and narrow-minded obstinacy to impose upon the highest works of Nature and Art his own personality and his petty onesideness.

To speak of works of art fitly and with true benefit to oneself and others, the discussion should take place only in the presence of the works themselves. Everything depends on the objects being in view; on whether something absolutely definite is suggested by the word with which one hopes to illuminate the work of art; for, otherwise, nothing is thought of at all. This is why it so often happens that the writer on art dwells merely on generalities, through which, indeed, ideas and sensations are aroused in all readers, but no satisfaction is given to the man who, book in hand, steps in front of the work of art itself. Precisely on this account, however, we may in several essays be in a position to arouse rather than to satisfy the desire of the readers; for nothing is more natural than that they should wish to have before their eyes immediately an excellent work of art which is minutely dissected, in order to enjoy the whole which we are discussing, and, so far as the parts are concerned, to subject to their own judgment the opinion which they read.

While the authors, however, write on the assumption that their readers either have seen the works, or will see them in the future, yet they hope to do everything in their power for those who are in neither case. We shall mention reproductions, shall indicate where casts of antique works of art and antique works themselves are accessible, particularly to Germans; and thus try, as far as we can, to minister to the genuine love and knowledge of art.

A history of art can be based only upon the highest and most detailed comprehension of art; only when one knows the finest things that man can produce can one trace the psychological and chronological course taken in art, as in other fields. This course began with a limited activity, busied about a dry and even gloomy imitation of the insignificant as well as the significant, whence developed a more amiable, more kindly feeling toward Nature, till finally, under favorable circumstances, accompanied by knowledge, regularity, seriousness, and severity, art rose to its height. There at last it became possible for the fortunate genius, surrounded by all these auxiliaries, to produce the charming and the complete.

Unfortunately, however, works of art with such ease of expression, which instil into man cheerfulness, freedom, and a pleasant feeling of his own personality, arouse in the striving artist the idea that the process of production is also agreeable. Since the pinnacle of what art and genius produce is an appearance of ease, the artists who come after are tempted to make things easy for themselves, and to work for the sake of appearances. Thus art gradually declines from its high position, as to the whole as well as details. But if we wish to gain a fair conception, we must come down to details of details, an occupation not always agreeable or charming, but by and by richly rewarded with a more certain view of the whole.

If the experience of observing ancient and mediaeval works of art has shown us that certain maxims hold good we need these most of all in judging the most recent modern productions; for, since personal relations, love and hatred of individuals, favor or disfavor of the multitude so easily enter into the valuation of living or recently deceased artists, we are in all the more need of principles in order to pass judgment on our contemporaries. The inquiry can be conducted in two ways: by diminishing the influence of caprice; by bringing the question before a higher tribunal. The principle can be tested as well as its application; and even if we should not agree, the point in dispute can still be definitely and clearly pointed out.

Especially should we wish that the vivifying artist, in whose works we might perhaps have found something to remember, might test our judgments carefully in this way; for everyone who deserves this name is forced in our times to form, as a result of his work and his reflections, a theory, or at least a certain conception of theoretical means, by the use of which he gets along tolerably well in a variety of cases. It will often be noticed, however, that in this way he sets up as laws such maxims as are in accordance with his talent, his inclination, and his convenience. He is subject to a fate that is common to all mankind. How many act in this very way in other fields! But we are not cultivating ourselves when we merely set in motion with ease and convenience that which lies in us. Every artist, like every man, is only an individual, and will always lean to one side. For that reason, man should pursue so far as possible, both theoretically and practically, that which is contrary to his nature. Let the easy-going seek what is serious and severe; let the stern keep before his eyes the light and agreeable; the strong, loveliness; the amiable, strength; and everyone will develop his own nature the more, the farther he seems to remove himself from it. Every art requires the whole man; the highest possible degree of art requires all mankind.

The practice of the plastic arts is mechanical, and the training of the artist rightly begins in his earliest youth with the mechanical side; the rest of his education, on the other hand, is often neglected, for it ought to be far more careful than the training of others who have opportunity of deriving advantage from life itself. Society soon makes a rough person courteous, a business life makes the most simple person prudent; literary labors, which through print come before a great public, find opposition and correction everywhere; only the plastic artist is, for the most part, limited to a lonely workshop; he has dealings almost solely with the man who orders and pays for his labor, with a public which frequently follows only certain morbid impressions, with connoisseurs who make him restless, with auctioneers who receive every new work with praise and estimates of value such as would fitly honor the most superlative production.

But it is time to conclude this introduction lest it anticipate and forestall the work, instead of merely preceding it. We have so far at least designated the point from which we intend to set out; how far our views can and will spread, must at first develop gradually. The theory and criticism of literary art will, we hope, soon occupy us; and whatever life, travel, and daily events suggest to us, shall not be excluded. In closing, let us say a word on an important concern of this moment.

For the training of the artist, for the enjoyment of the friend of art, it was from time immemorial of the greatest significance in what place the works of art happened to be. There was a time when, except for slight changes of location, they remained for the most part in one place; now, however, a great change has occurred, which will have important consequences for art in general and in particular. At present we have perhaps more cause than ever to regard Italy as a great storehouse of art—as it still was until recently. When it is possible to give a general review of it, then it will be shown what the world lost at the moment when so many parts were torn from this great and ancient whole.

What was destroyed in the very act of tearing away will probably remain a secret forever; but a description of the new storehouse that is being formed in Paris will be possible in a few years. Then the method by which an artist and a lover of art is to use France and Italy can be indicated; and a further important and fine question will arise: what are other nations, particularly Germany and England, to do in this period of scattering and loss, to make generally useful the manifold and widely strewn treasures of art—a task requiring the true cosmopolitan mind which is found perhaps nowhere purer than in the arts and sciences? And what are they to do to help to form an ideal storehouse, which in the course of time may perhaps happily compensate us for what the present moment tears away when it does not destroy?

So much in general of the purpose of a work in which we desire many earnest and friendly sympathizers

PREFACES TO VARIOUS
VOLUMES OF POEMS

BY WILLIAM WORDSWORTH

ADVERTISEMENT
TO LYRICAL BALLADS
(1798)

IT is the honourable characteristic of Poetry that its
materials are to be found in every subject which can
interest the human mind. The evidence of this fact
is to be sought, not in the writings of Critics, but in those
of Poets themselves.

The majority of the following poems are to be considered
as experiments. They were written chiefly with a view to
ascertain how far the language of conversation in the middle
and lower classes of society is adapted to the purposes of
poetic pleasure. Readers accustomed to the gaudiness and
inane phraseology of many modern writers, if they persist
in reading this book to its conclusion, will perhaps frequently
have to struggle with feelings of strangeness and awkwardness: they will look round for poetry, and will be induced
to inquire by what species of courtesy these attempts can be
permitted to assume that title. It is desirable that such readers, for their own sakes, should not suffer the solitary word
Poetry, a word of very disputed meaning, to stand in the way
of their gratification; but that, while they are perusing this
book, they should ask themselves if it contains a natural
delineation of human passions, human characters, and
human incidents; and if the answer be favourable to the
author's wishes, that they should consent to be pleased in

---

[1] William Wordsworth (1770-1850), probably the greatest of the poets of
the Romantic Movement in England, was also foremost in the critical defence of that movement. The Prefaces and Essays printed here form a
kind of manifesto of the reaction from the poetical traditions of the
eighteenth century; and contain besides some of the soundest theorizing
on the nature of poetry to be found in English. They afford an interesting comparison with the parallel protest in Victor Hugo's Preface to
"Cromwell," to be found later in the volume.

spite of that most dreadful enemy to our pleasures, our own pre-established codes of decision.

Readers of superior judgement may disapprove of the style in which many of these pieces are executed; it must be expected that many lines and phrases will not exactly suit their taste. It will perhaps appear to them, that wishing to avoid the prevalent fault of the day, the author has sometimes descended too low, and that many of his expressions are too familiar, and not of sufficient dignity. It is apprehended that the more conversant the reader is with our elder writers, and with those in modern times who have been the most successful in painting manners and passions, the fewer complaints of this kind will he have to make.

An accurate taste in poetry, and in all the other arts, Sir Joshua Reynolds has observed, is an acquired talent, which can only be produced by severe thought, and a long continued intercourse with the best models of composition. This is mentioned not with so ridiculous a purpose as to prevent the most inexperienced reader from judging for himself; but merely to temper the rashness of decision, and to suggest that if poetry be a subject on which much time has not been bestowed, the judgement may be erroneous, and that in many cases it necessarily will be so.

The tale of *Goody Blake and Harry Gill* is founded on a well-authenticated fact which happened in Warwickshire. Of the other poems in the collection, it may be proper to say that they are either absolute inventions of the author, or facts which took place within his personal observation or that of his friends. The poem of *The Thorn*, as the reader will soon discover, is not supposed to be spoken in the author's own person: the character of the loquacious narrator will sufficiently show itself in the course of the story. *The Rime of the Ancyent Marinere* was professedly written in imitation of the *style*, as well as of the spirit of the elder poets; but with a few exceptions, the Author believes that the language adopted in it has been equally intelligible for these three last centuries. The lines entitled *Expostulation and Reply*, and those which follow, arose out of conversation with a friend who was somewhat unreasonably attached to modern books of moral philosophy.

PREFACE TO LYRICAL BALLADS

(1800)

THE first volume of these Poems has already been submitted to general perusal. It was published, as an experiment, which, I hoped, might be of some use to ascertain, how far, by fitting to metrical arrangement a selection of the real language of men in a state of vivid sensation, that sort of pleasure and that quantity of pleasure may be imparted, which a Poet may rationally endeavour to impart.

I had formed no very inaccurate estimate of the probable effect of those Poems: I flattered myself that they who should be pleased with them would read them with more than common pleasure: and, on the other hand, I was well aware, that by those who should dislike them, they would be read with more than common dislike. The result has differed from my expectation in this only, that a greater number have been pleased than I ventured to hope I should please.

. . . .

Several of my Friends are anxious for the success of these Poems, from a belief, that, if the views with which they were composed were indeed realized, a class of Poetry would be produced, well adapted to interest mankind permanently, and not unimportant in the quality, and in the multiplicity of its moral relations: and on this account they have advised me to prefix a systematic defence of the theory upon which the Poems were written. But I was unwilling to undertake the task, knowing that on this occasion the Reader would look coldly upon my arguments, since I might be suspected of having been principally influenced by the selfish and foolish hope of *reasoning* him into an approbation of these particular Poems: and I was still more unwilling to undertake the task, because, adequately to display the opinions, and fully to enforce the arguments, would require a space wholly disproportionate to a preface. For, to treat the subject with the clearness and coherence of which it is susceptible, it would be necessary to give a full account of the present state of the public taste in this country, and to determine how far this taste is healthy or depraved; which, again, could not be determined, without pointing out in what manner language and the human mind act and re-act on each other, and without retracing the revolutions, not of literature alone, but likewise of society itself. I have therefore altogether declined to enter regularly upon this defence; yet I am sensible, that there would be something like impropriety in abruptly obtruding upon the Public, without a few words of introduction, Poems so materially different from those upon which general approbation is at present bestowed.

It is supposed, that by the act of writing in verse an Author makes a formal engagement that he will gratify certain known habits of association; that he not only thus apprises the Reader that certain classes of ideas and expressions will be found in his book, but that others will be carefully excluded. This exponent or symbol held forth by metrical language must in different eras of literature have excited very different expectations: for example, in the age of Catullus, Terence, and Lucretius, and that of Statius or Claudian; and in our own country, in the age of Shakespeare and Beaumont and Fletcher, and that of Donne and Cowley, or Dryden, or Pope. I will not take upon me to determine the exact import of the promise which, by the act of writing in verse, an Author in the present day makes to his reader: but it will undoubtedly appear to many persons that I have not fulfilled the terms of an engagement thus voluntarily contracted. They who have been accustomed to the gaudiness and inane phraseology of many modern writers, if they persist in reading this book to its conclusion, will, no doubt, frequently have to struggle with feelings of strangeness and awkwardness: they will look round for poetry, and will be induced to inquire by what species of courtesy these attempts can be permitted to assume that title. I hope therefore the reader will not censure me for attempting to state what I have proposed to myself to perform; and also (as far as the limits of a preface will permit) to explain some of the chief reasons which have determined me in the choice of my purpose: that at least he may be spared any unpleasant feeling of disappointment, and that I myself may be protected from one of the most dishonourable accusations which can be brought against an Author; namely, that of an indolence which prevents him from endeavouring to ascertain what is his duty, or, when his duty is ascertained, prevents him from performing it.

The principal object, then, proposed in these Poems was to choose incidents and situations from common life, and to relate or describe them, throughout, as far as was possible in a selection of language really used by men, and, at the same time, to throw over them a certain colouring of imagination, whereby ordinary things should be presented to the mind in an unusual aspect; and, further, and above all, to make these incidents and situations interesting by tracing in them, truly though not ostentatiously, the primary laws of our nature: chiefly, as far as regards the manner in which we associate ideas in a state of excitement. Humble and rustic life was generally chosen, because, in that condition, the essential passions of the heart find a better soil in which they can attain their maturity, are less under restraint, and speak a plainer and more emphatic language; because in that condition of life our elementary feelings coexist in a state of greater simplicity, and, consequently, may be more accurately contemplated, and more forcibly communicated; because the manners of rural life germinate from those elementary feelings, and, from the necessary character of rural occupations, are more easily comprehended, and are more durable; and, lastly, because in that condition the passions of men are incorporated with the beautiful and permanent forms of nature. The language, too, of these men has been adopted (purified indeed from what appear to be its real defects, from all lasting and rational causes of dislike or disgust) because such men hourly communicate with the best objects from which the best part of language is originally derived; and because, from their rank in society and the sameness and narrow circle of their intercourse, being less under the influence of social vanity, they convey their feelings and notions in simple and unelaborated expressions. Accordingly, such a language, arising out of repeated experience and regular feelings, is a more permanent, and a far more philosophical language, than that which is frequently substituted for it by Poets, who think that they are conferring honour upon themselves and their art, in proportion as they separate themselves from the sympathies of men, and indulge in arbitrary and capricious habits of expression, in order to furnish food for fickle tastes, and fickle appetites, of their own creation.[1]

I cannot, however, be insensible to the present outcry against the triviality and meanness, both of thought and language, which some of my contemporaries have occasionally introduced into their metrical compositions; and I acknowledge that this defect, where it exists, is more dishonourable to the Writer's own character than false refinement or arbitrary innovation, though I should contend at the same time, that it is far less pernicious in the sum of its consequences. From such verses the Poems in these volumes will be found distinguished at least by one mark of difference, that each of them has a worthy *purpose*. Not that I always began to write with a distinct purpose formerly conceived; but habits of meditation have, I trust, so prompted and regulated my feelings, that my descriptions of such objects as strongly excite those feelings, will be found to carry along with them a *purpose*. If this opinion be erroneous, I can have little right to the name of a Poet. For all good poetry is the spontaneous overflow of powerful feelings: and though this be true, Poems to which any value can be attached were never produced on any variety of subjects but by a man who, being possessed of more than usual organic sensibility, had also thought long and deeply. For our continued influxes of feeling are modified and directed by our thoughts, which are indeed the representatives of all our past feelings; and, as by contemplating the relation of these general representatives to each

[1] It is worth while here to observe, that the affecting parts of Chaucer are almost always expressed in language pure and universally intelligible even to this day.

other, we discover what is really important to men, so, by the repetition and continuance of this act, our feelings will be connected with important subjects, till at length, if we be originally possessed of much sensibility, such habits of mind will be produced, that, by obeying blindly and mechanically the impulses of those habits, we shall describe objects, and utter sentiments, of such a nature, and in such connexion with each other, that the understanding of the Reader must necessarily be in some degree enlightened, and his affections strengthened and purified.

It has been said that each of these poems has a purpose. Another circumstance must be mentioned which distinguishes these Poems from the popular Poetry of the day; it is this, that the feeling therein developed gives importance to the action and situation, and not the action and situation to the feeling.

A sense of false modesty shall not prevent me from asserting, that the Reader's attention is pointed to this mark of distinction, far less for the sake of these particular Poems than from the general importance of the subject. The subject is indeed important! For the human mind is capable of being excited without the application of gross and violent stimulants; and he must have a very faint perception of its beauty and dignity who does not know this, and who does not further know, that one being is elevated above another, in proportion as he possesses this capability. It has therefore appeared to me, that to endeavour to produce or enlarge this capability is one of the best services in which, at any period, a Writer can be engaged; but this service, excellent at all times, is especially so at the present day. For a multitude of causes, unknown to former times, are now acting with a combined force to blunt the discriminating powers of the mind, and, unfitting it for all voluntary exertion, to reduce it to a state of almost savage torpor. The most effective of these causes are the great national events which are daily taking place, and the increasing accumulation of men in cities, where the uniformity of their occupations produces a craving for extraordinary incident, which the rapid communication of intelligence hourly gratifies. To this tendency of life and manners the literature and theatrical exhibitions of the country have conformed themselves. The invaluable works of our elder writers, I had almost said the works of Shakespeare and Milton, are driven into neglect by frantic novels, sickly and stupid German Tragedies, and deluges of idle and extrava, gant stories in verse.—When I think upon this degrading thirst after outrageous stimulation, I am almost ashamed to have spoken of the feeble endeavour made in these volumes to counteract it; and, reflecting upon the magnitude of the general evil, I should be oppressed with no dishonourable melancholy, had I not a deep impression of certain inherent and indestructible qualities of the human mind, and likewise of certain powers in the great and permanent objects that act upon it, which are equally inherent and indestructible; and were there not added to this impression a belief, that the time is approaching when the evil will be systematically opposed, by men of greater powers, and with far more distinguished success.

Having dwelt thus long on the subjects and aim of these Poems, I shall request the Reader's permission to apprise him of a few circumstances relating to their *style,* in order, among other reasons, that he may not censure me for not having performed what I never attempted. The Reader will find that personifications of abstract ideas rarely occur in these volumes; and are utterly rejected, as an ordinary device to elevate the style, and raise it above prose. My purpose was to imitate, and, as far as possible, to adopt the very language of men; and assuredly such personifications do not make any natural or regular part of that language. They are, indeed, a figure of speech occasionally prompted by passion, and I have made use of them as such; but have endeavoured utterly to reject them as a mechanical device of style, or as a family language which Writers in metre seem to lay claim to by prescription. I have wished to keep the Reader in the company of flesh and blood, persuaded that by so doing I shall interest him. Others who pursue a different track will interest him likewise; I do not interfere with their claim, but wish to prefer a claim of my own. There will also be found in these volumes little of what is usually called poetic diction; as much pains has

been taken to avoid it as is ordinarily taken to produce it;
this has been done for the reason already alleged, to bring
my language near to the language of men; and further,
because the pleasure which I have proposed to myself to
impart, is of a kind very different from that which is
supposed by many persons to be the proper object of poetry.
Without being culpably particular, I do not know how to
give my Reader a more exact notion of the style in which it
was my wish and intention to write, than by informing
him that I have at all times endeavoured to look steadily at
my subject; consequently, there is I hope in these Poems
little falsehood of description, and my ideas are expressed
in language fitted to their respective importance.   Something must have been gained by this practice, as it is friendly
to one property of all good poetry, namely, good sense: but
it has necessarily cut me off from a large portion of phrases
and figures of speech which from father to son have long
been regarded as the common inheritance of Poets.   I have
also thought it expedient to restrict myself still further, having abstained from the use of many expressions, in themselves proper and beautiful, but which have been foolishly
repeated by bad Poets, till such feelings of disgust are
connected with them as it is scarcely possible by any art
of association to overpower.

If in a poem there should be found a series of lines, or
even a single line, in which the language, though naturally
arranged, and according to the strict laws of metre, does not
differ from that of prose, there is a numerous class of
critics, who, when they stumble upon these prosaisms, as
they call them, imagine that they have made a notable discovery, and exult over the Poet as over a man ignorant of
his own profession.   Now these men would establish a
canon of criticism which the Reader will conclude he must
utterly reject, if he wishes to be pleased with these volumes.
And it would be a most easy task to prove to him, that not
only the language of a large portion of every good poem,
even of the most elevated character, must necessarily, except with reference to the metre, in no respect differ from
that of good prose, but likewise that some of the most interesting parts of the best poems will be found to be strictly

the language of prose when prose is well written. The truth of this assertion might be demonstrated by innumerable passages from almost all the poetical writings, even of Milton himself. To illustrate the subject in a general manner, I will here adduce a short composition of Gray, who was at the head of those who, by their reasonings, have attempted to widen the space of separation betwixt Prose and Metrical composition, and was more than any other man curiously elaborate in the structure of his own poetic diction.

> In vain to me the smiling mornings shine,
> And reddening Phœbus lifts his golden fire:
> The birds in vain their amorous descant join,
> Or cheerful fields resume their green attire.
> These ears, alas! for other notes repine;
> *A different object do these eyes require;*
> *My lonely anguish melts no heart but mine;*
> *And in my breast the imperfect joys expire;*
> Yet morning smiles the busy race to cheer,
> And new-born pleasure brings to happier men;
> The fields to all their wonted tribute bear;
> To warm their little loves the birds complain.
> *I fruitless mourn to him that cannot hear,*
> *And weep the more because I weep in vain.*

It will easily be perceived, that the only part of this Sonnet which is of any value is the lines printed in Italics; it is equally obvious, that, except in the rhyme, and in the use of the single word 'fruitless' for fruitlessly, which is so far a defect, the language of these lines does in no respect differ from that of prose.

By the foregoing quotation it has been shown that the language of Prose may yet be well adapted to Poetry; and it was previously asserted, that a large portion of the language of every good poem can in no respect differ from that of good Prose. We will go further. It may be safely affirmed, that there neither is, nor can be, any *essential* difference between the language of prose and metrical composition. We are fond of tracing the resemblance between Poetry and Painting, and, accordingly, we call them Sisters: but where shall we find bonds of connexion sufficiently strict to typify the affinity betwixt metrical and prose composition? They both speak by and to the same organs; the bodies in

which both of them are clothed may be said to be of the
same substance, their affections are kindred, and almost
identical, not necessarily differing even in degree; Poetry[2]
sheds no tears 'such as Angels weep,' but natural and
human tears; she can boast of no celestial choir that distinguishes her vital juices from those of prose; the same
human blood circulates through the veins of them both,

If it be affirmed that rhyme and metrical arrangement
of themselves constitute a distinction which overturns what
has just been said on the strict affinity of metrical language
with that of prose, and paves the way for other artificial
distinctions which the mind voluntarily admits, I answer
that the language of such Poetry as is here recommended
is, as far as is possible, a selection of the language really
spoken by men; that this selection, wherever it is made with
true taste and feeling, will of itself form a distinction far
greater than would at first be imagined, and will entirely
separate the composition from the vulgarity and meanness of
ordinary life; and, if metre be superadded thereto, I believe
that a dissimilitude will be produced altogether sufficient for
the gratification of a rational mind. What other distinction
would we have? Whence is it to come? And where is it
to exist? Not, surely, where the Poet speaks through the
mouths of his characters: it cannot be necessary here, either
for elevation of style, or any of its supposed ornaments:
for, if the Poet's subject be judiciously chosen, it will
naturally, and upon fit occasion, lead him to passions the
language of which, if selected truly and judiciously, must
necessarily be dignified and variegated, and alive with
metaphors and figures. I forbear to speak of an incongruity
which would shock the intelligent Reader, should the Poet
interweave any foreign splendour of his own with that which
the passion naturally suggests: it is sufficient to say that
such addition is unnecessary. And, surely, it is more
probable that those passages, which with propriety abound

[2] I here use the word 'Poetry' (though against my own judgement) as
opposed to the word Prose, and synonymous with metrical composition.
But much confusion has been introduced into criticism by this contradis-
tinction of Poetry and Prose, instead of the more philosophical one of
Poetry and Matter of Fact, or Science. The only strict antithesis to Prose
is Metre; nor is this, in truth, a *strict* antithesis, because lines and passages
of metre so naturally occur in writing prose, that it would be scarcely
possible to avoid them, even were it desirable.

with metaphors and figures, will have their due effect, if, upon other occasions where the passions are of a milder character, the style also be subdued and temperate.

But, as the pleasure which I hope to give by the Poems now presented to the Reader must depend entirely on just notions upon this subject, and, as it is in itself of high importance to our taste and moral feelings, I cannot content myself with these detached remarks. And if, in what I am about to say, it shall appear to some that my labour is unnecessary, and that I am like a man fighting a battle without enemies, such persons may be reminded, that, whatever be the language outwardly holden by men, a practical faith in the opinions which I am wishing to establish is almost unknown. If my conclusions are admitted, and carried as far as they must be carried if admitted at all, our judgements concerning the works of the greatest Poets both ancient and modern will be far different from what they are at present, both when we praise, and when we censure: and our moral feelings influencing and influenced by these judgements will, I believe, be corrected and purified.

Taking up the subject, then, upon general grounds, let me ask, what is meant by the word Poet? What is a Poet? To whom does he address himself? And what language is to be expected from him?—He is a man speaking to men: a man, it is true, endowed with more lively sensibility, more enthusiasm and tenderness, who has a greater knowledge of human nature, and a more comprehensive soul, than are supposed to be common among mankind; a man pleased with his own passions and volitions, and who rejoices more than other men in the spirit of life that is in him; delighting to contemplate similar volitions and passions as manifested in the goings-on of the Universe, and habitually impelled to create them where he does not find them. To these qualities he has added a disposition to be affected more than other men by absent things as if they were present; an ability of conjuring up in himself passions, which are indeed far from being the same as those produced by real events, yet (especially in those parts of the general sympathy which are pleasing and delightful) do more nearly resemble the passions produced by real events, than anything which, from the motions of their own minds merely, other men are accustomed to feel in themselves:—whence, and from practice, he has acquired a greater readiness and power in expressing what he thinks and feels, and especially those thoughts and feelings which, by his own choice, or from the structure of his own mind, arise in him without immediate external excitement.

But whatever portion of this faculty we may suppose even the greatest Poet to possess, there cannot be a doubt that the language which it will suggest to him, must often, in liveliness and truth, fall short of that which is uttered by men in real life, under the actual pressure of those passions, certain shadows of which the Poet thus produces, or feels to be produced, in himself.

However exalted a notion we would wish to cherish of the character of a Poet, it is obvious, that while he describes and imitates passions, his employment is in some degree mechanical, compared with the freedom and power of real and substantial action and suffering. So that it will be the wish of the Poet to bring his feelings near to those of the persons whose feelings he describes, nay, for short spaces of time, perhaps, to let himself slip into an entire delusion, and even confound and identify his own feelings with theirs; modifying only the language which is thus suggested to him by a consideration that he describes for a particular purpose, that of giving pleasure. Here, then, he will apply the principle of selection which has been already insisted upon. He will depend upon this for removing what would otherwise be painful or disgusting in the passion; he will feel that there is no necessity to trick out or to elevate nature: and, the more industriously he applies this principle, the deeper will be his faith that no words, which *his* fancy or imagination can suggest, will be to be compared with those which are the emanations of reality and truth.

But it may be said by those who do not object to the general spirit of these remarks, that, as it is impossible for the Poet to produce upon all occasions language as exquisitely fitted for the passion as that which the real passion itself suggests, it is proper that he should consider himself as in the situation of a translator, who does not scruple to substitute excellencies of another kind for those which are unattainable by him; and endeavours occasionally to surpass his original, in order to make some amends for the general inferiority to which he feels that he must submit. But this would be to encourage idleness and unmanly despair. Further, it is the language of men who speak of what they do not understand; who talk of Poetry as of a matter of amusement and idle pleasure; who will converse with us as gravely about a *taste* for Poetry, as they express it, as if it were a thing as indifferent as a taste for rope-dancing, or Frontiniac or Sherry. Aristotle, I have been told, has said, that Poetry is the most philosophic of all writing: it is so: its object is truth, not individual and local, but general, and operative; not standing upon external testimony, but carried alive into the heart by passion; truth which is its own testimony, which gives competence and confidence to the tribunal to which it appeals, and receives them from the same tribunal. Poetry is the image of man and nature. The obstacles which stand in the way of the fidelity of the Biographer and Historian, and of their consequent utility, are incalculably greater than those which are to be encountered by the Poet who comprehends the dignity of his art. The Poet writes under one restriction only, namely, the necessity of giving immediate pleasure to a human Being possessed of that information which may be expected from him, not as a lawyer, a physician, a mariner, an astronomer, or a natural philosopher, but as a Man. Except this one restriction, there is no object standing between the Poet and the image of things; between this, and the Biographer and Historian, there are a thousand.

Nor let this necessity of producing immediate pleasure be considered as a degradation of the Poet's art. It is far otherwise. It is an acknowledgement of the beauty of the universe, an acknowledgement the more sincere, because not formal, but indirect; it is a task light and easy to him who looks at the world in the spirit of love: further, it is a homage paid to the native and naked dignity of man, to the grand elementary principle of pleasure, by which he knows, and feels, and lives, and moves. We have no sympathy but what is propagated by pleasure: I would not be misunderstood; but wherever we sympathize with pain, it will be found that the sympathy is produced and carried on by subtle combinations with pleasure. We have no knowledge, that is, no general principles drawn from the contemplation of particular facts, but what has been built up by pleasure, and exists in us by pleasure alone. The Man of science, the Chemist and Mathematician, whatever difficulties and disgusts they may have had to struggle with, know and feel this. However painful may be the objects with which the Anatomist's knowledge is connected, he feels that his knowledge is pleasure; and where he has no pleasure he has no knowledge. What then does the Poet? He considers man and the objects that surround him as acting and re-acting upon each other, so as to produce an infinite complexity of pain and pleasure; he considers man in his own nature and in his ordinary life as contemplating this with a certain quantity of immediate knowledge, with certain convictions, intuitions, and deductions, which from habit acquire the quality of intuitions; he considers him as looking upon this complex scene of ideas and sensations, and finding everywhere objects that immediately excite in him sympathies which, from the necessities of his nature, are accompanied by an overbalance of enjoyment.

To this knowledge which all men carry about with them, and to these sympathies in which, without any other discipline than that of our daily life, we are fitted to take delight, the Poet principally directs his attention. He considers man and nature as essentially adapted to each other, and the mind of man as naturally the mirror of the fairest and most interesting properties of nature. And thus the Poet, prompted by this feeling of pleasure, which accompanies him through the whole course of his studies, converses with general nature, with affections akin to those, which, through labour and length of time, the Man of science has raised up in himself, by conversing with those particular parts of nature which are the objects of his studies. The knowledge both of the Poet and the Man of science is pleasure; but the knowledge of the one cleaves to us as a necessary part of our existence, our natural and unalienable inheritance; the other is a personal and individual acquisition, slow to come to us, and by no habitual and direct sympathy connecting us with our fellow-beings. The Man of science seeks truth as a remote and unknown benefactor; he cherishes and loves it in his solitude: the Poet, singing a song in which all human beings join with him, rejoices in the presence of truth as our visible friend and hourly companion. Poetry is the breath and finer spirit of all knowledge; it is the impassioned expression which is in the countenance of all Science. Emphatically may it be said of the Poet, as Shakespeare hath said of man, 'that he looks before and after.' He is the rock of defence for human nature; an upholder and preserver, carrying everywhere with him relationship and love. In spite of difference of soil and climate, of language and manners, of laws and customs: in spite of things silently gone out of mind, and things violently destroyed; the Poet binds together by passion and knowledge the vast empire of human society, as it is spread over the whole earth, and over all time. The objects of the Poet's thoughts are everywhere; though the eyes and senses of man are, it is true, his favourite guides, yet he will follow wheresoever he can find an atmosphere of sensation in which to move his wings. Poetry is the first and last of all knowledge—it is as immortal as the heart of man. If the labours of Men of science should ever create any material revolution, direct or indirect, in our condition, and in the impressions which we habitually receive, the Poet will sleep then no more than at present; he will be ready to follow the steps of the Man of science, not only in those general indirect effects, but he will be at his side, carrying sensation into the midst of the objects of the science itself. The remotest discoveries of the Chemist, the Botanist, or Mineralogist, will be as proper objects of the Poet's art as any upon which it can be employed, if the time should ever come when these things shall be familiar to us, and the relations under which they are contemplated by the followers of these respective sciences shall be manifestly and palpably material to us as enjoying and suffering beings. If the time should ever come when what is now called science, thus familiarized to men, shall be ready to put on, as it

were, a form of flesh and blood, the Poet will lend his
divine spirit to aid the transfiguration, and will welcome the
Being thus produced, as a dear and genuine inmate of the
household of man.—It is not, then, to be supposed that any
one, who holds that sublime notion of Poetry which I have
attempted to convey, will break in upon the sanctity and
truth of his pictures by transitory and accidental ornaments,
and endeavour to excite admiration of himself by arts, the
necessity of which must manifestly depend upon the assumed
meanness of his subject.

What has been thus far said applies to Poetry in general;
but especially to those parts of composition where the Poet
speaks through the mouths of his characters; and upon this
point it appears to authorize the conclusion that there are
few persons of good sense, who would not allow that the
dramatic parts of composition are defective, in proportion
as they deviate from the real language of nature, and are
coloured by a diction of the Poet's own, either peculiar to
him as an individual Poet or belonging simply to Poets in
general; to a body of men who, from the circumstance of
their compositions being in metre, it is expected will employ
a particular language.

It is not, then, in the dramatic parts of composition that
we look for this distinction of language; but still it may be
proper and necessary where the Poet speaks to us in his own
person and character. To this I answer by referring the
Reader to the description before given of a Poet. Among
the qualities there enumerated as principally conducing to
form a Poet, is implied nothing differing in kind from other
men, but only in degree. The sum of what was said is, that
the Poet is chiefly distinguished from other men by a greater
promptness to think and feel without immediate external
excitement, and a greater power in expressing such thoughts
and feelings as are produced in him in that manner. But
these passions and thoughts and feelings are the general
passions and thoughts and feelings of men. And with what
are they connected? Undoubtedly with our moral sentiments
and animal sensations, and with the causes which excite
these; with the operations of the elements, and the appearances of the visible universe; with storm and sunshine,

with the revolutions of the seasons, with cold and heat, with loss of friends and kindred, with injuries and resentments, gratitude and hope, with fear and sorrow. These, and the like, are the sensations and objects which the Poet describes, as they are the sensations of other men, and the objects which interest them. The Poet thinks and feels in the spirit of human passions. How, then, can his language differ in any material degree from that of all other men who feel vividly and see clearly? It might be *proved* that it is impossible. But supposing that this were not the case, the Poet might then be allowed to use a peculiar language when expressing his feelings for his own gratification, or that of men like himself. But Poets do not write for Poets alone, but for men. Unless therefore we are advocates for that admiration which subsists upon ignorance, and that pleasure which arises from hearing what we do not understand, the Poet must descend from this supposed height; and, in order to excite rational sympathy, he must express himself as other men express themselves. To this it may be added, that while he is only selecting from the real language of men, or, which amounts to the same thing, composing accurately in the spirit of such selection, he is treading upon safe ground, and we know what we are to expect from him. Our feelings are the same with respect to metre; for, as it may be proper to remind the Reader, the distinction of metre is regular and uniform, and not, like that which is produced by what is usually called POETIC DICTION, arbitrary, and subject to infinite caprices upon which no calculation whatever can be made. In the one case, the Reader is utterly at the mercy of the Poet, respecting what imagery or diction he may choose to connect with the passion; whereas, in the other, the metre obeys certain laws, to which the Poet and Reader both willingly submit because they are certain, and because no interference is made by them with the passion, but such as the concurring testimony of ages has shown to heighten and improve the pleasure which co-exists with it.

It will now be proper to answer an obvious question, namely, Why, professing these opinions, have I written in verse? To this, in addition to such answer as is included in what has been already said, I reply, in the first place, Because,

however I may have restricted myself, there is still left open
to me what confessedly constitutes the most valuable object
of all writing, whether in prose or verse; the great and universal passions of men, the most general and interesting of
their occupations, and the entire world of nature before me—
to supply endless combinations of forms and imagery.
Now, supposing for a moment that whatever is interesting
in these objects may be as vividly described in prose, why
should I be condemned for attempting to superadd to such
description the charm which, by the consent of all nations,
is acknowledged to exist in metrical language? To
this, by such as are yet unconvinced, it may be answered that
a very small part of the pleasure given by Poetry depends
upon the metre, and that it is injudicious to write in metre,
unless it be accompanied with the other artificial distinctions
of style with which metre is usually accompanied, and that,
by such deviation, more will be lost from the shock which
will thereby be given to the Reader's associations than will
be counterbalanced by any pleasure which he can derive
from the general power of numbers. In answer to those
who still contend for the necessity of accompanying metre
with certain appropriate colours of style in order to the accomplishment of its appropriate end, and who also, in my
opinion, greatly underrate the power of metre in itself, it
might, perhaps, as far as relates to these Volumes, have been
almost sufficient to observe, that poems are extant, written
upon more humble subjects, and in a still more naked and
simple style, which have continued to give pleasure from
generation to generation. Now, if nakedness and simplicity
be a defect, the fact here mentioned affords a strong presumption that poems somewhat less naked and simple are
capable of affording pleasure at the present day; and, what
I wish *chiefly* to attempt, at present, was to justify myself for having written under the impression of this belief.

But various causes might be pointed out why, when the
style is manly, and the subject of some importance, words
metrically arranged will long continue to impart such a
pleasure to mankind as he who proves the extent of that
pleasure will be desirous to impart. The end of Poetry is
to produce excitement in co-existence with an overbalance

of pleasure; but, by the supposition, excitement is an unusual and irregular state of the mind; ideas and feelings do not, in that state, suceeed each other in accustomed order. If the words, however, by which this excitement is produced be in themselves powerful, or the images and feelings have an undue proportion of pain connected with them, there is some danger that the excitement may be carried beyond its proper bounds. Now the co-presence of something regular, something to which the mind has been accustomed in various moods and in a less excited state, cannot but have great efficacy in tempering and restraining the passion by an inter-texture of ordinary feeling, and of feeling not strictly and necessarily connected with the passion. This is unquestionably true; and hence, though the opinion will at first appear paradoxical, from the tendency of metre to divest language, in a certain degree, of its reality, and thus to throw a sort of half-consciousness of unsubstantial existence over the whole composition, there can be little doubt but that more pathetic situations and sentiments, that is, those which have a greater proportion of pain connected with them, may be endured in metrical composition, especially in rhyme, than in prose. The metre of the old ballads is very artless; yet they contain many passages which would illustrate this opinion; and, I hope, if the following Poems be attentively perused, similar instances will be found in them. This opinion may be further illustrated by appealing to the Reader's own experience of the reluctance with which he comes to the re-perusal of the distressful parts of *Clarissa Harlowe,* or *The Gamester;* while Shakespeare's writings, in the most pathetic scenes, never act upon us, as pathetic, beyond the bounds of pleasure —an effect which, in a much greater degree than might at first be imagined, is to be ascribed to small, but continual and regular impulses of pleasurable surprise from the metrical arrangement.—On the other hand (what it must be allowed will much more frequently happen) if the Poet's words should be incommensurate with the passion, and inadequate to raise the Reader to a height of desirable excitement, then (unless the Poet's choice of his metre has been grossly injudicious), in the feelings of pleasure which the Reader has been accustomed to connect with metre in general, and in the feeling, whether cheerful or melancholy, which he has been accustomed to connect with that particular movement of metre, there will be found something which will greatly contribute to impart passion to the words, and to effect the complex end which the Poet proposes to himself.

If I had undertaken a SYSTEMATIC defence of the theory here maintained, it would have been my duty to develop the various causes upon which the pleasure received from metrical language depends. Among the chief of these causes is to be reckoned a principle which must be well known to those who have made any of the Arts the object of accurate reflection; namely, the pleasure which the mind derives from the perception of similitude in dissimilitude. This principle is the great spring of the activity of our minds, and their chief feeder. From this principle the direction of the sexual appetite, and all the passions connected with it, take their origin: it is the life of our ordinary conversation; and upon the accuracy with which similitude in dissimilitude, and dissimilitude in similitude are perceived, depend our taste and our moral feelings. It would not be a useless employment to apply this principle to the consideration of metre, and to show that metre is hence enabled to afford much pleasure, and to point out in what manner that pleasure is produced. But my limits will not permit me to enter upon this subject, and I must content myself with a general summary.

I have said that poetry is the spontaneous overflow of powerful feelings: it takes its origin from emotion recollected in tranquillity: the emotion is contemplated till, by a species of reaction, the tranquillity gradually disappears, and an emotion, kindred to that which was before the subject of contemplation, is gradually produced, and does itself actually exist in the mind. In this mood successful composition generally begins, and in a mood similar to this it is carried on; but the emotion, of whatever kind, and in whatever degree, from various causes, is qualified by various pleasures, so that in describing any passions whatsoever, which are voluntarily described, the mind will, upon the whole, be in a state of enjoyment. If Nature be thus cautious to preserve in a state of enjoyment a being so employed, the Poet ought to profit by the lesson held forth to him, and ought especially to take care, that, whatever passions he communicates to his Reader, those passions, if his Reader's mind be sound and vigorous, should always be accompanied with an overbalance of pleasure. Now the music of harmonious metrical language, the sense of difficulty overcome, and the blind association of pleasure which has been previously received from works of rhyme or metre of the same or similar construction, an indistinct perception perpetually renewed of language closely resembling that of real life, and yet, in the circumstance of metre, differing from it so widely—all these imperceptibly make up a complex feeling of delight, which is of the most important use in tempering the painful feeling always found intermingled with powerful descriptions of the deeper passions. This effect is always produced in pathetic and impassioned poetry; while, in lighter compositions, the ease and gracefulness with which the Poet manages his numbers are themselves confessedly a principal source of the gratification of the Reader. All that it is *necessary* to say, however, upon this subject, may be effected by affirming, what few persons will deny, that, of two descriptions, either of passions, manners, or characters, each of them equally well executed, the one in prose and the other in verse, the verse will be read a hundred times where the prose is read once.

Having thus explained a few of my reasons for writing in verse, and why I have chosen subjects from common life, and endeavoured to bring my language near to the real language of men, if I have been too minute in pleading my own cause, I have at the same time been treating a subject of general interest; and for this reason a few words shall be added with reference solely to these particular poems, and to some defects which will probably be found in them. I am sensible that my associations must have sometimes been particular instead of general, and that, consequently, giving to things a false importance, I may have sometimes written upon unworthy subjects; but I am less apprehensive on this account, than that my language may frequently have suffered from those arbitrary connexions of feelings and ideas with particular words and phrases, from which no man can altogether protect himself. Hence I have no doubt, that, in some instances, feelings, even of the ludicrous, may be given to my Readers by expressions which appeared to me tender and pathetic. Such faulty expressions, were I convinced they were faulty at present, and that they must necessarily continue to be so, I would willingly take all reasonable pains to correct. But it is dangerous to make these alterations on the simple authority of a few individuals, or even of certain classes of men; for where the understanding of an Author is not convinced, or his feelings altered, this cannot be done without great injury to himself: for his own feelings are his stay and support; and, if he set them aside in one instance, he may be induced to repeat this act till his mind shall lose all confidence in itself, and become utterly debilitated. To this it may be added, that the critic ought never to forget that he is himself exposed to the same errors as the Poet, and, perhaps, in a much greater degree: for there can be no presumption in saying of most readers, that it is not probable they will be so well acquainted with the various stages of meaning through which words have passed, or with the fickleness or stability of the relations of particular ideas to each other; and, above all, since they are so much less interested in the subject, they may decide lightly and carelessly.

Long as the Reader has been detained, I hope he will permit me to caution him against a mode of false criticism which has been applied to Poetry, in which the language closely resembles that of life and nature. Such verses have been triumphed over in parodies, of which Dr. Johnson's stanza is a fair specimen:—

> I put my hat upon my head
> And walked into the Strand,
> And there I met another man
> Whose hat was in his hand.

Immediately under these lines let us place one of the most justly admired stanzas of the 'Babes in the Wood.'

> These pretty Babes with hand in hand
> Went wandering up and down;
> But never more they saw the Man
> Approaching from the Town.

In both these stanzas the words, and the order of the words, in no respect differ from the most unimpassioned conversation. There are words in both, for example, 'the Strand,' and 'the Town,' connected with none but the most familiar ideas; yet the one stanza we admit as admirable, and the other as a fair example of the superlatively contemptible. Whence arises this difference? Not from the metre, not from the language, not from the order of the words; but the *matter* expressed in Dr. Johnson's stanza is contemptible. The proper method of treating trivial and simple verses, to which Dr. Johnson's stanza would be a fair parallelism, is not to say, this is a bad kind of poetry, or, this is not poetry; but, this wants sense; it is neither interesting in itself nor can *lead* to anything interesting; the images neither originate in that sane state of feeling which arises out of thought, nor can excite thought or feeling in the Reader. This is the only sensible manner of dealing with such verses. Why trouble yourself about the species till you have previously decided upon the genus? Why take pains to prove than an ape is not a Newton, when it is self-evident that he is not a man?

One request I must make of my reader, which is, that in judging these Poems he would decide by his own feelings genuinely, and not by reflection upon what will probably be the judgement of others. How common is it to hear a person say, I myself do not object to this style of composition, or this or that expression, but, to such and such classes of people it will appear mean or ludicrous! This mode of criticism, so destructive of all sound unadulterated judgement, is almost universal: let the Reader then abide, independently, by his own feelings, and, if he finds himself affected, let him not suffer such conjectures to interfere with his pleasure.

If an Author, by any single composition, has impressed us with respect for his talents, it is useful to consider this as affording a presumption, that on other occasions where we have been displeased, he, nevertheless, may not have written ill or absurdly; and further, to give him so much credit for this one composition as may induce us to review what has displeased us, with more care than we should otherwise have bestowed upon it. This is not only an act of justice, but, in our decisions upon poetry especially, may conduce, in a high degree, to the improvement of our own taste; for an *accurate* taste in poetry, and in all the other arts, as Sir Joshua Reynolds has observed, is an *acquired* talent, which can only be produced by thought and a long continued intercourse with the best models of composition. This is mentioned, not with so ridiculous a purpose as to prevent the most inexperienced Reader from judging for himself (I have already said that I wish him to judge for himself), but merely to temper the rashness of decision, and to suggest, that, if Poetry be a subject on which much time has not been bestowed, the judgement may be erroneous; and that, in many cases, it necessarily will be so.

Nothing would, I know, have so effectually contributed to further the end which I have in view, as to have shown of what kind the pleasure is, and how that pleasure is produced, which is confessedly produced by metrical composition essentially different from that which I have here endeavoured to recommend: for the Reader will say that he has been pleased by such composition; and what more can be done for him? The power of any art is limited; and he will suspect, that, if it be proposed to furnish him with new friends, that can be only upon condition of his abandoning his old friends. Besides, as I have said, the Reader is himself conscious of the pleasure which he has received from such composition, composition to which he has peculiarly attached the endearing name of Poetry; and all men feel an habitual gratitude, and something of an honourable bigotry, for the objects which have long continued to please them: we not only wish to be pleased, but to be pleased in that particular way in which we have been accustomed to be pleased. There is in these feelings enough to resist a host of arguments; and I should be the less able to combat them successfully, as I am willing to allow, that, in order entirely to enjoy the Poetry which I am recommending, it would be necessary to give up much of what is ordinarily enjoyed. But, would my limits have permitted me to point out how this pleasure is produced, many obstacles might have been removed, and the Reader assisted in perceiving that the powers of language are not so limited as he may suppose; and that it is possible for poetry to give other enjoyments, of a purer, more lasting, and more exquisite nature. This part of the subject has not been altogether neglected, but it has not been so much my present aim to prove, that the interest excited by some other kinds of poetry is less vivid, and less worthy of the nobler powers of the mind, as to offer reasons for presuming, that if my purpose were fulfilled, a species of poetry would be produced, which is genuine poetry; in its nature well adapted to interest mankind permanently, and likewise important in the multiplicity and quality of its moral relations.

From what has been said, and from a perusal of the Poems, the Reader will be able clearly to perceive the object which I had in view: he will determine how far it has been attained; and, what is a much more important question, whether it be worth attaining: and upon the decision of these two questions will **rest my claim to the approbation of the Public.**

APPENDIX TO LYRICAL BALLADS

(1802)

ERHAPS, as I have no right to expect that attentive perusal, without which, confined, as I have been, to the narrow limits of a preface, my meaning cannot be thoroughly understood, I am anxious to give an exact notion of the sense in which the phrase poetic diction has been used; and for this purpose, a few words shall here be added, concerning the origin and characteristics of the phraseology, which I have condemned under that name.

The earliest poets of all nations generally wrote from passion excited by real events; they wrote naturally, and as men: feeling powerfully as they did, their language was daring, and figurative In succeeding times, Poets, and Men ambitious of the fame of Poets, perceiving the influence of such language, and desirous of producing the same effect without being animated by the same passion, set themselves to a mechanical adoption of these figures of speech, and made use of them, sometimes with propriety, but much more frequently applied them to feelings and thoughts with which they had no natural connexion whatsoever. A language was thus insensibly produced, differing materially from the real language of men in *any situation*. The Reader or Hearer of this distorted language found himself in a perturbed and unusual state of mind: when affected by the genuine language of passion he had been in a perturbed and unusual state of mind also: in both cases he was willing that his common judgement and understanding should be laid asleep, and he had no instinctive and infallible perception of the true to make him reject the false; the one served as a passport for the other. The emotion was in both cases delightful, and no wonder if he confounded the one with the other, and believed them both to be produced by the same, or similar causes. Besides, the Poet spake to him in the character of a man to be looked up to, a man of genius and authority. Thus, and from a variety of other causes, this distorted language was received with admiration; and Poets, it is probable, who had before contented themselves for the most part with misapplying only expressions which at first had been dictated by real passion, carried the abuse still further, and introduced phrases composed apparently in the spirit of the original figurative language of passion, yet altogether of their own invention, and characterized by various degrees of wanton deviation from good sense and nature.

It is indeed true, that the language of the earliest Poets was felt to differ materially from ordinary language, because it was the language of extraordinary occasions; but it was really spoken by men, language which the Poet himself had uttered when he had been affected by the events which he described, or which he had heard uttered by those around him. To this language it is probable that metre of some sort or other was early superadded. This separated the genuine language of Poetry still further from common life, so that whoever read or heard the poems of these earliest Poets felt himself moved in a way in which he had not been accustomed to be moved in real life, and by causes manifestly different from those which acted upon him in real life. This was the great temptation to all the corruptions which have followed: under the protection of this feeling succeeding Poets constructed a phraseology which had one thing, it is true, in common with the genuine language of poetry, namely, that it was not heard in ordinary conversation; that it was unusual. But the first Poets, as I have said, spake a language which, though unusual, was still the language of men. This circumstance, however, was disregarded by their successors; they found that they could please by easier means: they became proud of modes of expression which they themselves had invented, and which were uttered only by themselves. In process of time metre became a symbol or promise of this unusual language, and whoever took upon him to write in metre, according as he possessed more or less of true poetic genius, introduced less or more of this adulterated phraseology into his compositions, and the true and the false

were inseparately interwoven until, the taste of men becoming gradually perverted, this language was received
as a natural language: and at length, by the influence of
books upon men, did to a certain degree really become
so. Abuses of this kind were imported from one nation
to another, and with the progress of refinement this diction became daily more and more corrupt, thrusting out of
sight the plain humanities of nature by a motley mas-
querade of tricks, quaintnesses, hieroglyphics, and enigmas.
It would not be uninteresting to point out the causes
of the pleasure given by this extravagant and absurd
diction. It depends upon a great variety of causes, but
upon none, perhaps, more than its influence in impressing
a notion of the peculiarity and exaltation of the Poet's
character, and in flattering the Reader's self-love by bringing him nearer to a sympathy with that character; an effect
which is accomplished by unsettling ordinary habits of
thinking, and thus assisting the Reader to approach to
that perturbed and dizzy state of mind in which if he does
not find himself, he imagines that he is *balked* of a peculiar
enjoyment which poetry can and ought to bestow.

The sonnet quoted from Gray, in the Preface, except
the lines printed in italics, consists of little else but this diction, though not of the worst kind; and indeed, if one may
be permitted to say so, it is far too common in the best
writers both ancient and modern. Perhaps in no way,
by positive example could more easily be given a notion
of what I mean by the phrase *poetic diction* than by referring to a comparison between the metrical paraphrase
which we have of passages in the Old and New Testament,
and those passages as they exist in our common Translation. See Pope's *Messiah* throughout; Prior's 'Did sweeter
sounds adorn my flowing tongue,' &c. &c. 'Though I speak
with the tongues of men and of angels,' &c. &c., 1st
Corinthians, ch. xiii. By way of immediate example take
the following of Dr. Johnson:

> Turn on the prudent Ant thy heedless eyes,
> Observe her labours, Sluggard, and be wise;
> No stern command, no monitory voice,
> Prescribes her duties, or directs her choice;

Yet, timely provident, she hastes away
To snatch the blessings of a plenteous day;
When fruitful Summer loads the teeming plain,
She crops the harvest, and she stores the grain.
How long shall sloth usurp thy useless hours,
Unnerve thy vigour, and enchain thy powers?
While artful shades thy downy couch enclose,
And soft solicitation courts repose,
Amidst the drowsy charms of dull delight,
Year chases year with unremitted flight,
Till Want now following, fraudulent and slow,
Shall spring to seize thee, like an ambush'd foe.

From this hubbub of words pass to the original. 'Go
to the Ant, thou Sluggard, consider her ways, and be wise:
which having no guide, overseer, or ruler, provideth her
meat in the summer, and gathereth her food in the harvest.
How long wilt thou sleep, O Sluggard? when wilt thou
arise out of thy sleep? Yet a little sleep, a little slumber,
a little folding of the hands to sleep. So shall thy poverty
come as one that travelleth, and thy want as an armed
man.' Proverbs, ch. vi.

One more quotation, and I have done. It is from Cowper's Verses supposed to be written by Alexander Selkirk:

Religion! what treasure untold
Resides in that heavenly word!
More precious than silver and gold,
Or all that this earth can afford.
But the sound of the church-going bell
These valleys and rocks never heard,
Ne'er sighed at the sound of a knell,
Or smiled when a sabbath appeared.
Ye winds, that have made me your sport
Convey to this desolate shore
Some cordial endearing report
Of a land I must visit no more.
My Friends, do they now and then send
A wish or a thought after me?
O tell me I yet have a friend,
Though a friend I am never to see.

This passage is quoted as an instance of three different
styles of composition. The first four lines are poorly
expressed; some Critics would call the language prosaic;
the fact is, it would be bad prose, so bad, that it is scarcely

worse in metre. The epithet 'church-going' applied to a bell, and that by so chaste a writer as Cowper, is an instance of the strange abuses which Poets have introduced into their language, till they and their Readers take them as matters of course, if they do not single them out expressly as objects of admiration. The two lines 'Ne'er sighed at the sound,' &c., are, in my opinion, an instance of the language of passion wrested from its proper use, and, from the mere circumstance of the composition being in metre, applied upon an occasion that does not justify such violent expressions; and I should condemn the passage, though perhaps few Readers will agree with me, as vicious poetic diction. The last stanza is throughout admirably expressed: it would be equally good whether in prose or verse, except that the Reader has an exquisite pleasure in seeing such natural language so naturally connected with metre. The beauty of this stanza tempts me to conclude with a principle which ought never to be lost sight of, and which has been my chief guide in all I have said,—namely, that in works of *imagination and sentiment,* for of these only have I been treating, in proportion as ideas and feelings are valuable, whether the composition be in prose or in verse, they require and exact one and the same language. Metre is but adventitious to composition, and the phraseology for which that passport is necessary, even where it may be graceful at all will be little valued by the judicious.

PREFACE TO POEMS

(1815)

THE powers requisite for the production of poetry are:
first, those of Observation and Description,—i. e. the
ability to observe with accuracy things as they are in
themselves, and with fidelity to describe them, unmodified by
any passion or feeling existing in the mind of the describer;
whether the things depicted be actually present to the senses,
or have a place only in the memory. This power, though
indispensable to a Poet, is one which he employs only in submission to necessity, and never for a continuance of time:
as its exercise supposes all the higher qualities of the mind
to be passive, and in a state of subjection to external objects,
much in the same way as a translator or engraver ought to
be to his original. 2ndly, Sensibility,—which, the more
exquisite it is, the wider will be the range of a poet's per-
ceptions; and the more will he be incited to observe objects,
both as they exist in themselves and as re-acted upon by his
own mind. (The distinction between poetic and human sensibility has been marked in the character of the Poet delineated in the original preface.) 3rdly, Reflection,—which
makes the Poet acquainted with the value of actions, images,
thoughts, and feelings; and assists the sensibility in perceiving their connexion with each other. 4thly, Imagination
and Fancy,—to modify, to create, and to associate. 5thly,
Invention,—by which characters are composed out of materials supplied by observation; whether of the Poet's own
heart and mind, or of external life and nature; and such
incidents and situations produced as are most impressive to
the imagination, and most fitted to do justice to the characters, sentiments, and passions, which the Poet undertakes
to illustrate. And, lastly, Judgement, to decide how and
where, and in what degree, each of these faculties ought to
be exerted; so that the less shall not be sacrificed to the
greater; nor the greater, slighting the less, arrogate, to its
own injury, more than its due. By judgement, also, is

determined what are the laws and appropriate graces of every species of composition.[*]

The materials of Poetry, by these powers collected and produced, are cast, by means of various moulds, into divers forms. The moulds may be enumerated, and the forms specified, in the following order. 1st, The Narrative,—including the Epopœia, the Historic Poem, the Tale, the Romance, the Mock-heroic, and, if the spirit of Homer will tolerate such neighbourhood, that dear production of our days, the metrical Novel. Of this Class, the distinguishing mark is, that the Narrator, however liberally his speaking agents be introduced, is himself the source from which everything primarily flows. Epic Poets, in order that their mode of composition may accord with the elevation of their subject, represent themselves as *singing* from the inspiration of the Muse, ' Arma virumque *cano;* ' but this is a fiction, in modern times, of slight value: the *Iliad* or the *Paradise Lost* would gain little in our estimation by being chanted. The other poets who belong to this class are commonly content to *tell* their tale;—so that of the whole it may be affirmed that they neither require nor reject the accompaniment of music.

2ndly, The Dramatic,—consisting of Tragedy, Historic Drama, Comedy, and Masque, in which the Poet does not appear at all in his own person, and where the whole action is carried on by speech and dialogue of the agents; music being admitted only incidentally and rarely. The Opera may be placed here, inasmuch as it proceeds by dialogue; though depending, to the degree that it does, upon music, it has a strong claim to be ranked with the lyrical. The characteristic and impassioned Epistle, of which Ovid and Pope have given examples, considered as a species of monodrama, may, without impropriety, be placed in this class.

3rdly, The Lyrical,—containing the Hymn, the Ode, the Elegy, the Song, and the Ballad; in all which, for the production of their *full* effect, an accompaniment of music is indispensable.

4thly, The Idyllium,—descriptive chiefly either of the processes and appearances of external nature, as the *Seasons*

[*] As sensibility to harmony of numbers, and the power of producing it, are invariably attendants upon the faculties above specified, nothing has been said upon those requisites.

of Thomson; or of characters, manners, and sentiments, as are Shenstone's *Schoolmistress, The Cotter's Saturday Night* of Burns, *The Twa Dogs* of the same Author; or of these in conjunction with the appearances of Nature, as most of the pieces of Theocritus, the *Allegro* and *Penseroso* of Milton, Beattie's *Minstrel,* Goldsmith's *Deserted Village.* The Epitaph, the Inscription, the Sonnet, most of the epistles of poets writing in their own persons, and all loco-descriptive poetry, belonging to this class.

5thly, Didactic,—the principal object of which is direct instruction; as the Poem of Lucretius, the *Georgics* of Virgil, *The Fleece* of Dyer, Mason's *English Garden,* &c.

And, lastly, philosophical Satire, like that of Horace and Juvenal; personal and occasional Satire rarely comprehending sufficient of the general in the individual to be dignified with the name of poetry.

Out of the three last has been constructed a composite order, of which Young's *Night Thoughts,* and Cowper's *Task,* are excellent examples.

It is deducible from the above, that poems apparently miscellaneous, may with propriety be arranged either with reference to the powers of mind *predominant* in the production of them; or to the mould in which they are cast; or, lastly, to the subjects to which they relate. From each of these considerations, the following Poems have been divided into classes; which, that the work may more obviously correspond with the course of human life, and for the sake of exhibiting in it the three requisites of a legitimate whole, a beginning, a middle, and an end, have been also arranged, as far as it was possible, according to an order of time, commencing with Childhood, and terminating with Old Age, Death, and Immortality. My guiding wish was, that the small pieces of which these volumes consist, thus discriminated, might be regarded under a two-fold view; as composing an entire work within themselves, and as adjuncts to the philosophical Poem, *The Recluse.* This arrangement has long presented itself habitually to my own mind. Nevertheless, I should have preferred to scatter the contents of these volumes at random, if I had been persuaded that, by the plan adopted, anything material would be taken from the

naturai effect of the pieces, individually, on the mind of the
unreflecting Reader. I trust there is a sufficient variety in
each class to prevent this; while, for him who reads with
reflection, the arrangement will serve as a commentary
unostentatiously directing his attention to my purposes,
both particular and general. But, as I wish to guard against
the possibility of misleading by this classification, it is proper
first to remind the Reader, that certain poems are placed
according to the powers of mind, in the Author's conception,
predominant in the production of them; *predominant*, which
implies the exertion of other faculties in less degree. Where
there is more imagination than fancy in a poem, it is placed
under the head of imagination, and *vice versâ*. Both the above
classes might without impropriety have been enlarged from
that consisting of 'Poems founded on the Affections;' as
might this latter from those, and from the class 'proceeding
from Sentiment and Reflection.' The most striking characteristics of each piece, mutual illustration, variety, and proportion, have governed me throughout.

None of the other Classes, except those of Fancy and
Imagination, require any particular notice. But a remark
of general application may be made. All Poets, except the
dramatic, have been in the practice of feigning that their
works were composed to the music of the harp or lyre: with
what degree of affectation this has done in modern times, I
leave to the judicious to determine. For my own part, I have
not been disposed to violate probability so far, or to make
such a large demand upon the Reader's charity. Some of
these pieces are essentially lyrical; and, therefore, cannot
have their due force without a supposed musical accompaniment; but, in much the greatest part, as a substitute for the
classic lyre or romantic harp, I require nothing more than
an animated or impassioned recitation, adapted to the subject. Poems, however humble in their kind, if they be good
in that kind, cannot read themselves; the law of long syllable
and short must not be so inflexible,—the letter of metre must
not be so impassive to the spirit of versification,—as to
deprive the Reader of all voluntary power to modulate, in
subordination to the sense, the music of the poem;—in the
same manner as his mind is left at liberty, and even sum-

moned, to act upon its thoughts and images. But, though the accompaniment of a musical instrument be frequently dispensed with, the true Poet does not therefore abandon his privilege distinct from that of the mere Proseman;

> He murmurs near the running brooks
> A music sweeter than their own.

Let us come now to the consideration of the words Fancy and Imagination, as employed in the classification of the following Poems. 'A man,' says an intelligent author, ' has imagination in proportion as he can distinctly copy in idea the impressions of sense: it is the faculty which *images* within the mind the phenomena of sensation. A man has fancy in proportion as he can call up, connect, or associate, at pleasure, those internal images ($\phi \alpha \nu \tau \acute{\alpha} \zeta \epsilon \iota \nu$ is to cause to appear) so as to complete ideal representations of absent objects. Imagination is the power of depicting, and fancy of evoking and combining. The imagination is formed by patient observation; the fancy by a voluntary activity in shifting the scenery of the mind. The more accurate the imagination, the more safely may a painter, or a poet, undertake a delineation, or a description, without the presence of the objects to be characterized. The more versatile the fancy, the more original and striking will be the decorations produced.'—*British Synonyms discriminated, by W. Taylor.*

Is not this as if a man should undertake to supply an account of a building, and be so intent upon what he had discovered of the foundation, as to conclude his task without once looking up at the superstructure? Here, as in other instances throughout the volume, the judicious Author's mind is enthralled by Etymology; he takes up the original word as his guide and escort, and too often does not perceive how soon he becomes its prisoner, without liberty to tread in any path but that to which it confines him. It is not easy to find out how imagination, thus explained, differs from distinct remembrance of images; or fancy from quick and vivid recollection of them: each is nothing more than a mode of memory. If the two words bear the above meaning, and no other, what term is left to designate that faculty of which the Poet is 'all compact;' he whose eyes glances

from earth to heaven, whose spiritual attributes body forth
what his pen is prompt in turning to shape; or what is left
to characterize Fancy, as insinuating herself into the heart
of objects with creative activity?—Imagination, in the sense
of the word as giving title to a class of the following Poems,
has no reference to images that are merely a faithful copy,
existing in the mind, of absent external objects; but is a
word of higher import, denoting operations of the mind
upon those objects, and processes of creation or of composition, governed by certain fixed laws. I proceed to
illustrate my meaning by instances. A parrot *hangs* from
the wires of his cage by his beak or by his claws; or a
monkey from the bough of a tree by his paws or his tail.
Each creature does so literally and actually. In the first
Eclogue of Virgil, the shepherd, thinking of the time when
he is to take leave of his farm, thus addresses his goats:—

> Non ego vos posthac viridi projectus in antro
> Dumosa *pendere* procul de rupe videbo.
> ———— half way down
> *Hangs* one who gathers samphire,

is the well-known expression of Shakespeare, delineating an
ordinary image upon the cliffs of Dover. In these two
instances is a slight exertion of the faculty which I denom-
inate imagination, in the use of one word: neither the goats
nor the samphire-gatherer do literally hang, as does the
parrot or the monkey; but, presenting to the senses something of such an appearance, the mind in its activity, for
its own gratification, contemplates them as hanging.

> As when far off at sea a fleet descried
> *Hangs* in the clouds, by equinoctial winds
> Close sailing from Bengala, or the isles
> Of Ternate or Tidore, whence merchants bring
> Their spicy drugs; they on the trading flood
> Through the wide Ethiopian to the Cape
> Ply, stemming nightly toward the Pole; so seemed
> Far off the flying Fiend.

Here is the full strength of the imagination involved in
the word *hangs,* and exerted upon the whole image: First,
the fleet, an aggregate of many ships, is represented as one

mighty person, whose track, we know and feel, is upon the waters; but, taking advantage of its appearance to the senses, the Poet dares to represent it as *hanging in the clouds,* both for the gratification of the mind in contemplating the image itself, and in reference to the motion and appearance of the sublime objects to which it is compared.

From impressions of sight we will pass to those of sound; which, as they must necessarily be of a less definite character, shall be selected from these volumes:

> Over his own sweet voice the Stock-dove *broods;*

of the same bird,

> His voice was *buried* among trees,
> Yet to be come at by the breeze;
>
> O, Cuckoo! shall I call thee *Bird,*
> Or but a wandering *Voice?*

The stock-dove is said to *coo,* a sound well imitating the note of the bird; but, by the intervention of the metaphor *broods,* the affections are called in by the imagination to assist in marking the manner in which the bird reiterates and prolongs her soft note, as if herself delighting to listen to it, and participating of a still and quiet satisfaction, like that which may be supposed inseparable from the continuous process of incubation. 'His voice was buried among trees,' a metaphor expressing the love of *seclusion* by which this Bird is marked; and characterizing its note as not partaking of the shrill and the piercing, and therefore more easily deadened by the intervening shade; yet a note so peculiar and withal so pleasing, that the breeze, gifted with that love of the sound which the Poet feels, penetrates the shades in which it is entombed, and conveys it to the ear of the listener.

> Shall I call thee Bird,
> Or but a wandering *Voice?*

This concise interrogation characterizes the seeming ubiquity of the voice of the cuckoo, and dispossesses the creature almost of a corporeal existence; the Imagination being tempted to this exertion of her power by a consciousness in the memory that the cuckoo is almost perpetually heard throughout the season of spring, but seldom becomes an object of sight.

Thus far of images independent of each other, and immediately endowed by the mind with properties that do not inhere in them, upon an incitement from properties and qualities the existence of which is inherent and obvious. These processes of imagination are carried on either by conferring additional properties upon an object, or abstracting from it some of those which it actually possesses, and thus enabling it to react upon the mind which hath performed the process, like a new existence.

I pass from the Imagination acting upon an individual image to a consideration of the same faculty employed upon images in a conjunction by which they modify each other. The Reader has already had a fine instance before him in the passage quoted from Virgil, where the apparently perilous situation of the goat, hanging upon the shaggy precipice, is contrasted with that of the shepherd contemplating it from the seclusion of the cavern in which he lies stretched at ease and in security. Take these images separately, and how unaffecting the picture compared with that produced by their being thus connected with, and opposed to, each other!

> As a huge stone is sometimes seen to lie
> Couched on the bald top of an eminence,
> Wonder to all who do the same espy
> By what means it could thither come, and whence,
> So that it seems a thing endued with sense,
> Like a sea-beast crawled forth, which on a shelf
> Of rock or sand reposeth, there to sun himself.
>
> Such seemed this Man; not all alive or dead
> Nor all asleep, in his extreme old age.
>
>   .   .   .   .   .   .
>
> Motionless as a cloud the old Man stood,
> That heareth not the loud winds when they call,
> And moveth altogether if it move at all.

In these images, the conferring, the abstracting, and the modifying powers of the Imagination, immediately and mediately acting, are all brought into conjunction. The stone is endowed with something of the power of life to approxi-

mate it to the sea-beast; and the sea-beast stripped of some
of its vital qualities to assimilate it to the stone; which intermediate image is thus treated for the purpose of bringing
the original image, that of the stone, to a nearer resemblance
to the figure and condition of the aged Man; who is divested
of so much of the indications of life and motion as to bring
him to the point where the two objects unite and coalesce in
just comparison. After what has been said, the image of the
cloud need not be commented upon.

Thus far of an endowing or modifying power: but the
Imagination also shapes and *creates;* and how? By innumerable processes; and in none does it more delight than
in that of consolidating numbers into unity, and dissolving
and separating unity into number,—alternations proceeding
from, and governed by, a sublime consciousness of the soul
in her own mighty and almost divine powers. Recur to the
passage already cited from Milton. When the compact
Fleet, as one Person, has been introduced 'sailing from
Bengala,' 'They,' i. e. the 'merchants,' representing the
fleet resolved into a multitude of ships, 'ply' their voyage
towards the extremities of the earth: 'So' (referring to
the word 'As' in the commencement) 'seemed the flying
Fiend'; the image of his Person acting to recombine the
multitude of ships into one body,—the point from which
the comparison set out. 'So seemed,' and to whom seemed?
To the heavenly Muse who dictates the poem, to the eye
of the Poet's mind, and to that of the Reader, present at
one moment in the wide Ethiopian, and the next in the
solitudes, then first broken in upon, of the infernal regions!

> Modo me Thebis, modo ponit Athenis.

Hear again this mighty Poet,—speaking of the Messiah
going forth to expel from heaven the rebellious angels,

> Attended by ten thousand thousand Saints
> He onward came: far off his coming shone,—

the retinue of Saints, and the Person of the Messiah himself,
lost almost and merged in the splendour of that indefinite
abstraction 'His coming!'

As I do not mean here to treat this subject further

than to throw some light upon the present Volumes, and especially upon one division of them, I shall spare myself and the Reader the trouble of considering the Imagination as it deals with thoughts and sentiments, as it regulates the composition of characters, and determines the course of actions: I will not consider it (more than I have already done by implication) as that power which, in the language of one of my most esteemed Friends, 'draws all things to one; which makes things animate or inanimate, beings with their attributes, subjects with their accessories, take one colour and serve to one effect*.' The grand store-houses of enthusiastic and meditative Imagination, of poeti-cal, as contra-distinguished from human and dramatic Im-agination, are the prophetic and lyrical parts of the Holy Scriptures, and the works of Milton; to which I cannot forbear to add to those of Spenser. I select these writers in preference to those of ancient Greece and Rome, be-cause the anthropomorphitism of the Pagan religion sub-jected the minds of the greatest poets in those countries too much to the bondage of definite form; from which the Hebrews were preserved by their abhorrence of idolatry. This abhorrence was almost as strong in our great epic Poet, both from circumstances of his life, and from the constitution of his mind. However imbued the surface might be with classical literature, he was a Hebrew in soul; and all things tended in him towards the sublime. Spenser, of a gentler nature, maintained his freedom by aid of his allegorical spirit, at one time inciting him to create persons out of abstractions; and, at another, by a superior effort of genius, to give the universality and permanence of abstractions to his human beings, by means of attributes and emblems that belong to the highest moral truths and the purest sensations,—of which his character of Una is a glorious example. Of the human and dramatic Imagination the works of Shakespeare are an inexhaustible source.

> I tax not you, ye Elements, with unkindness,
> I never gave you kingdoms, call'd you Daughters!

And if, bearing in mind the many Poets distinguished

* Charles Lamb upon the genius of Hogarth.

by this prime quality, whose names I omit to mention; yet justified by recollection of the insults which the ignorant, the incapable, and the presumptuous, have heaped upon these and my other writings, I may be permitted to anticipate the judgment of posterity upon myself, I shall declare (censurable, I grant, if the notoriety of the fact above stated does not justify me) that I have given in these unfavourable times evidence of exertions of this faculty upon its worthiest objects, the external universe, the moral and religious sentiments of Man, his natural affections, and his acquired passions; which have the same ennobling tendency as the productions of men, in this kind, worthy to be holden in undying remembrance.

To the mode in which Fancy has already been characterized as the power of evoking and combining, or, as my friend Mr. Coleridge has styled it, 'the aggregative and associative power,' my objection is only that the definition is too general. To aggregate and to associate, to evoke and to combine, belong as well to the Imagination as to the Fancy; but either the materials evoked and combined are different; or they are brought together under a different law, and for a different purpose. Fancy does not require that the materials which she makes use of should be susceptible of change in their constitution, from her touch; and, where they admit of modification, it is enough for her purpose if it be slight, limited, and evanescent. Directly the reverse of these, are the desires and demands of the Imagination. She recoils from everything but the plastic, the pliant, and the indefinite. She leaves it to Fancy to describe Queen Mab as coming,

> In shape no bigger than an agate-stone
> On the fore-finger of an alderman.

Having to speak of stature, she does not tell you that her gigantic Angel was as tall as Pompey's Pillar; much less that he was twelve cubits, or twelve hundred cubits high; or that his dimensions equalled those of Teneriffe or Atlas;—because these, and if they were a million times as high it would be the same, are bounded: The expression is, 'His stature reached the sky!' the illimitable firma-

ment!—When the Imagination frames a comparison, if
it does not strike on the first presentation, a sense of the
truth of the likeness, from the moment that it is perceived,
grows—and continues to grow—upon the mind; the resemblance depending less upon outline of form and feature, than upon expression and effect; less upon casual
and outstanding, than upon inherent and internal, properties: moreover, the images invariably modify each other.
—The law under which the processes of Fancy are carried on is as capricious as the accidents of things, and the
effects are surprising, playful, ludicrous, amusing, tender,
or pathetic, as the objects happen to be appositely produced or fortunately combined. Fancy depends upon the
rapidity and profusion with which she scatters her thoughts
and images; trusting that their number, and the felicity
with which they are linked together, will make amends
for the want of individual value: or she prides herself
upon the curious subtilty and the successful elaboration
with which she can detect their lurking affinities. If she
can win you over to her purpose, and impart to you her
feelings, she cares not how unstable or transitory may
be her influence, knowing that it will not be out of her
power to resume it upon an apt occasion. But the Imagination is conscious of an indestructible dominion;—the Soul
may fall away from it, not being able to sustain its grandeur;
but, if once felt and acknowledged, by no act of any other
faculty of the mind can it be relaxed, impaired, or diminished.—Fancy is given to quicken and to beguile the temporal part of our nature, Imagination to incite and to support the eternal.—Yet is it not the less true that Fancy,
as she is an active, is also, under her own laws and in
her own spirit, a creative faculty? In what manner Fancy
ambitiously aims at a rivalship with Imagination, and Imagination stoops to work with the materials of Fancy, might
be illustrated from the compositions of all eloquent writers,
whether in prose or verse; and chiefly from those of our
own Country. Scarcely a page of the impassioned parts
of Bishop Taylor's Works can be opened that shall not afford
examples.—Referring the Reader to those inestimable volumes, I will content myself with placing a conceit (ascribed

to Lord Chesterfield) in contrast with a passage from the *Paradise Lost:*

> The dews of the evening most carefully shun,
> They are the tears of the sky for the loss of the sun.

After the transgression of Adam, Milton, with other appearances of sympathizing Nature, thus marks the immediate consequence,

> Sky lowered, and, muttering thunder, some sad drops
> Wept at completion of the mortal sin.

The associating link is the same in each instance: Dew and rain, not distinguishable from the liquid substance of tears, are employed as indications of sorrow. A flash of surprise is the effect in the former case; a flash of surprise, and nothing more; for the nature of things does not sustain the combination. In the latter, the effects from the act, of which there is this immediate consequence and visible sign, are so momentous, that the mind acknowledges the justice and reasonableness of the sympathy in nature so manifested; and the sky weeps drops of water as if with human eyes, as 'Earth had before trembled from her entrails, and Nature given a second groan.'

Finally, I will refer to Cotton's *Ode upon Winter,* an admirable composition, though stained with some peculiarities of the age in which he lived, for a general illustration of the characteristics of Fancy. The middle part of this ode contains a most lively description of the entrance of Winter, with his retinue, as 'A palsied king,' and yet a military monarch,—advancing for conquest with his army; the several bodies of which, and their arms and equipments, are described with a rapidity of detail, and a profusion of *fanciful* comparisons, which indicate on the part of the poet extreme activity of intellect, and a correspondent hurry of delightful feeling. Winter retires from the foe into his fortress, where

> a magazine
> Of sovereign juice is cellared in;
> Liquor that will the siege maintain
> Should Phœbus ne'er return again.

Though myself a water drinker, I cannot resist the pleasure
of transcribing what follows, as an instance still more happy
of Fancy employed in the treatment of feeling than, in its
preceding passages, the Poem supplies of her management
of forms.

'Tis that, that gives the poet rage,
And thaws the gelid blood of age;
Matures the young, restores the old,
And makes the fainting coward bold.

It lays the careful head to rest,
Calms palpitations in the breast,
Renders our lives' misfortune sweet;
. . . .

Then let the chill Sirocco blow,
And gird us round with hills of snow,
Or else go whistle to the shore,
And make the hollow mountains roar,

Whilst we together jovial sit
Careless, and crowned with mirth and wit,
Where, though bleak winds confine us home
Our fancies round the world shall roam.

We'll think of all the Friends we know,
And drink to all worth drinking to;
When having drunk all thine and mine,
We rather shall want healths than wine.

But where Friends fail us, we'll supply
Our friendships with our charity;
Men that remote in sorrows live,
Shall by our lusty brimmers thrive.

We'll drink the wanting into wealth,
And those that languish into health,
The afflicted into joy; th' opprest
Into security and rest.

The worthy in disgrace shall find
Favour return again more kind.
And in restraint who stifled lie,
Shall taste the air of liberty.

The brave shall triumph in success,
The lover shall have mistresses,
Poor unregarded Virtue, praise,
And the neglected Poet, bays.

Thus shall our healths do others good,
Whilst we ourselves do all we would;
For, freed from envy and from care,
What would we be but what we are?

When I sate down to write this Preface, it was my intention to have made it more comprehensive; but, thinking that I ought rather to apologize for detaining the reader so long, I will here conclude.

ESSAY SUPPLEMENTARY TO PREFACE

(1815)

WITH the young of both sexes, Poetry is, like love, a passion; but, for much the greater part of those who have been proud of its power over their minds, a necessity soon arises of breaking the pleasing bondage; or it relaxes of itself;—the thoughts being occupied in domestic cares, or the time engrossed by business. Poetry then becomes only an occasional recreation; while to those whose existence passes away in a course of fashionable pleasure, it is a species of luxurious amusement. In middle and declining age, a scattered number of serious persons resort to poetry, as to religion, for a protection against the pressure of trivial employments, and as a consolation for the afflictions of life. And, lastly, there are many, who, having been enamoured of this art in their youth, have found leisure, after youth was spent, to cultivate general literature; in which poetry has continued to be comprehended *as a study*.

Into the above classes the Readers of poetry may be divided; Critics abound in them all; but from the last only can opinions be collected of absolute value, and worthy to be depended upon, as prophetic of the destiny of a new work. The young, who in nothing can escape delusion, are especially subject to it in their intercourse with Poetry. The cause, not so obvious as the fact is unquestionable, is the same as that from which erroneous judgements in this art, in the minds of men of all ages, chiefly proceed; but upon Youth it operates with peculiar force. The appropriate business of poetry (which, nevertheless, if genuine, is as permanent as pure science), her appropriate employment, her privilege and her *duty*, is to treat of things not as they *are*, but as they *appear*; not as they exist in themselves, but as they *seem* to exist to the *senses*, and to the *passions*. What a world of

327

delusion does this acknowledged obligation prepare for the inexperienced! what temptations to go astray are here held forth for them whose thoughts have been little disciplined by the understanding, and whose feelings revolt from the sway of reason!—When a juvenile Reader is in the height of his rapture with some vicious passage, should experience throw in doubts, or common sense suggest suspicions, a lurking consciousness that the realities of the Muse are but shows, and that her liveliest excitements are raised by transient shocks of conflicting feeling and successive assemblages of contradictory thoughts—is ever at hand to justify extravagance, and to sanction absurdity. But, it may be asked, as these illusions are unavoidable, and, no doubt, eminently useful to the mind as a process, what good can be gained by making observations, the tendency of which is to diminish the confidence of youth in its feelings, and thus to abridge its innocent and even profitable pleasures? The reproach implied in the question could not be warded off, if Youth were incapable of being delighted with what is truly excellent; or, if these errors always terminated of themselves in due season. But, with the majority, though their force be abated, they continue through life. Moreover, the fire of youth is too vivacious an element to be extinguished or damped by a philosophical remark; and, while there is no danger that what has been said will be injurious or painful to the ardent and the confident, it may prove beneficial to those who, being enthusiastic, are, at the same time, modest and ingenuous. The intimation may unite with their own misgivings to regulate their sensibility, and to bring in, sooner than it would otherwise have arrived, a more discreet and sound judgement.

If it should excite wonder that men of ability, in later life, whose understandings have been rendered acute by practice in affairs, should be so easily and so far imposed upon when they happen to take up a new work in verse, this appears to be the cause;—that, having discontinued their attention to poetry, whatever progress may have been made in other departments of knowledge, they have not, as to this art, advanced in true discernment beyond the age of youth. If, then, a new poem fall in their way, whose attractions are of that kind which would have enraptured them during the heat of youth, the judgement not being improved to a degree that they shall be disgusted, they are dazzled; and prize and cherish the faults for having had power to make the present time vanish before them, and to throw the mind back, as by enchantment, into the happiest season of life. As they read, powers seem to be revived, passions are regenerated, and pleasures restored. The Book was probably taken up after an escape from the burden of business, and with a wish to forget the world, and all its vexations and anxieties. Having obtained this wish, and so much more, it is natural that they should make report as they have felt.

If Men of mature age, through want of practice, be thus easily beguiled into admiration of absurdities, extravagances, and misplaced ornaments, thinking it proper that their understandings should enjoy a holiday, while they are unbending their minds with verse, it may be expected that such Readers will resemble their former selves also in strength of prejudice, and an inaptitude to be moved by the unostentatious beauties of a pure style. In the higher poetry, an enlightened Critic chiefly looks for a reflection of the wisdom of the heart and the grandeur of the imagination. Wherever these appear, simplicity accompanies them; Magnificence herself, when legitimate, depending upon a simplicity of her own, to regulate her ornaments. But it is a well-known property of human nature, that our estimates are ever governed by comparisons, of which we are conscious with various degrees of distinctness. Is it not, then, inevitable (confining these observations to the effects of style merely) that an eye, accustomed to the glaring hues of diction by which such Readers are caught and excited, will for the most part be rather repelled than attracted by an original Work, the colouring of which is disposed according to a pure and refined scheme of harmony? It is in the fine arts as in the affairs of life, no man can *serve* (i. e. obey with zeal and fidelity) two Masters.

As Poetry is most just to its own divine origin when it administers the comforts and breathes the spirit of religion, they who have learned to perceive this truth, and who betake themselves to reading verse for sacred purposes, must be preserved from numerous illusions to which the two Classes of Readers, whom we have been considering, are liable. But, as the mind grows serious from the weight of life, the range of its passions is contracted accordingly; and its sympathies become so exclusive, that many species of high excellence wholly escape, or but languidly excite, its notice. Besides, men who read from religious or moral inclinations, even when the subject is of that kind which they approve, are beset with misconceptions and mistakes peculiar to themselves. Attaching so much importance to the truths which interest them, they are prone to over-rate the Authors by whom those truths are expressed and enforced. They come prepared to impart so much passion to the Poet's language, that they remain unconscious how little, in fact, they receive from it. And, on the other hand, religious faith is to him who holds it so momentous a thing, and error appears to be attended with such tremend-ous consequences, that, if opinions touching upon religion occur which the Reader condemns, he not only cannot sym-pathize with them, however animated the expression, but there is, for the most part, an end put to all satisfaction and enjoyment. Love, if it before existed, is converted into dislike; and the heart of the Reader is set against the Author and his book.—To these excesses, they, who from their pro-fessions ought to be the most guarded against them, are perhaps the most liable; I mean those sects whose religion, being from the calculating understanding, is cold and formal. For when Christianity, the religion of humility, is founded upon the proudest faculty of our nature, what can be ex-pected but contradictions? Accordingly, believers of this cast are at one time contemptuous; at another, being troubled, as they are and must be, with inward misgivings, they are jealous and suspicious;—and at all seasons, they are under temptation to supply by the heat with which they defend their tenets, the animation which is wanting to the constitution of the religion itself.

Faith was given to man that his affections, detached from the treasures of time, might be inclined to settle upon those of eternity;—the elevation of his nature, which this habit

produces on earth, being to him a presumptive evidence of
a future state of existence; and giving him a title to par-
take of its holiness. The religious man values what he sees
chiefly as an 'imperfect shadowing forth' of what he is incapable of seeing. The concerns of religion refer to indefinite
objects, and are too weighty for the mind to support them
without relieving itself by resting a great part of the burthen
upon words and symbols. The commerce between Man and
his Maker cannot be carried on but by a process where much
is represented in little, and the Infinite Being accommodates
himself to a finite capacity. In all this may be perceived
the affinity between religion and poetry; between religion—
making up the deficiencies of reason by faith; and poetry
—passionate for the instruction of reason; between religion—whose element is infinitude, and whose ultimate
trust is the supreme of things, submitting herself to cir-
cumscription, and reconciled to substitutions; and poetry
—ethereal and transcendent, yet incapable to sustain her
existence without sensuous incarnation. In this community
of nature may be perceived also the lurking incitements of
kindred error;—so that we shall find that no poetry has
been more subject to distortion, than that species, the argument and scope of which is religious; and no lovers of the
art have gone farther astray than the pious and the devout.

Whither then shall we turn for that union of qualifica-
tions which must necessarily exist before the decisions of
a critic can be of absolute value? For a mind at once
poetical and philosophical; for a critic whose affections are
as free and kindly as the spirit of society, and whose understanding is severe as that of dispassionate government?
Where are we to look for that initiatory composure of
mind which no selfishness can disturb? For a natural sensibility that has been tutored into correctness without losing
anything of its quickness; and for active faculties, capable
of answering the demands which an Author of original
imagination shall make upon them, associated with a judgement that cannot be duped into admiration by aught that is
unworthy of it?—among those and those only, who, never
having suffered their youthful love of poetry to remit much
of its force, have applied to the consideration of the laws

of this art the best power of their understandings. At the same time it must be observed—that, as this Class comprehends the only judgements which are trustworthy, so does it include the most erroneous and perverse. For to be mistaught is worse than to be untaught; and no perverseness equals that which is supported by system, no errors are so difficult to root out as those which the understanding has pledged its credit to uphold. In this Class are contained censors, who, if they be pleased with what is good, are pleased with it only by imperfect glimpses, and upon false principles; who, should they generalize rightly, to a certain point, are sure to suffer for it in the end; who, if they stumble upon a sound rule, are fettered by misapplying it, or by straining it too far; being incapable of perceiving when it ought to yeild to one of higher order. In it are found critics too petulant to be passive to a genuine poet, and too feeble to grapple with him; men, who take upon them to report of the course which *he* holds whom they are utterly unable to accompany,—confounded if he turn quick upon the wing, dismayed if he soar steadily 'into the region';—men of palsied imaginations and indurated hearts; in whose minds all healthy action is languid, who therefore feed as the many direct them, or, with the many, are greedy after vicious provocatives;—judges, whose censure is auspicious, and whose praise ominous! In this class meet together the two extremes of best and worst.

The observations presented in the foregoing series are of too ungracious a nature to have been made without reluctance; and, were it only on this account, I would invite the reader to try them by the test of comprehensive experience. If the number of judges who can be confidently relied upon be in reality so small, it ought to follow that partial notice only, or neglect, perhaps long continued, or attention wholly inadequate to their merits—must have been the fate of most works in the higher departments of poetry; and that, on the other hand, numerous productions have blazed into popularity, and have passed away, leaving scarcely a trace behind them: it will be further found, that when Authors shall have at length raised themselves into general admiration and maintained their ground, errors and prejudices have prevailed concerning their genius and their works, which the few who are conscious of those errors and prejudices would deplore; if they were not recompensed by perceiving that there are select Spirits for whom it is ordained that their fame shall be in the world an existence like that of Virtue, which owes its being to the struggles it makes, and its vigour to the enemies whom it provokes;—a vivacious quality, ever doomed to meet with opposition, and still triumphing over it; and, from the nature of its dominion, incapable of being brought to the sad conclusion of Alexander, when he wept that there were no more worlds for him to conquer.

Let us take a hasty retrospect of the poetical literature of this Country for the greater part of the last two centuries, and see if the facts support these inferences.

Who is there that now reads the *Creation* of Dubartas? Yet all Europe once resounded with his praise; he was caressed by kings; and, when his Poem was translated into our language, the *Faery Queen* faded before it. The name of Spenser, whose genius is of a higher order than even that of Ariosto, is at this day scarcely known beyond the limits of the British Isles. And if the value of his works is to be estimated from the attention now paid to them by his countrymen, compared with that which they bestow on those of some other writers, it must be pronounced small indeed.

> The laurel, meed of mighty conquerors
> And poets *sage*—

are his own words; but his wisdom has, in this particular, been his worst enemy: while its opposite, whether in the shape of folly or madness, has been *their* best friend. But he was a great power, and bears a high name: the laurel has been awarded to him.

A dramatic Author, if he write for the stage, must adapt himself to the taste of the audience, or they will not endure him; accordingly the mighty genius of Shakespeare was listened to. The people were delighted: but I am not sufficiently versed in stage antiquities to determine whether they did not flock as eagerly to the representation of many pieces of contemporary Authors, wholly undeserving to ap-

pear upon the same boards. Had there been a formal contest
for superiority among dramatic writers, that Shakespeare,
like his predecessors Sophocles and Euripides, would have
often been subject to the mortification of seeing the prize
adjudged to sorry competitors, becomes too probable, when
we reflect that the admirers of Settle and Shadwell were, in
a later age, as numerous, and reckoned as respectable, in
point of talent, as those of Dryden. At all events, that
Shakespeare stooped to accommodate himself to the People, is sufficiently apparent; and one of the most striking
proofs of his almost omnipotent genius is, that he could turn
to such glorious purpose those materials which the prepos-
sessions of the age compelled him to make use of. Yet even
this marvellous skill appears not to have been enough to
prevent his rivals from having some advantage over him
in public estimation; else how can we account for passages
and scenes that exist in his works, unless upon a supposition
that some of the grossest of them, a fact which in my own
mind I have no doubt of, were foisted in by the Players,
for the gratification of the many?

But that his Works, whatever might be their reception
upon the stage, made but little impression upon the ruling
Intellects of the time, may be inferred from the fact that
Lord Bacon, in his multifarious writings, nowhere either
quotes or alludes to him.[5] His dramatic excellence enabled
him to resume possession of the stage after the Restoration;
but Dryden tells us that in his time two of the plays of
Beaumont and Fletcher were acted for one of Shakespeare's.
And so faint and limited was the perception of the poetic
beauties of his dramas in the time of Pope, that, in his Edition of the Plays, with a view of rendering to the general
reader a necessary service, he printed between inverted commas those passages which he thought most worthy of notice.
At this day, the French Critics have abated nothing of
their aversion to this darling of our Nation: 'the English,
with their bouffon de Shakespeare,' is as familiar an ex-

---

[5] The learned Hakewill (a third edition of whose book bears date 1635),
writing to refute the error ' touching Nature's perpetual and universal
decay,' cites triumphantly the names of Ariosto, Tasso, Bartas, and Spenser,
as instances that poetic genius had not degenerated; but he makes no mention of Shakespeare.

pression among them as in the time of Voltaire. Baron
Grimm is the only French writer who seems to have perceived his infinite superiority to the first names of the French
Theatre; an advantage which the Parisian Critic owed to his
German blood and German education. The most enlightened
Italians, though well acquainted with our language, are
wholly incompetent to measure the proportions of Shakespeare. The Germans only, of foreign nations, are approaching towards a knowledge and feeling of what he is.
In some respects they have acquired a superiority over the
fellow countrymen of the Poet: for among us it is a current, I might say, an established opinion, that Shakespeare
is justly praised when he is pronounced to be 'a wild irregular genius, in whom great faults are compensated by
great beauties.' How long may it be before this miscon-
ception passes away, and it becomes universally acknowledged that the judgement of Shakespeare in the selection of
his materials, and in the manner in which he has made
them, heterogeneous as they often are, constitute a unity of
their own, and contribute all to one great end, is not less
admirable than his imagination, his invention, and his intuitive knowledge of human Nature?

There is extant a small Volume of miscellaneous poems,
in which Shakespeare expresses his own feelings in his own
person. It is not difficult to conceive that the Editor, George
Steevens, should have been insensible to the beauties of
one portion of that Volume, the Sonnets; though in no part
of the writings of this Poet is found, in an equal compass,
a greater number of exquisite feelings felicitously expressed.
But, from regard to the Critic's own credit, he would not
have ventured to talk of an[6] act of parliament not being
strong enough to compel the perusal of those little pieces,
if he had not known that the people of England were ignorant of the treasures contained in them: and if he had
not, moreover, shared the too common propensity of human
nature to exult over a supposed fall into the mire of a genius

[6] This flippant insensibility was publicly reprehended by Mr. Coleridge in
a course of Lectures upon Poetry given by him at the Royal Institution.
For the various merits of thought and language in Shakespeare's *Sonnets*,
see Nos. 27, 29, 30, 32, 33, 54, 64, 66, 68, 73, 76, 86, 91, 92, 93, 97, 98,
105, 107, 108, 109, 111, 113, 114, 116, 117, 129, and many others.

whom he had been compelled to regard with admiration, as an inmate of the celestial regions—'there sitting where he durst not soar.'

Nine years before the death of Shakespeare, Milton was born; and early in life he published several small poems, which, though on their first appearance they were praised by a few of the judicious, were afterwards neglected to that degree, that Pope in his youth could borrow from them without risk of its being known. Whether these poems are at this day justly appreciated, I will not undertake to decide: nor would it imply a severe reflection upon the mass of readers to suppose the contrary; seeing that a man of the acknowledged genius of Voss, the German poet, could suffer their spirit to evaporate; and could change their character, as is done in the translation made by him of the most popular of these pieces. At all events, it is certain that these Poems of Milton are now much read, and loudly praised; yet were they little heard of till more than 150 years after their publication; and of the Sonnets, Dr. Johnson, as appears from Boswell's *Life* of him, was in the habit of thinking and speaking as contemptuously as Steevens wrote upon those of Shakespeare.

About the time when the Pindaric odes of Cowley and his imitators, and the productions of that class of curious thinkers whom Dr. Johnson has strangely styled metaphysical Poets, were beginning to lose something of that extravagant admiration which they had excited, the *Paradise Lost* made its appearance. 'Fit audience find though few,' was the petition addressed by the Poet to his inspiring Muse. I have said elsewhere that he gained more than he asked; this I believe to be true; but Dr. Johnson has fallen into a gross mistake when he attempts to prove, by the sale of the work, that Milton's Countrymen were '*just* to it' upon its first appearance. Thirteen hundred Copies were sold in two years; an uncommon example, he asserts, of the prevalence of genius in opposition to so much recent enmity as Milton's public conduct had excited. But, be it remembered that, if Milton's political and religious opinions, and the manner in which he announced them, had raised him many enemies, they had procured him numerous friends; who, as all personal danger was passed away at the time of publication, would be eager to procure the master-work of a man whom they revered, and whom they would be proud of praising. Take, from the number of purchasers, persons of this class, and also those who wished to possess the Poem as a religious work, and but few I fear would be left who sought for it on account of its poetical merits. The demand did not immediately increase; 'for,' says Dr. Johnson, 'many more readers' (he means persons in the habit of reading poetry) 'than were supplied at first the Nation did not afford.' How careless must a writer be who can make this assertion in the face of so many existing title-pages to belie it! Turning to my own shelves, I find the folio of Cowley, seventh edition, 1681. A book near it is Flatman's Poems, fourth edition, 1686; Waller, fifth edition, same date. The Poems of Norris of Bemerton not long after went, I believe, through nine editions. What further demand there might be for these works I do not know; but I well remember that, twenty-five years ago, the booksellers' stalls in London swarmed with the folios of Cowley. This is not mentioned in disparagement of that able writer and amiable man; but merely to show that, if Milton's Works were not more read, it was not because readers did not exist at the time. The early editions of the *Paradise Lost* were printed in a shape which allowed them to be sold at a low price, yet only three thousand copies of the Work were sold in eleven years; and the Nation, says Dr. Johnson, had been satisfied from 1623 to 1664, that is, forty-one years, with only two editions of the Works of Shakespeare; which probably did not together make one thousand Copies; facts adduced by the critic to prove the 'paucity of Readers.'—There were readers in multitudes; but their money went for other purposes, as their admiration was fixed elsewhere. We are authorized, then, to affirm that the reception of the *Paradise Lost,* and the slow progress of its fame, are proofs as striking as can be desired that the positions which I am attempting to establish are not erroneous.[7]—How amusing to shape to one's self such a critique as

---

[7] Hughes is express upon this subject: in his dedication of Spenser's Works to Lord Somers, he writes thus: ' It was your Lordship's encouraging a beautiful edition of *Paradise Lost* that first brought that incomparable Poem to be generally known and esteemed.'

a Wit of Charles's days, or a Lord of the Miscellanies or trading Journalist of King William's time, would have brought forth, if he had set his faculties industriously to work upon this Poem, everywhere impregnated with *original* excellence.

So strange indeed are the obliquities of admiration, that they whose opinions are much influenced by authority will often be tempted to think that there are no fixed principles[8] in human nature for this art to rest upon. I have been honoured by being permitted to peruse in MS. a tract composed between the period of the Revolution and the close of that century. It is the Work of an English Peer of high accomplishments, its object to form the character and direct the studies of his son. Perhaps nowhere does a more beautiful treatise of the kind exist. The good sense and wisdom of the thoughts, the delicacy of the feelings, and the charm of the style, are, throughout, equally conspicuous. Yet the Author, selecting among the Poets of his own country those whom he deems most worthy of his son's perusal, particularizes only Lord Rochester, Sir John Denham, and Cowley. Writing about the same time, Shaftesbury, an author at present unjustly depreciated, describes the English Muses as only yet lisping in their cradles.

The arts by which Pope, soon afterwards, contrived to procure to himself a more general and a higher reputation than perhaps any English Poet ever attained during his lifetime, are known to the judicious. And as well known is it to them, that the undue exertion of those arts is the cause why Pope has for some time held a rank in literature, to which, if he had not been seduced by an over-love of immediate popularity, and had confided more in his native genius, he never could have descended. He bewitched the nation by his melody, and dazzled it by his polished style and was himself blinded by his own success. Having wandered from humanity in his Eclogues with boyish inexperience, the praise, which these compositions obtained, tempted him into a belief that Nature was not to be trusted, at least in pastoral Poetry. To prove this by example, he put his

[8] This opinion seems actually to have been entertained by Adam Smith, the worst critic, David Hume not excepted, that Scotland, a soil to which this sort of weed seems natural, has produced.

friend Gay upon writing those Eclogues which their author
intended to be burlesque. The instigator of the work, and
his admirers, could perceive in them nothing but what was
ridiculous. Nevertheless, though these Poems contain some
detestable passages, the effect, as Dr. Johnson well observes,
' of reality and truth became conspicuous even when the
intention was to show them grovelling and degraded.' The
Pastorals, ludicrous to such as prided themselves upon their
refinement, in spite of those disgusting passages, ' became
popular, and were read with delight, as just representations
of rural manners and occupations.'

Something less than sixty years after the publication of
the *Paradise Lost* appeared Thomson's *Winter;* which was
speedily followed by his other Seasons. It is a work of
inspiration; much of it is written from himself, and nobly
from himself. How was it received? ' It was no sooner
read,' says one of his contemporary biographers, ' than universally admired: those only excepted who had not been used
to feel, or to look for anything in poetry, beyond a *point*
of satirical or epigrammatic wit, a smart *antithesis* richly
trimmed with rime, or the softness of an *elegiac* complaint.
To such his manly classical spirit could not readily commend itself; till, after a more attentive perusal, they had
got the better of their prejudices, and either acquired or
affected a truer taste. A few others stood aloof, merely
because they had long before fixed the articles of their
poetical creed, and resigned themselves to an absolute despair of ever seeing anything new and original. These were
somewhat mortified to find their notions disturbed by the
appearance of a poet, who seemed to owe nothing but to
nature and his own genius. But, in a short time, the applause became unanimous; every one wondering how so
many pictures, and pictures so familiar, should have moved
them but faintly to what they felt in his descriptions. His
digressions too, the overflowings of a tender benevolent
heart, charmed the reader no less; leaving him in doubt,
whether he should more admire the Poet or love the Man.'

This case appears to bear strongly against us:—but
we must distinguish between wonder and legitimate admiration. The subject of the work is the changes produced in

the appearances of nature by the revolution of the year: and, by undertaking to write in verse, Thomson pledged himself to treat his subject as became a Poet. Now, it is remarkable that, excepting the nocturnal *Reverie of Lady Winchelsea,* and a passage or two in the *Windsor Forest* of Pope, the poetry of the period intervening between the publication of the *Paradise Lost* and the *Seasons* does not contain a single new image of external nature; and scarcely presents a familiar one from which it can be inferred that the eye of the Poet has been steadily fixed upon his object, much less that his feelings had urged him to work upon it in the spirit of genuine imagination. To what a low state knowledge of the most obvious and important phenomena had sunk, is evident from the style in which Dryden has executed a description of Night in one of his Tragedies, and Pope his translation of the celebrated moonlight scene in the *Iliad.* A blind man, in the habit of attending accurately to descriptions casually dropped from the lips of those around him, might easily depict these appearances with more truth. Dryden's lines are vague, bombastic, and senseless; [9] those of Pope, though he had Homer to guide him, are throughout false and contradictory. The verses of Dryden, once highly celebrated, are forgotten; those of Pope still retain their hold upon public estimation,—nay, there is not a passage of descriptive poetry, which at this day finds so many and such ardent admirers. Strange to think of an enthusiast, as may have been the case with thousands, reciting those verses under the cope of a moonlight sky, without having his raptures in the least disturbed by a suspicion of their absurdity!—If these two distinguished writers could habitually think that the visible universe was of so little consequence to a poet, that it was scarcely necessary for him to cast his eyes upon it, we may be assured that those passages of the elder poets which faithfully and poetically describe the phenomena of nature, were not at that

[9] CORTES, *alone in a night-gown.*
All things are hush'd as Nature's self lay dead;
The mountains seem to nod their drowsy head.
The little Birds in dreams their songs repeat,
And sleeping Flowers beneath the Night-dew sweat:
Even Lust and Envy sleep; yet Love denies
Rest to my soul, and slumber to my eyes.
                              DRYDEN'S *Indian Emperor.*

time holden in much estimation, and that there was little accurate attention paid to those appearances.

Wonder is the natural product of Ignorance; and as the
soil was *in such good condition* at the time of the publication
of the *Seasons* the crop was doubtless abundant. Neither individuals nor nations become corrupt all at once, nor are they
enlightened in a moment. Thomson was an inspired poet,
but he could not work miracles; in cases where the art
of seeing had in some degree been learned, the teacher would
further the proficiency of his pupils, but he could do little
more; though so far does vanity assist men in acts of self-
deception, that many would often fancy they recognized a
likeness when they knew nothing of the original. Having
shown that much of what his biographer deemed genuine
admiration must in fact have been blind wonderment—how
is the rest to be accounted for? —Thomson was fortunate
in the very title of his poem, which seemed to bring it home
to the prepared sympathies of every one: in the next place,
notwithstanding his high powers, he writes a vicious style;
and his false ornaments are exactly of that kind which would
be most likely to strike the undiscerning. He likewise
abounds with sentimental commonplaces, that, from the
manner in which they were brought forward, bore an imposing air of novelty. In any well-used copy of the *Seasons*
the book generally opens of itself with the rhapsody on love,
or with one of the stories(perhaps ' Damon and Musidora ') ;
these also are prominent in our collections of Extracts, and
are the parts of his Work which, after all, were probably
most efficient in first recommending the author to general
notice. Pope, repaying praises which he had received, and
wishing to extol him to the highest, only styles him ' an
elegant and philosophical Poet'; nor are we able to collect
any unquestionable proofs that the true characteristics of
Thomson's genius as an imaginative poet [10] were perceived,
till the elder Warton, almost forty years after the publication of the *Seasons,* pointed them out by a note in his

[10] Since these observations upon Thomson were written, I have perused
the second edition of his *Seasons,* and find that even *that* does not contain
the most striking passages which Warton points out for admiration; these,
with other improvements, throughout the whole work, must have been added
at a later period.

Essay on the *Life and Writings of Pope.* In the *Castle of Indolence* (of which Gray speaks so coldly) these characteristics were almost as conspicuously displayed, and in verse more harmonious and diction more pure. Yet that fine poem was neglected on its appearance, and is at this day the delight only of a few!

When Thomson died, Collins breathed forth his regrets in an Elegiac Poem, in which he pronounces a poetical curse upon *him* who should regard with insensibility the place where the Poet's remains were deposited. The Poems of the mourner himself have now passed through innumerable editions, and are universally known; but if, when Collins died, the same kind of imprecation had been pronounced by a surviving admirer, small is the number whom it would not have comprehended. The notice which his poems attained during his lifetime was so small, and of course the sale so insignificant, that not long before his death he deemed it right to repay to the bookseller the sum which he had advanced for them and threw the edition into the fire.

Next in importance to the *Seasons* of Thomson, though a considerable distance from that work in order of time, come the *Reliques of Ancient English Poetry;* collected, new-modelled, and in many instances (if such a contradiction in terms may be used) composed by the Editor, Dr. Percy. This work did not steal silently into the world, as is evident from the number of legendary tales, that appeared not long after its publication; and had been modelled, as the authors persuaded themselves, after the old Ballad. The Compilation was, however, ill suited to the then existing taste of city society; and Dr. Johnson, 'mid the little senate to which he gave laws, was not sparing in his exertions to make it an object of contempt. The critic triumphed, the legendary imitators were deservedly disregarded, and, as undeservedly, their ill-imitated models sank, in this country, into temporary neglect; while Bürger, and other able writers of Germany, were translating or imitating these Reliques, and composing, with the aid of inspiration thence derived, poems which are the delight of the German nation. Dr. Percy was so abashed by the ridicule flung upon his labours from the ignorance and insensibility of the persons with whom he lived, that,

though while he was writing under a mask he had not
wanted resolution to follow his genius into the regions of
true simplicity and genuine pathos (as is evinced by the exquisite ballad of *Sir Cauline* and by many other pieces),
yet when he appeared in his own person and character
as a poetical writer, he adopted, as in the tale of the *Hermit
of Warkworth*, a diction scarcely in any one of its features
distinguishable from the vague, the glossy, and unfeeling
language of his day.   I mention this remarkable fact[11] with
regret, esteeming the genius of Dr. Percy in this kind of
writing superior to that of any other man by whom in modern times it has been cultivated.   That even Bürger (to whom
Klopstock gave, in my hearing, a commendation which he
denied to Goethe and Schiller, pronouncing him to be a
genuine poet, and one of the few among the Germans whose
works would last) had not the fine sensibility of Percy,
might be shown from many passages, in which he has deserted his original only to go astray.   For example,

> Now daye was gone, and night was come,
> And all were fast asleepe,
> All save the Lady Emeline,
> Who sate in her bowre to weepe:

> And soone she heard her true Love's voice
> Low whispering at the walle,
> Awake, awake, my dear Ladye,
> 'Tis I thy true-love call.

Which is thus tricked out and dilated;

> Als nun die Nacht Gebirg' und Thal
> Vermummt in Rabenschatten,
> Und Hochburgs Lampen überall
> Schon ausgeflimmert hatten,
> Und alles tief entschlafen war;
> Doch nur das Fräulein immerdar,
> Voll Fieberangst, noch wachte,
> Und seinen Ritter dachte:

---

[11] Shenstone, in his *Schoolmistress,* gives a still more remarkable instance
of this timidity.   On its first appearance (see D'Israeli's 2d Series of the
Curiosities of Literature) the Poem was accompanied with an absurd prose
commentary, showing, as indeed some incongruous expressions in the text
imply, that the whole was intended for burlesque.   In subsequent editions,
the commentary was dropped, and the People have since continued to read
in seriousness, doing for the Author what he had not courage openly to
venture upon for himself.

Da horch! Ein susser Liebeston
Kam leis' empor geflogen.
'Ho, Trudchen, ho! Da bin ich schon!
Frisch auf! Dich angezogen!'

But from humble ballads we must ascend to heroics.
All hail, Macpherson! hail to thee, Sire of Ossian! The Phantom was begotten by the snug embrace of an impudent Highlander upon a cloud of tradition—it travelled southward, where it was greeted with acclamation, and the thin Consistence took its course through Europe, upon the breath of popular applause. The Editor of the *Reliques* had indirectly preferred a claim to the praise of invention, by not concealing that his supplementary labours were considerable! how selfish his conduct, contrasted with that of the disinterested Gael, who, like Lear, gives his kingdom away, and is content to become a pensioner upon his own issue for a beggarly pittance!—Open this far-famed Book!—I have done so at random, and the beginning of the *Epic Poem Temora,* in eight Books, presents itself. 'The blue waves of Ullin roll in light. The green hills are covered with day. Trees shake their dusky heads in the breeze. Grey torrents pour their noisy streams. Two green hills with aged oaks surround a narrow plain. The blue course of a stream is there. On its banks stood Cairbar of Atha. His spear supports the king; the red eyes of his fear are sad. Cormac rises on his soul with all his ghastly wounds.' Precious memorandums from the pocket-book of the blind Ossian!

If it be unbecoming, as I acknowledge that for the most part it is, to speak disrespectfully of Works that have enjoyed for a length of time a widely-spread reputation, without at the same time producing irrefragable proofs of their unworthiness, let me be forgiven upon this occasion.—Having had the good fortune to be born and reared in a mountainous country, from my very childhood I have felt the falsehood that pervades the volumes imposed upon the world under the name of Ossian. From what I saw with my own eyes, I knew that the imagery was spurious. In nature everything is distinct, yet nothing defined into absolute independent singleness. In Macpherson's work it is exactly

the reverse; everything (that is not stolen) is in this manner
defined, insulated, dislocated, deadened,—yet nothing distinct. It will always be so when words are substituted for
things. To say that the characters never could exist, that
the manners are impossible, and that a dream has more substance than the whole state of society, as there depicted, is
doing nothing more than pronouncing a censure which Macpherson defied; when, with the steeps of Morven before his
eyes, he could talk so familiarly of his Car-borne heroes;—
of Morven, which, if one may judge from its appearance at
the distance of a few miles, contains scarcely an acre of
ground sufficiently accommodating for a sledge to be trailed
along its surface.—Mr. Malcolm Laing has ably shown that
the diction of this pretended translation is a motley assemblage from all quarters; but he is so fond of making
out parallel passages as to call poor Macpherson to account
for his ' ands ' and his ' buts!' and he has weakened his
argument by conducting it as if he thought that every striking resemblance was a *conscious* plagiarism. It is enough
that the coincidences are too remarkable for its being probable or possible that they could arise in different minds
without communication between them. Now as the Translators of the Bible, and Shakespeare, Milton, and Pope,
could not be indebted to Macpherson, it follows that he
must have owed his fine feathers to them; unless we are
prepared gravely to assert, with Madame de Staël, that
many of the characteristic beauties of our most celebrated
English Poets are derived from the ancient Fingallian; in
which case the modern translator would have been but giving back to Ossian his own.—It is consistent that Lucien
Buonaparte, who could censure Milton for having surrounded Satan in the infernal regions with courtly and regal
splendour, should pronounce the modern Ossian to be the
glory of Scotland;—a country that has produced a Dunbar,
a Buchanan, a Thomson, and a Burns! These opinions are
of ill omen for the Epic ambition of him who has given
them to the world.

Yet, much as those pretended treasures of antiquity have
been admired, they have been wholly uninfluential upon the
literature of the Country. No succeeding writer appears to

have caught from them a ray of inspiration; no author, in the least distinguished, has ventured formally to imitate them—except the boy, Chatterton, on their first appearance. He had perceived, from the successful trials which he himself had made in literary forgery, how few critics were able to distinguish between a real ancient medal and a counterfeit of modern manufacture; and he set himself to the work of filling a magazine with *Saxon Poems,*—counterparts of those of Ossian, as like his as one of his misty stars is to another. This incapability to amalgamate with the literature of the Island is, in my estimation, a decisive proof that the book is essentially unnatural; nor should I require any other to demonstrate it to be a forgery, audacious as worthless.— Contrast, in this respect, the effect of Macpherson's publication with the *Reliques* of Percy, so unassuming, so modest in their pretensions!—I have already stated how much Germany is indebted to this latter work; and for our own country, its poetry has been absolutely redeemed by it. I do not think that there is an able writer in verse of the present day who would not be proud to acknowledge his obligations to the *Reliques;* I know that it is so with my friends; and, for myself, I am happy in this occasion to make a public avowal of my own.

Dr. Johnson, more fortunate in his contempt of the labours of Macpherson than those of his modest friend, was solicited not long after to furnish Prefaces biographical and critical for the works of some of the most eminent English Poets. The booksellers took upon themselves to make the collection; they referred probably to the most popular miscellanies, and, unquestionably, to their books of accounts; and decided upon the claim of authors to be admitted into a body of the most eminent, from the familiarity of their names with the readers of that day, and by the profits, which, from the sale of his works, each had brought and was bringing to the Trade. The Editor was allowed a limited exercise of discretion, and the Authors whom he recommended are scarcely to be mentioned without a smile. We open the volume of Prefatory Lives, and to our astonishment the *first* name we find is that of Cowley!—What is become of the morning-star of English Poetry? Where is the bright

Elizabethan constellation? Or, if names be more acceptable than images, where is the ever-to-be-honoured Chaucer? where is Spenser? where Sidney? and, lastly, where he, whose rights as a poet, contra-distinguished from those which he is universally allowed to possess as a dramatist, we have vindicated,—where Shakespeare?—These, and a multitude of others not unworthy to be placed near them, their contemporaries and successors, we have *not*. But in their stead, we have (could better be expected when precedence was to be settled by an abstract of reputation at any given period made, as in this case before us?) Roscommon, and Stepney, and Phillips, and Walsh, and Smith, and Duke, and King, and Spratt—Halifax, Granville, Sheffield, Congreve, Broome, and other reputed Magnates—metrical writers utterly worthless and useless, except for occasions like the present, when their productions are referred to as evidence what a small quantity of brain is necessary to procure a considerable stock of admiration, provided the aspirant will accommodate himself to the likings and fashions of his day.

As I do not mean to bring down this retrospect to our own times, it may with propriety be closed at the era of this distinguished event. From the literature of other ages and countries, proofs equally cogent might have been adduced, that the opinions announced in the former part of this Essay are founded upon truth. It was not an agreeable office, nor a prudent undertaking, to declare them; but their importance seemed to render it a duty. It may still be asked, where lies the particular relation of what has been said to these Volumes?—The question will be easily answered by the discerning Reader who is old enough to remember the taste that prevailed when some of these poems were first published, seventeen years ago; who has also observed to what degree the poetry of this Island has since that period been coloured by them; and who is further aware of the unremitting hostility with which, upon some principle or other, they have each and all been opposed. A sketch of my own notion of the constitution of Fame has been given; and, as far as concerns myself, I have cause to be satisfied. The love, the admiration, the indifference, the slight, the aversion, and even the contempt, with which these Poems have been received, knowing, as I do, the source within my own mind, from which they have proceeded, and the labour and pains, which, when labour and pains appeared needful, have been bestowed upon them, must all, if I think consistently, be received as pledges and tokens, bearing the same general impression, though widely different in value;—they are all proofs that for the present time I have not laboured in vain; and afford assurances, more or less authentic, that the products of my industry will endure.

If there be one conclusion more forcibly pressed upon us than another by the review which has been given of the fortunes and fate of poetical Works, it is this—that every author, as far as he is great and at the same time *original,* has had the task of *creating* the taste by which he is to be enjoyed: so has it been, so will it continue to be. This remark was long since made to me by the philosophical Friend for the separation of whose poems from my own I have previously expressed my regret. The predecessors of an original Genius of a high order will have smoothed the way for all that he has in common with them;—and much he will have in common; but, for what is peculiarly his own, he will be called upon to clear and often to shape his own road:—he will be in the condition of Hannibal among the Alps.

And where lies the real difficulty of creating that taste by which a truly original poet is to be relished? Is it in breaking the bonds of custom, in overcoming the prejudices of false refinement, and displacing the aversions of inexperience? Or, if he labour for an object which here and elsewhere I have proposed to myself, does it consist in divesting the reader of the pride that induces him to dwell upon those points wherein men differ from each other, to the exclusion of those in which all men are alike, or the same; and in making him ashamed of the vanity that renders him insensible of the appropriate excellence which civil arrangements, less unjust than might appear, and Nature illimitable in her bounty, had conferred on men who may stand below him in the scale of society? Finally, does it lie in establishing that dominion over the spirits of readers by which they are to be humbled and humanized, in order that they may be purified and exalted?

If these ends are to be attained by the mere communication of *knowledge,* it does *not* lie here.—TASTE, I would remind the reader, like IMAGINATION, is a word which has been forced to extend its services far beyond the point to which philosophy would have confined them. It is a metaphor, taken from a *passive* sense of the human body, and transferred to things which are in their essence *not* passive,—to intellectual *acts* and *operations.* The word, Imagination, has been overstrained, from impulses honourable to mankind, to meet the demands of the faculty which is perhaps the noblest of our nature. In the instance of Taste, the process has been reversed; and from the prevalence of dispositions at once injurious and discreditable, being no other than that selfishness which is the child of apathy,—which, as Nations decline in productive and creative power, makes them value themselves upon a presumed refinement of judging. Poverty of language is the primary cause of the use which we make of the word, Imagination; but the word, Taste, has been stretched to the sense which it bears in modern Europe by habits of self-conceit, inducing that inversion in the order of things whereby a passive faculty is made paramount among the faculties conversant with the fine arts. Proportion and congruity, the requisite knowledge being supposed, are subjects upon which taste may be trusted; it is competent to this office—for in its intercourse with these the mind is *passive,* and is affected painfully or pleasurably as by an instinct. But the profound and the exquisite in feeling, the lofty and universal in thought and imagination; or, in ordinary language, the pathetic and the sublime;—are neither of them, accurately speaking, objects of a faculty which could ever without a sinking in the spirit of Nations have been designated by the metaphor *Taste.* And why? Because without the exertion of a co-operating *power* in the mind of the reader, there can be no adequate sympathy with either of these emotions: without this auxiliary impulse, elevated or profound passion cannot exist.

Passion, it must be observed, is derived from a word which signifies *suffering;* but the connexion which suffering has with effort, with exertion, and *action,* is immediate and inseparable. How strikingly is this property of human nature exhibited by the fact that, in popular language, to be in a passion is to be angry! But,

> Anger in hasty *words* or *blows*
> Itself discharges on its foes.

To be moved, then, by a passion is to be excited, often to external, and always to internal, effort; whether for the continuance and strengthening of the passion, or for its suppression, accordingly as the course which it takes may be painful or pleasurable. If the latter, the soul must contribute to its support, or it never becomes vivid,—and soon languishes and dies. And this brings us to the point. If every great poet with whose writings men are familiar, in the highest exercise of his genius, before he can be thoroughly enjoyed, has to call forth and to communicate *power,* this service, in a still greater degree, falls upon an original writer, at his first appearance in the world.—Of genius the only proof is, the act of doing well what is worthy to be done, and what was never done before: Of genius, in the fine arts, the only infallible sign is the widening the sphere of human sensibility, for the delight, honour, and benefit of human nature. Genius is the introduction of a new element into the intellectual universe: or, if that be not allowed, it is the application of powers to objects on which they had not before been exercised, or the employment of them in such a manner as to produce effects hitherto unknown. What is all this but an advance, or a conquest, made by the soul of the poet? Is it to be supposed that the reader can make progress of this kind, like an Indian prince or general —stretched on his palanquin, and borne by his slaves? No; he is invigorated and inspirited by his leader, in order that he may exert himself; for he cannot proceed in quiescence, he cannot be carried like a dead weight. Therefore to create taste is to call forth and bestow power, of which knowledge is the effect; and *there* lies the true difficulty.

As the pathetic participates of an *animal* sensation, it

might seem—that, if the springs of this emotion were
genuine, all men, possessed of competent knowledge of
the facts and circumstances, would be instantaneously affected. And, doubtless, in the works of every true poet
will be found passages of that species of excellence which
is proved by effects immediate and universal. But there
are emotions of the pathetic that are simple and direct, and
others—that are complex and revolutionary; some—to
which the heart yields with gentleness; others—against
which it struggles with pride; these varieties are infinite
as the combinations of circumstance and the constitutions
of character. Remember, also, that the medium through
which, in poetry, the heart is to be affected, is language;
a thing subject to endless fluctuations and arbitrary associations. The genius of the poet melts these down for his
purpose; but they retain their shape and quality to him
who is not capable of exerting, within his own mind, a corresponding energy. There is also a meditative, as well as a
human, pathos; an enthusiastic, as well as an ordinary,
sorrow; a sadness that has its seat in the depths of reason,
to which the mind cannot sink gently of itself—but to which
it must descend by treading the steps of thought. And
for the sublime,—if we consider what are the cares that
occupy the passing day, and how remote is the practice and
the course of life from the sources of sublimity, in the
soul of Man, can it be wondered that there is little existing
preparation for a poet charged with a new mission to extend its kingdom, and to augment and spread its enjoyments?

Away, then, with the senseless iteration of the word
popular, applied to new works in poetry, as if there were
no test of excellence in this first of the fine arts but that
all men should run after its productions, as if urged by an
appetite, or constrained by a spell!—The qualities of writing best fitted for eager reception are either such as startle
the world into attention by their audacity and extravagance;
or they are chiefly of a superficial kind, lying upon the
surfaces of manners; or arising out of a selection and arrangement of incidents, by which the mind is kept upon
the stretch of curiosity, and the fancy amused without the

trouble of thought. But in everything which is to send the soul into herself, to be admonished of her weakness, or to be made conscious of her power;—wherever life and nature are described as operated upon by the creative or abstracting virtue of the imagination; wherever the instinctive wisdom of antiquity and her heroic passions uniting, in the heart of the poet, with the meditative wisdom of later ages, have produced that accord of sublimated humanity which is at once a history of the remote past and a prophetic enunciation of the remotest future, *there,* the poet must reconcile himself for a season to few and scattered hearers.—Grand thoughts (and Shakespeare must often have sighed over this truth), as they are most naturally and most fitly conceived in solitude, so can they not be brought forth in the midst of plaudits without some violation of their sanctity. Go to a silent exhibition of the productions of the sister Art, and be convinced that the qualities which dazzle at first sight, and kindle the admiration of the multitude, are essentially different from those by which permanent influence is secured. Let us not shrink from following up these principles as far as they will carry us, and conclude with observing—that there never has been a period, and perhaps never will be, in which vicious poetry, of some kind or other, has not excited more zealous admiration, and been far more generally read, than good; but this advantage attends the good, that the *individual,* as well as the species, survives from age to age; whereas, of the depraved, though the species be immortal, the individual quickly *perishes;* the object of present admiration vanishes, being supplanted by some other as easily produced; which, though no better, brings with it at least the irritation of novelty,—with adaptation, more or less skilful, to the changing humours of the majority of those who are most at leisure to regard poetical works when they first solicit their attention.

Is it the result of the whole, that, in the opinion of the Writer, the judgement of the People is not to be respected? The thought is most injurious; and, could the charge be brought against him, he would repel it with indignation. The People have already been justified, and their eulogium pronounced by implication, when it was said, above—that, of *good* poetry, the *individual,* as well as the species, *survives.* And how does it survive but through the People? What preserves it but their intellect and their wisdom?

> ——Past and future, are the wings
> On whose support, harmoniously conjoined,
> Moves the great Spirit of human knowledge——
> *MS.*

The voice that issues from this Spirit is that Vox Populi which the Deity inspires. Foolish must he be who can mistake for this a local acclamation, or a transitory outcry—transitory though it be for years, local though from a Nation. Still more lamentable is his error who can believe that there is anything of divine infallibility in the clamour of that small though loud portion of the community, ever governed by factitious influence, which, under the name of the Public, passes itself, upon the unthinking, for the People. Towards the Public, the Writer hopes that he feels as much deference as it is entitled to: but to the People, philosophically characterized, and to the embodied spirit of their knowledge, so far as it exists and moves, at the present, faithfully supported by its two wings, the past and the future, his devout respect, his reverence, is due. He offers it willingly and readily; and, this done, takes leave of his Readers, by assuring them—that, if he were not persuaded that the contents of these Volumes, and the Work to which they are subsidiary, evince something of the ' Vision and the Faculty divine '; and that, both in words and things, they will operate in their degree, to extend the domain of sensibility for the delight, the honour, and the benefit of human nature, nothwithstanding the many happy hours which he has employed in their composition, and the manifold comforts and enjoyments they have procured to him, he would not, if a wish could do it, save them from immediate destruction;—from becoming at this moment, to the world, as a thing that had never been.

PREFACE TO CROMWELL

BY VICTOR HUGO. (1827)

THE drama contained in the following pages has nothing to commend it to the attention or the good will of the public. It has not, to attract the interest of political disputants, the advantage of the veto of the official censorship, nor even, to win for it at the outset the literary sympathy of men of taste, the honour of having been formally rejected by an infallible reading committee.

It presents itself, therefore, to the public gaze, naked and friendless, like the infirm man of the Gospel—*solus, pauper, nudus.*

Not without some hesitation, moreover, did the author determine to burden his drama with a preface. Such things are usually of very little interest to the reader. He inquires concerning the talent of a writer rather than concerning his point of view; and in determining whether a work is good or bad, it matters little to him upon what ideas it is based, or in what sort of mind it germinated. One seldom inspects the cellars of a house after visiting its salons, and when one eats the fruit of a tree, one cares but little about its root.

On the other hand, notes and prefaces are sometimes a convenient method of adding to the weight of a book, and of magnifying, in appearance at least, the importance of a work; as a matter of tactics this is not dissimilar to that of the general who, to make his battle-front more imposing, puts everything, even his baggage-trains, in the line. And then, while critics fall foul of the preface and scholars of the notes, it may happen that the work itself will escape them, passing uninjured between their cross-fires, as an army extricates itself from a dangerous position between two skirmishes of outposts and rear-guards.

Victor Hugo (1802-1885) the chief of the romantic school in France, issued in the Preface to " Cromwell " the manifesto of the movement. Poet, dramatist, and novelist, Hugo remained through a long life the most conspicuous man of letters in France; and in the document here printed he laid down the principles which revolutionized the literary world of his time.

These reasons, weighty as they may seem, are not those which influenced the author. This volume did not need to be *inflated*, it was already too stout by far. Furthermore, and the author does not know why it is so, his prefaces, frank and ingenuous as they are, have always served rather to compromise him with the critics than to shield him. Far from being staunch and trusty bucklers, they have played him a trick like that played in a battle by an unusual and conspicuous uniform, which, calling attention to the soldier who wears it, attracts all the blows and is proof against none.

Considerations of an altogether different sort acted upon the author. It seemed to him that, although in fact, one seldom inspects the cellars of a building for pleasure, one is not sorry sometimes to examine its foundations. He will, therefore, give himself over once more, with a preface, to the wrath of the *feuilletonists*. *Che sara, sara.* He has never given much thought to the fortune of his works, and he is but little appalled by dread of the literary *what will people say*. In the discussion now raging, in which the theatre and the schools, the public and the academies, are at daggers drawn, one will hear, perhaps, not without some interest, the voice of a solitary *apprentice* of nature and truth, who has withdrawn betimes from the literary world, for pure love of letters, and who offers good faith in default of good taste, sincere conviction in default of talent, study in default of learning.

He will confine himself, however, to general considerations concerning the art, without the slightest attempt to smooth the path of his own work, without pretending to write an indictment or a plea, against or for any person whomsoever. An attack upon or defence of his book is of less importance to him than to anybody else. Nor is personal controversy agreeable to him. It is always a pitiful spectacle to see two hostile self-esteems crossing swords. He protests, therefore, beforehand against every interpretation of his ideas, every personal application of his words, saying with the Spanish fablist:—

> Quien haga aplicaciones
> Con su pan se lo coma.

In truth, several of the leading champions of "sound literary doctrines" have done him the honour to throw the gauntlet to him, even in his profound obscurity—to him, a simple, imperceptible spectator of this curious contest. He will not have the presumption to pick it up. In the following pages will be found the observations with which he might oppose them—there will be found his sling and his stone; but others, if they choose, may hurl them at the head of the classical Goliaths.

This said, let us pass on.

Let us set out from a fact. The same type of civilization, or to use a more exact, although more extended expression, the same society, has not always inhabited the earth. The human race as a whole has grown, has developed, has matured, like one of ourselves. It was once a child, it was once a man; we are now looking on at its impressive old age. Before the epoch which modern society has dubbed "ancient," there was another epoch which the ancients called "fabulous," but which it would be more accurate to call "primitive." Behold then three great successive orders of things in civilization, from its origin down to our days. Now, as poetry is always superposed upon society, we propose to try to demonstrate, from the form of its society, what the character of the poetry must have been in those three great ages of the world—primitive times, ancient times, modern times.

In primitive times, when man awakes in a world that is newly created, poetry awakes with him. In the face of the marvellous things that dazzle and intoxicate him, his first speech is a hymn simply. He is still so close to God that all his meditations are ecstatic, all his dreams are visions. His bosom swells, he sings as he breathes. His lyre has but three strings—God, the soul, creation; but this threefold mystery envelopes everything, this threefold idea embraces everything. The earth is still almost deserted. There are families, but no nations; patriarchs, but no kings. Each race exists at its own pleasure; no property, no laws, no contentions, no wars. Everything belongs to each and to all. Society is a community. Man is restrained in nought. He leads that nomadic pastoral

life with which all civilizations begin, and which is so well
adapted to solitary contemplation, to fanciful reverie. He
follows every suggestion, he goes hither and thither, at
random. His thought, like his life, resembles a cloud that
changes its shape and its direction according to the wind
that drives it. Such is the first man, such is the first
poet. He is young, he is cynical. Prayer is his sole religion, the ode is his only form of poetry.

This ode, this poem of primitive times, is Genesis.

By slow degrees, however, this youth of the world passes
away. All the spheres progress; the family becomes a
tribe, the tribe becomes a nation. Each of these groups
of men camps about a common centre, and kingdoms appear. The social instinct succeeds the nomadic instinct.
The camp gives place to the city, the tent to the palace,
the ark to the temple. The chiefs of these nascent states
are still shepherds, it is true, but shepherds of nations;
the pastoral staff has already assumed the shape of a
sceptre. Everything tends to become stationary and fixed.
Religion takes on a definite shape; prayer is governed by
rites; dogma sets bounds to worship. Thus the priest
and king share the paternity of the people; thus theocratic
society succeeds the patriarchal community.

Meanwhile the nations are beginning to be packed too
closely on the earth's surface. They annoy and jostle one
another; hence the clash of empires—war. They overflow upon another; hence, the migrations of nations—
voyages. Poetry reflects these momentous events; from
ideas it proceeds to things. It sings of ages, of nations,
of empires. It becomes epic, it gives birth to Homer.

Homer, in truth, dominates the society of ancient times.
In that society, all is simple, all is epic. Poetry is religion, religion is law. The virginity of the earlier age
is succeeded by the chastity of the later. A sort of solemn gravity is everywhere noticeable, in private manners
no less than in public. The nations have retained nothing
of the wandering life of the earlier time, save respect for
the stranger and the traveller. The family has a fatherland; everything is connected therewith; it has the cult
of the house and the cult of the tomb.

We say again, such a civilization can find its one expression only in the epic. The epic will assume diverse forms, but will never lose its specific character. Pindar is more priestlike than patriarchal, more epic than lyrical. If the chroniclers, the necessary accompaniments of this second age of the world, set about collecting traditions and begin to reckon by centuries, they labour to no purpose —chronology cannot expel poesy; history remains an epic. Herodotus is a Homer.

But it is in the ancient tragedy, above all, that the epic breaks out at every turn. It mounts the Greek stage without losing aught, so to speak, of its immeasurable, gigantic proportions. Its characters are still heroes, demigods, gods; its themes are visions, oracles, fatality; its scenes are battles, funeral rites, catalogues. That which the rhapsodists formerly sang, the actors declaim—that is the whole difference.

There is something more. When the whole plot, the whole spectacle of the epic poem have passed to the stage, the Chorus takes all that remains. The Chorus annotates the tragedy, encourages the heroes, gives descriptions, summons and expels the daylight, rejoices, laments, sometimes furnishes the scenery, explains the moral bearing of the subject, flatters the listening assemblage. Now, what is the Chorus, this anomalous character standing between the spectacle and the spectator, if it be not the poet completing his epic?

The theatre of the ancients is, like their dramas, huge, pontifical, epic. It is capable of holding thirty thousand spectators; the plays are given in the open air, in bright sunlight; the performances last all day. The actors disguise their voices, wear masks, increase their stature; they make themselves gigantic, like their rôles. The stage is immense. It may represent at the same moment both the interior and the exterior of a temple, a palace, a camp, a city. Upon it, vast spectacles are displayed. There is —we cite only from memory—Prometheus on his mountain; there is Antigone, at the top of a tower, seeking her brother Polynices in the hostile army (*The Phœnicians*); there is Evadne hurling herself from a cliff into the flames where the body of Capaneus is burning (*The Suppliants* of Euripides); there is a ship sailing into port and landing fifty princesses with their retinues (*The Suppliants* of Æschylus). Architecture, poetry, everything assumes a monumental character. In all antiquity there is nothing more solemn, more majestic. Its history and its religion are mingled on its stage. Its first actors are priests; its scenic performances are religious ceremonies, national festivals.

One last observation, which completes our demonstration of the epic character of this epoch: in the subjects which it treats, no less than in the forms it adopts, tragedy simply re-echoes the epic. All the ancient tragic authors derive their plots from Homer. The same fabulous exploits, the same catastrophes, the same heroes. One and all drink from the Homeric stream. The Iliad and Odyssey are always in evidence. Like Achilles dragging Hector at his chariot-wheel, the Greek tragedy circles about Troy.

But the age of the epic draws near its end. Like the society that it represents, this form of poetry wears itself out revolving upon itself. Rome reproduces Greece, Virgil copies Homer, and, as if to make a becoming end, epic poetry expires in the last parturition.

It was time. Another era is about to begin, for the world and for poetry.

A spiritual religion, supplanting the material and external paganism, makes its way to the heart of the ancient society, kills it, and deposits, in that corpse of a decrepit civilization, the germ of modern civilization. This religion is complete, because it is true; between its dogma and its cult, it embraces a deep-rooted moral. And first of all, as a fundamental truth, it teaches man that he has two lives to live, one ephemeral, the other immortal; one on earth, the other in heaven. It shows him that he, like his destiny, is twofold: that there is in him an animal and an intellect, a body and a soul; in a word, that he is the point of intersection, the common link of the two chains of beings which embrace all creation— of the chain of material beings and the chain of incorporeal beings; the first starting from the rock to arrive at man, the second starting from man to end at God.

A portion of these truths had perhaps been suspected by certain wise men of ancient times, but their full, broad, luminous revelation dates from the Gospels. The pagan schools walked in darkness, feeling their way, clinging to falsehoods as well as to truths in their haphazard journeying. Some of their philosophers occasionally cast upon certain subjects feeble gleams which illuminated but one side and made the darkness of the other side more profound. Hence all the phantoms created by ancient philosophy. None but divine wisdom was capable of substituting an even and all-embracing light for all those flickering rays of human wisdom. Pythagoras, Epicurus, Socrates, Plato, are torches: Christ is the glorious light of day.

Nothing could be more material, indeed, than the ancient theogony. Far from proposing, as Christianity does, to separate the spirit from the body, it ascribes form and features to everything, even to impalpable essences, even to the intelligence. In it everything is visible, tangible, fleshly. Its gods need a cloud to conceal themselves from men's eyes. They eat, drink, and sleep. They are wounded and their blood flows; they are maimed, and lo! they limp forever after. That religion has gods and halves of gods. Its thunderbolts are forged on an anvil, and among other things three rays of twisted rain (*tres imbris torti radios*) enter into their composition. Its Jupiter suspends the world by a golden chain; its sun rides in a four-horse chariot; its hell is a precipice the brink of which is marked on the globe; its heaven is a mountain.

Thus paganism, which moulded all creations from the same clay, minimizes divinity and magnifies man. Homer's heroes are of almost the same stature as his gods. Ajax defies Jupiter, Achilles is the peer of Mars. Christianity on the contrary, as we have seen, draws a broad line of division between spirit and matter. It places an abyss between the soul and the body, an abyss between man and God.

At this point—to omit nothing from the sketch upon which we have ventured—we will call attention to the fact that, with Christianity, and by its means, there entered into the mind of the nations a new sentiment, unknown to the ancients and marvellously developed among moderns, a sentiment which is more than gravity and less than sadness—melancholy. In truth, might not the heart of man, hitherto deadened by religions purely hierarchical and sacerdotal, awake and feel springing to life within it some unexpected faculty, under the breath of a religion that is human because it is divine, a religion which makes of the poor man's prayer, the rich man's wealth, a religion of equality, liberty and charity? Might it not see all things in a new light, since the Gospel had shown it the soul through the senses, eternity behind life?

Moreover, at that very moment the world was undergoing so complete a revolution that it was impossible that there should not be a revolution in men's minds. Hitherto the catastrophes of empires had rarely reached the hearts of the people; it was kings who fell, majesties that vanished, nothing more. The lightning struck only in the upper regions, and, as we have already pointed out, events seemed to succeed one another with all the solemnity of the epic. In the ancient society, the individual occupied so lowly a place that, to strike him, adversity must needs descend to his family. So that he knew little of misfortune outside of domestic sorrows. It was an almost unheard-of thing that the general disasters of the state should disarrange his life. But the instant that Christian society became firmly established, the ancient continent was thrown into confusion. Everything was pulled up by the roots. Events, destined to destroy ancient Europe and to construct a new Europe, trod upon one another's heels in their ceaseless rush, and drove the nations pell-mell, some into the light, others into darkness. So much uproar ensued that it was impossible that some echoes of it should not reach the hearts of the people. It was more than an echo, it was a reflex blow. Man, withdrawing within himself in presence of these imposing vicissitudes, began to take pity upon mankind, to reflect upon the bitter disillusionments of life. Of this sentiment, which to Cato the heathen was despair, Christianity fashioned melancholy.

At the same time was born the spirit of scrutiny and curiosity. These great catastrophes were also great spectacles, impressive cataclysms. It was the North hurling itself upon the South; the Roman world changing shape; the last convulsive throes of a whole universe in the death agony. As soon as that world was dead, lo! clouds of rhetoricians, grammarians, sophists, swooped down like insects on its immense body. People saw them swarming and heard them buzzing in that seat of putrefaction. They vied with one another in scrutinizing, commenting, disputing. Each limb, each muscle, each fibre of the huge prostrate body was twisted and turned in every direction. Surely it must have been a keen satisfaction to those anatomists of the mind, to be able, at their début, to make experiments on a large scale; to have a dead society to dissect, for their first " subject."

Thus we see melancholy and meditation, the demons of analysis and controversy, appear at the same moment, and, as it were, hand-in-hand. At one extremity of this era of transition is Longinus, at the other St. Augustine. We must beware of casting a disdainful eye upon that epoch wherein all that has since borne fruit was contained in germs; upon that epoch whose least eminent writers, if we may be pardoned a vulgar but expressive phrase, made fertilizer for the harvest that was to follow. The Middle Ages were grafted on the Lowei Empire.

Behold, then, a new religion, a new society; upon this twofold foundation there must inevitably spring up a new poetry. Previously—we beg pardon for setting forth a result which the reader has probably already foreseen from what has been said above—previously, following therein the course pursued by the ancient polytheism and philosophy, the purely epic muse of the ancients had studied nature in only a single aspect, casting aside without pity almost everything in art which, in the world subjected to its imitation, had not relation to a certain type of beauty. A type which was magnificent at first, but, as always happens with everything systematic, became in later times false, trivial and conventional. Christianity leads poetry to the truth. Like it, the modern muse will see things in a higher and broader light. It will realize that everything in creation is not humanly *beautiful*, that

the ugly exists beside the beautiful, the unshapely beside
the graceful, the grotesque on the reverse of the sublime,
evil with good, darkness with light. It will ask itself if
the narrow and relative sense of the artist should prevail
over the infinite, absolute sense of the Creator; if it is for
man to correct God; if a mutilated nature will be the
more beautiful for the mutilation; if art has the right
to duplicate, so to speak, man, life, creation; if things
will progress better when their muscles and their vigour
have been taken from them; if, in short, to be incomplete
is the best way to be harmonious. Then it is that, with
its eyes fixed upon events that are both laughable and
redoubtable, and under the influence of that spirit of
Christian melancholy and philosophical criticism which we
described a moment ago, poetry will take a great step,
a decisive step, a step which, like the upheaval of an earth-
quake, will change the whole face of the intellectual world.
It will set about doing as nature does, mingling in its creations—but without confounding them—darkness and light,
the grotesque and the sublime; in other words, the body
and the soul, the beast and the intellect; for the starting-
point of religion is always the starting-point of poetry. All
things are connected.

Thus, then, we see a principle unknown to the ancients,
a new type, introduced in poetry; and as an additional
element in anything modifies the whole of the thing, a new
form of the art is developed. This type is the grotesque;
its new form is comedy.

And we beg leave to dwell upon this point; for we have
now indicated the significant feature, the fundamental difference which, in our opinion, separates modern from ancient art, the present form from the defunct form; or,
to use less definite but more popular terms, *romantic* literature from *classical* literature.

"At last!" exclaim the people who for some time past
have seen what we were coming at, "at last we have you—
you are caught in the act. So then you put forward the
ugly as a type for imitation, you make the *grotesque* an
element of art. But the graces; but good taste! Don't
you know that art should correct nature? that we must

ennoble art? that we must *select?* Did the ancients ever exhibit the ugly or the grotesque? Did they ever mingle comedy and tragedy? The example of the ancients, gentlemen! And Aristotle, too; and Boileau; and La Harpe. Upon my word!"

These arguments are sound, doubtless, and, above all, of extraordinary novelty. But it is not our place to reply to them. We are constructing no system here—God protect us from systems! We are stating a fact. We are a historian, not a critic. Whether the fact is agreeable or not matters little; it is a fact. Let us resume, therefore, and try to prove that it is of the fruitful union of the grotesque and the sublime types that modern genius is born—so complex, so diverse in its forms, so inexhaustible in its creations; and therein directly opposed to the uniform simplicity of the genius of the ancients; let us show that that is the point from which we must set out to establish the real and radical difference between the two forms of literature.

Not that it is strictly true that comedy and the grotesque were entirely unknown to the ancients. In fact, such a thing would be impossible. Nothing grows without a root; the germ of the second epoch always exists in the first. In the Iliad Thersites and Vulcan furnish comedy, one to the mortals, the other to the gods. There is too much nature and originality in the Greek tragedy for there not to be an occasional touch of comedy in it. For example, to cite only what we happen to recall, the scene between Menelaus and the portress of the palace. (*Helen,* Act I), and the scene of the Phrygian (*Orestes,* Act IV). The Tritons, the Satyrs, the Cyclops are grotesque; Polyphemus is a terrifying, Silenus a farcical grotesque.

But one feels that this part of the art is still in its infancy. The epic, which at this period imposes its form on everything, the epic weighs heavily upon it and stifles it. The ancient grotesque is timid and forever trying to keep out of sight. It is plain that it is not on familiar ground, because it is not in its natural surroundings. It conceals itself as much as it can. The Satyrs, the Tritons, and the Sirens are hardly abnormal in form. The Fates and the Harpies are hideous in their attributes rather than in feature; the Furies are beautiful, and are called *Eumenides,* that is to say, *gentle, beneficent.* There is a veil of grandeur or of divinity over other grotesques. Polyphemus is a giant, Midas a king, Silenus a god.

Thus comedy is almost imperceptible in the great epic *ensemble* of ancient times. What is the barrow of Thespis beside the Olympian chariots? What are Aristophanes and Plautus, beside the Homeric colossi, Æschylus, Sophocles, Euripides? Homer bears them along with him, as Hercules bore the pygmies, hidden in his lion's skin!

In the idea of men of modern times, however, the grotesque plays an enormous part. It is found everywhere; on the one hand it creates the abnormal and the horrible, on the other the comic and the burlesque. It fastens upon religion a thousand original superstitions, upon poetry a thousand picturesque fancies. It is the grotesque which scatters lavishly, in air, water, earth, fire, those myriads of intermediary creatures which we find all alive in the popular traditions of the Middle Ages; it is the grotesque which impels the ghastly antics of the witches' revels, which gives Satan his horns, his cloven foot and his bat's wings. It is the grotesque, still the grotesque, which now casts into the Christian hell the frightful faces which the severe genius of Dante and Milton will evoke, and again peoples it with those laughter-moving figures amid which Callot, the burlesque Michelangelo, will disport himself. If it passes from the world of imagination to the real world, it unfolds an inexhaustible supply of parodies of mankind. Creations of its fantasy are the Scaramouches, Crispins and Harlequins, grinning silhouettes of man, types altogether unknown to serious-minded antiquity, although they originated in classic Italy. It is the grotesque, lastly, which, colouring the same drama with the fancies of the North and of the South in turn, exhibits Sganarelle capering about Don Juan and Mephistopheles crawling about Faust.

And how free and open it is in its bearing! how boldly it brings into relief all the strange forms which the preceding age had timidly wrapped in swaddling-clothes! Ancient poetry, compelled to provide the lame Vulcan with companions, tried to disguise their deformity by distributing it, so to speak, upon gigantic proportions. Modern genius retains this myth of the supernatural smiths, but gives it an entirely different character and one which makes it even more striking; it changes the giants to dwarfs and makes gnomes of the Cyclops. With like originality, it substitutes for the somewhat commonplace Lernæan hydra all the local dragons of our national legends—the gargoyle of Rouen, the *gra-ouilli* of Metz, the *chair sallée* of Troyes, the *drée* of Montlhéry, the *tarasque* of Tarascon—monsters of forms so diverse, whose outlandish names are an additional attribute. All these creations draw from their own nature that energetic and significant expression before which antiquity seems sometimes to have recoiled. Certain it is that the Greek Eumenides are much less horrible, and consequently less *true*, than the witches in *Macbeth*. Pluto is not the devil.

In our opinion a most novel book might be written upon the employment of the grotesque in the arts. One might point out the powerful effects the moderns have obtained from that fruitful type, upon which narrow-minded criticism continues to wage war even in our own day. It may be that we shall be led by our subject to call attention in passing to some features of this vast picture. We will simply say here that, as a means of contrast with the sublime, the grotesque is, in our view, the richest source that nature can offer art. Rubens so understood it, doubtless, when it pleased him to introduce the hideous features of a court dwarf amid his exhibitions of royal magnificence, coronations and splendid ceremonial. The universal beauty which the ancients solemnly laid upon everything, is not without monotony; the same impression repeated again and again may prove fatiguing at last. Sublime upon sublime scarcely presents a contrast, and we need a little rest from everything, even the beautiful. On the other hand, the grotesque seems to be a halting-place, a mean term, a starting-point whence one rises toward the beautiful with a fresher and keener perception. The salamander gives relief to the water-sprite; the gnome heightens the charm of the sylph.

And it would be true also to say that contact with the abnormal has imparted to the modern sublime a something purer, grander, more sublime, in short, than the beautiful of the ancients; and that is as it should be. When art is consistent with itself, it guides everything more surely to its goal. If the Homeric Elysium is a long, long way from the ethereal charm, the angelic pleasureableness of Milton's Paradise, it is because under Eden there is a hell far more terrible than the heathen Tartarus. Do you think that Francesca da Rimini and Beatrice would be so enchanting in a poet who should not confine us in the Tower of Hunger and compel us to share Ugolino's revolting repast? Dante would have less charm, if he had less power. Have the fleshly naiads, the muscular Tritons, the wanton Zephyrs, the diaphanous transparency of our water-sprites and sylphs? Is it not because the modern imagination does not fear to picture the ghastly forms of vampires, ogres, ghouls, snake-charmers and jinns prowling about graveyards, that it can give to its fairies that incorporeal shape, that purity of essence, of which the heathen nymphs fall so far short? The antique Venus is beautiful, admirable, no doubt; but what has imparted to Jean Goujon's faces that weird, tender, ethereal delicacy? What has given them that unfamiliar suggestion of life and grandeur, if not the proximity of the rough and powerful sculptures of the Middle Ages?

If the thread of our argument has not been broken in the reader's mind by these necessary digressions—which in truth, might be developed much further—he has realized, doubtless, how powerfully the grotesque—that germ of comedy, fostered by the modern muse—grew in extent and importance as soon as it was transplanted to a soil more propitious than paganism and the Epic. In truth, in the new poetry, while the sublime represents the soul as it is, purified by Christian morality, the grotesque plays the part of the human beast. The former type, delivered of all impure alloy, has as its attributes all the charms, all the graces, all the beauties; it must be able some day to create Juliet, Desdemona, Ophelia. The latter assumes all the absurdities, all the infirmities, all the blemishes. In this partition of mankind and of creation, to it fall the passions, vices, crimes; it is sensuous, fawning, greedy, miserly, false, incoherent, hypocritical; it is, in turn, Iago, Tartuffe, Basile, Polonius, Harpagon, Bartholo, Falstaff, Scapin, Figaro. The beautiful has but one type, the ugly has a thousand. The fact is that the beautiful, humanly speaking, is merely form considered in its simplest aspect, in its most perfect symmetry, in its most entire harmony with our make-up. Thus the *ensemble* that it offers us is always complete, but restricted like ourselves. What we call the ugly, on the contrary, is a detail of a great whole which eludes us, and which is in harmony, not with man but with all creation. That is why it constantly presents itself to us in new but incomplete aspects.

It is interesting to study the first appearance and the progress of the grotesque in modern times. At first, it is an invasion, an irruption, an overflow, as of a torrent that has burst its banks. It rushes through the expiring Latin literature, imparts some coloring to Persius, Petronius and Juvenal, and leaves behind it the *Golden Ass* of Apuleius. Thence it diffuses itself through the imaginations of the new nations that are remodelling Europe. It abounds in the work of the fabulists, the chroniclers, the romancists. We see it make its way from the South to the North. It disports itself in the dreams of the Teutonic nations, and at the same time vivifies with its breath the admirable Spanish *romanceros,* a veritable Iliad of the age of chivalry. For example, it is the grotesque which describes thus, in the *Roman de la Rose,* an august ceremonial, the election of a king:—

> "A long-shanked knave they chose, I wis,
> Of all their men the boniest."

More especially it imposes its characteristic qualities upon that wonderful architecture which, in the Middle Ages, takes the place of all the arts. It affixes its mark on the façades of cathedrals, frames its hells and purgatories in the ogive arches of great doorways, portrays them in brilliant hues on window-glass, exhibits its monsters, its bull-dogs, its imps about capitals, along friezes, on the edges of roofs. It flaunts itself in numberless shapes on the wooden façades of houses, on the stone façades of châteaux, on the marble façades of palaces. From the arts it makes its way into the national manners, and while it stirs applause from the people for the *graciosos* of comedy, it gives to the kings court-jesters. Later, in the age of etiquette, it will show us Scarron on the very edge of Louis the Fourteenth's bed. Meanwhile, it decorates coats-of-arms, and draws upon knights' shields the symbolic hieroglyphs of feudalism. From the manners, it makes its way into the laws; numberless strange customs attest its passage through the institutions of the Middle Ages. Just as it represented Thespis, smeared with wine-lees, leaping in her tomb, it dances with the *Basoche* on the famous marble table which served at the same time as a stage for the popular farces and for the royal banquets. Finally, having made its way into the arts, the manners, and the laws, it enters even the Church. In every Catholic city we see it organizing some one of those curious ceremonies, those strange processions, wherein religion is attended by all varieties of superstition—the sublime attended by all the forms of the grotesque. To paint it in one stroke, so great is its vigour, its energy, its creative sap, at the dawn of letters, that it casts, at the outset, upon the threshold of modern poetry, three burlesque Homers: Ariosto in Italy, Cervantes in Spain, Rabelais in France.

It would be mere surplusage to dwell further upon the influence of the grotesque in the third civilization. Everything tends to show its close creative alliance with the beautiful in the so-called "romantic" period. Even among the simplest popular legends there are none which do not somewhere, with an admirable instinct, solve this mystery of modern art. Antiquity could not have produced *Beauty and the Beast*.

It is true that at the period at which we have arrived the predominance of the grotesque over the sublime in literature is clearly indicated. But it is a spasm of reaction, an eager thirst for novelty, which is but temporary; it is an initial wave which gradually recedes. The type of the beautiful will soon resume its rights and its rôle, which is not to exclude the other principle, but to prevail over it. It is time that the grotesque should be content with a corner of the picture in Murillo's royal frescoes, in the sacred pages of Veronese; content to be introduced in two marvellous *Last Judgments,* in which art will take a just pride, in the scene of fascination and horror with which Michelangelo will embellish the Vatican; in those awe-inspiring representations of the fall of man which Rubens will throw upon the arches of the Cathedral of Antwerp. The time has come when the balance between the two principles is to be established. A man, a poet-king, *poeta soverano,* as Dante calls Homer, is about to adjust everything. The two rival genii combine their flames, and thence issues Shakespeare.

We have now reached the poetic culmination of modern times. Shakespeare is the drama; and the drama, which with the same breath moulds the grotesque and the sublime, the terrible and the absurd, tragedy and comedy—the drama is the distinguishing characteristic of the third epoch of poetry, of the literature of the present day.

Thus, to sum up hurriedly the facts that we have noted thus far, poetry has three periods, each of which corresponds to an epoch of civilization: the ode, the epic, and the drama. Primitive times are lyrical, ancient times epical, modern times dramatic. The ode sings of eternity, the epic imparts solemnity to history, the drama depicts life. The characteristic of the first poetry is ingenuousness, of the second, simplicity, of the third, truth. The rhapsodists mark the transition from the lyric to the epic poets, as do the romancists that from the lyric to the dramatic poets. Historians appear in the second period, chroniclers and critics in the third. The characters of the ode are colossi—Adam, Cain, Noah; those of the epic are giants—Achilles, Atreus, Orestes; those of the drama are men—Hamlet, Macbeth, Othello. The ode lives upon the ideal, the epic upon the grandiose, the drama upon the real. Lastly, this threefold poetry flows from three great sources—The Bible, Homer, Shakespeare.

Such then—and we confine ourselves herein to noting a single result—such are the diverse aspects of thought in the different epochs of mankind and of civilization. Such are its three faces, in youth, in manhood, in old age. Whether one examines one literature by itself or all literatures *en masse,* one will always reach the same result: the lyric poets before the epic poets, the epic poets before the dramatic poets. In France, Malherbe before Chapelain, Chapelain before Corneille; in ancient Greece, Orpheus before Homer, Homer before Æschylus; in the first of all books, *Genesis* before *Kings, Kings* before *Job;* or to come back to that monumental scale of all ages of poetry, which we ran over a moment since, The Bible before the *Iliad*, the *Iliad* before Shakespeare.

In a word, civilization begins by singing of its dreams, then narrates its doings, and, lastly, sets about describing what it thinks. It is, let us say in passing, because of this last, that the drama, combining the most opposed qualities, may be at the same time full of profundity and full of relief, philosophical and picturesque.

It would be logical to add here that everything in nature and in life passes through these three phases, the lyric, the epic, and the dramatic, because everything is born, acts, and dies. If it were not absurd to confound the fantastic conceits of the imagination with the stern deductions of the reasoning faculty, a poet might say that the rising of the sun, for example, is a hymn, noon-day a brilliant epic, and sunset a gloomy drama wherein day and night, life and death, contend for mastery. But that would be poetry— folly, perhaps—and *what does it prove?*

Let us hold to the facts marshalled above; let us supplement them, too, by an important observation, namely that we have in no wise pretended to assign exclusive limits to the three epochs of poetry, but simply to set forth their predominant characteristics. The Bible, that divine lyric monument, contains in germ, as we suggested a moment ago, an epic and a drama—*Kings* and *Job*. In the Homeric poems one is conscious of a clinging reminiscence of lyric poetry and of a beginning of dramatic poetry. Ode and drama meet in the epic. There is a touch of all in each; but in each there exists a generative element to which all the other elements give place, and which imposes its own character upon the whole.

The drama is complete poetry. The ode and the epic contain it only in germ; it contains both of them in a state of high development, and epitomizes both. Surely, he who said: "The French have not the epic brain," said a true and clever thing; if he had said, "The moderns," the clever remark would have been profound. It is beyond question, however, that there is epic genius in that marvellous *Athalie*, so exalted and so simple in its sublimity that the royal century was unable to comprehend it. It is certain, too, that the series of Shakespeare's chronicle dramas presents a grand epic aspect. But it is lyric poetry above all that befits the drama; it never embarrasses it, adapts itself to all its caprices, disports itself in all forms, sometimes sublime as in Ariel, sometimes grotesque as in Caliban. Our era being above all else dramatic, is for that very reason eminently lyric. There is more than one connection between the beginning and the end; the sunset has some features of the sunrise; the old man becomes a child once more. But this second childhood is not like the first; it is as melancholy as the other is joyous. It is the same with lyric poetry. Dazzling, dreamy, at the dawn of civilization, it reappears, solemn and pensive, at its decline. The Bible opens joyously with *Genesis* and comes to a close with the threatening *Apocalypse*. The modern ode is still inspired, but is no longer ignorant. It meditates more than it scrutinizes; its musing is melancholy. We see, by its painful labour, that the muse has taken the drama for her mate.

To make clear by a metaphor the ideas that we have ventured to put forth, we will compare early lyric poetry to a placid lake which reflects the clouds and stars; the epic is the stream which flows from the lake, and rushes on, reflecting its banks, forests, fields and cities, until it throws itself into the ocean of the drama. Like the lake, the drama reflects the sky; like the stream, it reflects its banks; but it alone has tempests and measureless depths.

The drama, then, is the goal to which everything in modern poetry leads. *Paradise Lost* is a drama before it is an epic. As we know, it first presented itself to the poet's imagination in the first of these forms, and as a drama it always remains in the reader's memory, so prominent is the old dramatic framework still beneath Milton's epic structure! When Dante had finished his terrible *Inferno,* when he had closed its doors and nought remained save to give his work a name, the unerring instinct of his genius showed him that that multiform poem was an emanation of the drama, not of the epic; and on the front of that gigantic monument, he wrote with his pen of bronze: *Divina Commedia.*

Thus we see that the only two poets of modern times who are of Shakespeare's stature follow him in unity of design. They coincide with him in imparting a dramatic tinge to all our poetry; like him, they blend the grotesque with the sublime; and, far from standing by themselves in the great literary *ensemble* that rests upon Shakespeare, Dante and Milton are, in some sort, the two supporting abutments of the edifice of which he is the central pillar, the buttresses of the arch of which he is the keystone.

Permit us, at this point, to recur to certain ideas already suggested, which, however, it is necessary to emphasize. We have arrived, and now we must set out again.

On the day when Christianity said to man: " Thou art twofold, thou art made up of two beings, one perishable, the other immortal, one carnal, the other ethereal, one enslaved by appetites, cravings and passions, the other borne aloft on the wings of enthusiasm and reverie—in a word, the one always stooping toward the earth, its mother, the other always darting up toward heaven, its fatherland"— on that day the drama was created. Is it, in truth, anything other than that contrast of every day, that struggle of every moment, between two opposing principles which are ever face to face in life, and which dispute possession of man from the cradle to the tomb?

The poetry born of Christianity, the poetry of our time, is, therefore, the drama; the real results from the wholly natural combination of two types, the sublime and the grotesque, which meet in the drama, as they meet in life and in creation. For true poetry, complete poetry, consists in the harmony of contraries. Hence, it is time to say aloud—and it is here above all that exceptions prove the rule—that everything that exists in nature exists in art.

On taking one's stand at this point of view, to pass judgment on our petty conventional rules, to disentangle all those scholastic labyrinths, to solve all those trivial problems which the critics of the last two centuries have laboriously built up about the art, one is struck by the promptitude with which the question of the modern stage is made clear and distinct. The drama has but to take a step to break all the spider's webs

with which the militia of Lilliput have attempted to fetter
its sleep.

And so, let addle-pated pedants (one does not exclude
the other) claim that the deformed, the ugly, the grotesque
should never be imitated in art; one replies that the grotesque is comedy, and that comedy apparently makes a part
of art. Tartuffe is not handsome, Pourceaugnac is not noble,
but Pourceaugnac and Tartuffe are admirable flashes of art.

If, driven back from this entrenchment to their second
line of custom-houses, they renew their prohibition of the
grotesque coupled with the sublime, of comedy melted into
tragedy, we prove to them that, in the poetry of Christian
nations, the first of these two types represents the human
beast, the second the soul. These two stalks of art, if we
prevent their branches from mingling, if we persistently
separate them, will produce by way of fruit, on the one
hand abstract vices and absurdities, on the other, abstract
crime, heroism and virtue. The two types, thus isolated
and left to themselves, will go each its own way, leaving
the real between them, at the left hand of one, at the right
hand of the other. Whence it follows that after all these
abstractions there will remain something to represent—
man; after these tragedies and comedies, something to
create—the drama.

In the drama, as it may be conceived at least, if not
executed, all things are connected and follow one another
as in real life. The body plays its part no less than the
mind; and men and events, set in motion by this twofold
agent, pass across the stage, burlesque and terrible in turn,
and sometimes both at once. Thus the judge will say:
"Off with his head and let us go to dinner!" Thus the
Roman Senate will deliberate over Domitian's turbot. Thus
Socrates, drinking the hemlock and discoursing on the immortal soul and the only God, will interrupt himself to
suggest that a cook be sacrificed to Æsculapius. Thus
Elizabeth will swear and talk Latin. Thus Richelieu will
submit to Joseph the Capuchin, and Louis XI to his barber,
Maître Olivier le Diable. Thus Cromwell will say: "I
have Parliament in my bag and the King in my pocket";
or, with the hand that signed the death sentence of Charles

the First, smear with ink the face of a regicide who smilingly returns the compliment. Thus Cæsar, in his triumphal car, will be afraid of overturning. For men of genius, however great they be, have always within them a touch of the beast which mocks at their intelligence. Therein they are akin to mankind in general, for therein they are dramatic. "It is but a step from the sublime to the ridiculous," said Napoleon, when he was convinced that he was mere man; and that outburst of a soul on fire illumines art and history at once; that cry of anguish is the résumé of the drama and of life.

It is a striking fact that all these contrasts are met with in the poets themselves, taken as men. By dint of meditating upon existence, of laying stress upon its bitter irony, of pouring floods of sarcasm and raillery upon our infirmities, the very men who make us laugh so heartily become profoundly sad. These Democrituses are Heraclituses as well. Beaumarchais was surly, Molière gloomy, Shakespeare melancholy.

The fact is, then, that the grotesque is one of the supreme beauties of the drama. It is not simply an appropriate element of it, but is oftentimes a necessity. Sometimes it appears in homogeneous masses, in entire characters, as Daudin, Prusias, Trissotin, Brid'oison, Juliet's nurse; sometimes impregnated with terror, as Richard III, Bégears, Tartuffe, Mephistopheles; sometimes, too, with a veil of grace and refinement, as Figaro, Osric, Mercutio, Don Juan. It finds its way in everywhere; for just as the most commonplace have their occasional moments of sublimity, so the most exalted frequently pay tribute to the trivial and ridiculous. Thus, often impalpable, often imperceptible, it is always present on the stage, even when it says nothing, even when it keeps out of sight. Thanks to it, there is no thought of monotony. Sometimes it injects laughter, sometimes horror, into tragedy. It will bring Romeo face to face with the apothecary, Macbeth with the witches, Hamlet with the grave-diggers. Sometimes it may, without discord, as in the scene between King Lear and his jester, mingle its shrill voice with the most sublime, the most dismal, the dreamiest music of the soul.

That is what Shakespeare alone among all has succeeded in doing, in a fashion of his own, which it would be no less fruitless than impossible to imitate—Shakespeare, the god of the stage, in whom, as in a trinity, the three characteristic geniuses of our stage, Corneille, Molière, Beaumarchais, seem united.

We see how quickly the arbitrary distinction between the species of poetry vanishes before common sense and taste. No less easily one might demolish the alleged rule of the two unities. We say *two* and not *three* unities, because unity of plot or of *ensemble,* the only true and well-founded one, was long ago removed from the sphere of discussion.

Distinguished contemporaries, foreigners and Frenchmen, have already attacked, both in theory and in practice, that fundamental law of the pseudo-Aristotelian code. Indeed, the combat was not likely to be a long one. At the first blow it cracked, so worm-eaten was that timber of the old scholastic hovel!

The strange thing is that the slaves of routine pretend to rest their rule of the two unities on probability, whereas reality is the very thing that destroys it. Indeed, what could be more improbable and absurd than this porch or peristyle or ante-chamber—vulgar places where our tragedies are obliging enough to develop themselves; whither conspirators come, no one knows whence, to declaim against the tyrant, and the tyrant to declaim against the conspirators, each in turn, as if they had said to one another in bucolic phrase:—

Alternis cantemus; amant alterna Camenæ.

Where did anyone ever see a porch or peristyle of that sort? What could be more opposed—we will not say to the truth, for the scholastics hold it very cheap, but to probability? The result is that everything that is too characteristic, too intimate, too local, to happen in the ante-chamber or on the street-corner—that is to say, the whole drama—takes place in the wings. We see on the stage only the elbows of the plot, so to speak; its hands are somewhere else. Instead of scenes we have narrative; instead of tableaux, descriptions. Solemn-faced characters,

placed, as in the old chorus, between the drama and ourselves, tell us what is going on in the temple, in the palace,
on the public square, until we are tempted many a time
to call out to them: "Indeed! then take us there! It
must be very entertaining—a fine sight!" To which they
would reply no doubt: "It is quite possible that it might
entertain or interest you, but that isn't the question; we are
the guardians of the dignity of the French Melpomene." And
there you are!

"But," someone will say, "this rule that you discard is
borrowed from the Greek drama." Wherein, pray, do the
Greek stage and drama resemble our stage and drama?
Moreover, we have already shown that the vast extent of
the ancient stage enabled it to include a whole locality, so
that the poet could, according to the exigencies of the plot,
transport it at his pleasure from one part of the stage to
another, which is practically equivalent to a change of stage-
setting. Curious contradiction! the Greek theatre, restricted
as it was to a national and religious object, was much more
free than ours, whose only object is the enjoyment, and, if
you please, the instruction, of the spectator. The reason is
that the one obeys only the laws that are suited to it, while the
other takes upon itself conditions of existence which are
absolutely foreign to its essence. One is artistic, the other
artificial.

People are beginning to understand in our day that exact
localization is one of the first elements of reality. The speaking or acting characters are not the only ones who engrave on
the minds of the spectators a faithful representation of the
facts. The place where this or that catastrophe took place
becomes a terrible and inseparable witness thereof; and the
absence of silent characters of this sort would make the
greatest scenes of history incomplete in the drama. Would
the poet dare to murder Rizzio elsewhere than in Mary
Stuart's chamber? to stab Henri IV elsewhere than in Rue
de la Ferronerie, all blocked with drays and carriages? to
burn Jeanne d'Arc elsewhere than in the Vieux-Marché? to
despatch the Duc de Guise elsewhere than in that château of
Blois where his ambition roused a popular assemblage to
frenzy? to behead Charles I and Louis XVI elsewhere than in

those ill-omened localities whence Whitehall or the Tuileries
may be seen, as if their scaffolds were appurtenances of their
palaces?

Unity of time rests on no firmer foundation than unity
of place. A plot forcibly confined within twenty-four hours
is as absurd as one confined within a peristyle. Every plot
has its proper duration as well as its appropriate place. Think
of administering the same dose of time to all events! of
applying the same measure to everything! You would laugh
at a cobbler who should attempt to put the same shoe on
every foot. To cross unity of time and unity of place like
the bars of a cage, and pedantically to introduce therein, in
the name of Aristotle, all the deeds, all the nations, all the
figures which Providence sets before us in such vast numbers
in real life,—to proceed thus is to mutilate men and things,
to cause history to make wry faces. Let us say, rather, that
everything will die in the operation, and so the dogmatic
mutilaters reach their ordinary result: what was alive in the
chronicles is dead in tragedy. That is why the cage of the
unities often contains only a skeleton.

And then, if twenty-four hours can be comprised in two,
it is a logical consequence that four hours may contain forty-
eight. Thus Shakespeare's unity must be different from
Corneille's. 'Tis pity!

But these are the wretched quibbles with which mediocrity, envy and routine has pestered genius for two centuries past! By such means the flight of our greatest poets
has been cut short. Their wings have been clipped with the
scissors of the unities. And what has been given us in exchange for the eagle feathers stolen from Corneille and
Racine? Campistron.

We imagine that someone may say: "There is something in too frequent changes of scene which confuses and
fatigues the spectator, and which produces a bewildering
effect on his attention; it may be, too, that manifold transitions from place to place, from one time to another time,
demand explanations which repel the attention; one should
also avoid leaving, in the midst of a plot, gaps which prevent the different parts of the drama from adhering closely
to one another, and which, moreover, puzzle the spectator

because he does not know what there may be in those gaps."
But these are precisely the difficulties which art has to meet.
These are some of the obstacles peculiar to one subject or
another, as to which it would be impossible to pass judgment
once for all. It is for genius to overcome, not for treatises
or poetry to evade them.

A final argument, taken from the very bowels of the art,
would of itself suffice to show the absurdity of the rule of
the two unities. It is the existence of the third unity, unity
of plot—the only one that is universally admitted, because it
results from a fact: neither the human eye nor the human
mind can grasp more than one *ensemble* at one time. This
one is as essential as the other two are useless. It is the one
which fixes the view-point of the drama; now, by that very
fact, it excludes the other two. There can no more be three
unities in the drama than three horizons in a picture. But
let us be careful not to confound unity with simplicity of
plot. The former does not in any way exclude the secondary
plots on which the principal plot may depend. It is necessary
only that these parts, being skilfully subordinated to the general plan, shall tend constantly toward the central plot and
group themselves about it at the various stages, or rather on
the various levels of the drama. Unity of plot is the stage law
of perspective.

"But," the customs-officers of thought will cry. "great
geniuses have submitted to these rules which you spurn!"
Unfortunately, yes. But what would those admirable men
have done if they had been left to themselves? At all events
they did not accept your chains without a struggle. You
should have seen how Pierre Corneille, worried and harassed
at his first step in the art on account of his marvellous work,
Le Cid, struggled under Mairet, Claveret, d'Aubignac and
Scudéri! How he denounced to posterity the violent attacks
of those men, who, he says, made themselves "all white with
Aristotle!" You should read how they said to him—and
we quote from books of the time: "Young man, you must
learn before you teach; and unless one is a Scaliger or a
Heinsius that is intolerable!" Thereupon Corneille rebels
and asks if their purpose is to force him "much below
Claveret." Here Scudéri waxes indignant at such a display

of pride, and reminds the "thrice great author of *Le Cid*
of the modest words in which Tasso, the greatest man of his
age, began his apology for the finest of his works against the
bitterest and most unjust censure perhaps that will ever be
pronounced. M. Corneille," he adds, "shows in his replies
that he is as far removed from that author's moderation as
from his merit." The young man *so justly and gently reproved*
dares to protest; thereupon Scudéri returns to the charge; he
calls to his assistance the *Eminent Academy:* "Pronounce,
O my Judges, a decree worthy of your eminence, which will
give all Europe to know that *Le Cid* is not the chef-d'œuvre
of the greatest man in France, but the least judicious performance of M. Corneille himself. You are bound to do it,
both for your own private renown; and for that of our people
in general, who are concerned in this matter; inasmuch as
foreigners who may see this precious masterpiece—they who
have possessed a Tasso or a Guarini—might think that our
greatest masters were no more than apprentices."

These few instructive lines contain the everlasting tactics
of envious routine against growing talent—tactics which are
still followed in our own day, and which, for example, added
such a curious page to the youthful essays of Lord Byron.
Scudéri gives us its quintessence. In like manner the earlier
works of a man of genius are always preferred to the newer
ones, in order to prove that he is going down instead of up—
Mélite and La Galérie du Palais placed above *Le Cid*. And
the names of the dead are always thrown at the heads of the
living—Corneille stoned with Tasso and Guarini (Guarini!),
as, later, Racine will be stoned with Corneille, Voltaire with
Racine, and as to-day, everyone who shows signs of rising is
stoned with Corneille, Racine and Voltaire. These tactics, as
will be seen, are well-worn; but they must be effective as they
are still in use. However, the poor devil of a great man still
breathed. Here we cannot help but admire the way in which
Scudéri, the bully of this tragic-comedy, forced to the wall,
blackguards and maltreats him, how pitilessly he unmasks
his classical artillery, how he shows the author of *Le Cid*
"what the episodes should be, according to Aristotle, who
tells us in the tenth and sixteenth chapters of his *Poetics*";
how he crushes Corneille, in the name of the same Aristotle

"in the eleventh chapter of his *Art of Poetry,* wherein we find the condemnation of *Le Cid*"; in the name of Plato, "in the tenth book of his *Republic*"; in the name of Marcellinus, "as may be seen in the twenty-seventh book"; in the name of "the tragedies of Niobe and Jephthah"; in the name of the "*Ajax* of Sophocles"; in the name of "the example of Euripides"; in the name of "Heinsius, chapter six of the *Constitution* of *Tragedy;* and the younger Scaliger in his poems"; and finally, in the name of the Canonists and Jurisconsults, under the title "Nuptials." The first arguments were addressed to the Academy, the last one was aimed at the Cardinal. After the pin-pricks the blow with a club. A judge was needed to decide the question. Chapelain gave judgment. Corneille saw that he was doomed; the lion was muzzled, or, as was said at the time, the crow (*Corneille*) was plucked. Now comes the painful side of this grotesque performance: after he had been thus quenched at his first flash, this genius, thoroughly modern, fed upon the Middle Ages and Spain, being compelled to lie to himself and to hark back to ancient times, drew for us that Castilian Rome, which is sublime beyond question, but in which, except perhaps in *Nicomède,* which was so ridiculed by the eighteenth century for its dignified and simple colouring, we find neither the real Rome nor the true Corneille.

Racine was treated to the same persecution, but did not make the same resistance. Neither in his genius nor in his character was there any of Corneille's lofty asperity. He submitted in silence and sacrificed to the scorn of his time his enchanting elegy of *Esther,* his magnificent epic, *Athalie.* So that we can but believe that, if he had not been paralyzed as he was by the prejudices of his epoch, if he had come in contact less frequently with the classic cramp-fish, he would not have failed to introduce Locuste in his drama between Narcisse and Neron, and above all things would not have relegated to the wings the admirable scene of the banquet at which Seneca's pupil poisons Britannicus in the cup of reconciliation. But can we demand of the bird that he fly under the receiver of an air-pump? What a multitude of beautiful scenes the *people*

of taste have cost us, from Scudéri to La Harpe! A noble
work might be composed of all that their scorching breath
has withered in its germ. However, our great poets have
found a way none the less to cause their genius to blaze
forth through all these obstacles. Often the attempt to
confine them behind walls of dogmas and rules is vain.
Like the Hebrew giant they carry their prison doors with
them to the mountains.

But still the same refrain is repeated, and will be, no
doubt, for a long while to come: "Follow the rules! Copy
the models! It was the rules that shaped the models."
One moment! In that case there are two sorts of models,
those which are made according to the rules, and, prior to
them, those according to which the rules were made. Now,
in which of these two categories should genius seek a place
for itself? Although it is always disagreeable to come in
contact with pedants, is it not a thousand times better to give
them lessons than to receive lessons from them? And
then—copy! Is the reflection equal to the light? Is the
satellite which travels unceasingly in the same circle equal
to the central creative planet? With all his poetry Virgil
is no more than the moon of Homer.

And whom are we to copy, I pray to know? The
ancients? We have just shown that their stage has nothing
in common with ours. Moreover, Voltaire, who will have
none of Shakespeare, will have none of the Greeks, either.
Let him tell us why: "The Greeks ventured to produce
scenes no less revolting to us. Hippolyte, crushed by his
fall, counts his wounds and utters doleful cries. Philoctetes
falls in his paroxysms of pain; black blood flows from his
wound. Œdipus, covered with the blood that still drops
from the sockets of the eyes he has torn out, complains
bitterly of gods and men. We hear the shrieks of Clytemnestra, murdered by her own son, and Electra, on the
stage, cries: 'Strike! spare her not! she did not spare
our father.' Prometheus is fastened to a rock by nails
driven through his stomach and his arms. The Furies reply
to Clytemnestra's bleeding shade with inarticulate roars.
Art was in its infancy in the time of Æschylus as it was
in London in Shakespeare's time."

Whom shall we copy, then? The moderns? What!
Copy copies! God forbid!

"But," someone else will object, "according to your
conception of the art, you seem to look for none but great
poets, to count always upon genius." Art certainly does
not count upon mediocrity. It prescribes no rules for it,
it knows nothing of it; in fact, mediocrity has no existence
so far as art is concerned; art supplies wings, not crutches.
Alas! D'Aubignac followed rules, Campistron copied models. What does it matter to art? It does not build its palaces for ants. It lets them make their ant-hill, without
taking the trouble to find out whether they have built their
burlesque imitation of its palace upon its foundation.

The critics of the scholastic school place their poets in a
strange position. On the one hand they cry incessantly:
"Copy the models!" On the other hand they have a habit
of declaring that "the models are inimitable"! Now,
if their craftsman, by dint of hard work, succeeds in forcing
through this dangerous defile some colourless tracing of
the masters, these ungrateful wretches, after examining the
new *refaccimiento,* exclaim sometimes: "This doesn't
resemble anything!" and sometimes: "This resembles
everything!" And by virtue of a logic made for the occasion each of these formulæ is a criticism.

Let us then speak boldly. The time for it has come, and
it would be strange if, in this age, liberty, like the light,
should penetrate everywhere except to the one place where
freedom is most natural—the domain of thought. Let us
take the hammer to theories and poetic systems. Let us
throw down the old plastering that conceals the façade
of art. There are neither rules nor models; or, rather,
there are no other rules than the general laws of nature,
which soar above the whole field of art, and the special
rules which result from the conditions appropriate to the
subject of each composition. The former are of the essence, eternal, and do not change; the latter are variable,
external, and are used but once. The former are the framework that supports the house; the latter the scaffolding
which is used in building it, and which is made anew for
each building. In a word, the former are the flesh and

bones, the latter the clothing, of the drama. But these rules are not written in the treatises on poetry. Richelet has no idea of their existence. Genius, which divines rather than learns, devises for each work the general rules from the general plan of things, the special rules from the separate *ensemble* of the subject treated; not after the manner of the chemist, who lights the fire under his furnace, heats his crucible, analyzes and destroys; but after the manner of the bee, which flies on its golden wings, lights on each flower and extracts its honey, leaving it as brilliant and fragrant as before.

The poet—let us insist on this point—should take counsel therefore only of nature, truth, and inspiration which is itself both truth and nature. " Quando he," says Lope de Vega,

" Quando he de escrivir una comedia,
Encierro los preceptos con seis llaves."

To secure these precepts " six keys " are none too many, in very truth. Let the poet beware especially of copying anything whatsoever—Shakespeare no more than Molière, Schiller no more than Corneille. If genuine talent could abdicate its own nature in this matter, and thus lay aside its original personality, to transform itself into another, it would lose everything by playing this rôle of its own double. It is as if a god should turn valet. We must draw our inspiration from the original sources. It is the same sap, distributed through the soil, that produces all the trees of the forest, so different in bearing power, in fruit, in foliage. It is the same nature that fertilizes and nourishes the most diverse geniuses. The poet is a tree that may be blown about by all winds and watered by every fall of dew; and bears his works as his fruit, as the *fablier* of old bore his fables. Why attach one's self to a master, or graft one's self upon a model? It were better to be a bramble or a thistle, fed by the same earth as the cedar and the palm, than the fungus or the lichen of those noble trees. The bramble lives, the fungus vegetates. Moreover, however great the cedar and the palm may be, it is not with the sap one sucks from them that one can become great one's self. A giant's parasite will be at best a dwarf.

The oak, colossus that it is, can produce and sustain nothing more than the mistletoe.

Let there be no misunderstanding: if some of our poets have succeeded in being great, even when copying, it is because, while forming themselves on the antique model, they have often listened to the voice of nature and to their own genius—it is because they have been themselves in some one respect. Their branches became entangled in those of the near-by tree, but their roots were buried deep in the soil of art. They were the ivy, not the mistletoe. Then came imitators of the second rank, who, having neither roots in the earth, nor genius in their souls, had to confine themselves to imitation. As Charles Nodier says: "After the school of Athens, the school of Alexandria." Then there was a deluge of mediocrity; then there came a swarm of those treatises on poetry, so annoying to true talent, so convenient for mediocrity. We were told that everything was done, and God was forbidden to create more Molières or Corneilles. Memory was put in place of imagination. Imagination itself was subjected to hard-and-fast rules, and aphorisms were made about it: "To imagine," says La Harpe, with his naïve assurance, "is in substance to remember, that is all."

But nature! Nature and truth!—And here, in order to prove that, far from demolishing art, the new ideas aim only to reconstruct it more firmly and on a better foundation, let us try to point out the impassable limit which in our opinion, separates reality according to art from reality according to nature. It is careless to confuse them as some ill-informed partisans of *romanticism* do. Truth in art cannot possibly be, as several writers have claimed, *absolute* reality. Art cannot produce the thing itself. Let us imagine, for example, one of those unreflecting promoters of absolute nature, of nature viewed apart from art, at the performance of a romantic play, say *Le Cid*. "What's that?" he will ask at the first word. "The Cid speaks in verse? It isn't *natural* to speak in verse."—"How would you have him speak, pray?"—"In prose." Very good. A moment later, "How's this!" he will continue, if he is consistent; "the Cid is speaking French!"—"Well?"—

"Nature demands that he speak his own language; he can't speak anything but Spanish."

We shall fail entirely to understand, but again—very good. You imagine that this is all? By no means: before the tenth sentence in Castilian, he is certain to rise and ask if the Cid who is speaking is the real Cid, in flesh and blood. By what right does the actor, whose name is Pierre or Jacques, take the name of the Cid? That is *false*. There is no reason why he should not go on to demand that the sun should be substituted for the footlights, *real* trees and *real* houses for those deceitful wings. For, once started on that road, logic has you by the collar, and you cannot stop.

We must admit, therefore, or confess ourselves ridiculous, that the domains of art and of nature are entirely distinct. Nature and art are two things—were it not so, one or the other would not exist. Art, in addition to its idealistic side, has a terrestrial, material side. Let it do what it will, it is shut in between grammar and prosody, between Vaugelas and Richelet. For its most capricious creations, it has formulæ, methods of execution, a complete apparatus to set in motion. For genius there are delicate instruments, for mediocrity, tools.

It seems to us that someone has already said that the drama is a mirror wherein nature is reflected. But if it be an ordinary mirror, a smooth and polished surface, it will give only a dull image of objects, with no relief—faithful, but colourless; everyone knows that colour and light are lost in a simple reflection. The drama, therefore, must be a concentrating mirror, which, instead of weakening, concentrates and condenses the coloured rays, which makes of a mere gleam a light, and of a light a flame. Then only is the drama acknowledged by art.

The stage is an optical point. Everything that exists in the world—in history, in life, in man—should be and can be reflected therein, but under the magic wand of art. Art turns the leaves of the ages, of nature, studies chronicles, strives to reproduce actual facts (especially in respect to manners and peculiarities, which are much less exposed to doubt and contradiction than are concrete facts), restores what the chroniclers have lopped off, harmonises what they have collected, divines and supplies their omissions, fills their gaps with imaginary scenes which have the colour of the time, groups what they have left scattered about, sets in motion anew the threads of Providence which work the human marionettes, clothes the whole with a form at once poetical and natural, and imparts to it that vitality of truth and brilliancy which gives birth to illusion, that prestige of reality which arouses the enthusiasm of the spectator, and of the poet first of all, for the poet is sincere. Thus the aim of art is almost divine: to bring to life again if it is writing history, to create if it is writing poetry.

It is a grand and beautiful sight to see this broad development of a drama wherein art powerfully seconds nature; of a drama wherein the plot moves on to the conclusion with a firm and unembarrassed step, without diffuseness and without undue compression; of a drama, in short, wherein the poet abundantly fulfills the multifold object of art, which is to open to the spectator a double prospect, to illuminate at the same time the interior and the exterior of mankind: the exterior by their speech and their acts, the interior, by asides and monologues; to bring together, in a word, in the same picture, the drama of life and the drama of conscience.

It will readily be imagined that, for a work of this kind, if the poet must *choose* (and he must), he should choose, not the *beautiful*, but the *characteristic*. Not that it is advisable to "make local colour," as they say to-day; that is, to add as an afterthought a few discordant touches here and there to a work that is at best utterly conventional and false. The local colour should not be on the surface of the drama, but in its substance, in the very heart of the work, whence it spreads of itself, naturally, evenly, and, so to speak, into every corner of the drama, as the sap ascends from the root to the tree's topmost leaf. The drama should be thoroughly impregnated with this colour of the time, which should be, in some sort, in the air, so that one detects it only on entering the theatre, and that on going forth one finds one's self in a different period and atmosphere. It requires some study, some labour, to attain this end; so much the better. It is well that the avenues of art should be obstructed by those brambles from which everybody recoils except those of powerful will. Besides, it is this very study, fostered by an ardent inspiration, which will ensure the drama against a vice that kills it—the *commonplace*. To be commonplace is the failing of short-sighted, short-breathed poets. In this tableau of the stage, each figure must be held down to its most prominent, most individual, most precisely defined characteristic. Even the vulgar and the trivial should have an accent of their own. Like God, the true poet is present in every part of his work at once. Genius resembles the die which stamps the king's effigy on copper and golden coins alike.

We do not hesitate—and this will demonstrate once more to honest men how far we are from seeking to discredit the art—we do not hesitate to consider verse as one of the means best adapted to protect the drama from the scourge we have just mentioned, as one of the most powerful dams against the irruption of the commonplace, which, like democracy, is always flowing between full banks in men's minds. And at this point we beg the younger literary generation, already so rich in men and in works, to allow us to point out an error into which it seems to have fallen —an error too fully justified, indeed, by the extraordinary aberrations of the old school. The new century is at that growing age at which one can readily set one's self right.

There has appeared of late, like a penultimate branching-out of the old classical trunk, or, better still, like one of those excrescences, those polypi, which decrepitude develops, and which are a sign of decomposition much more than a proof of life—there has appeared a strange school of dramatic poetry. This school seems to us to have had for its master and its fountain-head the poet who marks the transition from the eighteenth to the nineteenth century, the man of wearisome description and periphrases —that Delille who, they say, toward the close of his life, boasted, after the fashion of the Homeric catalogues, of having *made* twelve camels, four dogs, three horses, including Job's, six tigers, two cats, a chess-board, a backgammon-board, a checker-board, a billiard-table, several winters, many summers, a multitude of springs, fifty sunsets, and so many daybreaks that he had lost count of them.

Now, Delille went into tragedy. He is the father (he, and not Racine, God save the mark!) of an alleged school of refinement and taste which flourished until recently. Tragedy is not to this school what it was to Will Shakespeare, say, a source of emotions of every sort, but a convenient frame for the solution of a multitude of petty descriptive problems which it propounds as it goes along. This muse, far from spurning, as the true French classic school does, the trivial and degrading things of life, eagerly seeks them out and brings them together. The grotesque, shunned as undesirable company by the tragedy of Louis the Fourteenth's day, cannot pass unnoticed before her. *It must be. described,* that is to say, ennobled. A scene in the guard-house, a popular uprising, the fishmarket, the galleys, the wine-shop, the *poule au pot* of Henri Quatre, are treasure-trove in her eyes. She seizes upon this canaille, washes it clean, and sews her tinsel and spangles over its villainies; *purpureus assuitur pannus.* Her object seems to be to deliver patents of nobility to all these *roturiers* of the drama; and each of these patents under the great seal is a speech.

This muse, as may be imagined, is of a rare prudery. Wonted as she is to the caresses of periphrasis, plain-speaking, if she should occasionally be exposed to it, would horrify her. It does not accord with her dignity to speak naturally. She *underlines* old Corneille for his blunt way of speaking, as in,—

" *A heap of men* ruined by debt and crimes."

" Chimène, *who'd have thought it?* Rodrigue, *who'd have said it?* "

" When their Flaminius *haggled with* Hannibal."

" Oh! do not *embroil* me with the Republic."

She still has her " Tout beau, monsieur! " on her heart. And it needed many " seigneurs " and " madames " to pro-

cure forgiveness for our admirable Racine for his mono-
syllabic "dogs!" and for so brutally bestowing Claudius
in Agrippina's bed.

This Melpomene, as she is called, would shudder at the
thought of touching a chronicle. She leaves to the costumer the duty of learning the period of the dramas she
writes. In her eyes history is bad form and bad taste.
How, for example, can one tolerate kings and queens who
swear? They must be elevated from mere regal dignity
to tragic dignity. It was in a promotion of this sort that she
exalted Henri IV. It was thus that the people's king,
purified by M. Legouvé, found his "ventre-saint-gris"
ignominiously banished from his mouth by two sentences,
and that he was reduced, like the girl in the old *fabliau,*
to the necessity of letting fall from those royal lips only
pearls and sapphires and rubies: the apotheosis of falsity,
in very truth.

The fact is that nothing is so commonplace as this conventional refinement and nobility. Nothing original, no
imagination, no invention in this style; simply what one
has seen everywhere—rhetoric, bombast, commonplaces,
flowers of college eloquence, poetry after the style of
Latin verses. The poets of this school are eloquent after
the manner of stage princes and princesses, always sure of
finding in the costumer's labelled cases, cloaks and pinch-
beck crowns, which have no other disadvantage than that
of having been used by everybody. If these poets never
turn the leaves of the Bible, it is not because they have
not a bulky book of their own, the *Dictionnaire de rimes.*
That is the source of their poetry—*fontes aquarum.*

It will be seen that, in all this, nature and truth get
along as best they can. It would be great good luck if
any remnants of either should survive in this cataclysm
of false art, false style, false poetry. This is what has
caused the errors of several of our distinguished reformers.
Disgusted by the stiffness, the ostentation, the *pomposo,* of
this alleged dramatic poetry, they have concluded that the
elements of our poetic language were incompatible with the
natural and the true. The Alexandrine had wearied them
so often, that they condemned it without giving it a hear-

ing, so to speak, and decided, a little hastily, perhaps, that the drama should be written in prose.

They were mistaken. If in fact the false is predominant in the style as well as in the action of certain French tragedies, it is not the verses that should be held responsible therefore, but the versifiers. It was needful to condemn, not the form employed, but those who employed it: the workmen, not the tool.

To convince one's self how few obstacles the nature of our poetry places in the way of the free expression of all that is true, we should study our verse, not in Racine, perhaps, but often in Corneille and always in Molière. Racine, a divine poet, is elegiac, lyric, epic; Molière is dramatic. It is time to deal sternly with the criticisms heaped upon that admirable style by the wretched taste of the last century, and to proclaim aloud that Molière occupies the topmost pinnacle of our drama, not only as a poet, but also as a writer. *Palmas vere habet iste duas.*

In his work the verse surrounds the idea, becomes of its very essence, compresses and develops it at once, imparts to it a more slender, more definite, more complete form, and gives us, in some sort, an extract thereof. Verse is the optical form of thought. That is why it is especially adapted to the perspective of the stage. Constructed in a certain way, it communicates its relief to things which, but for it, would be considered insignificant and trivial. It makes the tissue of style finer and firmer. It is the knot which stays the thread. It is the girdle which holds up the garment and gives it all its folds. What could nature and the true lose, then, by entering into verse? We ask the question of our prose-writers themselves—what do they lose in Molière's poetry? Does wine—we beg pardon for another trivial illustration—does wine cease to be wine when it is bottled?

If we were entitled to say what, in our opinion, the style of dramatic poetry should be, we would declare for a free, outspoken, sincere verse, which dares say everything without prudery, express its meaning without seeking for words; which passes naturally from comedy to tragedy, from the sublime to the grotesque; by turns practical and poetical, both artistic and inspired, profound and impulsive, of wide range and true; verse which is apt opportunely to displace the cæsura, in order to disguise the monotony of Alexandrines; more inclined to the *enjambement* that lengthens the line, than to the inversion of phrases that confuses the sense; faithful to rhyme, that enslaved queen, that supreme charm of our poetry, that creator of our metre; verse that is inexhaustible in the verity of its turns of thought, unfathomable in its secrets of composition and of grace; assuming, like Proteus, a thousand forms without changing its type and character; avoiding long speeches; taking delight in dialogue; always hiding behind the characters of the drama; intent, before everything, on being in its place, and when it falls to its lot to be *beautiful,* being so only by chance, as it were, in spite of itself and unconsciously; lyric, epic, dramatic, at need; capable of running through the whole gamut of poetry, of skipping from high notes to low, from the most exalted to the most trivial ideas, from the most extravagant to the most solemn, from the most superficial to the most abstract, without ever passing beyond the limits of a spoken scene; in a word, such verse as a man would write whom a fairy had endowed with Corneille's mind and Molière's brain. It seems to us that such verse would be *as fine as prose.*

There would be nothing in common between poetry of this sort and that of which we made a *post mortem* examination just now. The distinction will be easy to point out if a certain man of talent, to whom the author of this book is under personal obligation, will allow us to borrow his clever phrase: the other poetry was descriptive, this would be picturesque.

Let us repeat, verse on the stage should lay aside all self-love, all exigence, all coquetry. It is simply a form, and a form which should admit everything, which has no laws to impose on the drama, but on the contrary should receive everything from it, to be transmitted to the spectator—French, Latin, texts of laws, royal oaths, popular phrases, comedy, tragedy, laughter, tears, prose and poetry. Woe to the poet whose verse does not speak out! But this form is a form of bronze which encases the thought in its metre beneath which the drama is indestructible, which engraves it more deeply on the actor's mind, warns him of what he omits and of what he adds, prevents him from changing his rôle, from substituting himself for the author, makes each word sacred, and causes what the poet has said to remain vivid a long while in the hearer's memory. The idea, when steeped in verse, suddenly assumes a more incisive, more brilliant quality.

One feels that prose, which is necessarily more timid, obliged to wean the drama from anything like epic or lyric poetry, reduced to dialogue and to matter-of-fact, is a long way from possessing these resources. It has much narrower wings. And then, too, it is much more easy of access; mediocrity is at its ease in prose; and for the sake of a few works of distinction such as have appeared of late, the art would very soon be overloaded with abortions and embryos. Another faction of the reformers incline to drama written in both prose and verse, as Shakespeare composed it. This method has its advantages. There might, however, be some incongruity in the transitions from one form to the other; and when a tissue is homogeneous it is much stouter. However, whether the drama should be written in prose is only a secondary question. The rank of a work is certain to be fixed, not according to its form, but according to its intrinsic value. In questions of this sort, there is only one solution. There is but one weight that can turn the scale in the balance of art— that is genius.

Meanwhile, the first, the indispensable merit of a dramatic writer, whether he write in prose or verse, is correctness. Not a mere superficial correctness, the merit or defect of the descriptive school, which makes Lhomond and Restaut the two wings of its Pegasus; but that intimate, deep-rooted, deliberate correctness, which is permeated with the genius of a language, which has sounded its roots and searched its etymology; always unfettered, because it is sure of its footing, and always more in harmony with the logic of the language. Our Lady Grammar leads the one in leading-strings; the other holds grammar in leash. It can venture anything, can create or invent its style; it

has a right to do so. For, whatever certain men may
have said who did not think what they were saying, and
among whom we must place, notably, him who writes these
lines, the French tongue is not *fixed* and never will be.
A language does not become fixed. The human intellect
is always on the march, or, if you prefer, in movement,
and languages with it. Things are made so. When the
body changes, how could the coat not change? The French
of the nineteenth century can no more be the French of
the eighteenth, than that is the French of the seventeenth,
or than the French of the seventeenth is that of the sixteenth. Montaigne's language is not Rabelais's, Pascal's
is not Montaigne's, Montesquieu's is not Pascal's. Each of
the four languages, taken by itself, is admirable because
it is original. Every age has its own ideas; it must have
also words adapted to those ideas. Languages are like the
sea, they move to and fro incessantly. At certain times
they leave one shore of the world of thought and overflow another. All that their waves thus abandon dries
up and vanishes. It is in this wise that ideas vanish,
that words disappear. It is the same with human tongues
as with everything. Each age adds and takes away something. What can be done? It is the decree of fate. In
vain, therefore, should we seek to petrify the mobile physiognomy of our idiom in a fixed form. In vain do our literary Joshuas cry out to the language to stand still; languages and the sun do not stand still. The day when
they become *fixed,* they are dead.—That is why the French
of a certain contemporary school is a dead language.

Such are, substantially, but without the more elaborate
development which would make the evidence in their favour
more complete, the *present* ideas of the author of this book
concerning the drama. He is far, however, from presuming to put forth his first dramatic essay as an emanation of these ideas, which, on the contrary, are themselves,
it may be, simply results of its execution. It would be
very convenient for him, no doubt, and very clever, to
rest his book on his preface, and to defend each by the
other. He prefers less cleverness and more frankness. He
proposes, therefore, to be the first to point out the ex-

treme tenuity of the thread connecting this preface with his drama. His first plan, dictated by his laziness, was to give the work to the public entirely unattended: *el demonio sin las cuernas,* as Yriarte said. It was only after he had duly brought it to a close, that, at the solicitations of a few friends, blinded by their friendship, no doubt, he determined to reckon with himself in a preface—to draw, so to speak, a map of the poetic voyage he had made, to take account of the acquisitions, good or bad, that he had brought home, and of the new aspects in which the domain of art had presented itself to his mind. Someone will take advantage of this admission, doubtless, to repeat the reproach already uttered by a critic in Germany, that he has written " a treatise in defence of his poetry." What does it matter? In the first place he was much more inclined to demolish treatises on poetry than to write them. And then, would it not be better always to write treatises based on a poem, than to write poems based on a treatise? But no, we repeat that he has neither the talent to create nor the presumption to put forth systems. " Systems," cleverly said Voltaire, "are like rats which pass through twenty holes, only to find at last two or three which will not let them through." It would have been, therefore, to undertake a useless task and one much beyond his strength. What he has pleaded, on the contrary, is the freedom of art against the despotism of systems, codes and rules. It is his habit to follow at all risks whatever he takes for his inspiration, and to change moulds as often as he changes metals. Dogmatism in the arts is what he shuns before everything. God forbid that he should aspire to be numbered among those men, be they romanticists or classicists, who compose *works according to their own systems,* who condemn themselves to have but one form in their minds, to be forever *proving* something, to follow other laws than those of their temperaments and their natures. The artificial work of these men, however talented they may be, has no existence so far as art is concerned. It is a theory, not poetry.

Having attempted, in all that has gone before, to point out what, in our opinion, was the origin of the drama, what its character is, and what its style should be, the time has come to descend from these exalted general considerations upon the art to the particular case which has led us to put them forth. It remains for us to discourse to the reader of our work, of this *Cromwell;* and as it is not a subject in which we take pleasure, we will say very little about it in very few words.

Oliver Cromwell is one of those historical characters who are at once very famous and very little known. Most of his biographers—and among them there are some who are themselves historical—have left that colossal figure incomplete. It would seem that they dared not assemble all the characteristic features of that strange and gigantic prototype of the religious reformation, of the political revolution of England. Almost all of them have confined themselves to reproducing on a larger scale the simple and ominous profile drawn by Bossuet from his Catholic and monarchical standpoint, from his episcopal pulpit supported by the throne of Louis XIV.

Like everybody else, the author of this book went no further than that. The name of Oliver Cromwell suggested to him simply the bare conception of a fanatical regicide and a great captain. Only on prowling among the chronicles of the times, which he did with delight, and on looking through the English memoirs of the seventeenth century, was he surprised to find that a wholly new Cromwell was gradually exposed to his gaze. It was no longer simply Bossuet's Cromwell the soldier, Cromwell the politician; it was a complex, heterogenous, multiple being, made up of all sorts of contraries—a mixture of much that was evil and much that was good, of genius and pettiness; a sort of Tiberius-Dandin, the tyrant of Europe and the plaything of his family; an old regicide, who delighted to humiliate the ambassadors of all the kings of Europe, and was tormented by his young royalist daughter; austere and gloomy in his manners, yet keeping four court jesters about him; given to the composition of wretched verses; sober, simple, frugal, yet a stickler for etiquette; a rough soldier and a crafty politician; skilled in theological disputation and very fond of it; a dull, diffuse, obscure orator, but clever in speaking the language of anybody whom he wished to influence; a hypocrite and a fanatic; a visionary swayed by phantoms of his childhood, believing in astrologers and banishing them; suspicious to excess, always threatening, rarely sanguinary; a strict observer of Puritan rules, and solemnly wasting several hours a day in buffoonery.; abrupt and contemptuous with his intimates, caressing with the secretaries whom he feared, holding his remorse at bay with sophistry, paltering with his conscience, inexhaustible in adroitness, in tricks, in resources; mastering his imagination by his intelligence; grotesque and sublime; in a word, one of those men who are " square at the base," as they were described by Napoleon, himself their chief, in his mathematically exact and poetically figurative language.

He who writes these lines, in presence of this rare and impressive *ensemble,* felt that Bossuet's impassioned sketch was no longer sufficient for him. He began to walk about that lofty figure, and he was seized by a powerful temptation to depict the giant in all his aspects. It was a rich soil. Beside the man of war and the statesman, it remained to draw the theologian, the pedant, the wretched poet, the seer of visions, the buffoon, the father, the husband, the human Proteus—in a word, the twofold Cromwell, *homo et vir.*

There is one period of his life, especially, in which this strange personality exhibits itself in all its forms. It is not as one might think at first blush, the period of the trial of Charles I, instinct as that is with depressing and terrible interest; but it is the moment when the ambitious mortal boldly attempted to pluck the fruit of that monarch's death; it is the moment when Cromwell, having attained what would have been to any other man the zenith of fortune—master of England, whose innumerable factions knelt silently at his feet; master of Scotland, of which he had made a satrapy, and of Ireland, which he had turned into a prison; master of Europe through his diplomacy and his fleets—seeks to fulfil the dream of his earliest childhood, the last ambition of his life; to make himself king. History never had a more im-

pressive lesson in a more impressive drama. First of all,
the Protector arranges to be urged to assume the crown:
the august farce begins by addresses from municipalities,
from counties; then there comes an act of Parliament.
Cromwell, the anonymous author of the play, pretends to
be displeased; we see him put out a hand toward the
sceptre, then draw it back; by a devious path he draws
near the throne from which he has swept the legitimate
dynasty. At last he makes up his mind, suddenly; by
his command Westminster is decked with flags, the dais
is built, the crown is ordered from the jewelers, the day
is appointed for the ceremony.—Strange dénouement! On
that very day, in presence of the populace, the troops,
the House of Commons, in the great hall of Westminster, on that dais from which he expected to descend
as king, suddenly, as if aroused by a shock, he seems
to awaken at the sight of the crown, asks if he is
dreaming, and what the meaning is of all this regal
pomp, and in a speech that lasts three hours declines the
kingly title.

Was it because his spies had warned him of two con-
spiracies formed by Cavaliers and Puritans in concert,
which were intended, taking advantage of this misstep, to
break out on the same day? Was it an inward revolution
caused by the silence or the murmurs of the populace,
discomposed to see their regicide ascend the throne? Or
was it simply the sagacity of genius, the instinct of a
far-seeing, albeit unbridled ambition, which realizes how
one step forward changes a man's position and attitude,
and which dares not expose its plebeian structure to the
wind of unpopularity? Was it all these at once? This
is a question which no contemporaneous document answers
satisfactorily. So much the better: the poet's liberty is
the more complete, and the drama is the gainer by the
latitude which history affords it. It will be seen that
here the latitude is ample and unique; this is, in truth,
the decisive hour, the turning-point in Cromwell's life.
It is the moment when his chimera escapes from him, when
the present kills the future, when, to use an expressive
colloquialism, his destiny *misses fire*. All of Cromwell is

at stake in the comedy being played between England and himself.

Such then is the man and such the period of which we have tried to give an idea in this book.

The author has allowed himself to be seduced by the childlike diversion of touching the keys of that great harpsichord. Unquestionably, more skillful hands might have evoked a thrilling and profound melody—not of those which simply caress the ear—but of those intimate harmonies which stir the whole man to the depths of his being, as if each key of the key-board were connected with a fibre of the heart. He has surrendered to the desire to depict all those fanaticisms, all those superstitions — maladies to which religion is subject at certain epochs; to the longing to "make playthings of all these men," as Hamlet says. To set in array about and below Cromwell, himself the centre and pivot of that court, of that people, of that little world, which attracts all to his cause and inspires all with his vigour, that twofold conspiracy devised by two factions which detest each other, but join hands to overthrow the man who blocks their path, but which unite simply without blending; and that Puritan faction, of divers minds, fanatical, gloomy, unselfish, choosing for leader the most insignificant of men for such a great part, the egotistical and cowardly Lambert; and the faction of the Cavaliers, featherheaded, merry, unscrupulous, reckless, devoted, led by the man who, aside from his devotion to the cause, was least fitted to represent it, the stern and upright Ormond; and those ambassadors, so humble and fawning before the soldier of fortune; and the court itself, an extraordinary mixture of upstarts and great nobles vying with one another in baseness; and the four jesters whom the contemptuous neglect of history permitted me to invent; and Cromwell's family, each member of which is as a thorn in his flesh; and Thurloe, the Protector's Achates; and the Jewish rabbi, Israel Ben-Manasseh, spy, usurer, and astrologer, vile on two sides, sublime on the third; and Rochester, the unique Rochester, absurd and clever, refined and crapulous, always cursing, always in love, and always tipsy, as he himself boasted to Bishop

Burnet—wretched poet and gallant gentleman, vicious
and ingenuous, staking his head and indifferent whether he
wins the game provided it amuses him—in a word, capable of everything, of ruse and recklessness, calculation
and folly, villainy and generosity; and the morose Carr,
of whom history describes but one trait, albeit a most characteristic and suggestive one; and those other fanatics,
of all ranks and varieties: Harrison, the thieving fanatic;
Barebones the shopkeeping fanatic; Syndercomb, the bravo;
Garland the tearful and pious assassin; gallant Colonel
Overton, intelligent but a little declamatory; the austere
and unbending Ludlow, who left his ashes and his epitaph
at Lausanne; and lastly, "Milton and a few other men
of mind," as we read in a pamphlet of 1675 (*Cromwell
the Politician*), which reminds one of "a certain Dante"
of the Italian chronicle.

We omit many less important characters, of each of
whom, however, the actual life is known, and each of
whom has his marked individuality, and all of whom contributed to the fascination which this vast historical scene
exerted upon the author's imagination. From that scene
he constructed this drama. He moulded it in verse, because he preferred to do so. One will discover on reading it how little thought he gave to his work while writing
this preface—with what disinterestedness, for instance,
he contended against the dogma of the unities. His drama
does not leave London; it begins on June 25, 1657, at three
in the morning, and ends on the 26th at noon. Observe
that he has almost followed the classic formula, as the
professors of poetry lay it down to-day. They need not,
however, thank him for it. With the permission of history,
not of Aristotle, the author constructed his drama thus;
and because, when the interest is the same, he prefers a
compact subject to a widely diffused one.

It is evident that, in its present proportions, this drama
could not be given at one of our theatrical performances.
It is too long. The reader will perhaps comprehend, none
the less, that every part of it was written for the stage.
It was on approaching his subject to study it that the
author recognized, or thought that he recognized, the im-

possibility of procuring the performance of a faithful reproduction of it on our stage, in the exceptional position
it now occupies, between the academic Charybdis and
the administrative Scylla, between the literary juries and
the political censorship. He was required to choose: either
the wheedling, tricky, false tragedy, which may be acted,
or the audaciously true drama, which is prohibited.
The first was not worth the trouble of writing, so he
preferred to attempt the second. That is why, hopeless
of ever being put on the stage, he abandoned himself, freely
and submissively, to the whims of composition, to the
pleasure of painting with a freer hand, to the developments which his subject demanded, and which, even if they
keep his drama off the stage, have at all events the advantage of making it almost complete from the historical
standpoint. However, the reading committees are an ob-
stacle of the second class only. If it should happen that
the dramatic censorship, realizing how far this harmless,
conscientious and accurate picture of Cromwell and his
time is removed from our own age, should sanction its
production on the stage, in that case, but only in that case,
the author might perhaps extract from this drama a play
which would venture to show itself on the boards, and
would be hissed.

Until then he will continue to hold aloof from the
theatre. And even then he will leave his cherished and
tranquil retirement soon enough, for the agitation and
excitement of this new world. God grant that he may
never repent of having exposed the unspotted obscurity
of his name and his person to the shoals, the squalls and
tempests of the pit, and above all (for what does a mere
failure matter?) to the wretched bickerings of the wings;
of having entered that shifting, foggy, stormy atmosphere,
where ignorance dogmatises, where envy hisses, where cabals
cringe and crawl, where the probity of talent has so
often been misrepresented, where the noble innocence of
genius is sometimes so out of place, where mediocrity
triumphs in lowering to its level the superiority which
obscures it, where one finds so many small men for a
single great one, so many nobodies for one Talma, so many

myrmidons for one Achilles! This sketch will seem ill-tempered perhaps, and far from flattering; but does it not fully mark out the distance that separates our stage, the abode of intrigues and uproar, from the solemn serenity of the ancient stage?

Whatever may happen, he feels bound to warn in advance that small number of persons whom such a production might attract, that a play made up of excerpts from *Cromwell* would occupy no less time then is ordinarily occupied by a theatrical performance. It is difficult for a *romantic* theatre to maintain itself otherwise. Surely, if people desire something different from the tragedies in which one or two characters, abstract types of a purely metaphysical idea, stalk solemnly about on a narrow stage occupied only by a few confidents, colourless reflections of the heroes, employed to fill the gaps in a simple, unified, single-stringed plot; if that sort of thing has grown tiresome, a whole evening is not too much time to devote to delineating with some fullness a man among men, a whole critical period: the one, with his peculiar temperament, his genius which adapts itself thereto, his beliefs which dominate them both, his passions which throw out of gear his temperament, his genius and his beliefs, his tastes which give colour to his passions, his habits which regulate his tastes and muzzle his passions, and with the innumerable procession of men of every sort whom these various elements keep in constant commotion about him; the other, with its manners, its laws, its fashions, its wit, its attainments, its superstitions, its events, and its people, whom all these first causes in turn mould like soft wax. It is needless to say that such a picture will be of huge proportions. Instead of one personality, like that with which the abstract drama of the old school is content, there will be twenty, forty, fifty,—who knows how many?—of every size and of every degree of importance. There will be a crowd of characters in the drama. Would it not be niggardly to assign it two hours only, and give up the rest of the performance to opera-comique or farce? to cut Shakespeare for Bobèche?— And do not imagine that, if the plot is well adjusted, the multitude of characters set in motion will cause fatigue to the spectator or confusion in the drama. Shakespeare, abounding in petty details, is at the same time, and for that very reason, imposing by the grandeur of the *ensemble*. It is the oak which casts a most extensive shadow with its myriads of slender leaves.

Let us hope that people in France will ere long become accustomed to devote a whole evening to a single play. In England and Germany there are plays that last six hours. The Greeks, about whom we hear so much, the Greeks—and after the fashion of Scudéri we will cite at this point the classicist Dacier, in the seventh chapter of his *Poetics*—the Greeks sometimes went so far as to have twelve or sixteen plays acted in a single day. Among a people who are fond of spectacles the attention is more lively than is commonly believed. The *Mariage de Figaro,* the connecting link of Beaumarchais's great trilogy, occupies the whole evening, and who was ever bored or fatigued by it. Beaumarchais was worthy to venture on the first step toward that goal of modern art at which it will be impossible to arrive in two hours, that profound, insatiable interest which results from a vast, life-like and multiform plot. " But," someone will say, "this performance, consisting of a single play, would be monotonous, would seem terribly long."—Not so. On the contrary it would lose its present monotony and tediousness. For what is done now? The spectator's entertainment is divided into two or three sharply defined parts. At first he is given two hours of serious enjoyment, then one hour of hilarious enjoyment; these, with the hour of entr' actes, which we do not include in the enjoyment, make four hours. What would the romantic drama do? It would mingle and blend artistically these two kinds of enjoyment. It would lead the audience constantly from sobriety to laughter, from mirthful excitement to heart-breaking emotion, " from grave to gay, from pleasant to severe." For, as we have already proved, the drama is the grotesque in conjunction with the sublime, the soul within the body; it is tragedy beneath comedy. Do you not see that, by affording you repose from one impression by means of another, by sharpening the tragic upon the comic, the merry upon the terrible, and at need calling in the charms of the opera, these performances, while presenting but one play, would be worth a multitude of others? The romantic stage would make a piquant, savoury, diversified dish of that which, on the classic stage, is a drug divided into two pills.

The author has soon come to the end of what he had to say to the reader. He has no idea how the critics will greet this drama and these thoughts, summarily set forth, stripped of their corollaries and ramifications, put together *currente calamo,* and in haste to have done with them. Doubtless they will appear to " the disciples of La Harpe " most impudent and strange. But if perchance, naked and undeveloped as they are, they should have the power to start upon the road of truth this public whose education is so far advanced, and whose minds so many notable writings, of criticism or of original thought, books or newspapers, have already matured for art, let the public follow that impulsion, caring naught whether it comes from a man unknown, from a voice with no authority, from a work of little merit. It is a copper bell which summons the people to the true temple and the true God.

There is to-day the old literary régime as well as the old political régime. The last century still weighs upon the present one at almost every point. It is notably oppressive in the matter of criticism. For instance, you find living men who repeat to you this definition of taste let fall by Voltaire: " Taste in poetry is no different from what it is in women's clothes." Taste, then, is coquetry. Remarkable words, which depict marvellously the painted, *moucheté,* powdered poetry of the eighteenth century— that literature in paniers, pompons and falbalas. They give an admirable résumé of an age with which the loftiest geniuses could not come in contact without becoming petty, in one respect or another; of an age when Montesquieu was able and apt to produce *Le Temple de Gnide,* Voltaire *Le Temple du Goût,* Jean-Jacques *Le Devin du Village.*

Taste is the common sense of genius. This is what will soon be demonstrated by another school of criticism, powerful, outspoken, well-informed,—a school of the cen-

tury which is beginning to put forth vigorous shoots under the dead and withered branches of the old school.
This youthful criticism, as serious as the other is frivolous,
as learned as the other is ignorant, has already established
organs that are listened to, and one is sometimes surprised to find, even in the least important sheets, excellent articles emanating from it. Joining hands with all
that is fearless and superior in letters, it will deliver us
from two scourges: tottering *classicism*, and false *romanticism*, which has the presumption to show itself at the feet
of the true. For modern genius already has its shadow,
its copy, its parasite, its *classic*, which forms itself upon it,
smears itself with its colours, assumes its livery, picks
up its crumbs, and, like *the sorcerer's pupil*, puts in play,
with words retained by the memory, elements of theatrical
action of which it has not the secret. Thus it does idiotic
things which its master many a time has much difficulty
in making good. But the thing that must be destroyed
first of all is the old false taste. Present-day literature
must be cleansed of its rust. In vain does the rust eat
into it and tarnish it. It is addressing a young, stern,
vigorous generation, which does not understand it. The
train of the eighteenth century is still dragging in the
nineteenth; but we, we young men who have seen Bona-
parte, are not the ones who will carry it.

We are approaching, then, the moment when we shall
see the new criticism prevail, firmly established upon a
broad and deep foundation. People generally will soon
understand that writers should be judged, not according to
rules and species, which are contrary to nature and art,
but according to the immutable principles of the art of
composition, and the special laws of their individual temperaments. The sound judgment of all men will be ashamed
of the criticism which broke Pierre Corneille on the wheel,
gagged Jean Racine, and which ridiculously rehabilitated
John Milton only by virtue of the epic code of Père le
Bossu. People will consent to place themselves at the
author's standpoint, to view the subject with his eyes, in
order to judge a work intelligently. They will lay aside
—and it is M. de Chateaubriand who speaks—" the paltry

criticism of defects for the noble and fruitful criticism of beauties." It is time that all acute minds should grasp the thread that frequently connects what we, following our special whim, call "defects" with what we call "beauty." Defects—at all events those which we call by that name —are often the inborn, necessary, inevitable conditions of good qualities.

Scit genius, natale comes qui temperat astrum.

Who ever saw a medal without its reverse? a talent that had not some shadow with its brilliancy, some smoke with its flame? Such a blemish can be only the inseparable consequence of such beauty. This rough stroke of the brush, which offends my eye at close range, completes the effect and gives relief to the whole picture. Efface one and you efface the other. Originality is made up of such things. Genius is necessarily uneven. There are no high mountains without deep ravines. Fill up the valley with the mountain and you will have nothing but a steppe, a plateau, the plain of Les Sablons instead of the Alps, swallows and not eagles.

We must also take into account the weather, the climate, the local influences. The Bible, Homer, hurt us sometimes by their very sublimities. Who would want to part with a word of either of them? Our infirmity often takes fright at the inspired bold flights of genius, for lack of power to swoop down upon objects with such vast intelligence. And then, once again, there are *defects* which take root only in masterpieces; it is given only to certain geniuses to have certain defects. Shakespeare is blamed for his abuse of metaphysics, of wit, of redundant scenes, of obscenities, for his employment of the mythological nonsense in vogue in his time, for exaggeration, obscurity, bad taste, bombast, asperities of style. The oak, that giant tree which we were comparing to Shakespeare just now, and which has more than one point of resemblance to him, the oak has an unusual shape, gnarled branches, dark leaves, and hard, rough bark; but it is the oak.

And it is because of these qualities that it is the oak.

If you would have a smooth trunk, straight branches, satiny leaves, apply to the pale birch, the hollow elder, the weeping willow; but leave the mighty oak in peace. Do not stone that which gives you shade.

The author of this book knows as well as any one the numerous and gross faults of his works. If it happens too seldom that he corrects them, it is because it is repugnant to him to return to a work that has grown cold. Moreover, what has he ever done that is worth that trouble? The labor that he would throw away in correcting the imperfections of his books, he prefers to use in purging his intellect of its defects. It is his method to correct one work only in another work.

However, no matter what treatment may be accorded his book, he binds himself not to defend it, in whole or in part. If his drama is worthless, what is the use of upholding it? If it is good, why defend it? Time will do the book justice or will wreak justice upon it. Its success for the moment is the affair of the publisher alone. If then the wrath of the critics is aroused by the publication of this essay, he will let them do their worst. What reply should he make to them? He is not one of those who speak, as the Castilian poet says, "through the mouths of their wounds."

Por la boca de su herida.

One last word. It may have been noticed that in this somewhat long journey through so many different subjects, the author has generally refrained from resting his personal views upon texts or citations of authorities. It is not, however, because he did not have them at his hand.

"If the poet establishes things that are impossible according to the rules of his art, he makes a mistake unquestionably; but it ceases to be a mistake when by this means he has reached the end that he aimed at; for he has found what he sought."—"They take for nonsense whatever the weakness of their intellects does not allow them to understand. They are especially prone to call absurd those wonderful passages in which the poet, in order the better to enforce his argument, departs, if we may so express it, from his argument. In fact, the precept which makes it a rule sometimes to disregard rules, is a mystery of the art which it is not easy to make men understand who are absolutely without taste and whom a sort of abnormality of mind renders insensible to those things which ordinarily impress men."

Who said the first? Aristotle. Who said the last? Boileau. By these two specimens you will see that the author of this drama might, as well as another, have shielded himself with proper names and taken refuge behind others' reputations. But he preferred to leave that style of argument to those who deem it unanswerable, universal and all-powerful. As for himself, he prefers reasons to authorities; he has always cared more for arms than for coats-of-arms.

October, 1827.

PREFACE TO LEAVES OF GRASS

BY WALT WHITMAN. (1855)

AMERICA does not repel the past or what it has produced under its forms or amid other politics or
the idea of castes or the old religions . . . accepts
the lesson with calmness . . . is not so impatient as has
been supposed that the slough still sticks to opinions and
manners and literature while the life which served its re-
quirements has passed into the new life of the new forms
. . . perceives that the corpse is slowly borne from the eat-
ing and sleeping rooms of the house . . . perceives that it
waits a little while in the door . . . that it was fittest for its
days . . . that its action has descended to the stalwart and
well shaped heir who approaches . . . and that he shall be
fittest for his days.

The Americans of all nations at any time upon the earth,
have probably the fullest poetical nature. The United
States themselves are essentially the greatest poem. In
the history of the earth hitherto the largest and most stirring appear tame and orderly to their ampler largeness and
stir. Here at last is something in the doings of man that
corresponds with the broadcast doings of the day and night.
Here is not merely a nation but a teeming nation of nations.
Here is action untied from strings necessarily blind to
particulars and details magnificently moving in vast masses.

Walt Whitman (1819-1892), the most original of American poets, was
born in West Hills, Long Island, educated in the Brooklyn Public Schools,
and apprenticed to a printer. As a youth he taught in a country school,
and later went into journalism in New York, Brooklyn, and New Orleans.
The first edition of "Leaves of Grass" appeared in 1855, with the remarkable preface here printed. During the war he acted as a volunteer
nurse in the army hospitals, and, when it closed, he became a clerk in the
government service at Washington. He continued to write almost till his
death.

Here is the hospitality which forever indicates heroes.
. . . Here are the roughs and beards and space and ruggedness and nonchalance that the soul loves. Here the
performance disdaining the trivial unapproached in the tre-
mendous audacity of its crowds and groupings and the push
of its perspective spreads with crampless and flowing breadth
and showers its prolic and splendid extravagance. One
sees it must indeed own the riches of the summer and winter,
and need never be bankrupt while corn grows from the
ground or the orchards drop apples or the bays contain fish
or men beget children upon women.

Other states indicate themselves in their deputies . . .
but the genius of the United States is not best or most in
its executives or legislatures, nor in its ambassadors or
authors or colleges or churches or parlors, nor even in its
newspapers or inventors . . . but always most in the common people. Their manners speech dress friendship—the
freshness and candor of their physiognomy—the picturesque looseness of their carriage . . . their deathless attachment to freedom—their aversion to anything indecorous
or soft or mean—the practical acknowledgment of the citizens of one state by the citizens of all other states—the
fierceness of their roused resentment—their curiosity and
welcome of novelty—their self-esteem and wonderful sympathy—their susceptibility to a slight—the air they have of
persons who never knew how it felt to stand in the presence
of superiors—the fluency of their speech—their delight in
music, the sure symptom of manly tenderness and native
elegance of soul . . . their good temper and open handed-
ness—the terrible significance of their elections—the President's taking off his hat to them, not they to him—these too
are unrhymed poetry. It awaits the gigantic and generous
treatment worthy of it.

The largeness of nature or the nation were monstrous
without a corresponding largeness and generosity of the
spirit of the citizen. Not nature nor swarming states nor
streets and steamships nor prosperous business nor farms
nor capital nor learning may suffice for the ideal of man
. . . nor suffice the poet. No reminiscences may suffice
either. A live nation can always cut a deep mark and

can have the best authority the cheapest . . . namely from
its own soul. This is the sum of the profitable uses of
individuals or states and of present action and grandeur
and of the subjects of poets.—As if it were necessary to
trot back generation after generation to the eastern records!
As if the beauty and sacredness of the demonstrable must
fall behind that of the mythical! As if men do not make
their mark out of any times! As if the opening of the
western continent by discovery and what has transpired
since in North and South America were less than the
small theatre of the antique or the aimless sleepwalking
of the middle ages! The pride of the United States leaves
the wealth and finesse of the cities and all returns of commerce and agriculture and all the magnitude of geography
or shows of exterior victory to enjoy the breed of full
sized men or one full sized man unconquerable and simple.

The American poets are to enclose old and new for
America is the race of races. Of them a bard is to be
commensurate with a people. To him the other continents
arrive as contributions . . . he gives them reception for
their sake and his own sake. His spirit responds to his
country's spirit . . . he incarnates its geography and natural life and rivers and lakes. Mississippi with annual fresh-
ets and changing chutes, Missouri and Columbia and Ohio
and St. Lawrence with the Falls and beautiful masculine
Hudson, do not embouchure where they spend themselves
more than they embouchure into him. The blue breadth
over the inland sea of Virginia and Maryland and the sea
off Massachusetts and Maine and over Manhattan bay and
over Champlain and Erie and over Ontario and Huron and
Michigan and Superior, and over the Texan and Mexican
and Flordian and Cuban seas, and over the seas off California
and Oregon, is not tallied by the blue breadth of the waters
below more than the breadth of above and below is tallied
by him. When the long Atlantic coast stretches longer and
the Pacific coast stretches longer he easily stretches with
them north or south. He spans between them also from
east to west and reflects what is between them. On him rise
solid growths that offset the growths of pine and cedar
and hemlock and live oak and locust and chestnut and cypress

and hickory and limetree and cottonwood and tuliptree and
cactus and wildvine and tamarind and persimmon . . .
and tangles as tangled as any canebrake or swamp . . . and
forests coated with transparent ice, and icicles hanging from
boughs and crackling in the wind . . . and sides and peaks
of mountains . . . and pasturage sweet and free as savan-
nah or upland or prairie . . . with flights and songs and
screams that answer those of the wild pigeon and high-
hold and orchard-oriole and coot and surf-duck and red-
shouldered-hawk and fish-hawk and white ibis and Indian-
hen and cat-owl and water-pheasant and qua-bird and pied-
sheldrake and blackbird and mockingbird and buzzard and
condor and night-heron and eagle. To him the hereditary
countenance descends both mother's and father's. To him
enter the essences of the real things and past and present
events—of the enormous diversity of temperature and agriculture and mines—the tribes of red aborigines—the weather-
beaten vessels entering new ports or making landings on
rocky coasts—the first settlements north or south—the rapid
stature and muscle—the haughty defiance of '76, and the war
and peace and formation of the constitution . . . the Union
always surrounded by blatherers and always calm and im-
pregnable—the perpetual coming of immigrants—the wharf-
hem'd cities and superior marine—the unsurveyed interior—
the loghouses and clearings and wild animals and hunters
and trappers . . . the free commerce—the fisheries and
whaling and gold-digging—the endless gestation of new
states—the convening of Congress every December, the
members duly coming up from all climates and the uttermost
parts . . . the noble character of the young mechanics
and of all free American workmen and workwomen . . .
the general ardor and friendliness and enterprise—the perfect equality of the female with the male . . . the large am-
ativeness—the fluid movement of the population—the fac-
tories and mercantile life and laborsaving machinery—the
Yankee swap—the New York firemen and the target excursion—the Southern plantation life—the character of the
northeast and of the northwest and southwest—slavery and
the tremulous spreading of hands to protect it, and the stern
opposition to it which shall never cease till it ceases or the

speaking of tongues and the moving of lips cease. For such the expression of the American poet is to be transcendent and new. It is to be indirect and not direct or descriptive or epic. Its quality goes through these to much more. Let the age and wars of other nations be chanted and their eras and characters be illustrated and that finish the verse. Not so the great psalm of the republic. Here the theme is creative and has vista. Here comes one among the well beloved stonecutters and plans with decision and science and sees the solid and beautiful forms of the future where there are now no solid forms.

Of all nations the United States with veins full of poetical stuff most need poets and will doubtless have the greatest and use them the greatest. Their Presidents shall not be their common referee so much as their poets shall. Of all mankind the great poet is the equable man. Not in him but off from him things are grotesque or eccentric or fail of their sanity. Nothing out of its place is good and nothing in its place is bad. He bestows on every object or quality its fit proportions neither more nor less. He is the arbiter of the diverse and he is the key. He is the equalizer of his age and land . . . he supplies what wants supplying and checks what wants checking. If peace is the routine out of him speaks the spirit of peace, large, rich, thrifty, building vast and populous cities, encouraging agriculture and the arts and commerce—lighting the study of man, the soul, immortality—federal, state or municipal government, marriage, health, freetrade, intertravel by land and sea . . . nothing too close, nothing too far off . . . the stars not too far off. In war he is the most deadly force of the war. Who recruits him recruits horse and foot . . . he fetches parks of artillery the best that engineer ever knew. If the time becomes slothful and heavy he knows how to arouse it . . . he can make every word he speaks draw blood. Whatever stagnates in the flat of custom or obedience or legislation he never stagnates. Obedience does not master him, he masters it. High up out of reach he stands turning a concentrated light . . . he turns the pivot with his finger . . . he baffles the swiftest runners as he stands and easily overtakes and envelopes them. The

time straying towards infidelity and confections and persi-
flage he withholds by his steady faith . . . he spreads out
his dishes . . . he offers the sweet firmfibred meat that
grows men and women. His brain is the ultimate brain.
He is no arguer . . . he is judgment. He judges not as
the judge judges but as the sun falling around a helpless
thing. As he sees the farthest he has the most faith.
His thoughts are the hymns of the praise of things. In
the talk on the soul and eternity and God off of his equal
plane he is silent. He sees eternity less like a play with
a prologue and denouement . . . he sees eternity in men
and women . . . he does not see men or women as dreams
or dots. Faith is the antiseptic of the soul . . . it pervades
the common people and preserves them . . . they never
give up believing and expecting and trusting. There is
that indescribable freshness and unconsciousness about an
illiterate person that humbles and mocks the power of the
noblest expressive genius. The poet sees for a certainty
how one not a great artist may be just as sacred and perfect as the greatest artist. . . . The power to destroy or
remould is freely used by him, but never the power of
attack. What is past is past. If he does not expose
superior models and prove himself by every step he takes
he is not what is wanted. The presence of the greatest
poet conquers . . . not parleying or struggling or any
prepared attempts. Now he has passed that way see after
him! There is not left any vestige of despair or misan-
thropy or cunning or exclusiveness or the ignominy of a
nativity or color or delusion of hell or the necessity of
hell . . . and no man thenceforward shall be degraded for
ignorance or weakness or sin.

The greatest poet hardly knows pettiness or triviality. If
he breathes into anything that was before thought small it
dilates with the grandeur and life of the universe. He is
a seer . . . he is individual . . . he is complete in himself
. . . the others are as good as he, only he sees it and they
do not. He is not one of the chorus . . . he does not
stop for any regulation . . . he is the president of regulation. What the eyesight does to the rest he does to the
rest. Who knows the curious mystery of the eyesight?

The other senses corroborate themselves, but this is removed from any proof but its own and foreruns the identities of the spiritual world. A single glance of it mocks
all the investigations of man and all the instruments and
books of the earth and all reasoning. What is marvellous? what is unlikely? what is impossible or baseless or
vague? after you have once just opened the space of a
peachpit and given audience to far and near and to the
sunset and had all things enter with electric swiftness
softly and duly without confusion or jostling or jam.

The land and sea, the animals fishes and birds, the sky of
heavens and the orbs, the forests mountains and rivers, are
not small themes . . . but folks expect of the poet to indicate more than the beauty and dignity which always attach
to dumb real objects . . . they expect him to indicate the
path between reality and their souls. Men and women
perceive the beauty well enough . . . probably as well as
he. The passionate tenacity of hunters, woodmen, early
risers, cultivators of gardens and orchards and fields, the
love of healthy women for the manly form, seafaring
persons, drivers of horses, the passion for light and the
open air, all is an old varied sign of the unfailing perception of beauty and of a residence of the poetic in outdoor
people. They can never be assisted by poets to perceive
. . . some may but they never can. The poetic quality is
not marshalled in rhyme or uniformity or abstract addresses to things nor in melancholy complaints or good
precepts, but is the life of these and much else and is in
the soul. The profit of rhyme is that it drops seeds of a
sweeter and more luxuriant rhyme, and of uniformity that
it conveys itself into its own roots in the ground out of
sight. The rhyme and uniformity of perfect poems show
the free growth of metrical laws and bud from them as
unerringly and loosely as lilacs and roses on a bush, and
take shapes as compact as the shapes of chestnuts and
oranges and melons and pears, and shed the perfume impalpable to form. The fluency and ornaments of the
finest poems or music or orations or recitations are not independent but dependent. All beauty comes from beautiful blood and a beautiful brain. If the greatnesses are in

conjunction in a man or woman it is enough . . . the fact
will prevail through the universe . . . but the gaggery and
gilt of a million years will not prevail. Who troubles himself about his ornaments or fluency is lost. This is what
you shall do: Love the earth and sun and the animals,
despise riches, give alms to every one that asks, stand up
for the stupid and crazy, devote your income and labor
to others, hate tyrants, argue not concerning God, have
patience and indulgence toward the people, take off your
hat to nothing known or unknown or to any man or
number of men, go freely with powerful uneducated persons and with the young and with the mothers of families,
read these leaves in the open air every season of every year
of your life, re-examine all you have been told at school or
church or in any book, dismiss whatever insults your own
soul; and your very flesh shall be a great poem and have
the richest fluency not only in its words but in the silent
lines of its lips and face and between the lashes of your
eyes and in every motion and joint of your body. . . . The
poet shall not spend his time in unneeded work. He shall
know that the ground is always ready ploughed and ma-
nured . . . others may not know it but he shall. He
shall go directly to the creation. His trust shall master
the trust of everything he touches . . . and shall master all
attachment.

The known universe has one complete lover and that is
the greatest poet. He consumes an eternal passion and is
indifferent which chance happens and which possible con-
tingency of fortune or misfortune and persuades daily and
hourly his delicious pay. What baulks or breaks others is
fuel for his burning progress to contact and amorous joy.
Other proportions of the reception of pleasure dwindle to
nothing to his proportions. All expected from heaven or
from the highest he is rapport with in the sight of the
daybreak or a scene of the winter woods or the presence
of children playing or with his arm round the neck of a
man or woman. His love above all love has leisure and
expanse . . . he leaves room ahead of himself. He is no
irresolute or suspicious lover . . . he is sure . . . he scorns
intervals. His experience and the showers and thrills are

not for nothing. Nothing can jar him . . . suffering and
darkness cannot—death and fear cannot. To him complaint and jealousy and envy are corpses buried and rotten
in the earth . . . he saw them buried. The sea is not surer
of the shore or the shore of the sea than he is of the
fruition of his love and of all perfection and beauty.

The fruition of beauty is no chance of hit or miss . . . it is
inevitable as life . . . it is as exact and plumb as gravitation.
From the eyesight proceeds another eyesight and from the
hearing proceeds another hearing and from the voice proceeds another voice eternally curious of the harmony of
things with man. To these respond perfections not only
in the committees that were supposed to stand for the rest
but in the rest themselves just the same. These understand the law of perfection in masses and floods . . . that
its finish is to each for itself and onward from itself . . .
that it is profuse and impartial . . . that there is not a
minute of the light or dark nor an acre of the earth and
sea without it—nor any direction of the sky nor any trade
or employment nor any turn of events. This is the reason
that about the proper expression of beauty there is precision
and balance . . . one part does not need to be thrust above
another. The best singer is not the one who has the most
lithe and powerful organ . . . the pleasure of poems is not
in them that take the handsomest measure and similes and
sound.

Without effort and without exposing in the least how it is
done the greatest poet brings the spirit of any or all events
and passions and scenes and persons some more and some
less to bear on your individual character as you hear or
read. To do this well is to compete with the laws that
pursue and follow time. What is the purpose must surely
be there and the clue of it must be there . . . and the
faintest indication is the indication of the best and then
becomes the clearest indication. Past and present and
future are not disjoined but joined. The greatest poet
forms the consistence of what is to be from what has been
and is. He drags the dead out of their coffins and stands
them again on their feet . . . he says to the past, Rise and
walk before me that I may realize you. He learns the

lesson . . . he places himself where the future becomes present. The greatest poet does not only dazzle his rays over character and scenes and passions . . . he finally ascends and finishes all . . . he exhibits the pinnacles that no man can tell what they are for or what is beyond . . . he glows a moment on the extremest verge. He is most wonderful in his last half-hidden smile or frown . . . by that flash of the moment of parting the one that sees it shall be encouraged or terrified afterward for many years. The greatest poet does not moralize or make applications of morals . . . he knows the soul. The soul has that measureless pride which consists in never acknowledging any lessons but its own. But it has sympathy as measureless as its pride and the one balances the other and neither can stretch too far while it stretches in company with the other. The inmost secrets of art sleep with the twain. The greatest poet has lain close betwixt both and they are vital in his style and thoughts.

The art of art, the glory of expression and the sunshine of the light of letters is simplicity. Nothing is better than simplicity . . . nothing can make up for excess or for the lack of definiteness. To carry on the heave of impulse and pierce intellectual depths and give all subjects their articulations are powers neither common nor very uncommon. But to speak in literature with the perfect rectitude and insouciance of the movements of animals and the unimpeachableness of the sentiment of trees in the woods and grass by the roadside is the flawless triumph of art. If you have looked on him who has achieved it you have looked on one of the masters of the artists of all nations and times. You shall not contemplate the flight of the gray gull over the bay or the mettlesome action of the blood horse or the tall leaning of sunflowers on their stalk or the appearance of the sun journeying through heaven or the appearance of the moon afterward with any more satisfaction than you shall contemplate him. The greatest poet has less a marked style and is more the channel of thoughts and things without increase or diminution and is the free channel of himself. He swears to his art, I will not be meddlesome, I will not have in my writing any elegance or effect or originality to hang in the way between me and the rest like curtains. I will have nothing hang in the way not the richest curtains. What I tell I tell for precisely what it is. Let who may exalt or startle or fascinate or soothe I will have purposes as health or heat or snow has and be as regardless of observation. What I experience or portray shall go from my composition without a shred of my composition. You shall stand by my side and look in the mirror with me.

The old red blood and stainless gentility of great poets will be proved by their unconstraint. A heroic person walks at his ease through and out of that custom or precedent or authority that suits him not. Of the traits of the brotherhood of writers savans musicians inventors and artists, nothing is finer than silent defiance advancing from new free forms. In the need of poems philosophy politics mechanism science behavior, the craft of art, an appropriate native grand-opera, shipcraft, or any craft, he is greatest for ever and for ever who contributes the greatest original practical example. The cleanest expression is that which finds no sphere worthy of itself and makes one. The messages of great poets to each man and woman are, Come to us on equal terms, Only then can you understand us, We are no better than you, What we enclose you enclose, What we enjoy you may enjoy. Did you suppose there could be only one Supreme? We affirm there can be unnumbered Supremes, and that one does not countervail another any more than one eyesight countervails another . . . and that men can be good or grand only of the consciousness of their supremacy within them. What do you think is the grandeur of storms and dismemberments and the deadliest battles and wrecks and the wildest fury of the elements and the power of the sea and the motion of nature and the throes of human desires and dignity and hate and love? It is that something in the soul which says, Rage on, Whirl on, I tread master here and everywhere, Master of the spasms of the sky and of the shatter of the sea, Master of nature and passion and death, And of all terror and all pain.

The American bards shall be marked for generosity and

affection and for encouraging competitors. . . . They shall be kosmos . . . without monopoly or secrecy . . . glad to pass anything to any one . . . hungry for equals night and day. They shall not be careful of riches and privilege . . . they shall be riches and privilege . . . they shall perceive who the most affluent man is. The most affluent man is he that confronts all the shows he sees by equivalents out of the stronger wealth of himself. The American bard shall delineate no class of persons nor one or two out of the strata of interests nor love most nor truth most nor the soul most nor the body most . . . and not be for the eastern states more than the western or the northern states more than the southern.

Exact science and its practical movements are no checks on the greatest poet but always his encouragement and support. The outset and remembrance are there . . . there the arms that lifted him first and brace him best . . . there he returns after all his goings and comings. The sailor and traveller . . . the anatomist chemist astronomer geologist phrenologist spiritualist mathematician historian and lexicographer are not poets, but they are the lawgivers of poets and their construction underlies the structure of every perfect poem. No matter what rises or is uttered they sent the seed of the conception of it . . . of them and by them stand the visible proofs of souls . . . always of their fatherstuff must be begotten the sinewy races of bards. If there shall be love and content between the father and the son and if the greatness of the son is the exuding of the greatness of the father there shall be love between the poet and the man of demonstrable science. In the beauty of poems are the tuft and final applause of science.

Great is the faith of the flush of knowledge and of the investigation of the depths of qualities and things. Cleaving and circling here swells the soul of the poet yet is president of itself always. The depths are fathomless and therefore calm. The innocence and nakedness are resumed . . . they are neither modest nor immodest. The whole theory of the special and supernatural and all that was twined with it or educed out of it departs as a dream.

What has ever happened . . . what happens and whatever may or shall happen, the vital laws enclose all . . . they are sufficient for any case and for all cases . . . none to be hurried or retarded . . . any miracle of affairs or persons inadmissible in the vast clear scheme where every motion and every spear of grass and the frames and spirits of men and women and all that concerns them are unspeakably perfect miracles all referring to all and each distinct and in its place. It is also not consistent with the reality of the soul to admit that there is anything in the known universe more divine than men and women.

Men and women and the earth and all upon it are simply to be taken as they are, and the investigation of their past and present and future shall be unintermitted and shall be done with perfect candor. Upon this basis philosophy speculates ever looking towards the poet, ever regarding the eternal tendencies of all toward happiness never inconsistent with what is clear to the senses and to the soul. For the eternal tendencies of all toward happiness make the only point of sane philosophy. Whatever comprehends less than that . . . whatever is less than the laws of light and of astronomical motion . . . or less than the laws that follow the thief the liar the glutton and the drunkard through this life and doubtless afterward . . . or less than vast stretches of time or the slow formation of density or the patient upheaving of strata—is of no account. Whatever would put God in a poem or system of philosophy as contending against some being or influence is also of no account. Sanity and ensemble characterize the great master . . . spoilt in one principle all is spoilt. The great master has nothing to do with miracles. He sees health for himself in being one of the mass . . . he sees the hiatus in singular eminence. To the perfect shape comes common ground. To be under the general law is great, for that is to correspond with it. The master knows that he is unspeakably great and that all are unspeakably great . . . that nothing for instance is greater than to conceive children and bring them up well . . . that to be is just as great as to perceive or tell.

In the make of the great masters the idea of political

liberty is indispensable. Liberty takes the adherence of
heroes wherever men and women exist . . . but never takes
any adherence or welcome from the rest more than from
poets. They are the voice and exposition of liberty.
They out of ages are worthy the grand idea . . . to them it
is confided and they must sustain it. Nothing has precedence of it and nothing can warp or degrade it. The
attitude of great poets is to cheer up slaves and horrify
despots. The turn of their necks, the sound of their feet,
the motions of their wrists, are full of hazard to the one
and hope to the other. Come nigh them awhile and
though they neither speak nor advise you shall learn the
faithful American lesson. Liberty is poorly served by men
whose good intent is quelled from one failure or two
failures or any number of failures, or from the casual
indifference or ingratitude of the people, or from the sharp
show of the tushes of power, or the bringing to bear
soldiers and cannon or any penal statutes. Liberty relies
upon itself, invites no one, promises nothing, sits in calmness and light, is positive and composed, and knows no
discouragement. The battle rages with many a loud alarm
and frequent advance and retreat . . . the enemy triumphs
. . . the prison, the handcuffs, the iron necklace and
anklet, the scaffold, garrote and leadballs do their work . . .
the cause is asleep . . . the strong throats are choked with
their own blood . . . the young men drop their eyelashes
toward the ground when they pass each other . . . and is
liberty gone out of that place? No never. When liberty
goes it is not the first to go nor the second or third to go
. . . it awaits for all the rest to go . . . it is the last. . . .
When the memories of the old martyrs are faded utterly
away . . . when the large names of patriots are laughed at
in the public halls from the lips of the orators . . . when
the boys are no more christened after the same but
christened after tyrants and traitors instead . . . when the
laws of the free are grudgingly permitted and the laws for
informers and bloodmoney are sweet to the taste of the
people . . . when I and you walk abroad upon the earth
stung with compassion at the sight of numberless brothers
answering our equal friendship and calling no man master

—and when we are elated with noble joy at the sight of slaves . . . when the soul retires in the cool communion of the night and surveys its experience and has much extasy over the word and deed that put back a helpless innocent person into the gripe of the gripers or into any cruel inferiority . . . when those in all parts of these states who could easier realize the true American character but do not yet—when the swarms of cringers, suckers, doughfaces, lice of politics, planners of sly involutions for their own preferment to city offices or state legislatures or the judiciary or congress or the presidency, obtain a response of love and natural deference from the people whether they get the offices or no . . . when it is better to be a bound booby and rogue in office at a high salary than the poorest free mechanic or farmer with his hat unmoved from his head and firm eyes and a candid and generous heart . . . and when servility by town or state or the federal government or any oppression on a large scale or small scale can be tried on without its own punishment following duly after in exact proportion against the smallest chance of escape . . . or rather when all life and all the souls of men and women are discharged from any part of the earth— then only shall the instinct of liberty be discharged from that part of the earth.

As the attributes of the poets of the kosmos concentre in the real body and soul and in the pleasure of things they possess the superiority of genuineness over all fiction and romance. As they emit themselves facts are showered over with light . . . the daylight is lit with more volatile light . . . also the deep between the setting and rising sun goes deeper many fold. Each precise object or condition or combination or process exhibits a beauty . . . the multiplication table its—old age its—the carpenter's trade its —the grand opera its—the hugehulled cleanshaped New-York clipper at sea under steam or full sail gleams with unmatched beauty. . . . the American circles and large harmonies of government gleam with theirs . . . and the commonest definite intentions and actions with theirs. The poets of the kosmos advance through all interpositions and coverings and turmoils and stratagems to first principles.

They are of use . . . they dissolve poverty from its need and riches from its conceit. You large proprietor, they say, shall not realize or perceive more than any one else. The owner of the library is not he who holds a legal title to it having bought and paid for it. Any one and every one is owner of the library who can read the same through all the varieties of tongues and subjects and styles, and in whom they enter with ease and take residence and force toward paternity and maternity, and make supple and powerful and rich and large. . . . These American states strong and healthy and accomplished shall receive no pleasure from violations of natural models and must not permit them. In paintings or mouldings or carvings in mineral or wood, or in the illustrations of books and newspapers, or in any comic or tragic prints, or in the patterns of woven stuffs or anything to beautify rooms or furniture or costumes, or to put upon cornices or monuments or on the prows or sterns of ships, or to put anywhere before the human eye indoors or out, that which distorts honest shapes or which creates unearthly beings or places or contingencies, is a nuisance and revolt. Of the human form especially, it is so great it must never be made ridiculous. Of ornaments to a work nothing outré can be allowed . . . but those ornaments can be allowed that conform to the perfect facts of the open air, and that flow out of the nature of the work and come irrepressibly from it and are necessary to the completion of the work. Most works are most beautiful without ornament . . . Exaggerations will be revenged in human physiology. Clean and vigorous children are jetted and conceived only in those communities where the models of natural forms are public every day . . . Great genius and the people of these states must never be demeaned to romances. As soon as histories are properly told there is no more need of romances.

The great poets are also to be known by the absence in them of tricks and by the justification of perfect personal candor. Then folks echo a new cheap joy and a divine voice leaping from their brains: How beautiful is candor! All faults may be forgiven of him who has perfect candor. Henceforth let no man of us lie, for we have seen that

openness wins the inner and outer world and that there is
no single exception, and that never since our earth gathered
itself in a mass have deceit or subterfuge or prevarication
attracted its smallest particle or the faintest tinge of a shade
—and that through the enveloping wealth and rank of a
state or the whole republic of states a sneak or sly person
shall be discovered and despised . . . and that the soul has
never once been fooled and never can be fooled . . . and
thrift without the loving nod of the soul is only a fœtid
puff . . . and there never grew up in any of the continents
of the globe nor upon any planet or satellite or star, nor
upon the asteroids, nor in any part of ethereal space, nor in
the midst of density, nor under the fluid wet of the sea, nor
in that condition which precedes the birth of babes, nor at
any time during the changes of life, nor in that condition
that follows what we term death, nor in any stretch of
abeyance or action afterward of vitality, nor in any process
of formation or reformation anywhere, a being whose instinct hated the truth.

Extreme caution or prudence, the soundest organic health,
large hope and comparison and fondness for women and
children, large alimentiveness and destructiveness and caus-
ality, with a perfect sense of the oneness of nature and
the propriety of the same spirit applied to human affairs
. . . these are called up of the float of the brain of the
world to be parts of the greatest poet from his birth out of
his mother's womb and from her birth out of her mother's.
Caution seldom goes far enough. It has been thought
that the prudent citizen was the citizen who applied himself to solid gains and did well for himself and for his family and completed a lawful life without debt or crime.
The greatest poet sees and admits these economies as he
sees the economies of food and sleep, but has higher notions
of prudence than to think he gives much when he gives
a few slight attentions at the latch of the gate. The
premises of the prudence of life are not the hospitality of
it or the ripeness and harvest of it. Beyond the indepen-
dence of a little sum laid aside for burial-money, and of
a few clapboards around and shingles overhead on a lot
of American soil owned, and the easy dollars that supply

the year's plain clothing and meals, the melancholy prudence of the abandonment of such a great being as a man is to the toss and pallor of years of money-making with all their scorching days and icy nights and all their stifling deceits and underhanded dodgings, or infinitesimals of parlors, or shameless stuffing while others starve . . . and all the loss of the bloom and odor of the earth and of the flowers and atmosphere and of the sea, and of the true taste of the women and men you pass or have to do with in youth or middle age, and the issuing sickness and desperate revolt at the close of a life without elevation or naivete, and the ghastly chatter of a death without serenity or majesty, is the great fraud upon modern civilization and forethought, blotching the surface and system which civilization undeniably drafts, and moistening with tears the immense features it spreads and spreads with such velocity before the reached kisses of the soul. . . . Still the right explanation remains to be made about prudence. The prudence of the mere wealth and respectability of the most esteemed life appears too faint for the eye to observe at all when little and large alike drop quietly aside at the thought of the prudence suitable for immortality. What is wisdom that fills the thinness of a year or seventy or eighty years to wisdom spaced out by ages and coming back at a certain time with strong reinforcements and rich presents and the clear faces of weddingguests as far as you can look in every direction, running gaily toward you? Only the soul is of itself . . . all else has reference to what ensues. All that a person does or thinks is of consequence. Not a move can a man or woman make that effects him or her in a day or a month or any part of the direct lifetime or the hour of death but the same affects him or her onward afterward through the indirect lifetime. The indirect is always as great and real as the direct. The spirit receives from the body just as much as it gives to the body. Not one name of word or deed . . . not of venereal sores or discolorations . . . not the privacy of the onanist . . . not of the putrid veins of gluttons or rumdrinkers . . . not peculation or cunning or betrayal or murder . . . no serpentine poison of those that seduce women . . . not the foolish yielding of women . . .

not prostitution . . . not of any depravity of young men
. . . not of the attainment of gain by discreditable means
. . . not any nastiness of appetite . . . not any harshness
of officers to men or judges to prisoners or fathers to
sons or sons to fathers or of husbands to wives or bosses
to their boys . . . not of greedy looks or malignant wishes
. . . nor any of the wiles practised by people upon themselves . . . ever is or ever can be stamped on the programme
but it is duly realized and returned, and that returned in
further performances . . . and they returned again. Nor
can the push of charity or personal force ever be anything
else than the profoundest reason, whether it bring argument
to hand or no. No specification is necessary . . . to add
or subtract or divide is in vain. Little or big, learned
or unlearned, white or black, legal or illegal, sick or well,
from the first inspiration down the windpipe to the last
expiration out of it, all that a male or female does that is
vigorous and benevolent and clean is so much sure profit
to him or her in the unshakable order of the universe and
through the whole scope of it for ever. If the savage or
felon is wise it is well . . . if the greatest poet or savan
is wise it is simply the same . . . if the President or chief
justice is wise it is the same . . . if the young mechanic
or farmer is wise it is no more or less . . . if the prostitute
is wise it is no more nor less. The interest will come round
. . . all will come round. All the best actions of war
and peace . . . all help given to relatives and strangers and
the poor and old and sorrowful and young children and
widows and the sick, and to all shunned persons . . . all
furtherance of fugitives and of the escape of slaves . . .
all the self-denial that stood steady and aloof on wrecks and
saw others take the seats of the boats . . . all offering of
substance or life for the good old cause, or for a friend's
sake or opinion's sake . . . all pains of enthusiasts scoffed
at by their neighbors . . . all the vast sweet love and precious sufferings of mothers . . . all honest men baffled in
strifes recorded or unrecorded . . . all the grandeur and
good of the few ancient nations whose fragments of annals
we inherit . . . and all the good of the hundreds of far
mightier and more ancient nations unknown to us by name or

date or location . . . all that was ever manfully begun,
whether it succeeded or no . . . all that has at any time been
well suggested out of the divine heart of man or by the
divinity of his mouth or by the shaping of his great hands
. . . and all that is well thought or done this day on any part
of the surface of the globe . . . or on any of the wandering
stars or fixed stars by those there as we are here . . . or that
is henceforth to be well thought or done by you whoever you
are, or by any one—these singly and wholly inured at their
time and inure now and will inure always to the identities
from which they sprung or shall spring. . . . Did you
guess any of them lived only its moment? The world does
not so exist . . . no parts palpable or impalpable so exist
. . . no result exists now without being from its long
antecedent result, and that from its antecedent, and so
backward without the farthest mentionable spot coming a
bit nearer the beginning than any other spot. . . . Whatever satisfies the soul is truth. The prudence of the greatest poet answers at last the craving and glut of the soul, is
not contemptuous of less ways of prudence if they conform
to its ways, puts off nothing, permits no let-up for its own
case or any case, has no particular sabbath or judgment-
day, divides not the living from the dead or the righteous
from the unrighteous, is satisfied with the present, matches
every thought or act by its correlative, knows no possible
forgiveness or deputed atonement . . . knows that the young
man who composedly perilled his life and lost it has done
exceeding well for himself, while the man who has not
perilled his life and retains to old age in riches and ease
has perhaps achieved nothing for himself worth mentioning
. . . and that only that person has no great prudence to
learn who has learnt to prefer real longlived things, and
favors body and soul the same, and perceives the indirect
assuredly following the direct, and what evil or good he
does leaping onward and waiting to meet him again—and
who in his spirit in any emergency whatever neither hurries
or avoids death.

The direct trial of him who would be the greatest poet
is to-day. If he does not flood himself with the immediate
age as with vast oceanic tides . . . and if he does not at-

tract his own land body and soul to himself, and hang on its neck with incomparable love and plunge his semitic muscle into its merits and demerits . . . and if he be not himself the age transfigured . . . and if to him is not opened the eternity which gives similitude to all periods and locations and processes and animate and inanimate forms, and which is the bond of time, and rises up from its inconceivable vagueness and infiniteness in the swimming shape of to-day, and is held by the ductile anchors of life, and makes the present spot the passage from what was to what shall be, and commits itself to the representation of this wave of an hour and this one of the sixty beautiful children of the wave—let him merge in the general run and wait his development. . . . Still the final test of poems or any character or work remains. The prescient poet projects himself centuries ahead and judges performer or performance after the changes of time. Does it live through them? Does it still hold on untired? Will the same style and the direction of genius to similar points be satisfactory now? Has no new discovery in science or arrival at superior planes of thought and judgment and behavior fixed him or his so that either can be looked down upon? Have the marches of tens and hundreds and thousands of years made willing detours to the right hand and the left hand for his sake? Is he beloved long and long after he is buried? Does the young man think often of him? and the young woman think often of him? and do the middle aged and the old think of him?

A great poem is for ages and ages in common, and for all degrees and complexions, and all departments and sects, and for a woman as much as a man and a man as much as a woman. A great poem is no finish to a man or woman but rather a beginning. Has any one fancied he could sit at last under some due authority and rest satisfied with explanations and realize and be content and full? To no such terminus does the greatest poet bring . . . he brings neither cessation or sheltered fatness and ease. The touch of him tells in action. Whom he takes he takes with firm sure grasp into live regions previously unattained . . . thenceforward is no rest . . . they see the space and ineffable sheen that turn the old spots and lights into dead vacuums. The companion of him beholds the birth and progress of stars and learns one of the meanings. Now there shall be a man cohered out of tumult and chaos . . . the elder encourages the younger and shows him how . . . they too shall launch off fearlessly together till the new world fits an orbit for itself and looks unabashed on the lesser orbits of the stars and sweeps through the ceaseless rings and shall never be quiet again.

There will soon be no more priests. Their work is done. They may wait awhile . . . perhaps a generation or two . . . dropping off by degrees. A superior breed shall take their place . . . the gangs of kosmos and prophets *en masse* shall take their place. A new order shall arise and they shall be the priests of man, and every man shall be his own priest. The churches built under their umbrage shall be the churches of men and women. Through the divinity of themselves shall the kosmos and the new breed of poets be interpreters of men and women and of all events and things. They shall find their inspiration in real objects to-day, symptoms of the past and future. . . . They shall not deign to defend immortality or God or the perfection of things or liberty or the exquisite beauty and reality of the soul. They shall arise in America and be responded to from the remainder of the earth.

The English language befriends the grand American expression . . . it is brawny enough and limber and full enough . . . on the tough stock of a race who through all change of circumstance was never without the idea of political liberty, which is the animus of all liberty, it has attracted the terms of daintier and gayer and subtler and more elegant tongues. It is the powerful language of resistance . . . it is the dialect of common sense. It is the speech of the proud and melancholy races and of all who aspire. It is the chosen tongue to express growth faith self-esteem freedom justice equality friendliness amplitude prudence decision and courage. It is the medium that shall well nigh express the inexpressible.

No great literature nor any like style of behavior or oratory or social intercourse or household arrangements or public institutions or the treatment of bosses of employed people, nor executive detail or detail of the army and navy, nor spirit of legislation or courts or police or tuition or architecture or songs or amusements or the costumes of young men, can long elude the jealous and passionate instinct of American standards. Whether or no the sign appears from the mouths of the people, it throbs a live interrogation in every freeman's and freewoman's heart after that which passes by or this built to remain. Is it uniform with my country? Are its disposals without ignominious distinctions? Is it for the ever growing communes of brothers and lovers, large, well-united, proud beyond the old models, generous beyond all models? Is it something grown fresh out of the fields or drawn from the sea for use to me today here? I know that what answers for me an American must answer for any individual or nation that serves for a part of my materials. Does this answer? or is it without reference to universal needs? or sprung of the needs of the less developed society of special ranks? or old needs of pleasure overlaid by modern science or forms? Does this acknowledge liberty with audible and absolute acknowledgment, and set slavery at nought for life and death? Will it help breed one goodshaped and wellhung man, and a woman to be his perfect and independent mate? Does it improve manners? Is it for the nursing of the young of the republic? Does it solve readily with the sweet milk of the nipples of the breasts of the mother of many children? Has it too the old ever-fresh forbearance and impartiality? Does it look for the same love on the last born and on those hardening toward stature, and on the errant, and on those who disdain all strength of assault outside their own?

The poems distilled from other poems will probably pass away. The coward will surely pass away. The expectation of the vital and great can only be satisfied by the demeanor of the vital and great. The swarms of the polished deprecating and reflectors and the polite float off and leave no remembrance. America prepares with composure and goodwill for the visitors that have sent word. It is not intellect that is to be their warrant and welcome. The talented, the artist, the ingenious, the editor, the statesman, the erudite . . . they are not unappreciated . . . they fall in their place and do their work. The soul of the nation also does its work. No disguise can pass on it . . . no disguise can conceal from it. It rejects none, it permits all. Only towards as good as itself and toward the like of itself will it advance half-way. An individual is as superb as a nation when he has the qualities which make a superb nation. The soul of the largest and wealthiest and proudest nation may well go half-way to meet that of its poets. The signs are effectual. There is no fear of mistake. If the one is true the other is true. The proof of a poet is that his country absorbs him as affectionately as he has absorbed it.

INTRODUCTION TO THE HISTORY OF ENGLISH LITERATURE

BY HIPPOLYTE ADOLPHE TAINE. (1863)

I

HISTORY, within a hundred years in Germany, and within sixty years in France, has undergone a transformation owing to a study of literatures.

The discovery has been made that a literary work is not a mere play of the imagination, the isolated caprice of an excited brain, but a transcript of contemporary manners and customs and the sign of a particular state of intellect. The conclusion derived from this is that, through literary monuments, we can retrace the way in which men felt and thought many centuries ago. This method has been tried and found successful.

We have meditated over these ways of feeling and thinking and have accepted them as facts of prime significance. We have found that they were dependent on most important events, that they explain these, and that these explain them, and that henceforth it was necessary to give them their place in history, and one of the highest. This place has been assigned to them, and hence all is changed in history—the aim, the method, the instrumentalities, and the

Hippolyte Adolphe Taine (b. 1828; d. 1893) was one of the most distinguished French critics of the nineteenth century. He held the chair of esthetics at the École des Beaux Arts, and wrote a large number of works in history, travel, and literary criticism. His " History of English Literature " is the most brilliant book on the subject ever written by a foreigner; and in this introduction he expounds the method of criticism which has come to be associated with his name, and in accordance with which he seeks to interpret the characteristics of English authors.

conceptions of laws and of causes. It is this change as now going on, and which must continue to go on, that is here attempted to be set forth.

On turning over the large stiff pages of a folio volume, or the yellow leaves of a manuscript, in short, a poem, a code of laws, a confession of faith, what is your first comment? You say to yourself that the work before you is not of its own creation. It is simply a mold like a fossil shell, an imprint similar to one of those forms embedded in a stone by an animal which once lived and perished. Beneath the shell was an animal and behind the document there was a man. Why do you study the shell unless to form some idea of the animal? In the same way do you study the document in order to comprehend the man; both shell and document are dead fragments and of value only as indications of the complete living being. The aim is to reach this being; this is what you strive to reconstruct. It is a mistake to study the document as if it existed alone by itself. That is treating things merely as a pedant, and you subject yourself to the illusions of a book-worm. At bottom mythologies and languages are not existences; the only realities are human beings who have employed words and imagery adapted to their organs and to suit the original cast of their intellects. A creed is nothing in itself. Who made it? Look at this or that portrait of the sixteenth century, the stern, energetic features of an archbishop or of an English martyr. Nothing exists except through the individual; it is necessary to know the individual himself. Let the parentage of creeds be established, or the classification of poems, or the growth of constitutions, or the transformations of idioms, and we have only cleared the ground. True history begins when the historian has discerned beyond the mists of ages the living, active man, endowed with passions, furnished with habits, special in voice, feature, gesture and costume, distinctive and complete, like anybody that you have just encountered in the street. Let us strive then, as far as possible, to get rid of this great interval of time which prevents us from observing the man with our eyes, *the eyes of our own head*. What revelations do we find in the calendared leaves of a modern poem? A modern poet, a man like De Musset, Victor Hugo, Lamartine, or Heine, graduated from a college and traveled, wearing a dress-coat and gloves, favored by ladies, bowing fifty times and uttering a dozen witticisms in an evening, reading daily newspapers, generally occupying an apartment on the second story, not over-cheerful on account of his nerves, and especially because, in this dense democracy in which we stifle each other, the discredit of official rank exaggerates his pretensions by raising his importance, and, owing to the delicacy of his personal sensations, leading him to regard himself as a Deity. Such is what we detect behind modern *meditations* and *sonnets*.

Again, behind a tragedy of the seventeenth century there is a poet, one, for example, like Racine, refined, discreet, a courtier, a fine talker, with majestic perruque and ribboned shoes, a monarchist and zealous Christian, " God having given him the grace not to blush in any society on account of zeal for his king or for the Gospel," clever in interesting the monarch, translating into proper French "the *gaulois* of Amyot," deferential to the great, always knowing how to keep his place in their company, assiduous and respectful at Marly as at Versailles, amid the formal creations of a decorative landscape and the reverential bows, graces, intrigues, and fineness of the braided seigniors who get up early every morning to obtain the reversion of an office, together with the charming ladies who count on their fingers the pedigrees which entitle them to a seat on a footstool. On this point consult Saint-Simon and the engravings of Pérelle, the same as you have just consulted Balzac and the water-color drawings of Eugène Lami.

In like manner, on reading a Greek tragedy, our first care is to figure to ourselves the Greeks, that is to say, men who lived half-naked in the gymnasiums or on a public square under a brilliant sky, in full view of the noblest and most delicate landscape, busy in rendering their bodies strong and agile, in conversing together, in arguing, in voting, in carrying out patriotic piracies, and yet idle and temperate, the furniture of their houses consisting of three earthen jars and their food of two pots of anchovies preserved in oil, served by slaves who afford them the time to

cultivate their minds and to exercise their limbs, with no
other concern that that of having the most beautiful city,
the most beautiful processions, the most beautiful ideas,
and the most beautiful men. In this respect, a statue like
the "Meleager" or the "Theseus" of the Parthenon, or
again a sight of the blue and lustrous Mediterranean, resembling a silken tunic out of which islands arise like marble
bodies, together with a dozen choice phrases selected from
the works of Plato and Aristophanes, teach us more than
any number of dissertations and commentaries.

And so again, in order to understand an Indian Purana,
one must begin by imagining the father of a family who,
"having seen a son on his son's knees," follows the law
and, with ax and pitcher, seeks solitude under a banyan
tree, talks no more, multiplies his fastings, lives naked with
four fires around him under the fifth fire, that terrible sun
which endlessly devours and resuscitates all living things;
who fixes his imagination in turn for weeks at a time on the
foot of Brahma, then on his knee, on his thigh, on his navel,
and so on, until, beneath the strain of this intense meditation, hallucinations appear, when all the forms of being,
mingling together and transformed into each other, oscillate
to and fro in this vertiginous brain until the motionless
man, with suspended breath and fixed eyeballs, beholds the
universe melting away like vapor over the vacant immensity
of the Being in which he hopes for absorption. In this
case the best of teachings would be a journey in India;
but, for lack of a better one, take the narratives of travelers
along with works in geography, botany, and ethnology. In
any event, there must be the same research. A language,
a law, a creed, is never other than an abstraction; the perfect thing is found in the active man, the visible corporeal
figure which eats, walks, fights, and labors. Set aside the
theories of constitutions and their results, of religions and
their systems, and try to observe men in their workshops or
offices, in their fields along with their own sky and soil,
with their own homes, clothes, occupations and repasts,
just as you see them when, on landing in England or in
Italy, you remark their features and gestures, their roads
and their inns, the citiizen on his promenades and the work-

man taking a drink. Let us strive as much as possible to
supply the place of the actual, personal, sensible observation that is no longer practicable, this being the only way
in which we can really know the man; let us make the past
present; to judge of an object it must be present; no
experience can be had of what is absent. Undoubtedly,
this sort of reconstruction is always imperfect; only an
imperfect judgment can be based on it; but let us do the
best we can; incomplete knowledge is better than none at
all, or than knowledge which is erroneous, and there is no
other way of obtaining knowledge approximatively of bygone times than by *seeing* approximatively the men of
former times.

Such is the first step in history. This step was taken in
Europe at the end of the last century when the imagination
took fresh flight under the auspices of Lessing and Walter
Scott, and a little later in France under Chateaubriand,
Augustin Thierry, Michelet, and others. We now come to
the second step.

II

On observing the visible man with your own eyes what do
you try to find in him? The invisible man. These words
which your ears catch, those gestures, those airs of the
head, his attire and sensible operations of all kinds, are,
for you, merely so many expressions; these express something, a soul. An inward man is hidden beneath the outward man, and the latter simply manifests the former. You
have observed the house in which he lives, his furniture,
his costume, in order to discover his habits and tastes, the
degree of his refinement or rusticity, his extravagance or
economy, his follies or his cleverness. You have listened
to his conversation and noted the inflexions of his voice,
the attitudes he has assumed, so as to judge of his spirit,
self-abandonment or gayety, his energy or his rigidity. You
consider his writings, works of art, financial and political
schemes, with a view to measure the reach and limits of his
intelligence, his creative power and self-command, to ascertain the usual order, kind, and force of his conceptions, in

what way he thinks and how he resolves. All these externals are so many avenues converging to one center, and you
follow these only to reach that center; here is the real
man, namely, that group of faculties and of sentiments
which produces the rest. Behold a new world, an infinite
world; for each visible action involves an infinite train of
reasonings and emotions, new or old sensations which have
combined to bring this into light and which, like long
ledges of rock sunk deep in the earth, have cropped out
above the surface and attained their level. It is this sub-
terranean world which forms the second aim, the special
object of the historian. If his critical education suffices, he
is able to discriminate under every ornament in architecture,
under every stroke of the brush in a picture, under each
phrase of literary composition, the particular sentiment out
of which the ornament, the stroke, and the phrase have
sprung; he is a spectator of the inward drama which has
developed itself in the breast of the artist or writer; the
choice of words, the length or shortness of the period, the
species of metaphor, the accent of a verse, the chain of
reasoning—all are to him an indication; while his eyes are
reading the text his mind and soul are following the steady
flow and ever-changing series of emotions and conceptions
from which this text has issued; he is working out its *psychology*. Should you desire to study this operation, regard
the promoter and model of all the high culture of the epoch,
Goethe, who, before composing his "Iphigenia" spent days
in making drawings of the most perfect statues and who,
at last, his eyes filled with the noble forms of antique
scenery and his mind penetrated by the harmonious beauty
of antique life, succeeded in reproducing internally, with such
exactness, the habits and yearnings of Greek imagination
as to provide us with an almost twin sister of the "Antigone" of Sophocles and of the goddesses of Phidias. This
exact and demonstrated divination of bygone sentiments
has, in our days, given a new life to history. There was
almost complete ignorance of this in the last century; men
of every race and of every epoch were represented as about
alike, the Greek, the barbarian, the Hindoo, the man of the
Renaissance and the man of the eighteenth century, cast in

the same mold and after the same pattern, and after a
certain abstract conception which served for the whole
human species. There was a knowledge of man but not
of men. There was no penetration into the soul itself;
nothing of the infinite diversity and wonderful complexity
of souls had been detected; it was not known that the
moral organization of a people or of an age is as special
and distinct as the physical structure of a family of plants
or of an order of animals. History to-day, like zoölogy, has
found its anatomy, and whatever branch of it is studied,
whether philology, languages or mythologies, it is in this
way that labor must be given to make it produce new fruit.
Among so many writers who, since Herder, Ottfried Müller,
and Goethe have steadily followed and rectified this great
effort, let the reader take two historians and two works, one
" The Life and Letters of Cromwell " by Carlyle, and the
other the " Port Royal " of Sainte-Beuve. He will see how
precisely, how clearly, and how profoundly we detect the
soul of a man beneath his actions and works; how, under
an old general and in place of an ambitious man vulgarly
hypocritical, we find one tormented by the disordered rev-
eries of a gloomy imagination, but practical in instinct
and faculties, thoroughly English and strange and incomprehensible to whoever has not studied the climate and the
race; how, with about a hundred scattered letters and a
dozen or more mutilated speeches, we follow him from his
farm and his team to his general's tent and to his Protector's
throne, in his transformation and in his development, in his
struggles of conscience and in his statesman's resolutions,
in such a way that the mechanism of his thought and action
becomes visible and the ever renewed and fitful tragedy,
within which wracked this great gloomy soul, passes like
the tragedies of Shakespeare into the souls of those who
behold them. We see how, behind convent disputes and
the obstinacy of nuns, we recover one of the great provinces
of human psychology; how fifty or more characters, rendered
invisible through the uniformity of a narration careful of
the proprieties, came forth in full daylight, each standing
out clear in its countless diversities; how, underneath theological dissertations and monotonous sermons, we dis-

cern the throbbings of ever-breathing hearts, the excitements and depressions of the religious life, the unforeseen reaction and pell-mell stir of natural feeling, the infiltrations of surrounding society, the intermittent triumphs of grace, presenting so many shades of difference that the fullest description and most flexible style can scarcely garner in the vast harvest which the critic has caused to germinate in this abandoned field. And the same elsewhere. Germany, with its genius, so pliant, so broad, so prompt in transformations, so fitted for the reproduction of the remotest and strangest states of human thought; England, with its matter-of-fact mind, so suited to the grappling with moral problems, to making them clear by figures, weights, and measures, by geography and statistics, by texts and common sense; France, at length, with its Parisian culture and drawing-room habits, with its unceasing analysis of characters and of works, with its ever ready irony at detecting weaknesses, with its skilled finesse in discriminating shades of thought—all have plowed over the same ground, and we now begin to comprehend that no region of history exists in which this deep sub-soil should not be reached if we would secure adequate crops between the furrows.

Such is the second step, and we are now in train to follow it out. Such is the proper aim of contemporary criticism. No one has done this work so judiciously and on so grand a scale as Sainte-Beuve; in this respect, we are all his pupils; literary, philosophic, and religious criticism in books, and even in the newspapers, is to-day entirely changed by his method. Ulterior evolution must start from this point. I have often attempted to expose what this evolution is; in my opinion, it is a new road open to history and which I shall strive to describe more in detail.

III

AFTER having observed in a man and noted down one, two, three, and then a multitude of, sentiments, do these suffice and does your knowledge of him seem complete? Does a memorandum book constitute a psychology? It is not a psychology, and here, as elsewhere, the search for causes must follow the collection of facts. It matters not what the facts may be, whether physical or moral, they always spring from causes; there are causes for ambition, for courage, for veracity, as well as for digestion, for muscular action, and for animal heat. Vice and virtue are products like vitriol and sugar; every complex fact grows out of the simple facts with which it is affiliated and on which it depends. We must therefore try to ascertain what simple facts underlie moral qualities the same as we ascertain those that underlie physical qualities, and, for example, let us take the first fact that comes to hand, a religious system of music, that of a Protestant church. A certain inward cause has inclined the minds of worshipers toward these grave, monotonous melodies, a cause much greater than its effect; that is to say, a general conception of the veritable outward forms of worship which man owes to God; it is this general conception which has shaped the architecture of the temple, cast out statues, dispensed with paintings, effaced ornaments, shortened ceremonies, confined the members of a congregation to high pews which cut off the view, and governed the thousand details of decoration, posture, and all other externals. This conception itself again proceeds from a more general cause, an idea of human conduct in general, inward and outward, prayers, actions, dispositions of every sort that man is bound to maintain toward the Deity; it is this which has enthroned the doctrine of grace, lessened the importance of the clergy, transformed the sacraments, suppressed observances, and changed the religion of discipline into one of morality. This conception, in its turn, depends on a third one, still more general, that of moral perfection as this is found in a perfect God, the impeccable judge, the stern overseer, who regards every soul as sinful, meriting punishment, incapable of virtue or of salvation, except through a stricken conscience which He provokes and the renewal of the heart which He brings about. Here is the master conception, consisting of duty erected into the absolute sovereign of human life, and which prostrates all other ideals at the feet of the moral ideal. Here we reach what is deepest in man; for, to explain this conception, we must consider the race he belongs to, say the German, the Northman, the formation and character of his intellect, his ways in general of thinking and feeling, that tardiness and frigidity of sensation which keeps him from rasmy and easily falling under the empire of sensual enjoyments, that bluntness of taste, that irregularity and those outbursts of conception which arrest in him the birth of refined and harmonious forms and methods; that disdain of appearances, that yearning for truth, that attachment to abstract, bare ideas which develop conscience in him at the expense of everything else. Here the search comes to an end. We have reached a certain primitive disposition, a particular trait belonging to sensations of all kinds, to every conception peculiar to an age or to a race, to characteristics inseparable from every idea and feeling that stir in the human breast. Such are the grand causes, for these are universal and permanent causes, present in every case and at every moment, everywhere and always active, indestructible, and inevitably dominant in the end, since, whatever accidents cross their path being limited and partial, end in yielding to the obscure and incessant repetition of their energy; so that the general structure of things and all the main features of events are their work, all religions and philosophies, all poetic and industrial systems, all forms of society and of the family, all, in fine, being imprints bearing the stamp of their seal.

IV

There is, then, a system in human ideas and sentiments, the prime motor of which consists in general traits, certain characteristics of thought and feeling common to men belonging to a particular race, epoch, or country. Just as crystals in mineralogy, whatever their diversity, proceed from a few simple physical forms, so do civilizations in history, however these may differ, proceed from a few spiritual forms. One is explained by a primitive geometrical element as the other is explained by a primitive psychological ele-

ment. In order to comprehend the entire group of miner-
alogical species we must first study a regular solid in the
general, its facets and angles, and observe in this abridged
form the innumerable transformations of which it is susceptible. In like manner, if we would comprehend the entire
group of historic varieties we must consider beforehand a
human soul in the general, with its two or three fundamental faculties, and, in this abridgment, observe the principal
forms it may present. This sort of ideal tableau, the geometrical as well as psychological, is not very complex, and
we soon detect the limitations of organic conditions to
which civilizations, the same as crystals, are forcibly confined. What do we find in man at the point of departure?
Images or representations of objects, namely, that which
floats before him internally, lasts a certain time, is effaced,
and then returns after contemplating this or that tree or
animal, in short, some sensible object. This forms the
material basis of the rest and the development of this
material basis is twofold, speculative or positive, just as
these representations end in a *general conception* or in an
active resolution. Such is man, summarily abridged. It
is here, within these narrow confines, that human diversities
are encountered, now in the matter itself and again in the
primordial twofold development. However insignificant in
the elements they are of vast significance in the mass, while
the slightest change in the factors leads to gigantic changes
in the results. According as the representation is distinct,
as if stamped by a coining-press, or confused and blurred;
according as it concentrates in itself a larger or smaller
number of the characters of an object; according as it is
violent and accompanied with impulsions or tranquil and
surrounded with calmness, so are all the operations and the
whole running-gear of the human machine entirely transformed. In like manner, again, according as the ulterior
development of the representation varies, so does the whole
development of the man vary. If the general conception
in which this ends is merely a dry notation in Chinese
fashion, language becomes a kind of algebra, religion and
poetry are reduced to a minimum, philosophy is brought
down to a sort of moral and practical common sense,

science to a collection of recipes, classifications, and utilitarian mnemonics, the mind itself taking a whole positive turn. If, on the contrary, the general conception in which the representation culminates is a poetic and figurative creation, a living symbol, as with the Aryan races, language becomes a sort of shaded and tinted epic in which each word stands as a personage, poesy and religion assume magnificent and inexhaustible richness, and metaphysics develops with breadth and subtlety without any consideration of positive bearings; the whole intellect, notwithstanding the deviation and inevitable weaknesses of the effort, is captivated by the beautiful and sublime, thus conceiving an ideal type which, through its nobleness and harmony, gathers to itself all the affections and enthusiasms of humanity. If, on the other hand, the general conception in which the representation culminates is poetic but abrupt, is reached not gradually but by sudden intuition, if the original operation is not a regular development but a violent explosion—then, as with the semitic races, metaphysical power is wanting; the religious conception becomes that of a royal God, consuming and solitary; science cannot take shape, the intellect grows rigid and too headstrong to reproduce the delicate ordering of nature; poetry cannot give birth to aught but a series of vehement, grandiose exclamations, while language no longer renders the concatenation of reasoning and eloquence, man being reduced to lyric enthusiasm, to ungovernable passion, and to narrow and fanatical action. It is in this interval between the particular representation and the universal conception that the germs of the greatest human differences are found. Some races, like the classic, for example, pass from the former to the latter by a graduated scale of ideas regularly classified and more and more general; others, like the Germanic, traverse the interval in leaps, with uniformity and after prolonged and uncertain groping. Others, like the Romans and the English, stop at the lowest stages; others, like the Hindoos and Germans, mount to the uppermost.

If, now, after considering the passage from the representation to the idea, we regard the passage from the representation to the resolution, we find here elementary differences of like importance and of the same order, according as the impression is vivid, as in Southern climes, or faint, as in Northern climes, as it ends in instantaneous action as with barbarians, or tardily as with civilized nations, as it is capable or not of growth, of inequality, of persistence and of association. The entire system of human passion, all the risks of public peace and security, all labor and action, spring from these sources. It is the same with the other primordial differences; their effects embrace an entire civilization, and may be likened to those algebraic formulæ which, within narrow bounds, describe beforehand the curve of which these form the law. Not that this law always prevails to the end; sometimes, perturbations arise, but, even when this happens, it is not because the law is defective, but because it has not operated alone. New elements have entered into combination with old ones; powerful foreign forces have interfered to oppose primitive forces. The race has emigrated, as with the ancient Aryans, and the change of climate has led to a change in the whole intellectual economy and structure of society. A people has been conquered like the Saxon nation, and the new political structure has imposed on its customs, capacities, and desires which it did not possess. The nation has established itself permanently in the midst of downtrodden and threatening subjects, as with the ancient Spartans, while the necessity of living, as in an armed encampment, has violently turned the whole moral and social organization in one unique direction. At all events, the mechanism of human history is like this. We always find the primitive mainspring consisting of some widespread tendency of soul and intellect, either innate and natural to the race or acquired by it and due to some circumstance forced upon it. These great given mainsprings gradually produce their effects, that is to say, at the end of a few centuries they place the nation in a new religious, literary, social, and economic state; a new condition which, combined with their renewed effort, produces another condition, sometimes a good one, sometimes a bad one, now slowly, now rapidly, and so on; so that the entire development of each distinct civilization may be considered as the effect of one permanent force which, at every moment, varies its work by modifying the circumstances where it acts.

V

THREE different sources contribute to the production of this elementary moral state, *race, environment,* and *epoch.* What we call *race* consists of those innate and hereditary dispositions which man brings with him into the world and which are generally accompanied with marked differences of temperament and of bodily structure. They vary in different nations.

Naturally, there are varieties of men as there are varieties of cattle and horses, some brave and intelligent, and others timid and of limited capacity; some capable of superior conceptions and creations, and others reduced to rudimentary ideas and contrivances; some specially fitted for certain works, and more richly furnished with certain instincts, as we see in the better endowed species of dogs, some for running and others for fighting, some for hunting and others for guarding houses and flocks. We have here a distinct force; so distinct that, in spite of the enormous deviations which both the other motors impress upon it, we still recognize, and which a race like the Aryan people, scattered from the Ganges to the Hebrides, established under all climates, ranged along every degree of civilization, transformed by thirty centuries of revolutions, shows nevertheless in its languages, in its religions, in its literatures, and in its philosophies, the community of blood and of intellect which still to-day binds together all its offshoots. However they may differ, their parentage is not lost; barbarism, culture and grafting, differences of atmosphere and of soil, fortunate or unfortunate occurrences, have operated in vain; the grand characteristics of the original form have lasted, and we find that the two or three leading features of the primitive imprint are again apparent under the subsequent imprints with which time has overlaid them. There is nothing surprising in this extraordinary tenacity. Although the immensity of the distance allows us to catch only a glimpse in a dubious light of the origin of species,[1] the events of history throw sufficient light on events anterior to history to explain the almost unshaken solidity of primordial traits. At the moment of encountering them, fifteen, twenty, and thirty centuries before our era, in an Aryan, Egyptian, or Chinese, they represent the work of a much greater number of centuries, perhaps the work of many myriads of centuries. For, as soon as an animal is born it must adapt itself to its surroundings; it breathes in another way, it renews itself differently, it is otherwise stimulated according as the atmosphere, the food, and the temperature are different. A different climate and situation create different necessities and hence activities of a different kind; and hence, again, a system of different habits, and, finally, a system of different aptitudes and instincts. Man, thus compelled to put himself in equilibrium with circumstances, contracts a corresponding temperament and character, and his character, like his temperament, are acquisitions all the more stable because of the outward impression being more deeply imprinted in him by more frequent repetitions and transmitted to his offspring by more ancient heredity. So that at each moment of time the character of a people may be considered as a summary of all antecedent actions and sensations; that is to say, as a quantity and as a weighty mass, not infinite,[2] since all things in nature are limited, but disproportionate to the rest and almost impossible to raise, since each minute of an almost infinite past has contributed to render it heavier, and, in order to turn the scale, it would require, on the other side, a still greater accumulation of actions and sensations. Such is the first and most abundant source of these master faculties from which historic events are derived; and we see at once that if it is powerful it is owing to its not being a mere source, but a sort of lake, and like a deep reservoir wherein other sources have poured their waters for a multitude of centuries.

When we have thus verified the internal structure of a race we must consider the *environment* in which it lives.

[1] Darwin, "The Origin of Species." Prosper Lucas, "De l'Hérédité."
[2] Spinosa, "Ethics," part iv., axiom.

For man is not alone in the world; nature envelops him
and other men surround him; accidental and secondary
folds come and overspread the primitive and permanent fold,
while physical or social circumstances derange or complete
the natural groundwork surrendered to them. At one time
climate has had its effect. Although the history of Aryan
nations can be only obscurely traced from their common
country to their final abodes, we can nevertheless affirm that
the profound difference which is apparent between the Germanic races on the one hand, and the Hellenic and Latin
races on the other, proceeds in great part from the differences between the countries in which they have established
themselves—the former in cold and moist countries, in the
depths of gloomy forests and swamps, or on the borders of
a wild ocean, confined to melancholic or rude sensations, inclined to drunkenness and gross feeding, leading a militant
and carnivorous life; the latter, on the contrary, living
amidst the finest scenery, alongside of a brilliant, sparkling
sea inviting navigation and commerce, exempt from the
grosser cravings of the stomach, disposed at the start to
social habits and customs, to political organization, to the
sentiments and faculties which develop the art of speaking,
the capacity for enjoyment and invention in the sciences, in
art, and in literature. At another time, political events
have operated, as in the two Italian civilizations: the first
one tending wholly to action, to conquest, to government,
and to legislation, through the primitive situation of a city
of refuge, a frontier *emporium,* and of an armed aristocracy
which, importing and enrolling foreigners and the vanquished under it, sets two hostile bodies facing each other,
with no outlet for its internal troubles and rapacious instincts but systematic' warfare; the second one, excluded
from unity and political ambition on a grand scale by the
permanency of its municipal system, by the cosmopolite
situation of its pope and by the military intervention of
neighboring states, and following the bent of its magnificent
and harmonious genius, is wholly carried over to the worship
of voluptuousness and beauty. Finally, at another time,
social conditions have imposed their stamp as, eighteen centuries ago, by Christianity, and twenty-five centuries ago, by

Buddhism, when, around the Mediterranean as in Hindostan, the extreme effects of Aryan conquest and organization led to intolerable oppression, the crushing of the individual, utter despair, the whole world under the ban of a curse, with the development of metaphysics and visions, until man, in this dungeon of despondency, feeling his heart melt, conceived of abnegation, charity, tender love, gentleness, humility, human brotherhood, here in the idea of universal nothingness and there under that of the fatherhood of God. Look around at the regulative instincts and faculties implanted in a race; in brief, the turn of mind according to which it thinks and acts at the present day; we shall find most frequently that its work is due to one of these prolonged situations, to these enveloping circumstances, to these persistent gigantic pressures brought to bear on a mass of men who, one by one, and all collectively, from one generation to another, have been unceasingly bent and fashioned by them, in Spain a crusade of eight centuries against the Mohammedans, prolonged yet longer even to the exhaustion of the nation through the expulsion of the Moors, through the spoliation of the Jews, through the establishment of the Inquisition, through the Catholic wars; in England, a political establishment of eight centuries which maintains man erect and respectful, independent and obedient, all accustomed to struggling together in a body under the sanction of law; in France, a Latin organization which, at first imposed on docile barbarians, than leveled to the ground under the universal demolition, forms itself anew under the latent workings of national instinct, developing under hereditary monarchs and ending in a sort of equalized, centralized, administrative republic under dynasties exposed to revolutions. Such are the most efficacious among the observable causes which mold the primitive man; they are to nations what education, pursuit, condition, and abode are to individuals, and seem to comprise all, since the external forces which fashion human matter, and by which the outward acts on the inward, are comprehended in them.

There is, nevertheless, a third order of causes, for, with the forces within and without, there is the work these have

already produced together, which work itself contributes
toward producing the ensuing work; beside the permanent
impulsion and the given environment there is the acquired
momentum. When national character and surrounding
circumstances operate it is not on a *tabula rasa,* but on one
already bearing imprints. According as this *tabula* is taken
at one or at another moment so is the imprint different, and
this suffices to render the total effect different. Consider,
for example, two moments of a literature or of an art,
French tragedy under Corneille and under Voltaire, and
Greek drama under Æschylus and under Euripides, Latin
poetry under Lucretius and under Claudian, and Italian
painting under Da Vinci and under Guido. Assuredly, there
is no change of general conception at either of these two
extreme points; ever the same human type must be por-
trayed or represented in action; the cast of the verse, the
dramatic structure, the physical form have all persisted. But
there is this among these differences, that one of the artists
is a precursor and the other a successor, that the first one
has no model and the second one has a model; that the
former sees things face to face, and that the latter sees them
through the intermediation of the former, that many departments of art have become more perfect, that the simplicity and grandeur of the impression have diminished,
that what is pleasing and refined in form has augmented
—in short, that the first work has determined the second.
In this respect, it is with a people as with a plant; the same
sap at the same temperature and in the same soil produces,
at different stages of its successive elaborations, different
developments, buds, flowers, fruits, and seeds, in such a way
that the condition of the following is always that of the
preceding and is born of its death. Now, if you no longer
regard a brief moment, as above, but one of those grand
periods of development which embraces one or many centuries like the Middle Ages, or our last classic period, the
conclusion is the same. A certain dominating conception
has prevailed throughout; mankind, during two hundred
years, during five hundred years, have represented to themselves a certain ideal figure of man, in mediæval times
the knight and the monk, in our classic period the courtier

and refined talker; this creative and universal conception has monopolized the entire field of action and thought, and, after spreading its involuntary systematic works over the world, it languished and then died out, and now a new idea has arisen, destined to a like domination and to equally multiplied creations. Note here that the latter depends in part on the former, and that it is the former, which, combining its effect with those of national genius and surrounding circumstances, will impose their bent and their direction on new-born things. It is according to this law that great historic currents are formed, meaning by this, the long rule of a form of intellect or of a master idea, like that period of spontaneous creations called the Renaissance, or that period of oratorical classifications called the Classic Age, or that series of mystic systems called the Alexandrine and Christian epoch, or that series of mythological efflorescences found at the origins of Germany, India, and Greece. Here as elsewhere, we are dealing merely with a mechanical problem: the total effect is a compound wholly determined by the grandeur and direction of the forces which produce it. The sole difference which separates these moral problems from physical problems lies in this, that in the former the directions and grandeur cannot be estimated by or stated in figures with the same precision as in the latter. If a want, a faculty, is a quantity capable of degrees, the same as pressure or weight, this quantity is not measurable like that of the pressure or weight. We cannot fix it in an exact or approximative formula; we can obtain or give of it only a literary impression; we are reduced to nothing and citing the prominent facts which make it manifest and which nearly, or roughly, indicate about what grade on the scale it must be ranged at. And yet, notwithstanding the methods of notation are not the same in the moral sciences as in the physical sciences, nevertheless, as matter is the same in both, and is equally composed of forces, directions, and magnitudes, we can still show that in one as in the other, the final effect takes place according to the same law. This is great or small according as the fundamental forces are great or small and act more or less precisely in the same sense, according as the distinct effects of race, environment and epoch combine to enforce each other or combine to neutralize each other. Thus are explained the long impotences and the brilliant successes which appear irregularly and with no apparent reason in the life of a people; the causes of these consist in internal concordances and contrarieties. There was one of these concordances when, in the seventeenth century, the social disposition and conversational spirit innate in France encountered drawing-room formalities and the moment of oratorical analysis; when, in the nineteenth century, the flexible, profound genius of Germany encountered the age of philosophic synthesis and of cosmopolite criticism. One of these contrarieties happened when, in the seventeenth century, the blunt, isolated genius of England awkwardly tried to don the new polish of urbanity, and when, in the sixteenth century, the lucid, prosaic French intellect tried to gestate a living poesy. It is this secret concordance of creative forces which produced the exquisite courtesy and noble cast of literature under Louis XIV. and Bossuet, and the grandiose metaphysics and broad critical sympathy under Hegel and Goethe. It is this secret contrariety of creative forces which produced the literary incompleteness, the licentious plays, the abortive drama of Dryden and Wycherly, the poor Greek importations, the gropings, the minute beauties and fragments of Ronsard and the Pleiad. We may confidently affirm that the unknown creations toward which the current of coming ages is bearing up will spring from and be governed by these primordial forces; that, if these forces could be measured and computed we might deduce from them, as from a formula, the characters of future civilization; and that if, notwithstanding the evident rudeness of our notations, and the fundamental inexactitude of our measures, we would nowadays form some idea of our general destinies, we must base our conjectures on an examination of these forces. For, in enumerating them, we run through the full circle of active forces; and when the race, the environment, and the moment have been considered,—that is to say the inner mainspring, the pressure from without, and the impulsion already acquired,—we have exhausted not only all real causes but again all possible causes of movement.

VI

THERE remains to be ascertained in what way these causes, applied to a nation or to a century, distribute their effects. Like a spring issuing from an elevated spot and diffusing its waters, according to the height, from ledge to ledge, until it finally reaches the low ground, so does the tendency of mind or soul in a people, due to race, epoch, or environment, diffuse itself in different proportions, and by regular descent, over the different series of facts which compose its civilization.[3] In preparing the geographical map of a country, starting at its watershed, we see the slopes, just below this common point, dividing themselves into five or six principal basins, and then each of the latter into several others, and so on until the whole country, with its thousands of inequalities of surface, is included in the ramifications of this network. In like manner, in preparing the psychological map of the events and sentiments belonging to a certain human civilization, we find at the start five or six well determined provinces—religion, art, philosophy, the state, the family, and industries; next, in each of these provinces, natural departments, and then finally, in each of these departments, still smaller territories until we arrive at those countless details of life which we observe daily in ourselves and around us. If, again, we examine and compare together these various groups of facts we at once find that they are composed of parts and that all have parts in common. Let us take first the three principal products of human intelligence—religion, art, and philosophy. What is a philosophy but a conception of nature and of its primordial causes under the form of abstractions and formulas? What underlies a religion and an art if not a conception of this same nature, and of these same primordial causes, under the form of more or less determinate symbols, and of more or less distinct personages, with this difference, that in the first case we believe that they exist, and in the second case that

[3] For this scale of coördinate effects consult, " Langues Sémitiques," by Renan, ch. 1; " Comparison des civilizations Grecque et Romaine," vol. i., ch. 1, 3d ed., by Mommsen; " Conséquences de la démocratie," vol. iii., by Tocqueville.

they do not exist. Let the reader consider some of the great creations of the intellect in India, in Scandinavia, in Persia, in Rome, in Greece, and he will find that art everywhere is a sort of philosophy become sensible, religion a sort of poem regarded as true, and philosophy a sort of art and religion, desiccated and reduced to pure abstractions. There is, then, in the center of each of these groups a common element, the conception of the world and its origin, and if they differ amongst each other it is because each combines with the common element a distinct element; here the power of abstraction, there the faculty of personifying with belief, and, finally, the talent for personifying without belief. Let us now take the two leading products of human association, the Family and the State. What constitutes the State other than the sentiment of obedience by which a multitude of men collect together under the authority of a chief? And what constitutes the Family other than the sentiment of obedience by which a wife and children act together under the direction of a father and husband? The Family is a natural, primitive, limited state, as the State is an artificial, ulterior, and expanded Family, while beneath the differences which arise from the number, origin, and condition of its members, we distinguish, in the small as in the large community, a like fundamental disposition of mind which brings them together and unites them. Suppose, now, that this common element receives from the environment, the epoch, and the race peculiar characteristics, and it is clear that *all the groups into which it enters will be proportionately modified.* If the sentiment of obedience is merely one of fear,[4] you encounter, as in most of the Oriental states, the brutality of despotism, a prodigality of vigorous punishments, the exploitation of the subject, servile habits, insecurity of property, impoverished production, female slavery, and the customs of the harem. If the sentiment of obedience is rooted in the instinct of discipline, sociability, and honor, you find, as in France, a complete military organization, a superb administrative hierarchy, a weak public spirit with outbursts of patriotism, the unhesitating

[4] " L'Esprit des Lois," by Montesquieu; the essential principles of the three governments.

docility of the subject along with the hot-headedness of
the revolutionist, the obsequiousness of the courtier along
with the reserve of the gentleman, the charm of refined
conversation along with home and family bickerings, con-
jugal equality together with matrimonial incompatibilities
under the necessary constraints of the law. If, finally, the
sentiment of obedience is rooted in the instinct of subordination and in the idea of duty, you perceive, as in Germanic
nations, the security and contentment of the household,
the firm foundations of domestic life, the slow and imperfect
development of worldly matters, innate respect for established rank, superstitious reverence for the past, maintenance of social inequalities, natural and habitual deference
to the law. Similarly in a race, just as there is a difference
of aptitude for general ideas, so will its religion, art, and
philosophy be different. If man is naturally fitted for
broader universal conceptions and inclined at the same time
to their derangement, through the nervous irritability of an
over-excited organization, we find, as in India, a surprising
richness of gigantic religious creations, a splendid bloom
of extravagant transparent epics, a strange concatenation
of subtle, imaginative philosophic systems, all so intimately
associated and so interpenetrated with a common sap, that
we at once recognize them, by their amplitude, by their
color, and by their disorder, as productions of the same
climate and of the same spirit. If, on the contrary, the
naturally sound and well-balanced man is content to restrict
his conceptions to narrow bounds in order to cast them in
more precise forms, we see, as in Greece, a theology of artists
and narrators, special gods that are soon separated from
objects and almost transformed at once into substantial
personages, the sentiment of universal unity nearly effaced
and scarcely maintained in the vague notion of destiny, a
philosophy, rather than subtle and compact, grandiose and
systematic, narrow metaphysically[5] but incomparable in its
logic, sophistry, and morality, a poesy and arts superior to

[5] The birth of the Alexandrine philosophy is due to contact with the
Orient.   Aristotle's metaphysical views stand alone.   Moreover, with him
as with Plato, they afford merely a glimpse.   By way of contrast see systematic power in Plotinus, Proclus, Schelling, and Hegel, or again in the
admirable boldness of Brahmanic and Buddhist speculation.

anything we have seen in lucidity, naturalness, proportion, truth, and beauty. If, finally, man is reduced to narrow conceptions deprived of any speculative subtlety, and at the same time finds that he is absorbed and completely hardened by practical interests, we see, as in Rome, rudimentary deities, mere empty names, good for denoting the petty details of agriculture, generation, and the household, veritable marriage and farming labels, and, therefore, a null or borrowed mythology, philosophy, and poesy. Here, as elsewhere, comes in the law of mutual dependencies.[6] A civilization is a living unit, the parts of which hold together the same as the parts of an organic body. Just as in an animal, the instincts, teeth, limbs, bones, and muscular apparatus are bound together in such a way that a variation of one determines a corresponding variation in the others, and out of which a skillful naturalist, with a few bits, imagines and reconstructs an almost complete body, so, in a civilization, do religion, philosophy, the family scheme, literature and the arts form a system in which each local change involves a general change, so that an experienced historian, who studies one portion apart from the others, sees beforehand and partially predicts the characteristics of the rest. There is nothing vague in this dependence. The regulation of all this in the living body consists, first, of the tendency to manifest a certain primordial type, and, next, the necessity of its possessing organs which can supply its wants and put itself in harmony with itself in order to live. The regulation in a civilization consists in the presence in each great human creation of an elementary producer equally present in other surrounding creations, that is, some faculty and aptitude, some efficient and marked disposition, which, with its own peculiar character, introduces this with that into all operations in which it takes part, and which, according to its variations, causes variation in all the works in which it coöperates.

[6] I have very often made attempts to state this law, especially in the preface to " Essais de Critique et d'Histoire."

VII

HAVING reached this point we can obtain a glimpse of
the principal features of human transformations, and can
now search for the general laws which regulate not only
events, but classes of events; not only this religion or that
literature, but the whole group of religions or of literatures.
If, for example, it is admitted that a religion is a metaphysical poem associated with belief; if it is recognized, besides, that there are certain races and certain environments
in which belief, poetic faculty, and metaphysical faculty
display themselves in common with unwonted vigor; if we
consider that Christianity and Buddhism were developed at
periods of grand systematizations and in the midst of sufferings like the oppression which stirred up the fanatics of
Cevennes; if, on the other hand, it is recognized that primitive religions are born at the dawn of human reason, during the richest expansion of human imagination, at times of
the greatest naïveté and of the greatest credulity; if we
consider, again, that Mohammedanism appeared along with
the advent of poetic prose and of the conception of material unity, amongst a people destitute of science and at the
moment of a sudden development of the intellect—we
might conclude that religion is born and declines, is reformed and transformed, according as circumstances fortify
and bring together, with more or less precision and energy,
its three generative instincts; and we would then comprehend why religion is endemic in India among specially exalted imaginative and philosophic intellects; why it blooms
out so wonderfully and so grandly in the Middle Ages, in
an oppressive society, amongst new languages and literature; why it develops again in the sixteenth century with
a new character and an heroic enthusiasm, at the time of
an universal renaissance and at the awakening of the Germanic races; why it swarms out in so many bizarre sects in
the rude democracy of America and under the bureaucratic
despotism of Russia; why, in fine, it is seen spreading out in
the Europe of to-day in such different proportions and with
such special traits, according to such differences of race and

of civilizations. And so for every kind of human production, for letters, music, the arts of design, philosophy, the sciences, state industries, and the rest. Each has some moral tendency for its direct cause, or a concurrence of moral tendencies; given the cause, it appears; the cause withdrawn, it disappears; the weakness or intensity of the cause is the measure of its own weakness or intensity. It is bound to that like any physical phenomenon to its condition, like dew to the chilliness of a surrounding atmosphere, like dilatation to heat. Couples exist in the moral world as they exist in the physical world, as rigorously linked together and as universally diffused. Whatever in one case produces, alters, or suppresses the first term, produces, alters, and suppresses the second term as a necessary consequence. Whatever cools the surrounding atmosphere causes the fall of dew. Whatever develops credulity, along with poetic conceptions of the universe, engenders religion. Thus have things come about, and thus will they continue to come about. As soon as the adequate and necessary condition of one of these vast apparitions becomes known to us our mind has a hold on the future as well as on the past. We can confidently state under what circumstances it will reappear, foretell without rashness many portions of its future history, and sketch with precaution some of the traits of its ulterior development.

VIII.

HISTORY has reached this point at the present day, or rather it is nearly there, on the threshold of this inquest. The question as now stated is this: Given a literature, a philosophy, a society, an art, a certain group of arts, what is the moral state of things which produces it? And what are the conditions of race, epoch, and environment the best adapted to produce this moral state? There is a distinct moral state for each of these formations and for each of their branches; there is one for art in general as well as for each particular art; for architecture, painting, sculpture, music, and poetry, each with a germ of its own in the large field of human psychology; each has its own law, and it is by virtue of this law that we see each shoot up, apparently haphazard, singly and alone, amidst the miscarriages of their neighbors, like painting in Flanders and Holland in the seventeenth century, like poetry in England in the sixteenth century, like music in Germany in the eighteenth century. At this moment, and in these countries, the conditions for one art and not for the others are fulfilled, and one branch only has bloomed out amidst the general sterility. It is these laws of human vegetation which history must now search for; it is this special psychology of each special formation which must be got at; it is the composition of a complete table of these peculiar conditions that must now be worked out. There is nothing more delicate and nothing more difficult. Montesquieu undertook it, but in his day the interest in history was too recent for him to be successful; nobody, indeed, had any idea of the road that was to be followed, and even at the present day we scarcely begin to obtain a glimpse of it. Just as astronomy, at bottom, is a mechanical problem, and physiology, likewise, a chemical problem, so is history, at bottom, a *problem of psychology*. There is a particular system of inner impressions and operations which fashions the artist, the believer, the musician, the painter, the nomad, the social man; for each of these, the filiation, intensity, and interdependence of ideas and of emotions are different; each has his own moral history, and his own special organization, along with some master tendency and with some dominant trait. To explain each of these would require a chapter devoted to a profound internal analysis, and that is a work that can scarcely be called sketched out at the present day. But one man, Stendhal, through a certain turn of mind and a peculiar education, has attempted it, and even yet most of his readers find his works paradoxical and obscure. His talent and ideas were too premature. His admirable insight, his profound sayings carelessly thrown out, the astonishing precision of his notes and logic, were not understood; people were not aware that, under the appearances and talk of a man of the world, he explained the most complex of internal mechanisms; that his finger touched the great mainspring, that he brought scientific processes to bear in the history of the heart, the art of employing figures, of decomposing, of deducing; that he was the first to point out fundamental causes such as nationalities, climates, and temperaments; in short, that he treated sentiments as they should be treated, that is to say, as a naturalist and physicist, by making classifications and estimating forces. On account of all this he was pronounced dry and eccentric and allowed to live in isolation, composing novels, books of travel and taking notes, for which he counted upon, and has obtained, about a dozen or so of readers. And yet his works are those in which we of the present day may find the most satisfactory efforts that have been made to clear the road I have just striven to describe. Nobody has taught one better how to observe with one's own eyes, first, to re-gard humanity around us and life as it is, and next, old and authentic documents; how to read more than merely the black and white of the page; how to detect under old print and the scrawl of the text the veritable senti-ment and the train of thought, the mental state in which the words were penned. In his writings, as in those of Sainte-Beuve and in those of the German critics, the reader will find how much is to be derived from a literary document; if this document is rich and we know how to interpret it, we will find in the psychology of a particular soul, often that of an age, and sometimes that of a race. In this respect, a great poem, a good novel, the confessions of a superior man, are more instructive than a mass of his-torians and histories; I would give fifty volumes of charters and a hundred diplomatic files for the memoirs of Cellini, the epistles of Saint Paul, the table-talk of Luther, or the comedies of Aristophanes. Herein lies the value of literary productions. They are instructive because they are beauti-ful; their usefulness increases with their perfection; and if they provide us with documents, it is because they are monuments. The more visible a book renders sentiments the more literary it is, for it is the special office of literature to take note of sentiments. The more important the senti-ments noted in a book the higher its rank in literature, for it is by representing what sort of a life a nation or an epoch leads, that a writer rallies to himself the sympathies of a nation or of an epoch. Hence, among the documents which bring before our eyes the sentiments of preceding generations, a literature, and especially a great literature, is incomparably the best. It resembles those admirable instruments of remarkable sensitiveness which physicists make use of to detect and measure the most profound and delicate changes that occur in a human body. There is nothing approaching this in constitutions or religions; the articles of a code or of a catechism do no more than depict mind in gross and without finesse; if there are any documents which show life and spirit in politics and in creeds, they are the eloquent discourses of the pulpit and the tribune, memoirs and personal confessions, all belonging to literature, so that, outside of itself, literature embodies whatever is good elsewhere. It is mainly in studying literatures that we are able to produce moral history, and arrive at some knowledge of the psychological laws on which events depend.

I have undertaken to write a history of a literature and to ascertain the psychology of a people; in selecting this one, it is not without a motive. A people had to be taken possessing a vast and complete literature, which is rarely found. There are few nations which, throughout their existence, have thought and written well in the full sense of the word. Among the ancients, Latin literature is null at the beginning, and afterward borrowed and an imitation. Among the moderns, German literature is nearly a blank for two centuries.[7] Italian and Spanish literatures come to an end in the middle of the seventeenth century. Ancient Greece, and modern France and England, alone offer a complete series of great and expressive monuments. I have chosen the English because, as this still exists and is open to direct observation, it can be better studied than that of an extinct civilization of which fragments only remain; and because, being different, it offers better than that of France very marked characteristics in the eyes of a Frenchman. Moreover, outside of what is peculiar to English civilization, apart from a spontaneous development, it presents a forced

[7] From 1550 to 1750.

deviation due to the latest and most effective conquest to which the country was subject; the three given conditions out of which it issues—race, climate, and the Norman conquest—are clearly and distinctly visible in its literary monuments; so that we study in this history the two most potent motors of human transformation, namely, nature and constraint, and we study them, without any break or uncertainty, in a series of authentic and complete monuments. I have tried to define these primitive motors, to show their gradual effects, and explain how their insensible operation has brought religious and literary productions into full light, and how the inward mechanism is developed by which the barbarous Saxon became the Englishman of the present day.

THE PUBLISHERS OF THE HAR-
VARD CLASSICS · DR. ELIOT'S
FIVE-FOOT SHELF OF BOOKS · ARE
PLEASED TO ANNOUNCE THE
PUBLICATION OF

THE JUNIOR CLASSICS
A LIBRARY FOR BOYS AND GIRLS

"The Junior Classics constitute a set
of books whose contents will delight
children and at the same time
satisfy the legitimate ethical require-
ments of those who have the children's
best interests at heart."

CHARLES W. ELIOT

THE COLLIER PRESS · NEW YORK
P · F · COLLIER & SON